D1055370

The New Novel

FROM QUENEAU TO PINGET

The New Novel

FROM QUENEAU
TO PINGET

by Vivian Mercier

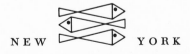

NEW YORK

Farrar, Straus and Giroux

Copyright © 1966, 1967, 1968, 1971 by Vivian Mercier
All rights reserved
Library of Congress catalog card number: 75-125158

FIRST EDITION, 1971

Printed in the United States of America
Published simultaneously in Canada by
Doubleday Canada Ltd., Toronto
DESIGNED BY HERB JOHNSON

LANSING COMMUNITY COLLEGE LIBRARY

Acknowledgments

THE late Cecil Hemley suggested the writing of this book; I deeply regret that he did not live to read it. Next, my warm thanks must go to the seven authors studied here: all of them have given me whatever help I asked for, and if I have asked less help from some than from others, the fault is mine. Samuel Beckett went out of his way to sponsor a fellow Irishman; I hesitate to embarrass him with my thanks. Frederick R. Karl, Jérôme Lindon, Barney Rosset, and Edwin Seaver also gave generous help. At Farrar, Straus and Giroux, I was guided, comforted, and admonished by Henry Robbins, Carmen Gomezplata, and Phyllis Skolnik. Special thanks are due Marilyn Abels, my typist, who can read my handwriting in both French and English. At one time or another since June 1964, virtually every member of the staff of Norlin Library at the University of Colorado has helped me in some way, and I thank them all.

Most of the time needed for writing this book and doing the necessary prior research was made available thanks to a year's sabbatical leave from The City College of the City University of New York, a Fellowship awarded by the American Council of Learned Societies, and a one-semester Faculty Fellowship recommended by the Committee on Research and Creative Work of the University of Colorado. All those who sponsored me for these awards or were instrumental in granting them have my deep gratitude.

Since I am a teacher of English, not of French, it may be in order for me to thank all those responsible for what I know of my ancestral language: my cousin the late Cora Mercier, who started me at French with a native speaker; S. B. Wynburne and his colleagues at Portora Royal School, Enniskillen; and the late Owen Sheehy Skeffington and his colleagues at Trinity College, Dublin.

Parts of this book have appeared as articles in *L'Esprit Créateur*, *Mundus Artium*, *Shenandoah*, and *TriQuarterly*. I thank the editors of those journals for permission to reprint. I have also written shorter articles and book reviews dealing with the French New Novel in *Book World*, *The Commonweal*, *The Hudson Review*, *The Nation*, and *The New York Times Book Review*; thus I may have unconsciously repeated an occasional sentence that has appeared in one of those periodicals.

I offer grateful acknowledgments to all those firms and individuals in France who have permitted me to quote copyright material in my own translation, as listed below.

To Raymond Queneau and Éditions Gallimard for quotations from the following works by M. Queneau:

Bâtons, chiffres et lettres, © 1950 Librairie Gallimard.

Le Chiendent, © 1933 Librairie Gallimard.

Les Enfants du limon, © 1938 Librairie Gallimard.

Entretiens avec Georges Charbonnier, © 1962 Éditions Gallimard.

Les Œuvres complètes de Sally Mara, © 1962 Éditions Gallimard.

Saint Glinglin, © 1948 Librairie Gallimard.

Si tu t'imagines 1920–1951, © 1952 Librairie Gallimard.

Le Vol d'Icare, © 1968 Éditions Gallimard.

To Robert Pinget and Les Éditions de Minuit for quotations from the following works by M. Pinget:

Baga, © 1958 Les Éditions de Minuit.

Clope au dossier, © 1961 Les Éditions de Minuit.

Graal Flibuste, © 1966 Les Éditions de Minuit.

L'Inquisitoire, © 1962 Les Éditions de Minuit.

Le Libera, © 1968 Les Éditions de Minuit.

Mahu ou le matériau, © 1952 Robert Laffont.

Quelqu'un, © 1965 Les Éditions de Minuit.

To Michel Butor and Les Éditions de Minuit for quotations from the following work by M. Butor:

Passage de Milan, © 1954 Les Éditions de Minuit.

To Alain Robbe-Grillet and Les Éditions de Minuit for quotations from the following work by M. Robbe-Grillet:

L'Immortelle, © 1963 Les Éditions de Minuit.

To Claude Mauriac and Éditions Albin Michel for quotations from the following work by M. Mauriac:

L'Agrandissement, © 1963 Éditions Albin Michel.

To Claude Mauriac and Éditions Bernard Grasset for quotations from the following work by M. Mauriac:

L'Oubli, © 1966 Éditions Bernard Grasset.

To Claude Simon and Calmann-Lévy, Éditeur, for quotations from the following work by M. Simon:

Le Sacre du printemps, © 1954 Calmann-Lévy.

To Jean-Jacques Pauvert for quotations from the following work by Raymond Roussel:

    Comment j'ai écrit certains de mes livres, © 1963 Jean-Jacques Pauvert, Éditeur.

I offer grateful acknowledgments to all those firms and individuals in the United States who have permitted me to quote from copyright material, as listed below.

To Barney Rosset and Grove Press, Inc., for quotations from the following works by Alain Robbe-Grillet, all translated by Richard Howard:

For a New Novel, © 1965 Grove Press, Inc.

In the Labyrinth, © 1960 Grove Press, Inc.

Jealousy, © 1959 Grove Press, Inc.

Last Year at Marienbad, © 1962 Grove Press, Inc.

La Maison de Rendez-vous, © 1966 Grove Press, Inc.

The Voyeur, © 1958 Grove Press, Inc.

To Barney Rosset and Grove Press, Inc., for quotations from the following works by Robert Pinget:

    Monsieur Levert, translated by Richard Howard, © 1961 Grove Press, Inc.

    L'Inquisitoire, © 1962 Les Éditions de Minuit.

    Quelqu'un, © 1965 Les Éditions de Minuit.

    (As already indicated, the last two works are quoted in my own translation, not in the translations published or to be published by Grove Press, Inc.)

To Barney Rosset and Grove Press, Inc., for a quotation from:

Molloy by Samuel Beckett, translated by Patrick Bowles in collaboration with the author, © 1955 Grove Press, Inc.

To George Braziller, Inc., for quotations from the following works by Nathalie Sarraute, all translated by Maria Jolas:

The Age of Suspicion, © 1963 George Braziller, Inc.

Between Life and Death, © 1969 George Braziller, Inc.

The Golden Fruits, © 1964 George Braziller, Inc.

Martereau, © 1953 Librairie Gallimard.

The Planetarium, © 1960 George Braziller, Inc.

Portrait of a Man Unknown, © 1958 George Braziller, Inc.

Tropisms, © 1963 John Calder Ltd.

To George Braziller, Inc., for quotations from the following works by Claude Simon, all translated by Richard Howard:

The Flanders Road, © 1961 George Braziller, Inc.

The Grass, © 1958 Les Éditions de Minuit.

Histoire, © 1968 George Braziller, Inc.

The Palace, © 1963 George Braziller, Inc.

The Wind, © 1957 Les Éditions de Minuit.

To George Braziller, Inc., for quotations from the following works by Claude Mauriac:

All Women Are Fatal, translated by Richard Howard, © 1964 George Braziller, Inc.

The Dinner Party, translated by Merloyd Lawrence, © 1960 George Braziller, Inc.

The Marquise Went Out at Five, translated by Richard Howard, © 1962 George Braziller.

To Simon and Schuster, Inc., for quotations from the following works by Michel Butor:

A Change of Heart, translated by Jean Stewart, © 1958 Michel Butor.

Degrees, translated by Richard Howard, © 1961 Simon and Schuster, Inc.

Passing Time, translated by Jean Stewart, © 1960 Faber and Faber Ltd.

To New Directions Publishing Corporation for quotations from the following works:

Our Exagmination Round His Factification for Incamination of Work in Progress by Samuel Beckett *et al.* All rights reserved.

The Skin of Dreams by Raymond Queneau, translated by H. J. Kaplan. All rights reserved.

Stephen Hero by James Joyce, Copyright 1944, 1955, © 1963 New Directions Publishing Corporation.

To Doubleday & Company, Inc., for a quotation from:

The Theatre of the Absurd by Martin Esslin, © 1961 Martin Esslin.

I offer grateful acknowledgments to all those firms in the United Kingdom that have permitted me to quote copyright material, as listed below.

To Associated Book Publishers (International) Ltd and Methuen and Co. Ltd for quotations from the following work by Michel Butor:

Degrees, translated by Richard Howard, © 1961 Simon and Schuster, Inc.

To Jonathan Cape Limited for quotations from the following works by Claude Simon, all translated by Richard Howard:

The Flanders Road, © 1961 George Braziller, Inc.

The Grass, © 1958 Les Éditions de Minuit.

Histoire, © 1968 George Braziller, Inc.

The Palace, © 1963 George Braziller, Inc.

To Faber and Faber Limited for quotations from the following works by Michel Butor, both translated by Jean Stewart:

Second Thoughts, © 1958 Michel Butor.

Passing Time, © 1960 Faber and Faber Limited.

To Calder and Boyars Limited for quotations from the following:

Molloy by Samuel Beckett, translated by Patrick Bowles in collaboration with the author, © 1955 Grove Press, Inc.

Raymond Roussel by Rayner Heppenstall, © 1967 Rayner Heppenstall.

To Calder and Boyars Limited for quotations from the following works by Claude Mauriac:

Dinner in Town, translated by Merloyd Lawrence, © 1960 George Braziller, Inc.

The Marquise Went Out at Five, translated by Richard Howard, © 1962 George Braziller.

L'Oubli, © 1966 Éditions Bernard Grasset. (Quoted in my own translation, not in that published or to be published by Calder and Boyars Limited.)

To Calder and Boyars Limited for quotations from the following works by Robert Pinget:

Baga, © 1958 Les Éditions de Minuit.

L'Inquisitoire, © 1962 Les Éditions de Minuit.

Mahu ou le matériau, © 1952 Robert Laffont.

Quelqu'un, © 1965 Les Éditions de Minuit.

(As already indicated, these four works are quoted in my own translation, not in the translations published or to be published by Calder and Boyars Limited.)

To Calder and Boyars Limited for quotations from the following work by Raymond Queneau:

Le Chiendent, © 1933 Librairie Gallimard. (Quoted in my own translation, not in that published by Calder and Boyars Limited.)

To Calder and Boyars Limited for quotations from the following works by Alain Robbe-Grillet, all translated by Richard Howard:

Jealousy, © 1959 Grove Press, Inc.

Last Year at Marienbad, © 1962 Grove Press, Inc.

The Voyeur, © 1958 Grove Press, Inc.

To Calder and Boyars Limited for quotations from the following works by Nathalie Sarraute, all translated by Maria Jolas:

Between Life and Death, © 1969 George Braziller, Inc.

The Golden Fruits, © 1964 George Braziller, Inc.

Martereau, © 1953 Librairie Gallimard.

The Planetarium, © 1960 George Braziller, Inc.

Portrait of a Man Unknown, © 1958 George Braziller, Inc.

Tropisms and The Age of Suspicion, © 1963 John Calder (Publishers) Ltd.

V. M.

Boulder, Colorado, 4 October, 1970

TO THE MEMORY OF MY FATHER

WILLIAM COCHRANE MERCIER

(1 8 8 5 – 1 9 5 4)

AND OF ALL OUR HUGUENOT ANCESTORS

IN IRELAND AS WELL AS FRANCE

Contents

The New Novel

FROM QUENEAU TO PINGET

I

Introduction

What is the New Novel?

THE basic premise of this book is that the growth of *le nouveau roman*, the New Novel in France, whose existence began to be recognized in 1953, was the result of a literary rather than a philosophic movement. To anyone who has not read recent French criticism, with its intensely philosophic orientation, this sentence will appear tautological. But in fact there has been strong insistence by the critics that, just as the drama and fiction of Sartre and Camus embodied existentialism, so the New Novel embodies phenomenology. Undeniably, new ways of conceiving human experience—and particularly the phenomenology of the German philosopher Husserl—had a powerful impact on those of the New Novelists who were capable of understanding them. Yet I believe that the primary impulse leading to the renewal of the French novel was a deep dissatisfaction with an art form now paying the penalty for the high degree of development it had achieved in the nineteenth century. The French novel of the first half of the twentieth century was technologically obsolescent or obsolete: it badly needed to "retool," following the lead of such English-language masters as Joyce, Faulkner, and Virginia Woolf, or such German-language ones as Kafka and Thomas Mann. It could also accept, at long last, the influence of Surrealism, which had transformed French poetry as early as the 1920's and was just beginning in the 1950's—after an abortive attempt in the 1920's—to renew French drama through the early plays of Adamov, Ionesco, and Beckett, the "theatre of the absurd." When the overdue renewal of the French novel finally took place, it could draw on all the innovations tested in other national literatures during the first half of the century and then go a step or two beyond them.

The history of the novel as a genre separate from the earlier narrative forms of romance and epic, when viewed in the broadest terms, may be summed up in a single phrase: the quest for realism. Realism is a convenient name for a set of literary conventions that claim to represent the reality of human experience. This set of conventions is not fixed, however. As the novelist's conception of reality changes, some conventions are dropped and others are added. In this sense, perhaps, the ideas of philosophers influence the techniques of novelists; but both the ideas and the techniques may express a new consensus—a "shift in sensibility," as it is sometimes called—tacitly adopted by the intelligentsia as a whole.

During the detailed examination of the seven novelists chosen for discussion here, it will become clear that they are all in some degree skeptical about "reality." Does it exist? And if it does exist, how can we attain any certain knowledge of it? In all probability, what we call reality is a mental construct imposed upon sensory data by the innate structure of the mind itself. If this construct be not reality, it may yet be all of reality that we can ever possibly know. These are the amateurish remarks of a literary critic untrained—and probably untrainable—in philosophic method, but any layman can see that some such doubts underlie the techniques and conventions employed by the New Novelists. Nathalie Sarraute coined the phrase the "age of suspicion" to define the attitude of the modern reader toward modern fiction; it also defines the attitude of the New Novelist toward human experience—his raw material.

The very phrase "human experience" begs the question,

for it implies on the one hand a *subject* in the technical sense
—a human being who experiences—and on the other hand
an *object*—something that is being experienced. The New
Novelist often finds himself unwilling or unable to make this
distinction between subject and object. As a writer, he must
then discover, consciously or unconsciously, a technique that
will force or inveigle his reader into a similar incapacity.
Beckett's *The Unnamable* and Robbe-Grillet's *Jealousy* exemplify two entirely different narrative techniques that achieve
this end. Joyce had achieved it earlier, on an enormous scale,
in *Finnegans Wake*; all discussions of who the dreamer is in
the *Wake* seem bound to prove fruitless: the dream dreams
itself, subject and object becoming one in the new language
coined by Joyce, just as form and content also become one.
However, for every reader who can penetrate far enough into
the *Wake* to have his consciousness radically modified, there
are probably ten who can perform the same feat by reading
Jealousy.

The new realism of the New Novel, then, may consist not
in *recording* reality—as Zola, for instance, believed he was
doing—but in *inventing* it. "I do not transcribe, I construct,"
writes Robbe-Grillet in his essay "From Realism to Reality,"
and he continues thus:

> This had been even the old ambition of Flaubert: to make
> something out of nothing, something that would stand alone,
> without having to lean on anything external to the work; today
> this is the ambition of the novel as a whole.[1]

The entire essay is of the greatest importance, beginning with
the very first sentence: "All writers believe they are realists."

If the New Novelist is so concerned with inventing, his
reader may be puzzled to find him engaging in minute description of familiar objects. Robbe-Grillet explains this seeming paradox in another essay, "Time and Description in
Fiction Today":

> Description once served to situate the chief contours of a
> setting, then to cast light on some of its particularly revealing

[1] *For a New Novel* (New York: Grove Press, 1966), p. 162.

elements; it no longer mentions anything except insignificant objects, or objects which it is concerned to make so. It once claimed to reproduce a pre-existing reality; it now asserts its creative function. Finally, it once made us see things, now it seems to destroy them, as if its intention to discuss them aimed only at blurring their contours, at making them incomprehensible, at causing them to disappear altogether.[2]

This is an accurate account of Robbe-Grillet's own practice of description, but just why his kind of description need appear in a novel at all is something he has never satisfactorily explained.

Under such conventions, fiction is fiction indeed, and the greatest realism may consist in constantly reminding the reader that he is reading a "made-up" story, not observing life. The struggle of the novelist, ever since Flaubert, to eliminate himself from his novel now becomes pointless. Claude Mauriac appears in person at some point in three of his novels—a device employed by Queneau also in *Les Enfants du limon* some twenty years before. This is only one of many ways invented by the New Novelist to put the reader on his guard. As the fundamental concept of reality has changed—and with it, of course, the definition of realism— much besides description that we took for granted in the "old" novel will tend to disappear or be transmuted: characters, plot, chronology, even dialogue.

Most readers find the disappearance of easily recognizable characters hardest to stomach. The protagonist of a New Novel (*Jealousy*, for instance) may not be identified even by a name, while the shadowy figures who flit around him either have no names or have several apiece, like "Lady Ava" in *La Maison de Rendez-vous*. We must read a long way into Butor's *A Change of Heart* before we learn the protagonist's full name—and then we promptly forget it. Since he tells his story entirely in the second person—"you" do this, "you" do that—we readers come to identify ourselves with him; we do the same with the nameless protagonist of *Jealousy*. Nathalie Sarraute gives no names to anyone in *Between Life and*

[2] *For a New Novel*, p. 147.

Death, but the reader may find himself even more disoriented when, as in *Martereau*, she names a *persona*. Throughout the book named after him, we can never decide whether Martereau is a fool, a knave, or a model of honesty and intelligence. Novels of this type bring home to us how much the identities of the people we meet every day are the products of our imagination, just as our own personalities are in large part the figments of others' imaginations and perhaps of our own. Much of our everyday activity is "creative" in exactly the sense of that word in the phrase "creative writing." Mme Sarraute also suggests to us that the persons we see speaking and acting with what appears to be full consciousness may only be the tip of the iceberg: below the surface their psyches and ours may meet and mingle in the collective unconscious, so that it might be unwise to distinguish separate individuals at all.

Another familiar reaction to the New Novel is the complaint that it "has no plot." Let us be sure what we mean by this criticism. E. M. Forster says in *Aspects of the Novel* that "The king died and then the queen died" is merely a story (one thing happens *after* another) whereas "The king died and then the queen died *of grief*" is a plot (one thing happens *because of* another). As we shall see, certain New Novels are very carefully plotted, but some of these plots turn out to be self-destroying. On the other hand, the absence of plot in most New Novels no doubt expresses the authors' skepticism about the possibility of establishing, with any degree of certainty, the causes of any particular event—or indeed of isolating such events at all from the continuum of experience.

That continuum—insofar as it exists, because trauma can of course suppress consciousness entirely for shorter or longer periods—explains the New Novelists' seemingly capricious handling of chronology. Our experience at the present moment may well consist of a memory of the past or a daydream of the future—indeed, our daydreams also invent or rearrange the past, though we can hardly be said to remember the future. Again, our dreams in sleep may be outside time altogether. It is a fairly widespread yet not very credible convention of the New Novel that when we think about past or future we are not aware of its being in a different time phase than the present. Robbe-Grillet in particular overworks this convention in both novels and films.

As for dialogue, most New Novels contain almost none, though some consist of little else. Yet all New Novel dialogue deviates—in style or content, or both—from what a tape recorder might capture. Generally, the style is extremely mannered, whether it tends toward the brevity of Hemingway's dialogue, as in Robbe-Grillet, or toward the prolixity of Faulkner's, as in Claude Simon. Pinget writes a more nearly colloquial—though not regional—dialogue than any of the others, but it often contains information that would rarely if ever be conveyed orally: for example, the inventories of furniture in *The Inquisitory*.

In the absence of so many elements that gave the traditional novel both interest and unity, the New Novelists have inevitably sought new principles of organization, ranging from train schedules to classical myths. The structure of a New Novel is generally more rigid than that of an "old" one, rather than less so. Extreme examples are found in Queneau and Butor: a Butor novel often resembles the solution of a problem in logistics rather than the product of artistic inspiration. Among other devices used by the New Novelists are the neo-classic standbys, unity of place and unity of time. The apartment house in Butor's *Passage de Milan* and the house on the banana plantation in *Jealousy* are perfect examples of unity of place. Unity of time is carried to fantastic lengths by Claude Mauriac, who would like to create an instantaneous novel and has succeeded in writing one, *L'Agrandissement*, that covers only two minutes—though it takes almost two hours to read. Cyclical time is used by Queneau in *Le Chiendent* and by Robbe-Grillet in *The Erasers*. The protagonist of Claude Simon's *The Flanders Road* remembers the events of many years of war and peace during a single night.

Some writers pursue analogies with the other arts, attempting to assimilate a novel to a painting, as in Claude Simon's

The Wind, subtitled "Attempted Restoration of a Baroque Altarpiece," or Robbe-Grillet's *In the Labyrinth,* which can be read as the bringing to life of the figures in an etching entitled "The Defeat of Reichenfels." In *Passing Time,* Butor makes similar use of a series of tapestries dealing with the mythical adventures of Theseus. Musical forms are less important, but there is frequent use of a leitmotiv in the manner of Wagner, and of variations upon a theme. In the chapter on Robbe-Grillet, a musical analogy for the development of *Jealousy* is explored in detail.

In short, the New Novelists experiment with form both negatively, because of what they discard that was essential to the traditional novel, and positively, because of their need to find substitutes for the discarded elements. Butor regards experiment with new forms and new techniques as an essential part of the novelist's task in every age, because these provide new instruments for his research into reality:

> . . . *des formes nouvelles révéleront dans la réalite des choses nouvelles, des liaisons nouvelles.* . . .[3]

The New Novel might well have been called the Experimental Novel had not Zola preempted that title in the nineteenth century for a volume of criticism in which he attempted to show that his Rougon-Macquart cycle of twenty novels conducted experiments in what we would now call the social sciences. Zola thus confused art and life in an unsophisticated way impossible, one would hope, for a New Novelist.

Who are the New Novelists?

Of the seven writers discussed in this book, three form the nucleus of the New Novel school: Alain Robbe-Grillet, Nathalie Sarraute, and Michel Butor. Robbe-Grillet, by virtue of his editorial post with the publishing firm of Les Éditions

[3] *Répertoire* (Paris: Les Éditions de Minuit, 1960), p. 9. I take this to mean "new forms will reveal new things, new relationships, within reality."

de Minuit, was in a good position to set himself at the head of a literary movement. Minuit had already published two of Samuel Beckett's novels in French, *Molloy* and *Malone meurt*, and the epoch-making play *En attendant Godot*, when Robbe-Grillet's first published novel, *Les Gommes* (*The Erasers*), appeared in 1953. In the following year Minuit published Butor's first novel, *Passage de Milan*. Other like-minded novelists, Robert Pinget and Claude Simon, whose first books had been published by other firms, were added to the Minuit list in 1956 and 1957, respectively. Nathalie Sarraute was already committed to the great publishing house of Gallimard —of which Queneau is an officer and by which he has almost always been published. Mme Sarraute's first novel, *Portrait d'un inconnu* (*Portrait of a Man Unknown*), had been published in 1948 by Robert Marin, with a preface by Jean-Paul Sartre, who coined the expression *anti-roman* ("anti-novel") to describe both her book and certain classic novels which he felt provided her with a tradition. Her second novel, *Martereau*, was brought out by Gallimard in the crucial year of 1953. Minuit did, however, give her its accolade by issuing the revised version of *Tropismes*, her 1939 volume of short fiction, in 1957.

Robbe-Grillet, Butor, and Mme Sarraute became known as members of a school partly because of their readiness to defend their novelistic practice in theoretical articles. The dates of publication of Robbe-Grillet's *Pour un nouveau roman* (*For a New Novel*) and Butor's first volume of collected criticism, *Répertoire*,[4] 1963 and 1960 respectively, are less important than the dates during the 1950's on which individual articles by them appeared. Mme Sarraute's *L'Ère du soupçon* (*The Age of Suspicion*), four essays on the novel, appeared more opportunely in 1956. Simon and Pinget have been unwilling to issue critical manifestoes, but their continued publication by Minuit has assured their identification with the New Novel group in the minds of readers.

⁴ Some of the most important essays on the novel from *Répertoire* and *Répertoire II* are translated in *Inventory*, ed. Richard Howard (New York: Simon and Schuster, 1968).

The American reputations of four of these five novelists have been well served by their New York publishers. The firm of George Braziller has published translations of virtually everything Mme Sarraute has written; Grove Press has done the same for Robbe-Grillet. Braziller has promptly translated every novel by Simon since *Le Vent* (*The Wind*), the first of his to be published by Minuit. Simon and Schuster has published all of Butor's four novels except the first, as well as *Mobile* and *Inventory*. One can only hope that more novels by Pinget will appear in translation, in addition to *Monsieur Levert* and *The Inquisitory*, the two already available.

Claude Mauriac has never been published by Minuit or Gallimard, nor can he be described as a friend of any of the novelists mentioned except Mme Sarraute. However, having published his first novel in 1957, he has been powerfully influenced by the New Novelists, and his work has come more and more to resemble theirs. Braziller took up his work enthusiastically for a time but dropped it after publishing three novels from the tetralogy. If Robbe-Grillet, Butor, Sarraute, and Simon may be said to have selected themselves for study here, the inclusion of Mauriac and Pinget has been my personal choice.

Still more personal is the inclusion of Raymond Queneau. Although Queneau had been writing works of fiction that show many characteristics of the New Novel for two decades before 1953, it seems likely that Robbe-Grillet, for one, was unaware of the fact until years after that date. Queneau has been recognized of late as at least a forerunner of the New Novel, but he has never been a personal friend of any of the five writers in the "inner" group. Had he not been so shamefully neglected until recently by both critics and publishers in the English-speaking world, he would not have had a chapter to himself but would have been grouped with other precursors in this introduction.

Of our seven writers, only three remain consistently loyal to the novel: Simon writes virtually nothing in any other form, while Pinget and Mme Sarraute have survived flirtations with broadcasting and the theatre. Robbe-Grillet and Mauriac devote a steadily increasing proportion of their energy to the cinema and the theatre, respectively. Queneau's most enduring love is lyric poetry, while Butor's aim is surely to transcend literature altogether in favor of some ultimate, multi-media art-to-end-art.

The arrangement and titling of the chapters on these seven authors require a brief explanation. In principle, the chapters follow the chronological order in which the authors "joined the movement." Queneau and Nathalie Sarraute were writing experimental fiction before there was a movement. Robbe-Grillet, Butor, and Simon then follow in the order in which they were first published by Les Éditions de Minuit. Claude Mauriac, as a late-comer, appears second-last. Pinget, however, has been removed from his rightful place after Nathalie Sarraute: his earliest experimental fiction, the short sketches entitled *Entre Fantoine et Agapa* ("Between Fantoine and Agapa"), dates from 1951 and his novel *Mahu* from 1952. In placing Pinget last, I am expressing the belief that of these novelists he is the one who most deserves to be better known in English-speaking countries. I am also expressing the hope that Pinget has not yet attained the peak of his career and may in time prove the greatest of the seven.

As for the subtitles of the chapters on individual authors, I hope they are not merely the result of misplaced ingenuity: in each case I have tried to define an aspect of the New Novel that is best represented by that particular author. In subtitling the chapter on Queneau "The Creator as Destroyer," I have pointed to the arbitrary structure that underpins so many Queneau novels—a structure that is sometimes demolished at the end of the work as if it were merely a scaffolding instead of something integral to the literary edifice. In "Nathalie Sarraute: From Jane Austen to Dostoevsky," I have tried to indicate Mme Sarraute's astonishing combination of satirical humor and depth psychology. Robbe-Grillet's two major concerns are without doubt "Description and Narration," though for a time I thought of putting down "Description *as* Narration." "The Schema and the Myth" refers to Butor's Queneau-like obsession with structure—complicated

and modified by an equal preoccupation with the anti-mecha-
nistic symbolism of ancient myth. The Simon subtitle is perhaps too complex and specific to be applicable to the New
Novel as a whole; yet we do see in Butor and Robbe-Grillet,
for example, on the one hand the attempt to strike a balance
between order and disorder, and on the other hand the subtle
way in which memory is distorted by desire. Mauriac's great
theme is nothing else than "The Immobilization of Time."
Pinget, at the opposite pole from the neat structures of
Queneau and Butor, seems to be offering us odd pieces from
a jigsaw puzzle and inviting us to construct our own picture,
filling the gaps ourselves. This invitation to the reader to
collaborate is endemic in the New Novel, but Pinget pushes it
further than any of his colleagues.

One further word about method: in most of the chapters on
individual authors—the exceptions are those on Mme Sarraute
and Mauriac—the book that I believe to be the novelist's
masterpiece, or at any rate his most characteristic work to
date, is analyzed first in great detail. The remaining novels
are treated more briefly in chronological order. In the Queneau
chapter, his first novel, *Le Chiendent*, happens to be his most
important and is discussed first; a later novel, *Saint Glinglin*,
is then taken out of chronological order and given second
place in the critical discussion.

Why renew the novel?

Each of our New Novelists had somewhat different reasons for
quarreling with the "old" novel—besides the excellent reason
that it was old. This quarrel with one's predecessors has
nothing unhealthy or negative about it. Two of the greatest
English novelists began their careers by parodying the most
fashionable novelists of their time: Fielding attacked Richard-
son's *Pamela* twice, first in *Shamela* and then in the purported
history of Pamela's brother, *Joseph Andrews*; Jane Austen
pilloried the entire "Gothic" novel school in *Northanger
Abbey*, her first major work, though published posthumously.

In certain of the chapters below, especially those on Robbe-Grillet and Mme Sarraute, we shall see the kind of complaint lodged by the New Novelists against their predecessors.

An observer from outside French culture may be excused for thinking that the French twentieth-century novel was in even poorer condition than the New Novelists alleged, however, and for the very reason that French fiction had developed so rapidly in the previous century. Only Russian fiction can be considered a worthy rival of French in the nineteenth century; while France has no second novelist of towering stature to set beside Balzac in competition with Tolstoy and Dostoevsky, the general level of French novelists—Hugo, Stendhal, Flaubert, Zola—is surely higher than that of comparable Russian writers.

In the first half of the twentieth century, on the other hand, France was the homeland of a number of competent nineteenth-century novelists and one great innovator—Marcel Proust. At first sight, Proust might be mistaken for a lesser Balzac, but in fact the twentieth-century novelist opened up whole territories undreamed of by the nineteenth-century one. Proust does not merely explore the unconscious mind: he introduces an entirely new concept of character portrayal. Where Balzac's characters are monolithic, and seem mysterious only until we get a look at the other, hidden side of them, Proust's characters do not merely reveal other aspects of themselves but actually have *changed* by the time we meet them again in a different period or place. To some extent all Proust's major characters disintegrate: we begin to wonder if we can see any permanent personality structure underlying all their metamorphoses. Also, Proust employs the Wagnerian leitmotiv technique of recurring phrases, as well as recurrent visual symbols, to lend unity to his long novel. Even so, Proust is not so great an innovator as the Joyce of *Ulysses*, not to mention the Joyce of *Finnegans Wake*: the stream-of-consciousness technique would have suited Proust's temperament admirably if he had hit upon it. It is ironical that Joyce borrowed the technique from a minor French novel of the

1880's, Édouard Dujardin's *Les Lauriers sont coupés* (translated as *We'll to the Woods No More*).

André Gide's experiments with the novel form, like all his other experiments, are rather cautious. *Les Caves du Vatican* (*Lafcadio's Adventures*) reminds one of Shaw's experiments with the drama: the reader's conventional expectations are just sufficiently disturbed to make him receptive to the author's rather subversive message. Innovation is pursued not for its own sake but in the interests of propaganda. All the fuss about the art of novel-writing in *Les Faux-monnayeurs* (*The Counterfeiters*) turns out to be in actuality a discussion of the relationship between life and art. The novel as an autonomous art form is a conception beyond Gide's ken. Gide's other works of fiction are more or less disguised confessions, though the best of them, *L'Immoraliste*, displays a beautiful symmetry in its three journeys—to Africa, back to Normandy, to Africa again.

Confessions, tales with a propagandist moral, and heavy-footed, pseudo-Balzacian series of novels—these are what French fiction of 1900–50 has to offer to the English-speaking critic. Very often he is much too tolerant of these works, for the simple reason that they are so easy to read. The "mandarin" French of the seventeenth and eighteenth centuries that he picked up in college will carry him through most allegedly twentieth-century French fiction. Even when Céline broke the language barrier with *Voyage au bout de la nuit* (1932), there were few to follow him in his attempt to put spoken French on paper.

In 1953, the novelists whom Robbe-Grillet, Beckett, and the others had to compete with for the allegiance of the intellectual reader—readers of best sellers went a different way, as always—were Camus and Sartre. I have no wish to belittle the achievements of these two gifted men of letters firmly situated in a French tradition that goes back to Voltaire, Diderot, and Rousseau; I must insist, however, that their creative endowment for novel-writing and their interest in the novel as an art form were little better than mediocre.

La Nausée (*Nausea*) and *L'Étranger* (*The Stranger*) may present a more realistic surface than *Candide*, but their reason for existence, like that of Voltaire's little masterpiece of fantasy, is the philosophic message they embody.

It was high time for Frenchmen to apply the doctrine of "art for art's sake" to the novel again, as Flaubert had done a century before, even if the special relationship between the novel and "reality" might once again thwart its full application. By showing interest in the novel as an art form, the New Novelists were not only turning back to Flaubert but looking outward from France to their contemporaries elsewhere. Queneau has written that it was English and American novelists, but Joyce above all, who taught him that a technique of the novel existed.

By no means all the New Novelists think of themselves exclusively as artists, however. Butor, Robbe-Grillet, and Mme Sarraute all hint in their essays at the possibility that they are scientists, capable of making new discoveries about human experience if they use their instrument, the novel, aright. The unpardonable crime, in novel-writing as in scientific research, is to make a discovery that you had "planted" in the first place. Conclusions, whether they be philosophical messages or merely endings to narratives, are hard to find in the New Novel. There is no compelling reason why Butor's *Degrees* or Pinget's *The Inquisitory* should end at the particular point it does. Beware of assuming that the rare works of fantasy written by the New Novelists—Pinget's *Graal Flibuste*, for instance—must be moral allegories; they are far more likely to be sheer storytelling for its own sake.

The reader who is encountering the New Novel for the first time should avoid hurrying "to get to the end." There may be no end: the narrative may simply be broken off, leaving jagged edges, or the end may rejoin the beginning like a snake with its tail in its mouth. It is the *process* of reading that supplies the enjoyment; at times the reader may find himself compelled to supplement what the author has given him with the products of his own imagination; he may even achieve the illusion that he and not the author is writing the book. In the words of Robert Louis Stevenson, "To travel hopefully is better than to arrive"; or, as Marshall McLuhan would say, "The medium is the message."

Some precursors: Kafka, Beckett, Roussel

Today, exponents of all the arts undergo incredibly diverse influences drawn from all the centuries and all the continents. Still, there are certain writers of fiction whose names the New Novelists continually invoke in interviews and critical essays: Dostoevsky, Joyce, Faulkner, Kafka, and of course their great countryman Proust. In later chapters, we shall see something of the influence of Dostoevsky on Mme Sarraute and of Faulkner on Claude Simon. Proust's influence can be seen almost everywhere, though most strikingly perhaps in Butor, Simon, and Pinget. The next section of this introductory chapter, based on a specialized knowledge of Joyce, tries to measure accurately the breadth and depth of his influence on the New Novel; even where no direct influence can be shown to exist, he and the New Novelists have gone far indeed upon parallel courses.

Some critics have noted points of comparison between the New Novel and the work of Jorge Luis Borges; Robbe-Grillet, Butor, and perhaps others of our writers are aware of his work. They share with him an insistence on the "fictionality" of fiction, but it might prove difficult to show a direct influence of the Argentinean writer on their novels.[5] Borges's reputation in France is comparatively recent, whereas Kafka's dates from before World War II, when his books became available in French translation. After World War II, Gide and Jean-Louis Barrault adapted *The Trial* for the French stage, with considerable commercial as well as artistic success. Some of the New Novelists must have absorbed the Kafka atmosphere in their teens, so that it pervades their work like an aroma. I

[5] Whether Pinget had read Borges at the time or not, the short, self-contained sketches—part essay, part story—in *Entre Fantoine et Agapa* and the second half of *Mahu* have most in common with Borges's work.

have therefore decided to stress, in the remainder of this section, the influence of Kafka, along with that of two French-language writers, Samuel Beckett and Raymond Roussel (1877–1933). Roussel's name is virtually unknown to English-speaking readers, but Butor's essay on him in *Répertoire* dates from 1950; Robbe-Grillet's in *For a New Novel* appeared in 1963.

Even the accidents of Kafka's career—his inability to finish his two great novels, *The Trial* and *The Castle,* and his consequent neglect to identify some major characters by anything more than initials—have proved useful to the New Novelists. Kafka's greatest contribution, however, has probably been the atmosphere of his major works, that feeling they give the reader of being awake and dreaming at the same time. Josef K. in *The Trial* loses his normal orientation mainly because the new and unfamiliar happenings in his life take place for the most part among familiar surroundings—his lodgings, his office. The subject/object confusion is present once again: the reader must ask himself whether the unexpected manifestations, such as the flagellation K. witnesses in a sort of closet at his place of work, are "really there" or are the products of dreaming and/or hallucination. Robbe-Grillet, it should be noted, insists on their reality, partly in order to defeat those who interpret Kafka allegorically. He insists that

> . . . if there is one thing of which an unprejudiced reading convinces us it is the absolute reality of the things Kafka describes. The visible world of his novels is certainly for him the real world, and what is behind (if there *is* something) seems without value, faced with the manifest nature of objects, gestures, words, etc. The hallucinatory effect derives from their extraordinary clarity and not from mystery or mist. Nothing is more fantastic, ultimately, than precision. Perhaps Kafka's staircases lead *elsewhere,* but they are *there.* . . .[6]

A brief look at several New Novels will give us some idea of the scope of Kafka's influence—or at any rate of the close

[6] *For a New Novel,* p. 165.

similarities between his work and that of the New Novelists, whether directly influenced or not. The nameless soldier of Robbe-Grillet's *In the Labyrinth*—constantly trying to deliver a package whose contents he is ignorant of to a person whose name he does not know in a street whose name he has forgotten—seems a more typical Kafka protagonist than any in Kafka's own work, until we reflect that the soldier displays no *Angst*: he hardly seems to care whether he completes his task or not, and he makes no passionate plea for recognition or justice. Jacques Revel, in Butor's *Passing Time*, feels as alien in Bleston as the surveyor protagonist of *The Castle* feels in the mysterious village ruled by the bureaucrats in the even more mysterious castle. The protagonists of both novels are comforted by women, only to find themselves more alienated than ever as a result. In Nathalie Sarraute's *Martereau*, the title character seems as ambiguous and enigmatic to the young narrator—himself almost as alienated as a Kafka protagonist—as K.'s lawyer or the painter Titorelli seems to K. in *The Trial*. A number of Pinget's protagonists feel impelled, like K. in *The Trial*, to defend themselves against obscure accusations: Clope, in *Clope au dossier*, seems to have compiled his defense in the form of a dossier; Monsieur Levert, in *Le Fiston*, writes on and on at his self-exculpatory letter to his runaway son. Most Kafka-like of all is the endless interrogation of the old manservant in *The Inquisitory*: he does not know who is being investigated—himself, his employers, their friends, another of their servants—or even whether a crime has been committed at all. Admittedly the influence of Kafka is everywhere in modern fiction, but the four New Novelists just mentioned have assimilated far more than a mere fashionable Kafkan veneer—doubtless because in part their aims are identical with his.

The contribution of Samuel Beckett to the theory and practice of the New Novel is essentially fourfold. The four elements may to some extent be found elsewhere, but Beckett's adoption of them reinforced the New Novelists' willingness to use them.

First, Beckett's work—especially *The Unnamable*—reveals once and for all the minima of the novel: no plot, an almost nonexistent protagonist, no setting.

Second, we have the apparently entirely original idea of the character who invents a life for himself: Malone in *Malone Dies*, for example. Pinget has played numerous variations on this theme: how much of *The Inquisitory* or *Quelqu'un* is supposed to be remembered and how much invented by the narrator? *Baga* is the extreme example of this self-invention among Pinget's novels.

Third, there is the awareness, so essential to Butor's *Passing Time* and Pinget's *Le Fiston* (*Monsieur Levert*), that words are the life of the fictional character. In *Malone Dies*, the protagonist dies when his hand stops writing the words— lying or truthful—that we are reading. In the introduction to *Last Year at Marienbad*, Robbe-Grillet makes a similar point when he insists that his film hero and heroine have no existence, past or future, except those moments when they appear before us on the screen.

Finally, Beckett reminds us again and again that fiction *is* fiction. For example, take the concluding words of *Molloy*:

> Then I went back into the house and wrote, It is midnight. The rain is beating on the windows. It was not midnight. It was not raining.

Although Butor and Robbe-Grillet have expressed keen admiration for Raymond Roussel, it is hard to say just how much their work has been influenced by his example. Robbe-Grillet's minute descriptions of inanimate objects such as cigarette packs and magazine illustrations, Butor's of works of art whether real or imaginary, and Simon's of a cigar box in *The Palace* or picture postcards and their stamps in *Histoire* —all these probably owe something indirectly to Roussel's *La Vue* (1904). As Rayner Heppenstall tells us:

> The title-piece in the volume *La Vue* is a poem of some two thousand lines. The volume contains two further poems, *Le Concert* and *La Source*, of about half that length. Each describes, in far more detail than it is possible to imagine being

physically visible, a miniature view. In *La Vue*, it is a sea-side
prospect engraved on a lens set into a penholder. In *Le
Concert*, it is the heading of a sheet of hotel writing paper,
showing the hotel itself, an omnibus standing before it, the
lake beyond and public gardens with a bandstand. In *La
Source*, the label on a bottle of mineral water shows the spring
itself and a girl in peasant costume serving customers with
the wholesome draught.[7]

Roussel, who was admired by some of the French Surrealists,
should be hailed on the strength of these poems as a patron
saint of Pop painting and sculpture. One cannot be sure, however, that the New Novelists ever read *La Vue*. What they did
read, apart from one or other of Roussel's strange and, to my
taste, intolerably tedious novels, *Impressions d'Afrique* (now
available in English as *Impressions of Africa*) or *Locus solus*,
was his posthumously published essay "*Comment j'ai écrit
certains de mes livres.*" None of the New Novelists, apparently,
has adopted precisely the method of stimulating the imagination advocated there, but the essay certainly encouraged some
of them—especially, perhaps, Butor in *Degrees* and Robbe-
Grillet in *La Maison de Rendez-vous*—to adopt arbitrary
structures and methods of procedure in writing their novels.
Queneau's essay, "*Délire typographique*" ("Typographical
Delirium"), now collected in his volume *Bâtons, chiffres et
lettres* but first published in 1938, mentions Roussel's *Nouvelles
impressions d'Afrique*, a poem very similar to *La Vue*; other
works by Roussel may have encouraged Queneau in the arbitrariness of his early novels. In any case, Queneau had been
a Surrealist himself in his formative years: it is hard to believe
that the New Novel movement would have taken quite the
path it did, had it not had the experiments of the Surrealists in
forms other than the novel to draw upon.

Roussel reveals the essence of his technique at the very
beginning of his essay:

I always intended to explain the way in which I had written

[7] Rayner Heppenstall, *Raymond Roussel* (Berkeley and Los Angeles:
University of California Press, 1967), p. 24.

certain of my books (*Impressions d'Afrique, Locus solus. L'Étoile au front* and *La Poussière de soleils*).

It's a matter of a very special procedure. And it seems to me my duty to reveal this technique, because I have the impression that some future writers might perhaps exploit it fruitfully.

Already while very young I wrote stories a few pages long using this procedure.

I used to choose two almost similar words (reminding one of *métagrammes*[8]). For example *billard* ("billiard table") and *pillard* ("plunderer"). Then I added to them words that were alike but taken in two different senses, and I thus obtained two almost identical sentences.

As far as *billard* and *pillard* are concerned, the two sentences I obtained were these:

1. *Les lettres du blanc sur les bandes du vieux billard . . .*
2. *Les lettres du blanc sur les bandes du vieux pillard.*

In the first, *lettres* ["letters"] was taken in the sense of "typographical signs," *blanc* ["white"] in the sense of "cube of chalk" and *bandes* ["bands"] in the sense of "cushions" on a billiard table.

In the second, *lettres* was taken in the sense of "missives," *blanc* in the sense of "white man," and *bandes* in the sense of "warrior hordes."

The two sentences once found, it was a matter of writing a story that could begin with the first sentence and end with the second.

Now, it was from the solution of this problem that I drew all my material.[9]

Not only did Roussel write a short story with the opening and closing sentences quoted, but twelve years later they provided the nucleus for his *Impressions of Africa*. He proceeds to give the word associations—derived at first from the master sentence and then from words chosen more or less

[8] Presumably a *métagramme* is what is often called a "word ladder" in English, where changing one letter at a time brings you from one word to another by a series of "steps":

BALD   BOLD   BOLT   BOOT

[9] Raymond Roussel, *Comment j'ai écrit certains de mes livres* (Paris: Jean-Jacques Pauvert, 1963), pp. 11–12. My translation.

arbitrarily—that provided him with the hidden structure of that astonishing if tedious novel. At the end of the essay, in the Pauvert edition, three early short stories are reprinted in which the final sentence echoes and puns on the opening one. Lest it be thought that Roussel was totally insane, here is a quotation drawn from the mid-point of the essay:

> This procedure, in short, is related to rhyme. In both cases there is unforeseen creation due to phonic combinations.
> It is essentially a poetic procedure.
> Furthermore, one has to know how to employ it. And just as with rhymes one can make either good or bad verses, so with this procedure one can compose either good or bad works.[10]

In proceeding thus as an author, Roussel was neither more nor less insane than Joyce in writing *Finnegans Wake*. Roussel himself points out that although he had traveled widely and gone around the world in 1920–21 (he was very wealthy), he did not make use of his travels in his books; as he writes, this fact "shows clearly that with me imagination is everything."

The greatest precursor: Joyce

The New Novelists to whom James Joyce has probably meant most—Butor, Claude Mauriac, and Queneau—have shown their devotion to him each in a distinctive way: Butor by his critical studies, Queneau by pastiche or parody, and Mauriac by quoting certain texts of the master in his two most important novels.

Butor, who is at least as fine a critic as he is a novelist, has written two long essays on Joyce, both published in *Répertoire* (1960). The first dates from 1948, years before Butor embarked on his first novel; it bears the modest title *"Petite croisière préliminaire à une reconnaissance de l'archipel Joyce"* ("A Little Cruise Preliminary to a Reconnaissance of the Joyce Archipelago"). Considerably less of a critical study than an expository introduction for the French reader, it covers Joyce's

[10] Roussel, p. 23.

entire *oeuvre*, leaning heavily on Stuart Gilbert's *James Joyce's Ulysses* and Campbell and Robinson's *Skeleton Key to Finnegans Wake*. Butor provides his own keen insights from time to time: for instance (p. 205), he stresses the point that Bloom is as much a portrait of and a spokesman for Joyce as Stephen is; this was certainly not a widely accepted view in 1948. The second essay, *"Esquisse d'un seuil pour Finnegan"* ("Sketch of a Threshold for Finnegan"), was originally published as a preface to a French translation of passages from *Finnegans Wake* in 1957. Butor stresses here the impossibility of any one reader's unaided interpretation of a passage agreeing precisely with that of any other reader: "Consequently it is a portrait of myself which takes shape as I let my glance travel over these pages. . . ." Joyce, I think, would not have approved of the extreme subjectivity of another comment describing the *Wake* as "a machine to provoke and facilitate my own dreams," but Butor goes on to correct this view: "It isn't only to the revelation of my private dream that Joyce invites me, but also to its situation within a vaster consciousness. . . ."

Claude Mauriac, in an interview (which forms part of a valuable series on the New Novelists conducted by André Bourin in *Les Nouvelles littéraires*, 1959–60), has stressed his early awareness of Joyce:

I am forty-five [in 1959]; I was sixteen when, thanks to my father, I read Proust. Then I discovered James Joyce's *Ulysses*. From that moment (around the years 1937–1938) I was convinced that one must start writing from *there*.

Presumably he means that a contemporary novelist must begin where *Ulysses* leaves off. In his most important novel so far, *The Marquise Went Out at Five*, Mauriac has his novelist-hero sum up his aims (p. 304) in two quotations: one from Joyce, "History is a nightmare from which I am trying to awake"; and the other from Paul Klee, "The temporal element must be eliminated: yesterday and today taken as simultaneity." (These quotations are anticipatorily referred to elsewhere in the book, for instance on pp. 117 and 248 of the American edition.) A somewhat different use of a quotation

from *Ulysses* will be found in *L'Agrandissement*: on page 61 it
is given in French translation, and on page 107 in the original
English: "Harsh gargoyle face that warred against me over
our mess of hash of lights in rue Saint-André-des-Arts. In
words of words for words, *palabras*." This recall of Joyce's
recollection of Synge is doubtless quoted chiefly because of its
reference to one of the streets that intersect at the Carrefour
de Buci, which forms the *locale* of both Mauriac novels.
(*L'Agrandissement*, though written after *The Marquise*, deals
with the genesis in Bertrand Carnéjoux's mind of a novel very
similar to *The Marquise*, which he plans to call *The Barricades of Paris*. Mauriac, speaking in his own person at the end
of *L'Agrandissement*, tells us, "This book is the story of a
gentleman who is wondering how he will write a novel that
I have already written.")

As for Raymond Queneau, anyone who consults the index
to his volume of essays, *Bâtons, chiffres et lettres* (1950), can
quickly find two formal acknowledgments of Joyce's influence.
In an essay on the technique of the novel, he speaks of "my
debt to the English and American novelists who taught me
that a technique of the novel existed, and very specially to
Joyce." In a radio interview, he tells how he planned his first
novel, *Le Chiendent*, "under the influence of Joyce and of
Faulkner [who had not yet been translated]. . . ." Most interesting of all, however, is "*Une Traduction en joycien*" ("A
Translation into Joycese"). This is prefaced by the following
remarks:

> To understand properly, nothing is better than practice.
> In order to *fairchtéer Finnegans Wake*, I tried a few years
> ago to apply the Joycean method to a text chosen at random.

(*Fairchtéer* is a French word coined by Queneau from the
German *verstehen*, "to understand.") Actually the text used
by Queneau is not chosen at random but forms the opening
paragraphs of his second novel, *Gueule de pierre* (1934).
Queneau retained some of the Joycisms when he revised the
passage for inclusion in *Saint Glinglin* (1948), the definitive
version and completion of *Gueule de pierre*.

This is not in fact the most ingenious or the most humorous of Queneau's tributes to Joyce. In 1947, under the pseudonym "Sally Mara," Queneau published a blackly humorous, semi-pornographic novel entitled *On est toujours trop bon avec les femmes* ("One Is Always Too Kind to Women"). It deals with a supposed episode of the 1916 Easter Rising in Dublin, and several of the Irish revolutionaries—Mat Dillon, Cissy Caffrey, Larry O'Rourke, and Corny Kelleher—bear names borrowed from *Ulysses*. At one point the eagerly violated heroine, Gertie Girdle, proclaims herself an agnostic; thereupon Cissy Caffrey remarks, "Well, we're learning new words today. You can see we're in the native land of James Joyce." A footnote by the author points out: "There is a slight anachronism here, but Caffrey, being illiterate, could not have known in 1916 that *Ulysses* had not yet been published."

The other New Novelists have less to say about Joyce, but this does not always mean that they have not been influenced by him. Mme Sarraute and Robbe-Grillet, however, while very much aware of him, have clearly not always followed his lead. In her book of essays on the novel, *The Age of Suspicion*, Mme Sarraute mentions Joyce at least half a dozen times but never gives him more than a sentence. As her own novels would suggest, Kafka, Virginia Woolf, Faulkner, and even Ivy Compton-Burnett receive far more critical attention in these essays than Joyce does. Similarly, Robbe-Grillet mentions Joyce only three times in the whole of *Pour un nouveau roman* (*For a New Novel*). Even Queneau, whom Robbe-Grillet seems to have read only recently, receives more space than Joyce. Flaubert, Proust, Kafka, Faulkner, and Beckett form the essential tradition for Robbe-Grillet, though he makes some grudging acknowledgments in the direction of Sartre's *Nausea* and Camus's *The Stranger*.

Claude Simon, who began as a painter, is not given to literary criticism, but he volunteered to Bourin a very full and frank list of literary ancestors: Dostoevsky, Chekhov, "the Anglo-Americans."

"I have read Proust and Joyce a great deal."

[Bourin] "Faulkner too, I think."

[Simon] "I had joined a lending library: it was there that I came across *Sanctuary*, which I didn't much care for, and *The Sound and the Fury*, which truly revealed to me what writing could be. But what I prefer in Faulkner is his Joycean and Proustian side. Besides, in him one rediscovers all the literary culture of the West. Faulkner is the Picasso of literature."

Since a Simon novel translated by an American reads so like a Faulkner novel, it is interesting to have this testimony about Joyce and Proust.

I have not been able to trace any interviews or manifestoes by Pinget, who perhaps follows Beckett, as Beckett follows Joyce, in refusing to grant or issue any. Nevertheless, Pinget could not be so close a friend of Beckett's as he is without hearing a good deal about Joyce, and I think internal evidence shows that he has learned a good deal from *Ulysses* and perhaps something also from *Finnegans Wake*. Thus, out of our list of seven New Novelists we find only one, Pinget, who does not explicitly admit knowledge of Joyce.

The more one reads the New Novelists, the more one feels that there are among them two contrasting "temperaments," the expansive and the constrictive, which result, broadly speaking, in the existence of both a school of Joyce and a school of Kafka. The words "expansive" and "constrictive" are used rather than "extrovert" and "introvert" in order to stress that these temperaments are a matter of literary expression and do not necessarily provide an index of the writers' personality structures. Although Butor and Robbe-Grillet or Mauriac and Sarraute seem to stand very close together in matters of aesthetic theory, the novels of the first member in each pair are expansive and those of the second constrictive. Butor in *Degrees* and Mauriac in *The Marquise Went Out at Five* paint on a very wide canvas containing a large number of what used to be called "characters" but which might better be called "figures," and the whole of contemporary society is somehow implicit in their books. Although both restrict time to a single hour and observe the unity of place, a great many lives intersect at a given point, whether that be a classroom or, in Mauriac's case, literally an intersection, a crossroads, a *carrefour* in Paris. Robbe-Grillet and Sarraute, however, prefer to limit the number of figures— sometimes to as few as three, in *Jealousy* or *Portrait of a Man Unknown*. Admittedly, such generalizations can only be partly true, since in Butor's *A Change of Heart* we have a triangular situation and in Sarraute's *The Golden Fruits* there are a number of figures, each very briefly treated. Nevertheless, one can point without misgivings to a number of "wide-angle" novels in the tradition of *Ulysses*, including Queneau's *Le Chiendent* and *Les Enfants du limon*; Butor's *Passage de Milan*, *Passing Time*, and *Degrees*; Mauriac's *The Marquise* and *L'Agrandissement*; Pinget's *Monsieur Levert* and especially *The Inquisitory*, which mentions some six hundred names or nicknames. Beckett, on the other hand, for all his admiration of Joyce, shows the constrictive temperament, narrowing his list of characters to one in *The Unnamable* and leaving us very much in doubt about the existence of even that one.

Certain specific characteristics of *Ulysses* and/or *Finnegans Wake* have been fruitfully imitated by one or more of our seven novelists. First in point of importance is overall structure, which can be shown in Joyce to have an arithmetical basis, as indeed it does in *Tom Jones*; by its concern with arithmetic, as Queneau has suggested, the structured novel finds an equivalent for the arithmetic of prosody—or for the all-embracing arithmetical structure of the *Divine Comedy*. We are familiar with the tripartite structure of *Ulysses*, with its three main divisions into Telemachia, Odyssey, and Nostos, indicated by Roman numerals; we know also that each of these three divisions contains three or a multiple of three episodes. *Finnegans Wake* is similarly divided into four, each main division except the last containing four or a multiple of four subdivisions.

Queneau has pointed out on several occasions that his first novel, *Le Chiendent*, contains seven chapters, each divided into thirteen sections; the last section in each of the first six chapters stands apart, being non-narrative, whereas the last section of the seventh becomes narrative to round out the book. Queneau has also indicated the arithmetical structure of two other early novels, *Les derniers jours* and *Gueule de pierre*. He does not tell us, but the reader can easily discover for himself, that *Les Enfants du limon* is divided into eight books of exactly twenty-one chapters each. Furthermore, the appendix to Claude Simonnet's *Queneau déchiffré* attempts to reconstruct the table of organization used by Queneau in working on *Le Chiendent*—similar to but less complex than that used by Joyce for *Ulysses*.

Butor employed a similar arithmetical structure in *Degrees*. He has expounded it in detail in an interview with Professor F. C. St Aubyn. The book is divided into three parts, each containing seven divisions. Characters are introduced by threes in each section of the first part, giving us, in all, eleven teachers and ten students. Fourteen more students are introduced two by two in the seven sections of the second part, and seven more one by one in the third part, giving a grand total of eleven teachers and thirty-one students.

A structural geometry as well as a structural arithmetic can be found in *Finnegans Wake*. We know that the book forms a circle, though Queneau could not have known this for certain in 1933, when he gave a circular form to *Le Chiendent*. Clive Hart, in *Structure and Motif in Finnegans Wake*, has shown that the *Wake* also contains crosses, squares, triangles, and rhombuses. An analogous preoccupation, though probably not the direct influence of Joyce, led Claude Simon to conceive the structure of his war novel, *The Flanders Road*,

> . . . in the form of the ace of clubs, which one cannot draw without lifting pencil from paper except by passing three times over the same point. That point, in *The Flanders Road*, is the dead horse toward which, in their wanderings, the cavalrymen return three times.

A further example of geometric structure can be found in Robbe-Grillet's *The Voyeur*, where we are constantly presented with objects taking the form of a figure eight, a pattern followed by the itinerary of the protagonist around the island which is the *locale* of the novel. Indeed, it might not be too much to say that the plan of the whole book is in the form of a figure eight.

In *The Erasers*, his first published novel, Robbe-Grillet adopted another structural device which this time seems directly traceable to Joyce's example. Just as Joyce patterned *Ulysses* upon the *Odyssey*, so Robbe-Grillet patterned his pseudo-detective story upon the Oedipus myth. In spite of the quotation from Sophocles on the title page, only Beckett is supposed to have noticed the parallel without further prompting from the author. Wallas, the clumsy detective, kills the supposed murder victim, Dupont, without realizing that Dupont is his own father. The numerous references to the Oedipus myth throughout the book have been carefully traced by Bruce Morrissette in an article and in his book, *Les Romans de Robbe-Grillet*. Butor has also used myths as structural elements in several of his books: Cain and Abel and Theseus and Ariadne in *Passing Time*, for instance. Queneau's use of Gnostic mythology in several novels has been insisted on quite convincingly by Simonnet in *Queneau déchiffré* ("Queneau Deciphered"), which is primarily a study of *Le Chiendent*.

Joyce's treatment of time in *Ulysses* and *Finnegans Wake* has influenced the New Novelists far more strongly than Proust's. Certainly Proust's use of involuntary memory and the consequent invasion of the present by the past can be found in Robbe-Grillet's *Jealousy*, Butor's *A Change of Heart*, and Simon's *The Flanders Road*, to give only three examples. Claude Mauriac evokes the past in a strictly Proustian manner in his first novel, *All Women Are Fatal*. But, generally speaking, the example of Joyce is decisive, in at least three different ways.

Most obvious is the restriction of time to twenty-four hours or less, in the manner of *Ulysses* and *Finnegans Wake*. This practice can be readily accepted by writers whose formal education has laid so much stress on the French classical drama. The so-called unity of time is rigorously observed by Molière, Marivaux, and Beaumarchais, as well as by the tragic dramatists—Corneille, Racine, and their imitators. Robbe-Grillet's *The Erasers* fills exactly twenty-four hours, from 7:30 p.m. on one day, when Dupont is supposedly murdered, to 7:30 p.m. on the next, when Wallas actually kills him—or alternatively from 6:00 a.m. the day after the supposed murder until the corresponding time next day. Everything else is either prologue or epilogue. Butor's *A Change of Heart* takes less than twenty-four hours, the length of an overnight journey by rail from Paris to Rome. Mauriac's *The Dinner Party* begins with the guests sitting down at table and ends as they stand up after the meal. Pinget's *The Inquisitory* records a single uninterrupted session of a legal interrogation. Butor's *Degrees* is focused on a single class hour in a secondary school, although it reaches backwards and forwards into time from that point. Mauriac's *The Marquise* covers a single hour in the life of the Carrefour de Buci, while *L'Agrandissement* ("The Enlargement") deals with just *two minutes* of that same hour.

Simultaneity is another aspect of time by which Joyce was greatly fascinated. One remembers the cloud that casts a chill over both Stephen and Bloom, who are separated by many miles of Dublin and many pages of *Ulysses*, or Stephen's being caught sight of from the mourners' coach as he is leaving Sandymount Strand, many pages after his seaside soliloquy is over. Above all, one remembers the "Wandering Rocks" episode, in which the doings of people all over Dublin are coordinated in relation to time. This was a side of Joyce that Virginia Woolf imitated meticulously in *Mrs. Dalloway*. Pinget does the same sort of thing in *Monsieur Levert* and *Clope au dossier*; incidentally, *Clope* seems to be restricted to twenty-four hours also. Claude Mauriac is compelled to stress simultaneity in *The Marquise* and its sequel because of the narrow limits in space and time that he has imposed on himself.

But there is another kind of simultaneity, as *Finnegans Wake* reminds us. At every moment of that book, past, present, *and* future are simultaneously "present" or at any rate implicit. Proust's Marcel, in his moments of involuntary memory, sees

the present as invaded and occupied by the past, but he can
still distinguish which is which; it is not so with the dreamer
or the reader of *Finnegans Wake*. Nor is it so with the reader
of Robbe-Grillet's *Jealousy* or the viewer of *Last Year at
Marienbad*. In the most original and disturbing of all his
essays, *"Temps et description dans le récit d'aujourd'hui"*
("Time and Description in the Narrative of Today"), Robbe-
Grillet makes the following comments about the works just
mentioned:

> The universe in which the whole film [*Marienbad*] unreels
> is, in characteristic fashion, that of a perpetual present which
> renders all recourse to memory impossible. It is a world with-
> out a past. . . . This man, this woman begin to exist only
> when they appear on the screen for the first time. . . . Their
> existence lasts only as long as the film does. . . . During the
> entire projection of the film we were in last year and . . . we
> were at Marienbad. . . .
>
> Similarly, it was absurd to believe that in the novel
> *Jealousy* . . . there existed an order of events, clear and un-
> equivocal, which was not the order of the sentences in the
> book, as though I had amused myself by jumbling a pre-
> established calendar, as one shuffles a deck of cards. On the
> contrary, the narrative was constructed in such a fashion that
> any attempt to reconstitute an exterior chronology would
> sooner or later come up against a series of contradictions, a
> dead end therefore.[11]

It is difficult to give the essence of this closely argued essay
in a few quotations, but two other brief ones may help to
sum it up: ". . . In the modern narrative, one might say that
time is cut off from its temporality. It no longer flows"; and
again, ". . . If temporality fulfills anticipation, instantaneity
disappoints it. . . ."
What Robbe-Grillet does, or intends to do, in these works
is not identical with Joyce's achievement or intention in
Finnegans Wake, but in their treatment of time both writers
have more in common with each other than they have with

---

[11] *Pour un nouveau roman* (Paris: Les Éditions de Minuit, 1963),
pp. 131–2. Translation mine.

Proust. The title of Proust's great novel, À la recherche du temps perdu (literally, "In Search of Lost Time"), implies that there *was* a past, which simply has to be rediscovered (as in the volume entitled Le Temps retrouvé), not invented or re-invented. Claude Mauriac, too, in L'Agrandissement, makes Bertrand Carnéjoux express, in capital letters, his ultimate ideal for the novel as "THE IMMOBILIZATION OF TIME, MY DEAR FELLOW, NEITHER MORE NOR LESS: THE IMMOBILIZATION OF TIME."

In discussing the circle among the spatial forms employed as structural elements, I purposely omitted any consideration of the cyclical treatment of time. Everybody knows that Finnegans Wake ends in mid-sentence and that the reader must turn back to the beginning of the book to find the end of that sentence; in other words, he cannot finish the book without beginning it again. Similarly, the last two sentences of Queneau's Le Chiendent are identical with the first two. But to return to the beginning in this way is also to have gotten nowhere, so that time in a sense has been annihilated. In Robbe-Grillet's The Erasers, the twenty-four hours between the firing of the two shots, which form a sort of cycle, are symbolized as being outside of time by the fact that Wallas's watch, having stopped at 7:30 p.m., the time of the first shot, starts working again when the second shot is fired. Cyclical form is a method of calling in question and annihilating both time and content. Queneau quotes as the epigraph of his humorous novel, Zazie dans le métro, which itself has an almost circular form, a fragment attributed to Aristotle: ho plasas ēphanisen ("He who created it destroyed it.") This sentence could serve as the epigraph to many a New Novel.

Having begun with overall structure and temporal orientation, one should logically continue by dealing with narrative techniques before focusing on the smaller structural units and ultimately on the smallest—individual words. Everything implicit in the technical use of the term "point of view" would seem to require discussion in a review of the relationship between Joyce and the New Novelists. Unfortunately, a full treatment of this subject would require a whole chapter. The

New Novelists know about Henry James as well as James Joyce. Robbe-Grillet's *Jealousy*, for instance, is an extraordinary tour de force in the use of point of view. Everything is seen through the eyes of the jealous husband, though he cannot distinguish between his mind's eye and his body's. At first we think that we are peering through the lens of a camera, but eventually we realize that this is no machine but an all-too-human human being. Yet we are never allowed to know what he thinks, only what he sees or imagines he sees.

On the other hand, the New Novelists feel utterly free to violate all the so-called "rules" of point of view, precisely because they are so keenly aware of them. And here Joyce, as well as Gide, has been of the greatest service to them. Having shown in *A Portrait of the Artist* that he could write an entire novel from a single, rigorously controlled point of view, Joyce cast off Henry James for good in *Ulysses*, where the point of view is different in almost every episode. More important, the point of view can shift within a single episode, as it does in "Nausica," where we are given first Gertie MacDowell's reverie and then Bloom's. And what are we to make of the "Cyclops" episode? The main narrative here is supplied by "Noman," the anonymous Dubliner whose command of slang surpasses that of Ferdinand in Céline's *Journey to the End of the Night* and possibly inspired that novel. But Noman's narrative is interspersed with wild parodies of every type of inflated literature, from classical and Celtic epics to modern journalism. *Whose* point of view is expressed in these parodies or in the dryly scientific questions and answers of the "Ithaca" episode? In *Finnegans Wake*, similar shifts of viewpoint are constantly occurring; moreover, it seems that Joyce there allows himself the one freedom that he had still abstained from in *Ulysses*, that of speaking at times in his own person.

It might even require a book rather than a chapter to examine closely all the permutations of point of view explored by the New Novelists. Butor's use of second-person narrative in *A Change of Heart* and to some extent in *Degrees* has been commented on in several reviews and articles. As indicated above, Mauriac speaks in his own person at the end of three of his novels. Queneau, perhaps imitating Gide in *Lafcadio's Adventures*, shows great ingenuity in destroying the illusion of impersonality at some point in virtually all his books. The crux for any critic of Pinget's *Monsieur Levert* must be to decide whether M. Levert is the narrator of the whole novel or not—and, if he is, why he speaks of himself so often in the third person. The same problem arises in Pinget's *Clope au dossier*. Is Clope the narrator, and if so, how can he observe the other characters when he is not present? In the middle of a coldly impersonal narrative about the domestic activities of a young mother named Simone Brize, the time comes for her to take a bath. Suddenly the mask of impersonality drops and the unidentified narrator becomes an eager observer; in fact, a *voyeur*:

> Then under the arms then that's it here we are the pink breasts turning brown at the tips let's savor it, she rinses, then more soap from the soap dish let's savor it the wash cloth she passes it between her legs. . . .

And so on and so on. Suddenly, too, the narrator will pass from omniscience to humorous nescience, unable to remember whether the saucepan of water on Simone's stove is full or not. Another fascinating variation on point of view is found in certain episodes of Nathalie Sarraute's *The Planetarium*: one character will try so hard to penetrate the thoughts of another that we soon forget whether the episode is being narrated via the consciousness of the first character or that of the second.

Hardly less prominent than this virtuosity in the use of point of view is the use of interior monologue and stream of consciousness, which are of course themselves variations of point of view. (I make the distinction that stream of consciousness admits sense impressions from the outside world but interior monologue does not.) Stream of consciousness and interior monologue have been so widely adopted, however, that they can hardly be described as experimental techniques any longer; they certainly do not distinguish the New Novelists from their predecessors, since Sartre and Camus, for instance, have employed these techniques when necessary. Experiments with viewpoint do not distinguish the New Novelists from their predecessors either: remember the famous shift from third person to first in *The Plague*. The difference is one of degree rather than kind.

Two further essential features of Joyce's technique must also be discussed in relation to the New Novelists. One is his use of different levels of discourse, which gives even *A Portrait of the Artist*, but especially *Ulysses* and *Finnegans Wake*, such variety of texture. The other is, of course, his experimentation with the basic unit, the individual word.

In the second of these features he has been followed hardly at all by the New Novelists, perhaps because they felt that enough had been done along those lines by the Surrealists. Queneau, who began his literary career as a Surrealist camp follower, has included portmanteau words sparingly in *Saint Glinglin*. He has also attracted a lot of attention in France for his phonetic spelling of certain word groups as single words. More truly Joycean in inspiration, perhaps, is his tour de force, *Exercices de style* (*Exercises in Style*), in which he recounts a banal anecdote in no fewer than ninety-nine different styles, many of which involve assaults upon the integrity of the word.

Aside from Queneau, the only verbal experimenter among our novelists is Pinget, particularly in *Le Renard et la boussole* and *Graal Flibuste*, two early books. His best novel, *L'Inquisitoire*, however, shows his brilliant verbal imagination in the naming of persons and places. Naturally, it is the more broadly humorous names that are most memorable, just as the puns we remember best from Joyce are relatively crude in every sense of the word. The name of Monseigneur Bougecroupe ("Monsignor Budgebottom"), the local bishop, is a case in point, but to name the local gossip Sophie Narre (*narre*, "narrates") is perhaps more subtle. Even the names of streets need to be scrutinized; for instance, the rue Sam runs into the rue des Irlandais, which reminds us that Pinget's friend Sam Beckett is an Irishman.

The counterpointing of different levels of discourse has

proved much more popular with the New Novelists. Again it is the expansive rather than the constrictive writers who have found this useful. The texture of a novel by Robbe-Grillet or Sarraute is relatively homogeneous. Queneau, Butor, Simon, Mauriac, and Pinget, on the other hand, take pleasure in varying the texture of their work. In addition to changing the level of discourse, they like to employ a technique somewhat like the Cubist painters' collage. Just as Picasso would cut shapes from newspapers, menus, or wallpaper and paste them on his canvas, thus inserting little bits of undigested reality into his abstract compositions, so these New Novelists like to excerpt passages from existing documents and incorporate them in the artistic structure of their novels. Besides Joyce, Dos Passos among novelists and Eliot and Pound among poets have used this technique. Two well-known Surrealist "novels," Louis Aragon's *Le Paysan de Paris* and André Breton's *Nadja* (in its illustrations), carried the technique a step farther by incorporating photographic or typographical reproductions of documents. Queneau, however, discovered that two English humorists, E. V. Lucas and George Morrow, both on the staff of *Punch*, had invented collage in 1911 in their book *What a Life!* With scissors and paste and a copy of Whiteley's mail-order catalogue, they concocted a series of bizarre illustrations and then wrote a pseudo-autobiography to fit the pictures. Even Breton's fertile imagination seems pallid beside Lucas's and Morrow's.

Butor's *Degrees* and Mauriac's *The Marquise Went Out at Five* make very serious use of documentary material: Butor's comes from geography and history textbooks and the classics of Greek, Roman, and French literature; Mauriac has traced the history of the Carrefour de Buci in excerpts ranging from the Middle Ages to *Ulysses* and the memoirs of Simone de Beauvoir. Pinget, who was trained in the law, from time to time makes use of modern and medieval legal documents, whether genuine or imitated it is difficult to tell. The description of an engraving of a female centaur that we find in Simon's *The Flanders Road*, supposedly translated from Italian into archaic French, looks authentic, yet it seems too symbolically apt in the context to be a genuine *objet trouvé*. Queneau's rather unsatisfactory novel, *Les Enfants du limon,* is a unique example of collage, for he has incorporated into it much of the results of his research into *les fous littéraires,* authentic French crackpots of the nineteenth century (he had failed to find a publisher for a non-fiction book on the subject). Other examples of collage, such as the excerpts from provincial newspapers in Pinget's *Mahu ou le matériau* and Queneau's *Le Chiendent,* are not documents at all but parodies and therefore closer to Joyce than to Pound, say.

To introduce documents is in itself a shift in the level of discourse, but not the most radical. A change from narrative or dialogue to documents is but a change from one form of prose to another. Queneau and Pinget have been known to shift from prose to verse. One of the seven parts of *Saint Glinglin* consists entirely of free verse in the manner of Claudel (or of Whitman). A whole chapter in Pinget's *Graal Flibuste* is written in that kind of verse, and one or two chapters in *Les Enfants du limon* are in the form of doggerel. Queneau, a fine poet of the school of Apollinaire, refuses to draw a hard-and-fast line between the novel and poetry, and Butor for one agrees with him. As a matter of fact, Queneau has written a novel in verse, *Chêne et chien* ("Oak and Dog"), about his childhood and his psychoanalysis, which is one of the finest longer poems of this century. It is a long poem in the same sense as Tennyson's *Maud* or *In Memoriam*—a closely related sequence of shorter poems.

One final aspect of shifting levels of discourse, the counterpointing of the formal with the colloquial, plays a significant part in many New Novels, again recalling the "Cyclops" episode of *Ulysses.* In Pinget's *The Inquisitory* this counterpoint is the fundamental structural element, for the official or officials who are interrogating the deaf, elderly protagonist must write down all their questions. Their clipped bureaucratic formality alternates with the rich colloquial language, almost a stream of consciousness, that pours from the garrulous old servant. Proverbs, argot, malapropisms mingle in his shrewd yet naïve commentary on his former employers, his neighbors, and life in general. Not even Céline at his best can match Pinget's mastery of spoken French, which is comparable to Mark Twain's spoken American or the spoken Irish-English of Joyce or O'Casey.

Queneau, too, used to be fascinated by spoken French, whose syntax, he has never tired of pointing out, resembles that of Chinook and other American-Indian languages more than it does the syntax of written French. Although his *dialogue* is authentic, Queneau has never succeeded in writing more than brief passages of *narrative* in the spoken language. The philosophical passages in all his novels, however, from *Le Chiendent* to *Zazie dans le métro*, take the form of spoken or silent meditations in a colloquial language liberally sprinkled with argot. Here the counterpoint is not so much one of style against style as of style against subject matter.

The vast variety of characters in *The Marquise Went Out at Five* gives Mauriac many opportunities for counterpointing different styles of speech and thought, but the most interesting occurs in *L'Agrandissement*. As Bertrand meditates on the novel he is going to write and lets one character or another speak for a page or two, there rises from his unconscious mind the voice of an American professor lecturing at some future date upon the novels of that rather overrated writer, Bertrand Carnéjoux. Not only does the professor's formal discourse contrast with the speech of Bertrand's Parisians, but the professor's own thoughts about a beautiful and bored coed in his class, Miss Fowling by name, serve as a counterpoint to his lecture.

I have discussed at length what the New Novelists learned or could have learned from Joyce's technique, but I don't feel competent to judge whether he and they view the world from the same philosophic standpoint. One broad generalization is possible, however. A recurrent theme of the critical essays written by the New Novelists is the inseparability of form and content. Robbe-Grillet, Sarraute, and Butor all stress it, and it is everywhere implicit in Queneau. Beckett has written of *Finnegans Wake*:

Here form *is* content, content *is* form. You complain that
this stuff is not written in English. It is not written at all. It is
not to be read—or rather it is not only to be read. It is to be
looked at and listened to. His writing is not *about* something; *it is that something itself*.[12]

In the same way, a New Novel that began as a hypothesis or
an experiment may end as part of the reality of which it went
in search. Not "about something" but "something itself"—to
write such a work is the ambition of every New Novelist, as it
was that of their great precursor and exemplar, James Joyce.

What have the New Novelists achieved?

Butor, Robbe-Grillet, and Mme Sarraute have never denied
that the New Novel would sooner or later become the Old
Novel. Indeed, they have insisted that every good novelist of
the past was "new" in his own day. Robbe-Grillet, in his
earlier polemics, did tend to denounce Balzac, but Butor, in
perhaps the most brilliant of all his essays, "Balzac and
Reality," points out

. . . the extent to which Balzac is deliberately and systematically an innovator, how conscious he is of his originality as a
novelist, the degree to which he considered his technique and
his technical invention to be open, capable of surprising developments, far from hardening into that academicism which
is attributed to him as the result of a complete misunderstanding, and in which his false disciples are trapped.[13]

Balzac, then, was a New Novelist, and the New Novelists of
today are his true disciples.

As *le nouveau roman* passes into history, to be succeeded
in its turn by *le nouveau nouveau roman*, which itself will
pass into history—to be succeeded by what?—we can say that
its first achievement was precisely its attempt to be new. Not

[12] Samuel Beckett, "Dante . . . Bruno . Vico . . Joyce," in *Our
Exagmination Round His Factification for Incamination of Work in
Progress* (London: Faber & Faber, 1929, 1961), p. 14. Beckett's italics.
[13] *Inventory*, p. 102.

only did the New Novelists' critical essays make both the critic and the common reader reexamine their stereotyped views on the novel, but, conversely, by attempting to renovate the French novel, Butor achieved an insight into the problems of the innovator that enabled him to write so perceptively about Balzac. Robbe-Grillet's criticism, too, profited immensely by his experience as an innovating novelist. In *For a New Novel* he has had the courage to present his essays, unchanged, in the order of their original publication. We can thus follow his rapid progress from the naïveté of 1956 to the richness and subtlety of 1963, but his evolving thought does show some fidelity to its beginnings.

In addition to stirring up the pool of novel criticism—a peculiarly stagnant one in France at the time—the New Novelists did write a number of important novels. It is of course possible to argue, as many critics still do, that the reach of Robbe-Grillet and the rest far exceeded their grasp: that their actual as opposed to their ideal novels are either so brief and lacking in content as to be negligible—Robbe-Grillet and Mme Sarraute—or concerned with working out an obsessive pattern at such enormous length as to be boring—Butor, Queneau, Mauriac. As for Simon and Pinget, they may be seen as innocents ruined by evil company—potentially great, warmhearted writers who have made their books unreadable by forcing good meat through the sausage-machine of dogmatic theory.

It can also be argued of course that, even if this is so, these writers have prepared the soil for a new crop of French novelists—men and women who can treat the genre with the greatest possible freedom because the New Novelists have swept away restrictive conventions and the crippling preconceptions of the average novel reader, 1900–50. Only time can test the validity of this view, for the hypothetical geniuses have not yet, in 1970, manifested themselves.

I believe, however, that the novels I have selected for intensive study (one in each chapter) are not inferior to any seven novels written during a comparable period of time in the history of French literature. Indeed, if we omit Queneau's

Le Chiendent, published in 1933, we are left with six novels all published within five years: Robbe-Grillet's *La Jalousie* (1957), Butor's *La Modification* (1957), Mme Sarraute's *Le Planétarium* (1959), Simon's *La Route des Flandres* (1960), Mauriac's *La Marquise sortit à cinq heures* (1961), and Pinget's *L'Inquisitoire* (1962). English translations are readily obtainable; let the skeptical reader go off and read them for himself before proceeding any further. I very much doubt if he can produce six novels first published in English anywhere in the world in 1957–62 that, on the one hand, are as interesting in traditional novelistic ways as these six and, on the other hand, illuminate the technical problems and possibilities of the novel as searchingly.

Even considered as social history—an aspect of the traditional novel that the New Novelists themselves scoff at—these six works are of the greatest interest. They portray life in a colony or ex-colonial country, in Paris, in provincial towns and villages, and in the countryside. Their characters range in social class from the aristocracy in its châteaux, through Parisian middle-class intellectuals and businessmen, and small-town shopkeepers, down to domestic servants and a jockey. We learn from *La Marquise* about eight centuries of life in Paris; from *La Route des Flandres* about cavalry tactics and prison-camp life in World War II; from *La Jalousie* about the care of banana plantations; and from *La Modification* about the growth of a new international managerial class as a result of the European Common Market.

There is no point in attempting to summarize the achievement of these six novels plus *Le Chiendent* here. They are dealt with at length in the chapters that follow. The door stands open; the hesitant reader is warmly invited to enter.

2

Raymond Queneau

THE CREATOR AS DESTROYER

THE one New Novelist who has rendered brief and tardy justice to Raymond Queneau is Alain Robbe-Grillet, in the final essay of his volume of criticism, *Pour un nouveau roman* (1963). He is stressing the abandonment of a narrow realism in favor of what he calls "reality," and insists, "I do not transcribe, I construct."

> . . . the "probable" and the "true-to-type" are no longer remotely capable of serving as criteria. Indeed, it is very much as if the *false*—that is to say, the possible, the impossible, the hypothesis, the lie, etc.—had become one of the privileged themes of modern fiction. . . . I must underline here the importance, from this point of view, of the novels of Raymond Queneau (*Le Chiendent* and *Loin de Rueil* especially), whose texture often and whose movement always are strictly those of the imagination. (pp. 139–40, my translation)[1]

Jacques Roudaut, in his critical study, *Michel Butor ou le livre futur* (1964, pp. 230–4), points out how much at fault are those critics who do not refer to Queneau in connection with the contemporary renewal of the French novel. Georges Charbonnier, in one of his radio interviews with Queneau,

---

[1] Barbara Wright, in her introduction to *The Bark-Tree*, says that Robbe-Grillet recently called *Le Chiendent* "the New Novel, twenty years ahead of its time."

drew an analogy between the structure of Butor's *Degrees* and that of Queneau's *Chiendent*, but went on to remark that the former is visible whereas the latter is concealed. In reply, Queneau suggested that in 1933 people had not yet learned to look for structure in the novel: "Perhaps this construction of *Le Chiendent* would be very obvious to present-day critics."

It certainly should become obvious in the course of this chapter that *Le Chiendent* (1933) and *Saint Glinglin* (1948) show many of the preoccupations and the literary and philosophical influences now familiar to us in the works of Robbe-Grillet, Butor, and their fellow New Novelists. One reason why English-speaking critics of the New Novel have so little to say about Queneau may be simply that one of his two most important novels, *Saint Glinglin*, has not yet been translated into English. The other, *Le Chiendent*, was translated only in 1968.[2]

Undoubtedly, Queneau was born before his time. His early novels were both more experimental and more ambitious than his later, better-known ones. Perhaps, consciously or unconsciously, Queneau became discouraged by the poor reception accorded his early experiments and allowed his energy to be diverted into other channels, notably his poetry and the immense enterprise of the *Encyclopédie de la Pléiade*, the planning and editing of which required all his vast knowledge as a modern polymath. Poetry and encyclopedic learning coalesce in his extraordinary work, *Petite cosmogonie portative* ("A Little Portable Cosmogony"), which takes for its province the history of the solar system, the evolution of life on earth, and the progress of human knowledge and invention down to the computer. (Published in 1950, it appeared too soon to include the exploration of outer space.) Its division into six *chants* challenges direct comparison with Lucretius' *De Rerum Natura*. While relatively shorter (it contains 1,400 alexandrines) than the great works of antiquity, *Petite cosmogonie*

---

[2] See *The Bark-Tree*, tr. Barbara Wright (London: Calder and Boyars, 1968). M. Queneau has kindly granted me permission to use my own translations of the passages from his works quoted throughout this chapter.

portative, by virtue of its tremendous range, entitles Queneau to be considered a modern Lucretius or Hesiod—endowed, however, with a sense of humor that his great predecessors might have considered a handicap.

Queneau's poetry, lyrical as well as didactic, falls outside the scope of this chapter, but the reader should bear in mind the possibility that Queneau may win his most lasting reputation as a poet rather than a novelist. Since Queneau himself has called his autobiographical *Chêne et chien* ("Oak Tree and Dog") a novel in verse, we shall be able to consider it here, but otherwise we must confine ourselves to his work in prose fiction. A preliminary summary of the resemblances— and differences—between this and the work of the later New Novelists may be helpful.

First of all, there are the common influences. Queneau has a thorough knowledge of English, having translated a number of works from that language into French. Aside from some poems by American poets—Whitman, Hart Crane, Wallace Stevens, William Carlos Williams, and others—the works translated are of no particular significance and were probably assigned him by the publishers. The crucial influences were Joyce's *Ulysses* and Faulkner's *Sanctuary*. Queneau first read Joyce carefully as early as 1929—perhaps in the French translation which appeared that year—and he has explicitly stated that he read Faulkner before Faulkner was translated into French. Conrad's *Lord Jim* also influenced *Le Chiendent*. Later Queneau discovered *Tom Jones*, which he described as "constructed with extraordinary care and skill." Other important later discoveries were the notebooks of Henry James, *The Making of Americans* and other works by Gertrude Stein, and Edmund Wilson's *Axel's Castle*. This of course does not exhaust Queneau's knowledge of English literature, which can be traced in the excellent index to his volume of selected criticism, *Bâtons, chiffres, et lettres* (1950), a title hereafter abbreviated to *BCL*. In *"Technique du roman,"* which forms part of that volume, he acknowledges a general debt "to the English and American novelists who taught me that a technique of the novel existed, and above all to Joyce."

A carefully planned—and carefully concealed—structure, so important in the novels of Robbe-Grillet, Butor, and (sometimes) Simon, almost became a fetish with Queneau during the years of his discipleship to Joyce. Presumably he had read, either in the *Nouvelle revue française* (April 1922) or elsewhere, Valéry Larbaud's famous lecture on Joyce. Either from it or from Stuart Gilbert's *James Joyce's Ulysses* (first published in London in 1930) he could have learned of the elaborate plan employed by Joyce in constructing the eighteen episodes of *Ulysses*, all but one of which correspond to episodes in the *Odyssey*. In Larbaud's words,

> Thus each episode will deal with a particular science or art, will contain a particular symbol, will represent a given organ of the human body, will have its own color, its appropriate technique, and, as an episode, will correspond to one of the hours of the day.

Gilbert reprinted almost the complete table of correspondences used by Joyce. In *Entretiens avec Georges Charbonnier*,[3] Queneau said that he drew up similar tables, "as formal as a chess game," for *Le Chiendent* and must still have them somewhere among his papers. In his critical study of *Le Chiendent*, entitled *Queneau déchiffré*, Claude Simonnet attempted to reconstruct these tables, apparently without assistance from Queneau.[4]

Queneau could hardly have known in 1933 of the variations upon a four-part organization that *Finnegans Wake* (then known as *Work in Progress*) would display when finally published in 1939. But, besides being as fascinated by numerical symbolism as Joyce was, he had an almost professional knowledge of mathematics entirely outside the scope of the Irish writer. As Queneau reveals in *"Technique du roman,"* two of his first three novels had elaborate arithmetical structures. *Le Chiendent* consists of seven chapters, each containing thirteen sections; of these,

[3] Paris: Gallimard, 1962, p. 49.
[4] Paris: Julliard, 1962, pp. 166ff.

. . . every thirteenth (the last in each chapter, consequently) is situated *outside* of this chapter, in another direction or dimension; they are pauses and their genre can only be monologue, report of a dream, or newspaper clipping. Naturally, the 91st breaks the rule and becomes narrative once more to end the whole. (*BCL*, p. 25)

The first and ninety-first ($7 \times 13 = 91$) sections, incidentally, are the only numbered ones; each chapter except the first, however, has its number clearly spelled out.

Les derniers jours (1936) was originally planned to have $(8 \times 6) + 1 = 49$ chapters, with every sixth forming a pause; however, the published version has only 38, Queneau having "taken away the scaffolding and syncopated the rhythm" by suppressing certain chapters. *Gueule de pierre* (1934) is less complex, mathematically at least. It consists of only three parts, each in a different technique: "monologue of the solitary man in the first, narrative and conversations when he returns to the people of the Native City, a poem finally in the third part when he *elevates himself. . . .*" However, each of the three parts also corresponds to one of the domains of nature—animal, vegetable, and mineral—and the third contains all twelve signs of the zodiac.

The structure of *Le Chiendent* will be examined in more detail later; that of *Gueule de pierre* will be considered also, to the extent that a revised version of this novel forms part of *Saint Glinglin*. However, a general statement about the structure of Queneau's novels needs to be quoted in full as a warning to critics and students and even to casual readers:

I wrote other novels [besides *Le Chiendent*] with this idea of rhythm, this intention of making a sort of poem out of the novel. It is possible to make situations or characters rhyme together just as one makes words rhyme; it is even possible to content oneself with mere alliteration.

Even in linear novels—*récits*, to use Gide's term—I always compelled myself to follow certain rules which had no justification other than their satisfying my taste for figures or some purely personal whims. Once again, this can't have been so

very arbitrary, since nobody ever noticed it, let alone re-
proached me for it.

To sum up, I have never seen any essential differences between the kind of novels I want to write and poetry. (*BCL*,
p. 34)

Implicit in this quotation is an attitude toward the reader
which Queneau shares in greater or lesser degree with all the
New Novelists. He is an author of the "age of suspicion," to
employ Nathalie Sarraute's term, and the reader must be
constantly on the alert to make sure the author is not out-
witting him in some way. Even so popular a book as Queneau's
Pierrot mon ami conceals something basic from the unwary
reader, namely an important complication of the plot; this in
addition to whatever philosophical concepts, learned allusions,
or symbolism there may be lurking for the more sophisticated
reader to ferret out.

For Nathalie Sarraute, the mutual distrust between novelist
and reader is primarily a result of their mutual inability to
believe in the novelist's characters. Here again, Queneau has
from the beginning taken full advantage of his awareness that
he is writing in an age of suspicion. By the end of *Le Chiendent*
it is impossible for any reader, however naïve, to believe that
the characters are real people, but an explicit warning is given
much earlier. Pierre le Grand, the intelligent observer through
whose eyes we watch much of the early action, tells Narcense,
"I am observing a man." "You don't say! Are you a novelist?"
"No. A character." In other words, the person we readers have
hitherto been most ready to identify with tells Narcense and
us explicitly that he is nothing more than a character in a
novel. And this on page 25!

Occasionally, in Queneau's later books, one finds a character
one can believe in, but by so believing, one probably thwarts
the conscious intent of the author. In *Odile*, perhaps the most
autobiographical of the novels, it is hard not to believe in
Anglarès, a character universally acknowledged to be based
on André Breton, the leader of the Surrealist movement.
Lehameau, the protagonist of *A Hard Winter*, partly based on
Queneau's father, is another convincing character, in this case

a sympathetic one. Finally, the delightful Valentin of Queneau's sunniest book, *Le Dimanche de la vie* ("The Sunday
of Life"), makes us want to believe in him, though some of
the events of his life are wildly improbable and though the
other characters he is involved with are transparently puppets.
Zazie, the adolescent "heroine" of Queneau's best-known book,
is a piece of machinery.

One apparent link between Queneau and certain of the
New Novelists—Robbe-Grillet, Claude Mauriac—is his devotion to the film. In 1945 he described himself as one of "those
who . . . were born more or less with the cinema and have
frequented the darkened rooms at least three times a week
for more than thirty-five years. . . ." The protagonist of *Loin
de Rueil* is a movie-struck youngster who grows up to be a
film star; Paul in *Saint Glinglin* becomes obsessed by the
screen personality of a star named Alice Phaye, whom he
ultimately marries. Queneau's heart is with the silent films,
however—*Zazie* being a mixture of *The Perils of Pauline* and
the Keystone Cops—as some nostalgic lines about "Charlot"
Chaplin in *Chêne et chien* demonstrate. *Zazie* itself has become a successful but far-from-silent film. However, besides
writing a scenario for a silent short film, Queneau has written
commentaries for a number of other short subjects, song lyrics
for *Gervaise* (the screen adaptation of Zola's *L'Assommoir*),
and dialogue for two full-length films, *Monsieur Ripois* and
Luis Buñuel's *La Mort en ce jardin.* Although he wrote the
commentary for a short subject by Alain Resnais, *Le Chant du
styrène,* Queneau may be dubious about the value of the kind
of collaboration between literature and the cinema represented
by Robbe-Grillet and Resnais's *Last Year at Marienbad.* At
any rate, in 1945 he commented that although the cinema is
an art, "it has as little relationship to literature (or as much)
as sculpture has to music. The cinema had its birth outside
'intellectual' circles . . ." (*BCL*, p. 145).

Queneau, like most of the New Novelists, has drawn on the
experiments in sentence structure, punctuation, verbal "montage," and point of view engaged in by Joyce, Faulkner, and
others, especially the Dadaist and Surrealist poets, between

the world wars. Curiously, however, he has made almost no use of their very free handling of time: with the minor exception of certain passages in *Les Enfants du limon* and *Loin de Rueil*, we find in his novels no flashbacks, no simultaneity, and none of what one may call the "flashforward."[5] Generally speaking, his narratives follow the accepted chronological order, and the only freedom he regularly allows himself is that of discontinuity: he will break off his narrative abruptly and resume it hours, days, or years later without any explicit indication of the passage of time, though of course implicit indications soon appear. There is one major exception (seemingly) to the above generalizations about Queneau's use of time—namely, the circular form of *Le Chiendent*, in which all the characters resume their original positions in time and space during the concluding sentences, the last two of which reproduce the two opening sentences of the novel. Yet this exception is only apparent. The entire book, up to the last two paragraphs, moves in one direction through time and can only be represented graphically as a straight line. Though Queneau himself has described the book as circular, one of his characters (p. 295) gives a better description of its ultimate effect by saying, *Alors comme ça, l'temps, c'est rien du tout?* Time is nothing at all (and cannot properly be represented spatially by either a straight line or a circle). To give Queneau full credit for his originality, we should take note that the circular structure of *Finnegans Wake*—which "ends" in the middle of a sentence, the continuation of which "begins" the book again—was not fully revealed until its publication in 1939.

Queneau differs most sharply from the New Novelists in the scope of his experiments with language. Like Joyce, though not to the same extreme point, he cannot remain content to experiment with word order, punctuation, and sentence structure; the individual word must also be liberated from convention. Most important among Queneau's linguistic preoccupations is his awareness of the gulf between most

[5] His freest use of time will be found in a more recent novel, *Les Fleurs bleues* (1965). See the end of this chapter.

written and most spoken French. In both his novels and his poetry he constantly strives to write the spoken language. It may seem curious that the French poets were at least fifty years ahead of the French novelists in adopting the spoken language. On reflection, however, one realizes that poetry is oral in its origins, whereas prose depends far more on the written and printed word. From Rimbaud, Laforgue, and Corbière onwards, there has been a colloquial line of tradition in modern French poetry which leads naturally by way of Apollinaire to the poetry of Queneau. It was during a journey to Greece in 1932 that Queneau took note of the two living traditions in modern Greek literature: one which tries to keep the language as close as possible to classical Greek and the other which emphasizes the spoken language. He then became conscious of a similar divorce between written and spoken French and conceived the project of turning a philosophical work—Descartes's *Discourse on Method*—into the spoken language. Instead, he began to translate the British philosopher J. W. Dunne's *An Experiment with Time* (1927) into French; this book prompted him to embark on *Le Chiendent*, a novel experimenting with time, parts of which are in spoken French.

Ironically, *Le Chiendent* appeared a year too late. Louis-Ferdinand Céline's novel, *Voyage au bout de la nuit* (*Journey to the End of the Night*), published in 1932, has the honor of being the first serious French novel written entirely in the spoken language. Novelists, since Zola if not before, had done a great deal to bring their dialogue in line with the contemporary spoken language, but Céline was the first, as Queneau handsomely acknowledges, to write *all* his narrative passages too in the spoken tongue, something Queneau has never brought himself to do.

Queneau's copious use of argot, the French equivalent of slang, partly explains why so few of his novels have been translated into English. Many Frenchmen, one imagines, need to consult an up-to-date dictionary of argot while reading him, but their problem is minor compared to that of a translator. Once the translator is sure what Queneau means, his real work begins: he must find an equivalent slang word or phrase in English—but *which* English? A translator's version will vary a good deal depending on whether he is native to Dublin, London, New York, San Francisco, or Sydney. At the very least, separate versions for America and the British Isles would seem necessary.

Queneau, through reading Vendryès's *Language*, became conscious of something that Céline may have grasped unconsciously: to write true spoken French is as much a matter of syntax as of vocabulary. One of Queneau's five essays on the subject reprinted in *Bâtons, chiffres et lettres* bears the intriguing title *"Connaissez-vous le Chinook?"* ("Do You Know Chinook?"). Vendryès pointed out that the syntax of spoken French often resembles that of certain American-Indian languages: the first part of the sentence "contains all the grammatical indications (that is to say, the 'morphemes') and the second all the concrete data (the 'semantemes')." Thus, in spoken French one doesn't say, "Your cousin hasn't yet traveled in Africa" but "She hasn't yet there traveled, your cousin, in Africa." The opening sentence of *Le Dimanche de la vie* could be translated literally: "He didn't suspect that every time he passed in front of her store, she was watching him, the storekeeper the soldier Brû." Because this construction sounds so unfamiliar in English, an intelligent translator might not render it literally, but in French it manages to be both familiar and unfamiliar—familiar to the ear, unfamiliar to the eye.

Much of Queneau's attempt to capture the spoken language is, paradoxically, directed to the eye rather than the ear, through the use of phonetic spelling. The first "word" of *Zazie* in French is "Doukipudonktan," a phonetic rendering of the sentence *"D'où qu'ils puent donc tant?"* which Barbara Wright translates "Howcanaystinkso." A favorite condensation of Queneau's, which he will use even in otherwise fairly formal expository prose, is *"spa"* for *"n'est-ce pas?"* Another is *"xa"* for *"que ça."* Actually, he uses this phonetic spelling with discretion; his most startling arabesques clearly have a humorous intent, as when a youngster cries out twice in *Saint*

Glinglin, "Imélamin'hocudlastar!" Queneau would have no qualms about indicating more clearly that Paul's amorous hand was upon the film star's *derrière*; he simply wants to render the breathless cry of the youngster in all its immediacy.

Another Queneau quirk that may puzzle the English-speaking reader more than the French one is his "Francizing." Many English words have found their way into written French unaltered, but spoken French gives them a quite un-English pronunciation. Queneau insists on spelling them phonetically, so that "weekend" becomes *"véquande,"* "W.C." becomes *"vécé,"* and the great Sir Isaac Newton becomes on at least one occasion "Nioutone," thus retaining the correct English pronunciation by virtue of transliteration.

As a disciple of Joyce, Queneau does not balk at neologisms and portmanteau words, although he uses them sparingly. In *Bâtons, chiffres et lettres* (pp. 172–3), he presents a translation into Joycean of the opening passage of *Gueule de pierre*. It shows a great many characteristics of the style of *Finnegans Wake*, though the basic language is French instead of English. When Queneau published a revised version of *Gueule de pierre* in *Saint Glinglin*, his revision of the passage retained only two of the many Joycisms used in his translation, but incorporated a pair of new ones. The passage as it now stands seems to allude to Joyce without really imitating him. The French word *existence* occurs here as *aiguesistence*; since the existence of fish is being discussed, the element *aigue-* is particularly appropriate: in a compound like *aiguemarine* ("aquamarine") or in a place name like *Aiguesmortes* it shows its derivation from Latin *aqua* ("water"). Queneau is also making the phonetic point that the letter *x* in *existence* is pronounced "gz" instead of "ks." Almost everywhere that this word occurs in *Saint Glinglin* it is either spelled phonetically or punned on. We read for instance of *l'ogresistence du homard* (p. 17), which goes comfortably into English as "the ogresistence of the lobster."

Queneau's Joycean talents are perhaps most seriously employed in *Petite cosmogonie portative*, though even here he seems to be having a good deal of fun, coining words for convenience of rhyme (*estomace* for *estomac*, p. 65) as well as for condensation of meaning (*représentasillon* for *représentation*, p. 64). Another product, perhaps fully as serious, of his discipleship to Joyce is the extraordinary *Exercices de style* (1947), in which a brief prose anecdote is recounted in ninety-nine different styles. Among the weirdest variations are those called "Permutations": one written in groups of from two to five letters; one in groups of from five to eight; one in groups of from nine to twelve. Here we see again the mind of a mathematician rather than of a literary artist at work. The only similar permutations I can think of—and they are far from identical—are found in Beckett's second novel in English, *Watt* (completed in 1945, though not published until 1953). Any attempt to describe the astonishing variety of styles in *Exercices* would soon become wearisome; fortunately the book has been translated with amazing fidelity and fortitude by Barbara Wright (London, 1958).

The literary critic who must analyze *Le Chiendent* cannot help wishing that Queneau shared still another trait of the New Novelists, their tendency to eliminate plot. In this work, as in almost all his novels, Queneau provides a most elaborate one, full of complications, coincidences, concealments, and discoveries. The reader, alternately baffled and surprised, wonders why Queneau felt it necessary to work so hard. To understand why, we must bear in mind Queneau's analogy between the novel and poetry—a very traditional kind of poetry, furthermore. In discussing *Le Chiendent* he has said:

> I set up for myself rules as strict as those of the sonnet. The characters do not appear and disappear by chance, nor do the scenes, nor the different modes of expression. (*BCL*, p. 34)

Paradoxically, in *Le Chiendent* and *Pierrot mon ami* at least, this extreme artifice has at times the effect of naturalism; the arbitrariness of the plot resembles the arbitrariness of life, so that a single impulsive deviation from everyday routine can set off a chain of unforeseeable consequences prolonged virtually to infinity. Étienne's whim, prompted by a sign he sees from his commuter train, to stop at Blagny and eat *frites*, leads him into undreamed-of complications. Narcisse, on impulse, joins a friend, Potice, who is engaged in his favorite pastime of following a woman; Potice is run over and killed, but Narcense becomes obsessed by the woman—Étienne's wife, as it happens—and his whole life pattern changes. (No doubt the names of these two characters were originally *Narcisse*—"Narcissus"—and *Potence*—meaning "crutch," "gallows," "derrick," etc., but with overtones of the English word "potency" —until Queneau decided to transpose their syllables.)

But this is not the whole story: interrupt a man's routine and ultimately his whole personality may change—at least in *Le Chiendent*. To remove him from his routine, even for a few hours, is to change his environment, and the influence of environment is shown to be decisive for several of the characters. Others, like the malign dwarf Bébé Toutout, have been given such a definitive mold by heredity or catastrophe that they are incapable of further change. Thus the arbitrary and complex plot not only has the effect of making characters and situations rhyme together; it also serves to emphasize the impermanence and malleability of personality and the omnipresence of chance. The determining factor in Étienne's change and intellectual growth is something even more trivial than his whim to eat fried potatoes; one day, while hurrying from his work to the subway, he is distracted by an advertising stunt in a shop window—two celluloid ducks floating in a waterproof hat full of water. He stops to look, is late for his train, and cannot get his usual seat on it. "Something had changed." He is surprised to learn from his stepson that the ducks had been in the window for at least two years before he noticed them.

It becomes imperative at this point to outline the rest of the plot. Étienne Marcel, although the central character of the book, pursues a course largely tangential to the main plot elements. He becomes too involved with the astonishing intellectual developments taking place within him to pay full attention to the events taking place around him, even when they closely concern his wife, Alberte, and his stepson, Théo.

At first, when he has no personality, we see him through the eyes of the observer, Pierre le Grand, to whom he appears merely a silhouette headed from the bank where he works to the subway entrance. Then comes the day when he turns to look at the ducks; looking at his back, Pierre becomes conscious of him as "a flat being." The next evening it rains and Étienne has to seek shelter; he misses his usual suburban train, and Pierre, following him onto a later train, becomes conscious that Étienne "is filling out gently, is maturing."

On this very evening the "Narcense Plot" begins. Unaware that Potice has been killed, Narcense follows Alberte to her home in Obonne. Returning to a bar near the station, he meets Pierre, who is also at loose ends after following Étienne. Pierre thus discovers the link between Étienne and Narcense, of which neither of them is yet aware.

Narcense writes love letters to Alberte, which she tears up and throws in the wastebasket. Théo pieces them together and writes taunting replies to Narcense. Narcense, furious, invites Théo to meet him in the woods near Obonne at midnight so that he can have the pleasure of hanging him. Théo agrees. True to an old convention of French humorous literature, Narcense's concierge, Saturnin Belhôtel, has been reading his correspondence and determines to prevent the murder of Théo. He tells his widowed sister, Mme Cloche, a midwife and abortionist, of his plan. Now, Mme Cloche happened to witness the accident which killed Potice. Watching at the same place next evening in morbid expectation of another accident, she sees Étienne struck a glancing blow by Pierre's taxi. Pierre and Étienne meet in this way and travel to Obonne together.

To complicate matters further, the restaurant at Blagny where Étienne goes to eat french fries is owned by Saturnin's brother, Dominique. Mme Cloche arrives there to cause the abortion of the waitress, Ernestine, whom Dominique has made pregnant. She recognizes Étienne and introduces herself. During Étienne's second visit to the restaurant, Mme Cloche tells the story of Saturnin, Narcense, and Théo, and discovers Étienne's unconscious involvement in it. Étienne, alerted, also plans to prevent the murder. Mme Cloche, still thirsty for blood, plans to make her own way to Obonne. Since Théo does not show up at the rendezvous, Narcense tries to hang himself, but is rescued by Étienne and Saturnin. Mme Cloche arrives after everything is over.

Saturnin takes Narcense home next day and the Narcense Plot falls into abeyance, its place being taken by the "Taupe Plot." Old Taupe (whose name means "Mole") is a junk dealer who lives in a shack on a garbage dump in Blagny and is in love with Ernestine, the waitress. Clovis Belhôtel, Dominique's son, overhears Pierre and Étienne talking about Taupe and mistakenly concludes that they think he is a millionaire. He tells his aunt, Mme Cloche, who swears him to secrecy. She then tries to persuade Ernestine to marry Taupe and share his wealth with her. Ernestine is at first unwilling, so Mme Cloche makes the mistake of telling her "secret" to Narcense; she has by now become convinced that Pierre and Étienne are international crooks and that Narcense belongs to a rival gang. Meanwhile, Ernestine changes her mind and decides to encourage Taupe's advances.

Three of the book's seven chapters are now complete. Chapter 4 is an interlude at a seaside resort to which young Théo has run away with a middle-aged neighbor, Mme Pigeonnier. He has sent a postcard to Narcense, not realizing that his stepfather is in touch with Narcense. In fact, Narcense has revealed to Étienne that Pierre had known of the whole Narcense-Alberte-Théo complication. Étienne thinks none the worse of Pierre, whose help he feels he needs in his intellectual development. Pierre, Alberte, and Étienne arrive at the resort in Pierre's car and find Théo, but Alberte and Étienne do not suspect his relationship with Mme Pigeonnier. Narcense turns up too, half crazy with frustrated love and money worries. Pierre becomes the lover of Catherine, Mme Pigeonnier's maid.

The fifth chapter deals entirely with the wedding day of Taupe and Ernestine. Both, for their different reasons, are radiant. A wildly humorous and satirical account of the wedding banquet follows. Suddenly Ernestine becomes ill, and in an hour or two she is dead from unexplained causes; poison is suspected, but, if Queneau supplied a clue to the poisoner, it has escaped the notice of at least this reader. (Mme Cloche wrongly blames Pierre and Étienne.) Ernestine delivers a deathbed speech, which sounds like an existential version of Socrates' as recorded by Plato except that it is couched in modern slang. She denounces priests and discusses the nature of existence and her disbelief in a life after death. At whatever cost, the seemingly inevitable mutual disillusionment of the radiantly happy Taupe and Ernestine is skillfully averted by this intervention of chance—or, rather, of the author. The chapter ends with the thwarted Mme Cloche ready to murder Taupe, but Dominique refuses to help her.

In the sixth chapter the Taupe Plot ends. Mme Cloche, Narcense, and Saturnin have become convinced that a door which Taupe keeps in his shack is where he has hidden his wealth. Actually, he treasures it because he and a girl he loved wrote their names on it before her death. Mme Cloche, disguised as a priest, gains access to the shack and behaves in a most unpriestlike manner until Taupe drives her away. (The unwary reader may fail to recognize Mme Cloche in disguise and think that Queneau is being anti-clerical to the point of insanity.) Next, Narcense and Saturnin break in and steal the door. Taupe dies, presumably of a broken heart, but the two thieves of course find nothing. Finally Clovis explains to his father how the misunderstanding about Taupe's alleged fortune came about.

As the Taupe Plot peters out, the "Bébé Toutout Plot" commences. Long before, when Narcense was particularly bitter against Théo, he had met the dwarf on a train. Learning that Bébé Toutout was a parasite who specialized in terrorizing children, Narcense gave him Étienne's address, hoping that he would terrorize Théo. Unfortunately, Narcense also managed to arouse the implacable hatred of Bébé Toutout against himself. Having run out of other victims for the moment, the dwarf now appears at Étienne's home and soon installs himself there permanently, in spite of Étienne's and

Alberte's attempts to get rid of him. Théo becomes his willing slave. Étienne, having lost touch with Pierre, feels himself slowly, gently diminishing. His intellectual adventures are over.

In the seventh and final chapter, all pretense at realism rapidly disappears. France and the "Etruscans," whose queen is Miss Aulini (Mussolini?), declare war on one another. Pierre and Catherine happen to be abroad at the time and escape the war, but everybody else is affected by it. Étienne, Saturnin, and Narcense are drafted. Alberte, unable to cope with Bébé Toutout any longer, goes to live in Paris with Mme Pigeonnier; she meets Narcense again there and becomes his mistress at last. Dominique and his wife have sold their restaurant and bought a brothel in Épinal, a garrison town; Bébé Toutout and Théo turn the Marcel home into another brothel, staffed by Théo's friends among the local high-school girls. Narcense deserts from the French Army; Bébé Toutout gives anonymous information to the authorities; Narcense is arrested, court-martialed, and executed by a firing squad.

The war drags on for decades. The last few French soldiers, including Étienne and Saturnin, are captured by the remaining Etruscans, whose queen, now that she is much older, calls herself Missize Aulini. She turns out to be our old friend Mme Cloche. She, her brother, and Étienne have a drunken feast together. Finally, she bets Saturnin that he can no longer count to ten. He refuses to accept the bet, suspecting a trick, so she tells him to count after her as follows: *nain, deuil, toit, carte, sein, scie, sexe, huître, oeuf et disque.* These are words which sound like the French numerals from one to ten but actually mean "dwarf, mourning, roof, card, breast, saw, sex, oyster, egg and disc." Saturnin and Étienne are delighted with the joke.

> "I didn't think that up myself," said the queen. "It's in the book."
> "What book?" asked the two errant Marshals of France.
> "Why, this one. This one we're in now, which repeats everything we say as we say it. . . ." (p. 294)

After some criticism of the book, they decide to start from the beginning again, and we reach the last two sentences, identical with the first two:

> The silhouette of a man profiled itself; simultaneously, thousands of others. There were thousands upon thousands of them.

So much—so very much—for the plot of *Le Chiendent*. But what has happened to the idea of translating Descartes into spoken French? Well, Descartes is not so much translated as exemplified; Étienne's mental growth is a sort of expansion of the philosopher's most famous axiom, *Cogito, ergo sum* (I think, therefore I exist). Take, for example, this extract from Étienne's meditation (pp. 79–80) when at last he begins to think:

> . . . I've changed a lot lately I see it now yes the world is not what it seems to be, at least when you live the same thing every day you see nothing any more yet there are people who live like that always me, at bottom I didn't exist, all that began with the little ducks before that I didn't think I didn't exist so to speak at any rate I don't remember any more the others were living beside me things were there there or elsewhere and I didn't see anything yet I must still look the same and the others if they're like I was before perhaps the others don't think don't exist they come and go like I came and went but that bears no relation to anything so to speak that would be curious all the same perhaps on the contrary it's me who was an exception I was the only one not existing and when I looked at the world I began to exist perhaps in philosophy books they say all that they explain perhaps what sort of book could give me the information Le Grand must know he's living he's always existed he sees everything he knows how to go about thinking I haven't read books when I was little I must have existed for instance when I was five I cried when the cat died I existed then for sure . . . I'm getting very smart it's fun like that to direct one's thoughts to talk to oneself before when I woke up in the night I looked at the fifth acanthus leaf on the wallpaper now I know how to say things to myself that aren't ordinary I wonder if all that is written in books. . . .

It *is* written in books, but hardly in the style in which Queneau makes him talk to himself.

On page 93 Étienne comes to a profound realization: "It isn't happiness that preoccupies me but existence." By page 125 he and Pierre le Grand are having a conversation which suggests that Étienne is beginning to outdistance his wealthy and better-educated friend and indeed is reaching areas of philosophy which have more to do with twentieth-century existentialism than with Descartes:

"If I overlook the practical side of a manufactured object . . ." said Étienne.

"You're dabbling in aesthetics," interrupted Pierre. "Or in magic."

"But I don't want to dabble in aesthetics or magic," Étienne protested. "Men think they're making one thing, and then they make another. They think they're making a pair of scissors, and it's something else they're making. Sure, it *is* a pair of scissors, it's made to cut and it cuts, but it's also something quite different."

"Why scissors?"

"Or any other manufactured object, every manufactured object. A table even. A house. It's a house, since you live in it, but it's something else too. That's not aesthetics, because it's not a matter of beauty or ugliness. And as for magic, I don't understand."

"What would be interesting would be to say what that 'something else' is."

"No doubt. But it isn't possible. That depends on circumstances, or else one can't express it. Words too are manufactured objects. One can consider them independently of their sense." (p. 125)

Of all the novels in which characters "talk philosophy"—one thinks at once of Dostoevsky—*Le Chiendent* is probably the earliest which shares the preoccupations of mid-twentieth-century philosophers. This is hardly an accident; Georges Bataille wrote in 1948 that this novel marked "a beginning of existential philosophy in France." He went on to say:

Le Chiendent would deserve this mention in the history of thought: in it for the first time attentive reflection, shaped by the refined methods of German phenomenology, laid open to metaphysics thanks to the interrogation of Heidegger, addressed itself to the most pitiful and degraded forms of life.[6]

Queneau himself tells us that he and Bataille were reading and discussing together, in the period 1929–32, not only books by Wahl, Gurvitch, and Lévinas dealing with Hegel, Husserl, and current German philosophy in general, but also the works by Heidegger and Husserl first published in French in 1931.[7] In other words, Queneau and Bataille were reading some of the philosophers who later helped Sartre to develop his existentialist philosophy; at the time, however, Sartre himself was not quite ready to understand them. Simone de Beauvoir admits that she and Sartre read the translation of Heidegger's *Was ist Metaphysik?* which appeared in the periodical *Bifur* in 1931 without understanding a word of it. Bataille and Queneau, presumably, understood it better.

The philosophic discussions in *Le Chiendent* are far from an irrelevant excrescence on the novel. Many of them arise out of the experiences of Étienne. For instance, when Pierre finally reveals to him that he, Pierre, took Narcense in his car to the woods at Obonne on the night of the rendezvous with Théo, Étienne begins to doubt his own existence and that of everybody around him. "Théo? Who is he? It's very simple: I don't know a thing about it. . . . And I myself, who am I? I've already told you, I don't know who I am. And what's more, does that question have a meaning? . . . Has the phrase 'to be' a meaning?" Pierre can only answer, "You've made great strides in metaphysics." It is hard for one who is not a professional philosopher to say whether Étienne's later meditation on appearance and reality (pp. 222–5), centered on the right shoe of a man opposite him in the train, represents any further progress in metaphysics; probably not.

Actually, the most startling philosophical passage in the book is the work not of Étienne but of Saturnin, the concierge,

[6] Georges Bataille, *"La Méchanceté du langage,"* Critique, IV (décembre 1948), 1059.

[7] Raymond Queneau, *"Premières confrontations avec Hegel,"* Critique, XIX (août–septembre 1963), 697.

who wants to be a writer but has apparently never learned to
spell. His philosophical discourse, delivered viva voce to the
bored Narcense, begins:

> You understand, philosophy, it's made two great mistakes;
> two great oversights; first it forgot to study the different ways
> of being, firstly; and that's no small oversight. But that's
> nothing yet; it's overlooked what's the most important, the
> different ways of not being. For instance, a pat of butter, I'm
> taking the first thing that comes into my head, a pat of butter
> for example, that's not a caravanserai, or a fork, or a cliff, or a
> down quilt. And take notice that this way of not being is pre-
> cisely its way of being. I'll come back to that. There's another
> way of not being; for example, the pat of butter that ain't on
> that table, is not. It's a degree higher of not-being. In between
> the two, there's no-longer-being and not-yet-having-been.
> Everything, like that, gives rise to heaps of non-bein's: The
> pat of butter is not everything that it ain't, it is not everywhere
> that it ain't, it prevents everything from being where it is, it
> hasn't always been, and it won't always be, ekcetera, ekcetera.
> So, a pretty infinite infinity of not being. That way, you can
> say that this pat of butter is in over its head in the infinity
> of nonbein, and what seems most important finally, tain't
> being but nonbein.[8] (pp. 256–7)

Over a page more of the same type of argument follows,
culminating in the setting forth of these formulas:

> Being is, nonbein is not,
> Being is not, nonbein is,
> Being is, nonbein is,
> Being is not, nonbein is not,

all of which reveal an aspect of truth; even together, all four,
they don't reveal the totality, because to admit that there ain't
but four possible formulas, that'd be to admit, firstly a limitation and secondly the legitimacy of the prirfciple of contra-
diction which as a matter of fact we said wasn't legitimate
when it wuz a matter of the totality. Which brings it about
that the truth is somewheres else yet. (pp. 258–9)

[8] "Nonbein" for "Non-being" is an attempt to approximate Queneau's
"le nonnête" for *"le non-être."*

Amen! One would like to hear a professional philosopher's comments upon such janitorial philosophy, but the layman can only gape at what appears to be an insanely logical argument whose method seems more appropriate to mathematics than to philosophy. But, then, there is reason to believe that Queneau, whose university studies were primarily in philosophy, has become a more formidable mathematician than philosopher.

Concern with plot and with philosophic content has led us to slight an important aspect of *Le Chiendent*: its experiments in the technique of narration and dialogue. It is true that these are not as radical as Queneau's experiments in philosophic exposition; probably no narrative device used by him is more than a variation on something already to be found in Joyce, the Surrealists, Rabelais, or Sterne. Indeed, one has to admit that certain passages in *Tristram Shandy*, which expound or exemplify—or simply plagiarize—the theory of association of ideas as treated in John Locke's *Essay Concerning Human Understanding*, anticipate Queneau's attempts to present philosophic ideas in colloquial language.

Queneau must have been considerably daunted by the very brief review by Jean Guérin accorded *Le Chiendent* in the *Nouvelle revue française* (XLII, 727), the leading literary periodical in the world at that time. It begins as follows: "Fifteen years ago, this book would have been a revelation," a sentence which might well make any author shrivel. However, the second sentence of this four-sentence review is more reassuring: "But if its audacities of form and thought are not entirely new, one is aware almost continuously of the presence of a real temperament." The reviewer did not, one assumes, really grasp how audacious some of the thought was; his highest praise is reserved for some of the book's humorous effects, especially the account of the wedding of old Taupe.

Yet the ninety-one sections of *Le Chiendent* display a technical virtuosity akin to that of Joyce's *Ulysses*. Joyce employed a different technique in each of his eighteen episodes; Queneau does not claim to have employed ninety-one different techniques, but he has gone a good distance in that direction:

no section is exactly like those which immediately precede
and follow it.

> Each of the sections of *Le Chiendent* is a unity, with two
> or three exceptions which I could justify if I wished. Each is
> a unity, first of all, as a tragedy is—that is to say, it observes
> the rule of the three unities. It is a unity not only in regard to
> time, place and action but also in regard to genre: pure narra-
> tion, narration interrupted by recorded dialogue, pure conver-
> sation (which tends toward dramatic style); interior mono-
> logue in "I," recorded monologue (as if the author were
> penetrating the slightest thoughts of his characters), or mono-
> logue spoken aloud (another equally dramatic mode); letters
> (of which some famous novels are entirely made up), journals
> (not private diaries, but account books or clippings from daily
> papers), or reports of dreams (which must be used sparingly,
> so greatly is this genre falling into disrepute). (*BCL*, pp.
> 24–5)

There is no way of conveying Queneau's technical virtuosity
short of compiling an anthology. I hope the passages already
quoted from *Le Chiendent* may give some idea of its extraordinary range. Two more follow: a brief example of Queneau
at his most lighthearted, and another of his more frequent
"black" humor. Chapter 4, which takes place at the seaside
resort, concludes with a parody of the local newspaper.
Among the news items is this:

> Théodore Marcel, aged fifteen, at present on vacation at
> X . . . , has just finished reading the third volume of *Les
> Misérables*. Compliments and congratulations to this youthful
> representative of French Intellect.

The other example (pp. 48–9) is the account of the funeral of
Narcense's grandmother as seen through the eyes of a dog
named Jupiter, who, though unusually intelligent (his master,
if he had had the time, would have taught him arithmetic and
perhaps the elements of formal logic), can make very little
sense of the proceedings:

> Then a big packing case is brought out into the street; he goes
> over to sniff at it; it smells of the old lady. A kick in the ribs
> teaches him respect for the dead.

> . . . Everybody has stopped around a hole. In the middle of
> the group, the man-woman growls a threatening song; the
> urchins are waving smoking teapots. Two qualified drunkards
> lower the box to the bottom of the hole. Then the guests
> throw drops of water.

Poor Jupiter unwittingly desecrates the grave and is put to
death by his master next morning.

Reluctantly, we must take leave of *Le Chiendent*, which, in
spite of its careful structure, does not succeed in conveying
the idea of a fundamental unity underlying its almost infinite
variety. Perhaps the point implicit in its return to the *status
quo ante* at the end is that no final resolution is possible for
all the contradictions presented by life. The strange title of
the novel may help us here. Etymologically, *chiendent* is presumably a compound of *chien* and *dent* ("dog-tooth"), but it
literally means a weed with similar properties to that nemesis
of suburban American lawns, crab grass. However, the proverbial phrase *"Voilà le chiendent!"* means "There's the rub!"
or "There's the snag!" or "There's the fly in the ointment!"
Some such meaning should presumably be given the title of
Queneau's novel; it must refer to some basic imperfection of
human life, perhaps Étienne's "something else" that we can
never know, perhaps death—so eloquently discoursed on by
Ernestine. Pierre believes that life lacks any meaning, but
Étienne refuses to accept this view. Ultimately, each reader
must give his own meaning to the title of *Le Chiendent*.

Queneau's second novel, *Gueule de pierre* ("Face of Stone"),
was published in 1934, a year after *Le Chiendent*. While much
shorter than the previous work, it is if anything more original,
representing the first wave of an inspiration which culminated
in *Saint Glinglin* (1948). The second wave did not break until
1941, when the second part of *Gueule de pierre*, *Les Temps
mêlés* ("Mixed Weather") was published. Finally, seven years
later, the two parts were revised and added to under the new
overall title of *Saint Glinglin*. This last work, which super-
sedes the two earlier volumes, will be dealt with at once, in
disregard of chronology, for it is sufficiently unified in style

and spirit to be regarded as a product of Queneau's first creative explosion. After World War II, Queneau undoubtedly experienced another tremendous upsurge of creative activity which produced, among other things, many of his best shorter poems, the *Exercices de style*, the *Petite cosmogonie*, and *Le Dimanche de la vie*; this may have helped supply the energy needed for the revision and completion of *Saint Glinglin*, but the characters, the style, and the basic plot had been established in 1934. Nevertheless, one must admit the possibility that Queneau had no intention of writing a sequel or sequels when he first published *Gueule de pierre*. He has said:

> I never have any plans for the future. Admittedly there is one of my novels [*Saint Glinglin*] which took me almost fifteen years to finish, but it presents many internal discontinuities.

Saint Glinglin might be described as the perfect foil to *Le Chiendent* in both form and content. To the complex plotting of the earlier book it opposes the broad, free movement of myth. In place of the rigorous intellectual discipline of logic, existential philosophy, and mathematics, it offers the less stringent methods of the social sciences: anthropology, sociology, psychology (a freewheeling Freudianism). Though *Saint Glinglin* contains two lengthy philosophical meditations, the intellectual life is on the whole subordinated to the instinctual. Furthermore, although three of its leading characters perish for their ideals—two defeated and one victorious— *Saint Glinglin* opposes a tempered optimism to the nihilistic pessimism of *Le Chiendent* and concludes with these auspicious words, "unchangeable fine weather."

Even the settings of the two books are sharply contrasted. *Le Chiendent* takes place mainly against the urban and suburban landscape of Paris and Obonne, both setting and events being fairly realistically described; *Saint Glinglin*, on the other hand, takes place in and around the archetypal Ville Natale ("Birthplace" or "Hometown"), whose patron saint is the apocryphal Glinglin. In colloquial French, to promise to love someone until Saint Glinglin's Day (*jusqu'à la Saint Glinglin*) means that one's love will last forever; conversely, to promise to do something on that mythical saint's day means putting it off indefinitely. The Romans had an equivalent expression, "Till the Greek Kalends"—the Greek calendar having no kalends. Many Irishmen still use a similar expression, "Till St. Tibb's Eve" (usually shortened to "Till Tibb's Eve").

Queneau has said that his first three novels—*Le Chiendent*, *Gueule de pierre*, *Les derniers jours*—are all circular in form. In *Gueule de pierre*, however, "the circular movement does not regain its point of departure but a homologous point, and forms a spiral arc; the final sign of the zodiac, the Fishes, is not situated on the same plane as fishes which are animals." He gives us some other hints about the book, including the fact that its three parts correspond to the three kingdoms of nature—animal, vegetable, and mineral.

Les Temps mêlés was also tripartite in form, but its first part, consisting of short poems, was suppressed in the revision. Since the third and final section of *Gueule de pierre* was also in verse, it is possible that the structure of *Les Temps mêlés* was intended to form a mirror image of that of *Gueule de pierre*; it would begin with verse rather than ending with it, and the three kingdoms would run in reverse order—mineral, vegetable, animal. The two surviving sections of *Les Temps mêlés*, which constitute the fourth and fifth sections of *Saint Glinglin*, certainly have a good deal to say about vegetable and mammalian behavior, respectively.

Saint Glinglin now consists of seven chapters, tabulated below, four of which are associated with the four children of Nabonide, the great mayor and culture hero of La Ville Natale:

   I. *Les Poissons* (The Fish)—Pierre
  II. *Le Printanier* (Rite of Spring)
 III. *Le Caillou* (The Rock)—Jean
  IV. *Les Ruraux* (The Country People)—Paul
   V. *Les Touristes* (The Tourists)
  VI. *Les Étrangers* (The Foreigners)—Hélène
 VII. *Saint Glinglin*

Chapter 1 is the monologue of Pierre—perhaps better described as a diary without dates—revolving around the lives of

fish. Its opening words are *Drôle de vie, la vie de poisson!*
("Funny life, a fish's!"). Pierre is a young man who has been
sent by his domineering father, Nabonide, the mayor of La
Ville Natale, to study the language of La Ville Étrangère so
that he can act as guide and interpreter for tourists in his
hometown; his father, obviously, thinks that's all he's good
for. Pierre finds it impossible to learn the foreign language and
instead becomes fascinated by the fish in the huge aquarium
of the foreign city. The basic theme of his meditation upon
fish is an existentialist one, the alienation of man from nature.
"It is not possible," he reflects, "to have human contacts with
a fish." Some fish are even less human than others—the ray,
for example, of which he says that its existence is impossible.
Nevertheless, it exists. The lobster too, which is still more
alien. Tropical fish seem to have a certain human gaiety; but
then he discovers the cave-dwelling fish, blind and colorless,
which have evolved from more normal species through countless generations of living in darkness; their existence reduces
him to tears. Eventually he concludes that there is one category of experience that man, the lobster, and the oyster have
in common—fear. Sometimes Queneau uses for "fear" the
word *angoisse*, the French equivalent of *Angst*, that favorite
term of German existentialism. Cave-dwelling fish and the sea
slug of the ocean depths are exempt from fear and therefore
totally inhuman.

The culmination of his studies in the aquarium is the establishment of two groups of categories, one human, the other
inhuman:

Human	Inhuman
Renewal	Silence
Light	Obscurity
Movement	Immobility
Diversity	Unity
Unrest	Rest
Fear	Calm

The first of these groups belongs to the future and is called
Glory; the second, which is the life of the human fetus, among
other creatures, belongs to the past and is called Happiness.

Pierre is not perhaps perfect as a systematic philosopher, but his attacks of vertigo make him sure of his vocation as a prophet or shaman. He resolves to deliver his prophetic message in the form of a lecture when he returns to his hometown for the Feast of St. Glinglin.

Chapter 2, which takes the form of narrative liberally interspersed with dialogue, relates the events of this particular feast day. Like every St. Glinglin's Day in the Ville Natale, it involves certain rituals and customs. In the morning, the males start drinking early; the only acceptable drink is a local wine called *fifrequet*. Meanwhile, the women are preparing a vast soup called *brouchtoucaille*, made up of every variety of vegetable, meat, and spice known to the inhabitants. At noon the official festivities begin with the blowing up of a huge balloon, unequivocally phallic in shape. Next follows the smashing by the male population of the masses of crockery exposed for this purpose by the chief citizens in the main square of the town. This ceremonial is strongly reminiscent both of the "potlatch" ritual of the Kwakiutl Indians and of the crockery smashing which forms a part of Italian ritual on New Year's Eve. The greatest honor, naturally, goes to the one who sacrifices the most crockery. This year, in order to compensate for Pierre's return in disgrace, Nabonide has contributed an unprecedented number of items, nearly four hundred thousand in all, including 317,000 egg cups. But instead of allowing others to smash them, he violates tradition by destroying them all himself with his mayoral tommy gun. After a lunch of *brouchtoucaille*, both sexes gather to watch the male competition called *Le Printanier*. The nature of this competition is never fully revealed; about the most explicit description is that "people mime with their fingers the growth of plants." A number of hints suggest that this Rite of Spring—not without precedent among primitive peoples—consists of a phallic display and perhaps public masturbation. At any rate, the winner of this year's triumphal prize is an elderly drunkard named Bonjean; the year's vintage of *fifrequet* will be associated with his name.

After this, while the citizens are enjoying the fun of the fair, Pierre announces his lecture, and the whole population eventually crowd in to hear it. Nabonide tries to break up the meeting by asking his son whether cave-dwelling fish are edible and by telling the audience to go home. They refuse. Pierre embarks upon his conclusion, "a subject precise and concrete: the situation created for the poor fish when they are removed from their humid space." At this, the entire audience bursts out laughing. Pierre blames his father for this disastrous reception and promises to kill him. Nabonide seems unmoved by this. Later, when Paul, his middle son, tells him that Pierre and Jean have set out for their grandmother's farm near the Arid Hills and that the sons have made "a discovery," Nabonide suddenly becomes greatly disturbed. While abroad, Pierre had been receiving cryptic messages about this discovery from his younger brothers.

Chapter 3 takes the form of an epic poem recited and doubtless composed by Jean. The verse form is unmetered and unrhymed, but with an incantatory tone reminiscent of the Psalms and some of the prophetic books of the Bible. In the original French it is strongly reminiscent also of similar verse by Paul Claudel; if translated into English, it would sound rather like Whitman.

In summary, it narrates the following events: The three brothers—Pierre, Paul, and Jean—have a sister, Hélène, whose existence Jean only recently discovered. Insane from birth, but very beautiful, she has been sequestered by Nabonide in an old mill on his witchlike mother's farm. Nabonide loves Hélène more than anything else in the world and has complete faith in her prophetic powers. He goes regularly to consult her and guides his life by what she tells him. Dismayed at his sons' discovery, he rushes to the mill and takes his daughter with him up into the Arid Hills. Jean, finding the squalid mill empty except for the rotting food and excreta left by Hélène, pursues his father and is now joined by Pierre. The father fires one shot at them but deliberately misses. Instead of fighting his sons, Nabonide plunges into the Petrifying Fountain and is

turned into stone. Jean goes abroad with Hélène while Pierre
returns to La Ville Natale, where he becomes mayor and has
his petrified father set up as a statue in the main square.

Originally, in *Gueule de pierre*, this chapter was divided
into twelve sub-sections, each preceded by a sign of the
zodiac. In the current edition of *Saint Glinglin*, the chapter is
divided into only ten parts, separated by blank spaces. However, this is probably an error on the part of the printer. There
should be a space on p. 103 after *"par notre vérité"* and on
p. 112 after *"Elle fuyait avec lui."* The chapter begins with the
first sign, Aries (the Ram), and ends with the twelfth, Pisces
(the Fishes), under which Queneau was born on February 21.
In *Gueule de pierre*, each of the twelve sections was headed
by the name of one of the twelve signs, in their traditional
order. One can still find allusions to all twelve signs, but no
longer in order except for the first and the last. The signs now
run as follows:

Page	Latin Name	English of Latin	French Keyword	English
100	Aries	Ram	*béliers*	rams
101	Capricornus	Goat	*cabreux*	goatherd?
105	Gemini	Twins	*jumeaux*	twins
106	Aquarius	Water Pourer	(Nabonide has urinated)	
110	Taurus	Bull	*taureau*	bull
111	Virgo	Virgin	(Hélène is kept a virgin)	
113	Libra	Scales	*justice, liberté*	(A pun: Justice bears scales and Libra suggests French *libre*, "free")
115	Scorpio	Scorpion	*scorpion*	scorpion
117	Cancer	Crab	*chancres*	cankers, chancres, cancers
118	Leo	Lion	*lion*	lion
120	Sagittarius	Archer	*sagittaire*	archer
124	Pisces	Fishes	*poissons*	fishes

Chapter 4 consists of Paul's meditation on the alienation
of man from nature and it is, if anything, more remarkable
than Pierre's. Whereas Pierre's "diary" is divided by blank
spaces into eighteen sub-sections, Paul's monologue is con-

tinuous and considerably shorter than his brother's. Paul is on vacation in the countryside and he hates it—"the long sheet of boredom and chlorophyll in which the Countryfolk enwind themselves day and night." Not only is vegetation alien to man, but those who live in the country and undergo its influence lose their humanity. The town, however, is a man-made world and its beauty a man-made beauty: that of the cinema, for example, recently introduced into La Ville Natale. And the beauty of the female stars themselves is man-made; encased in girdles, brassières, and silk stockings (which Paul has seen in importers' windows), their bodies are more beautiful and desirable than any nude body could ever be. Paul has fallen completely in love with the screen image of one star, Alice Phaye (whose name is perilously close to that of Alice Faye, an indispensable cast member of most Hollywood musicals of the 1930's).

In Chapter 5 we are on the eve of Pierre's first St. Glinglin's Day as mayor. The style is the same as in Chapter 2. Alice Phaye is being shown round La Ville Natale by a learned ethnologist named Dussouchel. She has come straight from *Le Bois Sacré* ("The Sacred Wood"; i.e., Hollywood). She admires the petrified body of Nabonide, with some misgivings about its nakedness. Dussouchel and she drink with some of the natives, who hint that tomorrow's festival may represent a disastrous break with tradition. While the star and the ethnologist are visiting Pierre in his office, Paul enters, sees Alice, and faints. By nighttime Alice and Paul are embracing so shamelessly, more or less in public, that Pierre feels obliged to marry them at once in his capacity as mayor. Although he had previously promised Dussouchel that the next day's feast would remain traditional, Pierre now threatens to make it rain. It is ominous that the objects he puts out for the crockery-smashing ceremony are all made of glass, aquariums and goldfish bowls! Sure enough, next day he throws the magic cloud-chaser (*le chasse-nuages*), which has given La Ville Natale its permanent fine weather, into the town dump (*le fourre-tout*). On the stroke of noon it begins to pour and Pierre's aquariums and fish bowls fill with water, though there are as yet no fish to put in them. The petrified form of Nabonide begins to melt in the downpour. Pierre is ejected from his office by the leading citizens, and Paul is appointed mayor in his place.

Chapter 6 consists of the monologue of Hélène, now living abroad with her brother Jean. To her, in her madness, it is the human world that is alien and the non-human insect world that is familiar. She identifies herself with some tiny blind creature that can do nothing but hop. To a worm she gives the name of her brother Jean; she imagines that it sings in the moonlight. A wood louse she names after Paul, and she watches him dance in the moonlight. To a winged beetle that lives under a flat stone she gives the name of Pierre. The world of the foreign population around her is described in terms of papers: identity papers, toilet paper, paper money are all interchangeable for her. Also, there are boxes: some are called houses, some apartments; at the theatre, the stage is one kind of box and the auditorium another. This description of the human world shows a certain failure of Queneau's imagination, but the pages on Hélène's view of the insect world are the work of a true poet.

Chapter 7 brings us back to La Ville Natale on the eve of the next feast of Saint Glinglin. It has not stopped raining since the last one, and the cellars of the town are full of water and fish, so that the bottles of *fifrequet* have to be stored in lofts. Pierre has been allowed to stay in the town on condition that he carve a statue of his father to replace the petrified body that melted. He is progressing very slowly. Paul has had the main square dug out to form a swimming pool, and it is rumored that Alice will swim there in the presence of the male population, as a substitute for the crockery-smashing. A number of the leading citizens are indignantly conspiring against Paul's regime.

On Saint Glinglin's Day many things happen. Jean and Hélène return to the town, both dressed alike as tourists in shorts. They meet their mother, an unimportant figure in the book. Their grandmother finally dies. Alice swims in her two-piece bathing suit and causes every man in her audience to

have an erection. Immediately after this ceremony, the grandmother's corpse is taken to *le fourre-tout* and thrown in; the
swamp soon engulfs it. Pierre stands looking at the mud.

"There must be funny creatures in there," he murmured.
"Big insects, little beasties," murmured Hélène. "Together.
They make little scratching noises at night. Little feet. Big
wings."
"They're alive!" murmured Pierre. "They're alive! It's difficult to imagine that. To be born, to endure, to die perhaps:
obscure, blind."
"In my hiding place," said Hélène, "I became so pale and
bleached. But I never cried out. Never."
"It's when I lose life as man understands it," said Pierre,
"that I attain the object of my search." (p. 253)

Pierre goes back and finishes the statue in a burst of inspiration, but the rain does not stop as people hoped it would.
Jean then puts forward his plan for stopping the rain. Some
of the citizens have their doubts; any change might be for the
worse. But what could be worse than rain? "Snow or hail" is
the answer. Most citizens do not know what these things are
and are horrified to learn of the existence of such monstrous
phenomena. Jean persists, and eventually his plan is accepted:
he gets into an airport wind-indicator sleeve and has himself
hoisted to the top of a mast, like the old *chasse-nuages*, where
Hélène feeds him with vitamins. Gradually, the good weather
returns. Paul resigns and goes abroad with Alice; Manuel
Bonjean becomes mayor. As the weather gets hotter, Pierre's
statue of his father melts and is thrown in *le fourre-tout*,
where Pierre soon joins it. Jean dies and becomes mummified
in the dry air at the top of the mast.[9] Hélène, in despair, flees
to the Arid Hills and disappears. None of the Nabonide children remains alive in their native town, but Jean is canonized
under the name of Saint Glinglin and a feast day is observed
in his honor:

[9] In the manner of Raymond Roussel (see the previous chapter),
Queneau calls this new totem *la nasse-chuages* (from *nasse*, a kind of
net).

In the morning, receptacles are smashed; in the afternoon, people mime with their fingers the growth of (rare) plants; in the evening, a fireworks display causes no atmospheric perturbation, for the fine weather is solidly established.

Thus *Saint Glinglin*, like *Le Chiendent*, proves to be circular in form: the essentials of life in La Ville Natale return to what they were at the beginning of the book. The rebellion of the sons against the father has proved abortive. Pierre, having willed the destruction of his father, has been forced to recreate him through art. Jean, the initiator of the rebellion, eventually has to sacrifice himself to undo all the harm the sons have done; in a sense he takes his father's place, because it is implied, if not clearly stated, that *le chasse-nuages* was Nabonide's invention. In spite of the misfortunes which befall all the siblings except Paul—Alice and he presumably live happily ever after and certainly have scads of babies (*des chiées de mômes*)—the total effect of *Saint Glinglin* is optimistic, since the reestablished *status quo* is a benign one, not a miserable one as in *Le Chiendent*.

Despite a certain amount of willfully self-indulgent whimsicality on Queneau's part, *Saint Glinglin* is a remarkable work of fiction. While not as ambitious as *The Magic Mountain* or *Ulysses*, it can be mentioned without incongruity in the company of those tragicomic masterpieces. In its own way, it has something of their encyclopedic quality: instead of discussing some of the great ideas of the nineteenth and twentieth centuries, it exemplifies them in rather lighthearted parables. Existentialist philosophy in its German manifestation, Freudian psychology (at least in regard to father-son relationships), and some of the discoveries of cultural anthropology are implicit in the structure of *Saint Glinglin*. The epic poem of Chapter 3 and Pierre's statue-carving remind us of Freud's hints about the origin of art in guilt feelings, particularly his famous study of Dostoevsky. Nor is Queneau entirely derivative: Paul's approving treatment of the synthetic beauty of film stars, Hélène's identification with the insects, and much of the detail in Pierre's existentialist meditation, all strike one as profoundly original. *Saint Glinglin* is by turns strange,

beautiful, ludicrous, and intellectually stimulating. Nothing in
Queneau's later work except *Petite cosmogonie portative*
reaches the same level.

Returning to chronological sequence, we come to *Les
derniers jours* ("The Last Days"), Queneau's next novel after
Gueule de pierre. Jean Queval, in his *Essai sur Raymond
Queneau*, says that Queneau does not wish this novel to be
reprinted. After reading it, one understands why, for it is the
nearest thing to a dull book that Queneau has written. One
might suspect, also, that Queneau was embarrassed by the
apparent self-portrait in it (Vincent Tuquedenne, the young
student who has just arrived in Paris). However, he has not
repudiated the far more intimate and factual self-revelation in
Chêne et chien (1937), his novel in verse, which we will consider now. Martin Esslin says: "The oak and the dog are, in
Queneau's view, the two possible etymologies of his name. . . ."
It is clear from the poem itself that these etymologies symbolize the two aspects of Queneau's nature and that the psychoanalysis which he underwent (from 1933 until 1939, according
to Queval) helped him to reconcile the two conflicting sides
of his personality.

Chêne et chien, explicitly subtitled "A Novel in Verse," falls
into three parts. Part I, untitled, has an epigraph from Boileau:

> . . . When I write verses, I always try to say what has not yet
> been said in our language. That is what I have principally
> aimed at in a new epistle. . . . In it I tell everything I have
> done since I came into the world. I set down in it my faults,
> my age, my inclinations, my manners and morals. I tell what
> father and mother I was born to. . . .

In the thirteen rhymed poems of this part, Queneau tries to
follow Boileau's program; the first three lines give us some
vital statistics: "I was born in Le Havre on a twenty-first of
February / in nineteen hundred and three. / My father was a
haberdasher and my mother a haberdasher's wife. . . ." He
evokes for us the stuffy haberdashery and its employees; the
lycée of Le Havre; childhood fears and friendships; trips to
Fécamp and Paris; childhood illnesses and his reading during

convalescence; country vacations; his traumatic realization of his parents' sexual relationship; various world events from the coronation of George V to the outbreak of World War I; his father's "defeatism" during the war; the decline of the family business in wartime and consequent visits to the cinema with his father; his reaching adolescence in 1916. The final poem of this part shows his parents reproaching him for his early attempts to write novels and his ambitious extracurricular reading, which have led him to neglect his schoolwork; it ends as follows: "Then I set to work / and pulled down more than one diploma. / Alas! what a poo-oor young man / I later became."

Part II, also untitled, consists of nine poems and deals with Queneau's psychoanalysis. For epigraph it bears two wonderfully appropriate lines (quoted in English) from Thomas Traherne:

> To Infancy, O Lord, again I come
> That I my Manhood may improve.

The first poem begins as follows:

> I lay down on a couch / and began to tell the story of my life, / what I thought was my life. / My life, what did I know about it? / And your life, what do you know about it? / And that man there, does he know / his life? / All of them imagine / that in this great big set-up / they act as they want to / as if they knew what they wanted / as if they wanted what they wanted / as if they wanted what they knew / as if they knew what they knew. / Anyway here I am lying down / on a couch near Passy. / I tell everything I please: / I'm under psychoanalysis.

He begins with recent events which he thinks are important; his main problem is that he is unable to work. But very soon the psychoanalyst is probing back into his early life. Queneau has forgotten his unhappy childhood, like the character Roland Travy in *Odile*, and must be made to remember it. The poet relates a dream: a man and a woman are walking by a river; a crocodile follows them like a dog. The man and woman are his parents and he is the crocodile, the psychoanalyst suggests.

And so the long game of hide-and-seek begins, using association of ideas. The third poem of Part II is a brilliant tour de
force: the psychoanalyst offers symbols and asks for associations; the poet claims he has none.

> The grass: I have nothing to say about the grass / but still
> what are these noises / these noises by day and by night / The
> wind: I have nothing to say about the wind.

And so we proceed via the oak tree, the rat, the sand, the rock,
the star, the moon, the dog, the city, the heart—doubtless all
features of the same or different dreams—until we reach the
sun,

> The sun: O monster, O Gorgon, Medusa / O sun.

At last an association has been established, and we recall a
shocking line from Part I: "The maternal sun is a black excrement . . ." which perhaps ties in with a yet earlier memory: "I
used to spy on my mother going to the toilet." The fourth
poem of Part II explores in great detail this association of the
sun with everything evil. The painful process of opening up
the unconscious continues in the fifth poem:

> Like Raymond, I carry off a bleeding nun / and the nun is my
> mother—after associations.

At this point, the patient's growing hostility to the analyst
explodes in the indignant cry, "Sir . . . this is going beyond a
joke!" The analysis is temporarily broken off but is soon resumed. Going to Passy becomes a daily routine, but still the
progress of the analysis is irritating, for no detail is ever insignificant. Half humorously, Queneau notes that if he considers the analyst's nose a little too big, that too must
compromise him (Queneau). Nevertheless, everything must
be said. The poet finds it easier to tell about his sexual
aberrations than to speak directly "about death and tortures /
and quarterings. . . ."

> But these bonds in their turn will be untied, / the symptoms
> find their explanation / like the crime at the end of a detective
> story: / but it isn't a crime! / For if as a child, deprived of
> love, you wished to kill / you yourself were the victim.

The second-last poem of this part is a humorous interlude: the time has come to pay, and the patient is cut to the quick. He pleads with the analyst: what has become of the latter's love of humanity and his devotion to science? From pleading he turns to indignation: the analyst is a bandit. To get his money, the doctor must reason sweetly with the patient, who eventually concedes that he is now able to work again and that the analyst is entitled to be paid for *his* work.

The final poem of the second part begins: "Oak tree and dog, these are my two names. . . ." The poet goes on to analyze his conflict in terms of these two opposed symbols. The dog "is ferocious and impulsive, / we know where he likes to shove his nose." The oak, on the other hand, "is noble and tall . . ." and its branches reach toward the sky. The psychoanalyst has made the poet clairvoyant, and now that the latter can see the shadows and phantoms of the unconscious clearly, they paradoxically tend to disappear: "I did not despise the unclean thing, / but of itself it went away." And the poem concludes triumphantly—perhaps also a little prematurely—with the lines, "The dog descends again to hell. / The oak rises up—at last!" After that follows a line of prose: "He begins to march toward the summit of the mountain."

The third part, "The Feast Day in the Village," abandons the rhymed verse of the first two parts for the Biblical free verse which had already appeared in *Gueule de pierre*. This chant of triumph and praise of the joy of life describes a sort of medieval kermess, Mardi Gras, or May Day celebration. It symbolically celebrates the poet's liberation from his old hostilities and fears.

Chêne et chien represents yet another brilliantly original achievement on the part of Queneau. Although it was his first published volume of poems, he had been writing verse intermittently since at least 1920. Without this long apprenticeship, he could not possibly have transmuted into true poetry the banalities and anguish of his psychoanalysis—"a subject," as he once remarked, "which is not generally considered especially poetic. . . ." His own summary of the poem runs as follows: "In the first part I tell of my childhood, which wasn't gay, and in the second I tell of a psychoanalytic treatment, which wasn't gay either" (*BCL*, pp. 34–5). The poem, except for Part III, can hardly be described as gay either, but it never falls into self-pity; the poet views himself always with irony or humor, without belittling the terrors which every human being must face, in the world within as in the world without.

The vein of pessimism in Queneau's novels was not entirely banished by his psychoanalysis, as we shall see.[10] Nevertheless, *Odile*, the short novel in prose also published in 1937, was a story of release and fulfillment. In technique and content it is the most straightforward and least characteristic of his novels. Accordingly, there is no need to deal with it here.

Les Enfants du limon shows far more of Queneau's idiosyncratic style and vision, but it must be reckoned an ambitious failure. Considering the antagonistic elements of which it is composed, one is amazed that the book has managed to achieve a certain precarious unity. To have made such an eccentric medley readable at all is in a sense a triumph, except that the experienced reader of Queneau has come to take his readability for granted, even in his least conventional works of fiction.

In an essay on a forgotten pioneer of science fiction named Defontenay, Queneau has told us something of the origin of *Les Enfants du limon*:

> When I began, in 1930, to track down "literary madmen" along the kilometers of bookstacks in the Bibliothèque Nationale, I was ambitious of discovering a significant number of "unappreciated geniuses." At the end of some years I had written a manuscript of 700 pages, unpublishable and unpublished, unorganized and unorganizable. (Later, parts of it were reworked in a novel [*Les Enfants du limon*]). The result was nothing remarkable. Hardly anybody was unearthed who was not either a reactionary paranoiac or a senile bore. "Interesting" delirium was rare. (*BCL*, p. 179)

[10] After reading this chapter in typescript, M. Queneau told me that his analyst was so dismayed by *Les Enfants du limon* that the analysis was resumed in 1938–39.

Such raw material, partly summarized, partly anthologized, makes up some 125 pages out of a total of 310 in *Les Enfants du limon*, or slightly over forty percent. Certain examples of the New Novel, particularly Claude Mauriac's *The Marquise Went Out at Five* and Butor's *Degrees*, incorporate non-fictional material: *Marquise* includes a number of historical references to the Parisian *carrefour* (intersection) which is its subject, and *Degrees* includes many quotations from textbooks and from the classic literary texts of French, Latin, and Greek literature. Neither, however, displays such an excessive proportion of non-fiction to fiction as does Queneau's novel.

The fictional portion of *Les Enfants du limon* takes the form of a family chronicle covering approximately the period 1914–35 in France. The principal characters are descendants or relatives by marriage of a certain Jules-Jules Limon, for many years a successful pioneer in the French radio industry. Most of them are listed in a sort of *Who's Who* entry on pp. 40–1 of the novel. Limon's surname suggests one meaning for the title, "The Children of Monsieur Limon," but it can also mean "The Children of the Clay" or even "The Children of the Bitter Lime"; either of these punning titles can be justified as the story unfolds.

The most important characters are three grandchildren of Limon—Daniel, Agnès, and Noémi Chambernac—and their uncle Astolphe Limon, who is less than two years older than the eldest of them. Daniel, who suffers from asthma, is a seeker after God and something of an ascetic, like other Queneau characters. Agnès is a superb athlete of great beauty, narcissistic and egotistical to such a point that she eventually imagines herself a latter-day Joan of Arc. The humble Noémi has been fascinated since childhood by her brilliant, unstable Uncle Astolphe, a setter of fashions—intellectual and otherwise—in high society. Their mother, Sophie, a World War I widow, takes as her second husband a Jewish financier, Baron Hachamoth; she is a volubly pious Catholic.

Around Agnès there gravitate a number of admirers: some from her own class, including Denis Coltet, whom she marries; others from a lower class, such as the Italian greengrocer

and fruiterer, Gramigni,[11] who comforts himself by marrying
a misshapen yet attractive illegitimate daughter of old Limon,
named Clémence.

The three children have an uncle on their father's side,
M. Chambernac, a retired high-school principal; his lifework
is the compilation of a work on "literary madmen," which he
calls *The Encyclopedia of Inexact Sciences.* He has a wife but
no children, except an illegitimate son named Robert Bossu,
an unwilling member of the lower classes, who also admires
Agnès from afar and reappears from time to time in the novel.
Chambernac is aided in his researches by Purpulan, a demon
trained by Bébé Toutout of *Le Chiendent*, who has tried to
blackmail Chambernac but, outwitted, is forced to become
his slave.

The novel consists of eight "books," each containing twenty-
one chapters. (The number $3 \times 7 = 21$ is a favorite with
Queneau, who was born on February 21.) All are set in the
late 1920's or early 1930's except Book Four, which is a brief
"flashback" to World War I. The Great Depression of the
1930's brings financial disaster upon the elder Limon, who
commits suicide, with characteristic modernity, by jumping
from an airplane. His family is not really ruined but has to
reduce its scale of living drastically. Astolphe, having obtained
a papal dispensation, marries his niece Noémi and sets himself
up as a dealer in rags and wastepaper. Agnès opposes the marriage bitterly and persuades Noémi to end her first pregnancy
by an abortion. Daniel's asthma returns in acute form, as does
his concern with the classic problem of why evil and suffering
should exist if God is all-loving and all-powerful. Agnès founds
an organization called La Nation Sans Classes ("The Classless
Nation") or N.S.C., which is meant to counterbalance both
Communism and Fascism, but which in fact attracts only
Fascists.

Chambernac, who has carried forward his researches from
would-be squarers of the circle, by way of flat-earthers and
other eccentric cosmogonists, to the self-styled messiahs of

---

[11] M. Queneau told me that his name is the Italian equivalent of
chiendent.

nineteenth-century France, also falls on evil days. With the help of Bébé Toutout, Purpulan has somehow escaped from his pact with Chambernac, has poisoned Mme Chambernac, and has enticed Chambernac into homosexual debauchery. Eventually Chambernac flees and takes refuge with his sister-in-law. He insists on reading aloud his chapters on the "messiahs"; Agnès is profoundly impressed by her own similarity to some of these lunatics and admits that the N.S.C. is collapsing. Nevertheless, she becomes involved in the abortive fascist uprising of le six février (February 6, 1934) in Paris and is killed. Purpulan finds Chambernac again, but Chambernac throws him into the Seine, where he melts under the horrified eyes of Robert Bossu. Daniel, after a period of vagabondage, rejoins Astolphe and Noémi. Astolphe has finally settled down happily to his redemption of waste matter; the book ends hopefully with the birth of a child to him and Noémi. One must cultivate one's garden, or one's rag pile.

In the penultimate chapter, however, Queneau has a quirk in store for us. Chambernac, having failed to find a publisher for his *Encyclopedia*, decides not to publish it at his own expense, for fear he might himself become one of his "literary madmen." One day, a man who has seen him at the offices of Queneau's publisher, the *N.R.F.*, approaches him and asks if he may see the manuscript. Chambernac makes him a present of it. His new acquaintance explains that he is writing a novel and would like to attribute the *Encyclopedia* to one of his characters. Of course he would put Chambernac's name with his own on the title page of the novel. No, Chambernac doesn't care about that. He's glad to get rid of his incubus, but he asks:

> "What sort of person is this character?"
> "He's the principal of a little *lycée* in the provinces. He's married, he has no children. One day a demon forces his way into his bathroom."
> "Wait. It's best that I should tell you the story of my life. Wait. I don't think it's extraordinary, but it might give reality to your little book."
> "I don't know how to thank you."

"Not at all, I assure you, dear sir, dear Mr. ———?"
"Queneau."
"Not at all, dear Mr. Queneau. I assure you, it's nothing."
(p. 315)

This is only one of the many devices used by Queneau throughout his works to remind us that we are reading fiction. Recall, for instance, the ending of *Le Chiendent.*

There are some other interesting new technical devices in *Les Enfants du limon,* such as the occasional employment of doggerel verse and the printing of interior monologues or relevant Biblical quotations on the right half of the page only, to distinguish them from the narrative or dialogue to which they supply a commentary. The critic must ask one key question about this novel, however: is the *Encyclopedia* of Chambernac integrated with the rest of the book? The answer, regrettably, is no. At just one point (pp. 270–82), non-fiction and fiction come together. Agnès realizes that she is "no more Joan of Arc than was Amélie Seulart [one of Chambernac's false messiahs]." Also, one can argue that in a general way the follies of all Chambernac's nineteenth-century monomaniacs provide a commentary on twentieth-century follies: those of Astolphe, for example, who takes up with all kinds of pseudo-scientific as well as scientific movements (and who can tell one from the other at this short distance?). But in the long run this huge load of ballast overbalances the book.

The fact that we are asked to accept the literal presence of a demon within an otherwise fairly realistic novel will also give many readers pause. Bébé Toutout in *Le Chiendent* is never explicitly identified as a demon, but we would be ready to accept him as such in the seventh chapter, when the book shifts conclusively from realism to fantasy. In *Les Enfants du limon,* however, we have the irreducible "fact" of Purpulan's demonic nature set squarely before us almost from his first appearance. Until he has been disposed of, the redemption or deliverance of the surviving characters cannot be accomplished. It is significant that the last words of the book, after Noémi's child has been born, are *"Dans un bassin saignait la délivrance."* Literally, these words mean, "The afterbirth was bleeding in a basin," but *délivrance* can mean "deliverance" as well as "afterbirth." The child born to Noémi and Astolphe is in some sense a Savior, a Redeemer.

In *Queneau déchiffré*, Simonnet devotes an entire chapter (pp. 131–53) to the subject of Gnosticism, not merely in *Le Chiendent*, but in almost all the novels of Queneau. Simonnet speaks of Queneau's "profound dualism," which is so striking in *Chêne et chien*; he sees a conflict between the good and evil angels taking place in almost every novel by Queneau from *Le Chiendent* to *Zazie dans le métro*—where the chief antagonists are the significantly named Gabriel and the policeman Trouscaillon. Gnostic mythology is saturated with dualism and thus supplies Queneau with a convenient frame of reference to which he constantly alludes. Valentinus, the greatest of the Gnostic writers, is almost certainly the source of the given name of Valentin Brû, hero of *Le Dimanche de la vie*. The allusions are so widespread that Simonnet, in spite of his erudition, overlooks some of them. Sophie Hachamoth's name recalls that of the fallen goddess Sophia Achamoth in the Valentinian mythology. In other Gnostic systems her place is taken by the beautiful Helena, who is held captive by the powers of this world in conditions of extreme degradation, sometimes even of prostitution; surely Hélène in *Saint Glinglin* is based upon this mythological figure?

We need not assume that Queneau actually believes in Gnosticism, but apparently he regards its mythology, demons and all, as presenting a more believable "model" of the real world than, say, Christianity. He uses it as a partial scaffolding on which to construct his novels, just as Joyce used the myth of Odysseus in *Ulysses*; it is neither more nor less significant than the mathematical structures which he employs in the same way. But in *Les Enfants du limon* he went a step farther: part of the scaffolding, in the person of Purpulan, is not removed but built into the façade of the final edifice. We must conclude that Queneau felt this was a mistake, since we do not encounter any recognizable angels or demons in his later novels—they are disguised as more or less believable human

beings. Nevertheless, all the novels contain a quest, successful
or not, for salvation, for redeeming wisdom, for *gnosis*.

Queneau's period of radical experiment in the novel form
was beginning to draw to a close. In December 1939 he published *Un rude hiver* (*A Hard Winter*), which, like *Odile*, is a
short exercise in the traditional novel. Unlike *Odile*, however,
this little work is a masterpiece, written with the precision
and economy of a craftsman who has learned most of what
there is to know about narration. Queneau, in fact, has never
had much difficulty in telling a fascinating story; his self-
imposed difficulties have arisen from his desire to make the
novel do so much more than this: to become a poem, a myth,
a philosophic discourse.

The changing circumstances of Queneau's life had much to
do with the change in his novelistic methods. As he told
Georges Charbonnier in referring to his earlier, more ambitious, more highly structured novels,

> . . . they are novels written at a period of my life when I
> could write them in a relatively short time because I could
> devote myself entirely to them during the required period;
> later, that is to say after *Pierrot mon ami*, since much of my
> time was taken up elsewhere, the other books that I have
> written took a much longer time to write, sometimes seven or
> eight years, and accordingly they are much freer from that
> kind of preoccupation [with structure, etc.]. (*Entretiens,*
> p. 55)

World War II did not make severe demands on Queneau's
time. Having done his military service, mainly in North
Africa, during 1925–27, he had experienced combat in the
Riff War; but, mobilized as a private in 1939, he spent most
of this period under arms "in a depot with rejects." However,
his appointment in 1941 as general secretary to the firm of
Gallimard–N.R.F., which had been his publisher since 1933,
made serious inroads into the time he had available for creative
work. Later, his position as general editor of *L'Encyclopédie*

de la Pléiade for the same firm made even greater demands upon his time.

Pierrot mon ami (1942), an enigmatic, wryly humorous short novel, has attained greater popularity in France than any other work by Queneau except possibly *Zazie dans le métro*. It was the first book by him to appear in a pocket edition. No doubt it took its readers' minds off the war, but underneath the humor may lie almost the same intense pessimism as we saw˙ in *Le Chiendent*. Pierrot, one of those Queneau characters who are doomed to defeat before they start, ends the book laughing over all his missed opportunities. But the reader, who has come to sympathize with him, finds it hard to laugh.

Pierrot is a born loser. When we first see him, aged twenty-eight, he is, as usual, in a new job. The scene is a side show called Le Palais de la Rigolade (The Fun Palace), part of a big fairground in Paris called L'Uni-Park. His chief duty is to "assist" girls who have just scrambled through a sort of obstacle course: he supports them firmly by the wrists and, when they have regained their equilibrium, holds them, equally firmly, over a jet of air which blows their skirts up for the delectation of a group of paying patrons called "the philosophers." (Queneau had observed all this at Le Palais du Rire in Luna-Park.) Very shortly, Pierrot gets into a fight with some dissatisfied philosophers and the police shut down the Fun Palace for the night. Pierrot picks up a girl named Yvonne, who runs a shooting gallery, and takes her for a ride on the "Dodgem" cars. Her father, furious at her neglecting the job, chases her; Pierrot knocks the intruder down, only to discover that his victim is not only the father of the girl he has fallen hopelessly in love with but also the proprietor of the Uni-Park, M. Pradonet.

Most of Pierrot's jobs end with similar abruptness; the others he quits himself because they do not interest him sufficiently. Among the other characters in the book are two who share his guilelessness—Pradonet himself, a warmhearted man who bears no real malice against Pierrot, and Mounnezergues, a maker of figures for wax museums. This last personage owns a little enclave in the Uni-Park, formerly his vegetable garden, which Pradonet dearly wants to buy. But Mounnezergues absolutely refuses because the garden is now the site of the tomb and chapel of a "Poldevian" prince who met with a riding accident, supposedly fatal, in Mounnezergues's garden twenty years before. Mounnezergues seems not to know that there is no such place as Poldevia; although his salary as custodian of the chapel has not been paid for many, many years, he regards the preservation of the hallowed spot as his true lifework. Furthermore, having taken a liking to Pierrot, he wishes to make him his heir, on condition that Pierrot will continue the duties of custodian. He even makes out a codicil to his will to this effect, but characteristically Pierrot loses it.

Contrasting with these guileless characters are the guileful ones, among whom the three chief are Pradonet's common-law wife, the widow Léonie Prouillot; his daughter, Yvonne; and a certain Jojo Mouilleminche, alias the Poldevian prince, alias the animal trainer Voussois. Léonie loved and lost Jojo twenty years before the book begins; suddenly she recognizes the "Algerian" fakir Crouïa-Bey as Jojo's brother; the fakir tells her a cock-and-bull story about Jojo's dying for love of a girl ten years ago, but unwisely mentions that this took place in Palinsac, where Jojo now lives under the name of Voussois. (Only a very careful reader will discover that the "dead prince" is in reality Jojo-Voussois. Even Pierrot, who learns a good many of the hidden facts, does not realize this.)

In the course of a cunningly entangled plot, Léonie makes her way to Palinsac, where Pierrot has also gone to return two trained animals to Voussois; Pierrot witnesses her accidental meeting with and recognition of Voussois. The two former lovers marry and proceed to elaborate a conspiracy against poor Pradonet, whose Uni-Park has burned down a short while before. With the pretext that it would desecrate the Poldevian chapel, they prevent his rebuilding the amusement park on a far vaster scale; they manage to gain possession of the burnt-out site and instead turn it into a supposedly educational zoo. Yvonne, who has never cared for Pierrot though she has been willing to make use of him on occasion, marries Paradis, his former colleague at the Fun Palace; she deserts her defeated father for her bar-sinister stepmother; when we last see her, she is taking over the house of Mounnezergues, who has presumably died. No doubt the chapel and its enclave will not exist much longer. It is even possible that Paradis, before he married her, set fire to the Uni-Park because he too had lost his job at the Fun Palace.

In an interesting article dealing with *Pierrot mon ami* and two other novels by Queneau, Alexandre Kojève—one of Queneau's teachers and a great authority on Hegel—puts forward the idea that Pierrot has mastered true wisdom in the Hegelian definition of that term:

> For Hegel . . . Wisdom is nothing other than perfect satisfaction accompanied by a plenitude of self-consciousness.

Pierrot seems hardly satisfied enough or self-conscious enough to fulfill Hegel's requirements; Valentin in *Le Dimanche de la vie* is a great deal more successful in this regard. Nevertheless, we ought at least to consider the possibility that Pierrot's laughter at the end of the book is philosophical and without bitterness.

In 1944, the year of the liberation of Paris, Queneau published another short novel, *Loin de Rueil*.[12] Although this is a rather lighthearted piece of work with a transparently incredible and romantic plot, it contains an anticipation of Robbe-Grillet which is almost entirely new in Queneau's work: the hallucinatory daydream. (It is worth noting again that Robbe-Grillet has praised *Loin de Rueil*.) True, Narcense has a daydream on pp. 141–4 of *Le Chiendent*, but he hardly goes so far as to confuse his dream with reality. Jacques L'Aumône, the central character in *Loin de Rueil*, is, however, so addicted to daydreaming from early childhood that both he and the reader find it difficult to tell where dream ends and reality begins. The habit starts with his early visits to the cinema: he cannot watch a cowboy silent film without becoming its hero

[12] The title means literally "Far from Rueil," but the only English translation is entitled *The Skin of Dreams*.

for the duration. Soon, this habit persists outside what Queneau has called "the darkened rooms." Little Jacques imagines
that he is of aristocratic descent and not the child of his petit-
bourgeois parents in the little suburban town of Rueil, near
Paris. Later, although he has had no training, he manages to
convince others and himself for a while that he is a gifted
research chemist. He appears to have genuine talent as a
boxer, but he lacks the patience to persevere; one wonders
whether he was ever amateur welterweight champion of either
France or Paris, though at various times he claims to have
been both. For a time he strives to divest himself of all
ambition and become a saint; but this, of course, proves to be
the most presumptuous ambition of all: as long as he consciously nourishes it, it is impossible to achieve the true
humility of a saint. At this time he is working as an extra in
films, where his docility and boxing talent bring him steady
work until the day he knocks out a male star. After considerable success with women and marriage to a waitress, Suzanne,
he suffers a disappointment in his love for a childhood friend,
Dominique, also married.

This traumatic experience strips Jacques of his daydreams,
but paradoxically the result is to turn them into realities: after
working in documentary films in South America (truly "far
from Rueil," as the French title says), he becomes a Hollywood star, using the name James Charity (English translation of "Jacques L'Aumône"). In his greatest film, *The Skin
of Dreams*, he plays himself, opposite his new wife, Lulu
L'Aumône (a former domestic servant from Rueil), who plays
herself, naturally. The film recapitulates, with the usual Hollywood poetic license, his life story from daydream to reality,
and ends with him signing the contract for his next film, *The
Skin of Dreams*.

Contrasted with Jacques's eventful life is that of Louis-
Philippe des Cigales, the (unpublished) Poet of Rueil. Of
aristocratic descent, he suffers from "ontalgia . . . an existential
disease . . . it resembles asthma but it's more distinguished."
Jacques's father and other Rueil bourgeois admire des Cigales
for his literary talent, and so he lives his life out in the little

town, gradually accepting himself for what he is. Jacques's deserted wife, Suzanne, and his son, Michou, come to live with Jacques's parents; des Cigales becomes Suzanne's lover. One day des Cigales and Michou see *The Skin of Dreams*, though Suzanne cannot bring herself to go. Afterwards, des Cigales tells Suzanne, as they go to bed together, that he liked the film:

> "Something struck me as odd," he went on; "the actors; they were new ones, but I had a feeling I've already seen them somewhere."
> "One imagines things sometimes," said Suzanne, stretching out on the bed.
> "Of course," said des Cigales. "Of course."[13]

So ends this brilliant tour de force. Not even Paul's meditation in *Saint Glinglin* gives quite so vivid an expression of Queneau's half-mocking, half-adoring attitude toward the films as does *The Skin of Dreams*. And what is this "skin of dreams" (*La Peau des rêves* in French)? Surely it is the photographic film itself (*pellicule* in French, from a Latin word meaning "little skin"), the "skin" on which the director's and the audience's "dreams" are registered. One sees anticipations of Fellini's famous autobiographical fantasy, $8\frac{1}{2}$, in the imaginary movie with which Queneau ends his novel.

Queneau, by virtue of his high position in the Gallimard firm, which has held a unique place in French publishing for the past fifty years, played a big part in the revival of French culture after the Liberation. From 1944 through 1947 he was a member of various committees and held various posts concerned with literature, broadcasting, the theatre, and journalism. Necessarily during this period his literary activity was somewhat marginal. He did, however, find time to publish two short volumes of poetry and the display of verbal virtuosity, *Exercices de Style* (1947).

From September 29, 1944, through November 12, 1945, Queneau wrote a column of comment on new books for the

[13] *The Skin of Dreams*, tr. H. J. Kaplan (Norfolk, Conn., 1948), p. 115.

newspaper *Front national.* In an entry dated December 29, 1944, he discussed George Orwell's essay "Raffles and Miss Blandish," which had just appeared in the English magazine *Horizon.* Orwell, it will be recalled, viewed with surprise and uneasiness the wartime popularity in England of James Hadley Chase's sadistic, pseudo-American gangster novel, *No Orchids for Miss Blandish.* Queneau comments:

> That this novel and others similar to it describe "fascist" be-
> havior . . . and that these adventures (which, when trans-
> ferred to the political plane, arouse horror) should delight a
> democratic reading public—all this is the best possible illustra-
> tion of the difference between literature and life. (*BCL*,
> p. 113)

In all probability Queneau obtained and read a copy of Chase's book; in 1947 he published, under the pseudonym of "Sally Mara," a novel outwardly at least as sadistically erotic as Chase's, *On est toujours trop bon avec les femmes* ("One Is Always Too Kind to Women"). Any reader who does not himself suffer from sadistic obsessions will find, if he does not abandon the book in disgust, that Queneau's "novel" is a parody of the genre. The "difference between literature and life" is made abundantly clear, for the horrors are described in such an insouciant, non-obsessive manner that eventually we laugh at them and can see the book as a not entirely successful example of "black humor."

The chief indication to the well-read reader that *On est toujours trop bon* should not be taken too seriously lies in its frequent allusions to the work of James Joyce. A group of seven Irish revolutionaries capture a branch post office (not the famous General Post Office) during the Dublin rising of Easter Week, 1916. Led by John MacCormack, a namesake of a great Irish tenor, the revolutionaries include the following people named after minor characters in *Ulysses*: Corny Kelle-her, Larry O'Rourke, Mat Dillon, and Cissy Caffrey; the last-named is a man—and, incidentally, not one of the two homosexuals in the group—though Joyce's Cissy was a girl.

The two other revolutionaries are named Callinan and Gallager [sic], names also probably borrowed from Joyce. The password of the revolutionaries is "Finnegans wake!"

When the post office is captured and its other employees killed or chased away, Gertie Girdle, an English girl, is in the ladies' lavatory. Eventually this virgin, engaged to a British naval officer, is discovered and made prisoner. MacCormack is extremely anxious that she be correctly treated, lest the honor of the rebels become tarnished. Gertie, however, has other ideas. Callinan, finding her willing, takes her virginity; a second bout introduces her to orgasm. She then practices fellatio on the "correct" MacCormack, who cannot bring himself to sully his lips by accusing her of what she has done. Caffrey is enjoying her favors when his head is blown off by a British shell. Undaunted, she attempts to seduce Dillon, one of the homosexuals. Larry O'Rourke, torn between desire and the prohibitions of his religion, attacks her, but his piety disgusts her and she hits him a low blow. Finally, all five heterosexuals are killed by the bombardment, before the unlucky Gallager has had his turn. In the hope of shocking Gertie into keeping her mouth shut when they are captured by the British, the second homosexual, Kelleher, violates her anally. When Commodore Cartwright, her fiancé, rescues her, he asks whether Dillon and Kelleher have been "correct" with her. "No," said Gertie. "They tried to lift up my beautiful white dress to look at my ankles." Outraged, Cartwright has the two rebels executed on the spot, but not before Kelleher has had time to say, "One is always too kind to women."

The year 1948, as we know, saw the publication of *Saint Glinglin*. In 1949 Queneau, continuing to emulate the ambition of the men of the Renaissance to prove themselves universal geniuses, held an exhibition of his gouaches and watercolors. Two years before, he had published a little volume, *Pictogrammes*, containing his attempts to write both prose and poetry in his own version of American Indian picture writing. These date from 1928, during his Surrealist period, and have been reprinted in *Bâtons, chiffres et lettres* (1950),

the fascinating selection of his occasional writings on literature, art, and mathematics that has been frequently quoted
here. Its title describes the studies of a French first-grader:
"pothooks," figures, and letters. In 1950 there also appeared
Petite cosmogonie portative and, again under a pseudonym,
the *Journal intime* of Sally Mara, supposed authoress of *On est
toujours trop bon avec les femmes*.

In 1951, the year Queneau was raised to the relative eminence of membership in the Académie Goncourt, his last really
significant work of fiction, *Le Dimanche de la vie* ("The
Sunday of Life"), was published. The title is derived from
Hegel, but we are not told from which of that philosopher's
voluminous works the epigraph of the novel comes:

> . . . it is the Sunday of life, which puts everything on the same
> level and keeps away everything that is evil; men endowed
> with so much good humor cannot be fundamentally evil or
> contemptible.

One wonders what class or era of humanity such favored
beings come from; at any rate, Queneau has succeeded in
creating as the "hero" and "heroine" of his novel two characters
to whom this quotation applies. Julia Julie Antoinette Ségovie,
a middle-aged spinster, owner of a haberdashery, and Valentin
Brû, the private barely more than half her age whom she
marries, are two of the most engaging characters in fiction.
They are not entirely exempt from original sin or even from a
certain commercial shrewdness, but they preserve through all
the vicissitudes of life an unshakable good humor—more evident on Valentin's part than on Julia's, for she has a sharp
tongue, although she always treats her husband with in-
dulgence. The pair remain essentially faithful to one another
throughout a married life that is not greatly blessed with
wealth or even, in Julia's case, with health.

Contrasted with this couple are Julia's sister, Chantal,
and her husband, Paul. Chantal perennially cuckolds her
husband with a variety of men—she even flirts with Valentin
at one point—while Paul, with the traditional cuckold's luck,
proceeds unerringly toward ever greater success in terms of

wealth and social status. Paul is so eminently the average successful bourgeois that his creator can never remember his last name, calling him by a number of trisyllables beginning with "B": Bolucra, Bulocra, Boulingra, Brolugat, Botugat, Botegat, Botrula, etc., etc. For a brief period there is even some uncertainty about Paul's first name. It would be a mistake, however, to consider this couple as really hostile to Valentin and Julia. Although their interests and sympathies often conflict, the two couples tolerate one another wonderfully well.

After their marriage in Bordeaux, Julia decides that she cannot afford to close up her business even for a day, so she sends Valentin to Paris alone for the honeymoon. This is characteristic of the absurd situations into which the pair maneuver themselves. Later they move to Paris, where Valentin learns his mother-in-law's trade of picture framing and takes over her store when she dies. Julia grows very tired of being alone most of the day and decides to make use of her gift of second sight as a fortune teller. When she is felled by a stroke, she persuades Valentin to dress as a woman and take over the crystal ball. Without Julia's natural talent, he manages to do better than she by drawing on a combination of guesswork and neighborhood gossip.

Valentin, like Étienne in *Le Chiendent*, has his intellectual side, however humble. During his military service, he read right through that famous French dictionary-encyclopedia, the *Petit Larousse illustré*, including the pink pages (which contain famous quotations). To improve his education, he decides to read books by authors who have lent their names to streets in his neighborhood: Baudelaire, Taine, Diderot, Ledru-Rollin. This highly original, if eclectic, plan of study comes to an abrupt end when he cannot find any of the works of the last-named, a nineteenth-century democratic politician, in his local library.

Valentin, for some unexplained reason, has always been interested in the Battle of Jéna, a name which has associations with Hegel, who was living in Jéna then and on the day of the battle called Napoleon "the World-Soul sitting on a horse."

At a séance, Valentin learns that he had an ancestor at the battle, who announced that he brought seriousness, with bared saber, into German philosophy. Eventually Valentin has his wish and visits the battlefield of Jéna on a vacation excursion; because of this trip he is suspected of German sympathies during World War II.

Valentin's greatest philosophic enterprise consists of trying to think of nothing and watch time passing. He stares at the hands of a big clock face but seems never to be able to concentrate on this task for more than four minutes. Eventually, thanks to a broom sold him by a mad beggarman, he is able to sweep away distracting images long enough to watch the passage of time for seven minutes. This remains his record performance, for he decides that he ought to kill time instead of following it. Later, mobilized for World War II, he attempts to become a saint, emulating such earlier Queneau characters as Daniel Chambernac and Jacques L'Aumône. Unfortunately, when he deliberately gets himself assigned to clean out the latrines daily in order to attain merit through self-abnegation, he soon finds that he takes keen pleasure in the chore and therefore cannot be acquiring any merit whatever.

At the end of the German conquest of France in 1940, Paul, Julia, and Chantal set out in search of Valentin. Paul is very anxious to ask him what the future has in store for France. A fellow soldier who is a priest in civilian life tells them that Valentin has been a sort of ascetic during the war but is, as a benign atheist, forever separated from God. Eventually Julia catches up with her demobilized husband at a railroad station. She bursts out laughing when she first sees him, for he is helping three young girls in shorts through the window of a crowded train: it gives him an excuse to put his hands on their behinds.

In *Le Dimanche de la vie* Queneau has succeeded in creating a world virtually without dualism, without conflict. Even World War II, as presented here, becomes part of "the Sunday of life," and its real horrors are ignored. The corrupted matter of the latrines has been redeemed, whether in Gnostic fashion or otherwise. If this be a Hegelian novel, it represents

a period of synthesis in which the conflict of thesis and antithesis has been resolved. Here at last Queneau has escaped
from the pessimism of his earlier work, and it is significant
that Valentin is characterized not as a Gnostic but as a "benign
atheist." His atheism, far from being a revolt against a God
who permits evil, allows him a vision of the world that lies
beyond good and evil. In spite of its characteristic touches of
originality, this book is in no sense a New Novel. Perhaps its
optimism would be sufficient to disqualify it, but in any case
it is a carefully disguised didactic novel, more closely related
to the *romans philosophiques* of Voltaire than to any later
school of novel-writing.

In the nearly twenty years since 1951, Queneau has published at least five new volumes of verse and only three novels:
Zazie dans le métro (1959), *Les Fleurs bleues* (1965), and
Le Vol d'Icare (1968). Each of these novels has its own
peculiar charm and originality, but none seriously changes
the picture already given of Queneau's gifts as a novelist.

Zazie is a precocious pre-teen girl who is left in charge of
her Uncle Gabriel in Paris for the weekend while her mother
visits a lover. Zazie assumes that every adult male except
Uncle Gabriel wishes to rape her, but she feels well able to
take care of herself. Her father, having been denied marital
relations by her mother, had tried to violate Zazie when he
was drunk. The mother used this as a pretext to kill the father
with an ax and was acquitted of murder. Then the lover who
had lent her the ax began to show an interest in Zazie and had
to be sent packing. Her new lover will not be allowed to see
her daughter at all. Uncle Gabriel, apparently happily married to Marceline, is not interested in little girls, we discover.
Gabriel dances in a night club as a female impersonator, but
it is not until the end of the book that we learn Marceline is
a man named Marcel in "drag."

A policeman named Trouscaillon is suspicious of Gabriel
and pursues him and Zazie in various disguises throughout
the book. After a variety of adventures, including a fight in
the night club where Gabriel works, Zazie is returned intact to

her mother early on Monday morning. When the mother asks about her weekend, all Zazie can tell her is "I've grown older."

Zazie's dearest wish is to ride the Métro, the Paris subway. During the weekend, the subway is on strike. Eventually, on Monday morning, the Métro starts running again and Zazie rides it, but she is fast asleep and does not realize what is happening. The whole eventful weekend seems as though it had never occurred.

The chief reason for the popularity of *Zazie dans le métro* in France was the precocious, highly slangy dialect spoken by Zazie. She knows all about her mother's crime and about her lovers—and indeed about homosexuality and most other human aberrations. Not yet sexually awakened herself, Zazie speaks of sex with a cynical knowledge but no emotional understanding. She is another, younger Sally Mara or Gerty Girdle. Besides her precocity, she amuses us by her rudeness to adults. Almost anything an adult says to her, especially in reproof, is likely to be repeated back to him or her by Zazie with *mon cul* ("my ass") tacked on at the end. Queneau also employs the highest percentage of phonetic spelling that has yet appeared in any of his works. His interest in the spoken language, having achieved this comic apotheosis, now begins to wane.

Les Fleurs bleues (*Blue Flowers*) is concerned with dreams, as its title would suggest to any Frenchman. (Zazie says "*Bonnes fleurs bleues*" to another character, meaning "Sweet dreams.") Two characters in the novel, the Duc d'Auge and Cidrolin, dream each other's lives. Cidrolin lives on a barge in modern Paris; the Duke approaches him through history in leaps of 175 years at a time. When one is asleep and dreaming, the other is up and about. Beginning in 1264, the Duke makes his way to 1964 via 1439, 1614, and 1789. This last date of course marks the beginning of the French Revolution, but the others are of some importance in French history also. After they meet in 1964, the Duke and Cidrolin can both remain awake (or asleep) simultaneously.

Every morning, insulting remarks about Cidrolin are painted on the fence that separates his mooring place from the boule-

vard. He spends the day painting over them. This is virtually
his only occupation besides drinking. His daughters keep
"house" for him. After the last one is married, Cidrolin takes
a "fiancée" in her place. Eventually, Cidrolin himself is caught
writing the insults on the fence after dark. Lalix, his fiancée,
becomes convinced that he is mad and leaves him, but the
Duke persuades her to return. The Duke and his retinue
commandeer the barge and sail back to Normandy in it, while
Cidrolin and Lalix slip away to the bank in the dinghy. A
tremendous flood covers the land; when it recedes, the house-
boat is aground on the top of a donjon, perhaps the Duke's
own. "A layer of mud still covered the earth, but, here and
there, little blue flowers were already blooming." No doubt
the entire book has been a dream as well as an experiment
with time—a huge angel-food cake sprinkled here and there
with talking horses, learned puns, medieval spelling, and
occasional fragments of phonetic speech.

In *Le Vol d'Icare* ("The Flight of Icarus"), as in Part I of
Pinget's *Mahu*, we encounter a world where novelists' characters literally come to life. Since there is nothing new under
the sun, one hesitates to grant priority in this kind of fantasy
to the Irish writer Flann O'Brien, whose *At Swim-Two-Birds*
appeared in 1939 with a partial cast of such characters. What
is certain is that Queneau knew O'Brien's book, for the French
translation, *Kermesse irlandaise* (1964), was published by
Gallimard.

Icare escapes from the early pages of a novel by Hubert
Lubert in the Paris of 1895. Although Hubert sets a stupid
detective on the trail and some of Hubert's fellow novelists
seek to entrap Icare for their own books, the errant character
eludes capture. True to the legend of his classical forerunner,
Icarus, he becomes a pioneer aviator and crashes to his death
on the first flight with a passenger—his beloved LN (Hélène).
Hubert has the last word: closing his manuscript after the
crash, he says, "Everything happened as I had foreseen; my
novel is ended." So is Queneau's.

For the first time, Queneau has written an entire novel in
the form of a play—seventy-four little scenes in all, with

dialogue, identification of each speaker, and stage directions. The entire book is a gay, iridescent soap bubble that swells and swells, floats away, and bursts—leaving nothing behind. Any attempt to analyze this entertaining trifle would destroy it, whereas its chief reason for existing is to destroy itself. After all, we know the *real* history of aviation, don't we?

The fact that the milieu of the book is so literary allows Queneau to make many sly comments upon writers and writing, including the Decadent school of poetry current in France in the 1890's, but naturally it is the novelists of every period that bear the brunt of his raillery. Hubert says of Icare, after he has first disappeared:

> I am preparing him for a melancholy existence which would hardly displease him since he knows no other. I'd like him to like moonlit nights, fairy roses, exotic nostalgias, springtime languors, *fin de siècle* neuroses—all of them things that I abominate but that, in our day, look good in a novel. (p. 17)

Another novelist, Jacques, decides to have a mauve adultery in his novel: if he cannot avoid the hackneyed subject, at least he can give it an up-to-date color. It is the same Jacques who is delighted when he has to fight a duel with Hubert (so do his fellow novelists Jean and Surget): his novel is to have a duel in it, and he will be able to take notes so as to falsify the realism of his description. "How modern you are!" says Jean. Clearly Jacques is introduced so that Queneau can make fun of Robbe-Grillet. Later Jacques says to his doctor, "I'm a descriptive. Nothing but description. If pushed to it, I could do without characters" (p. 115). After being wounded in his duel, Jacques is able to give a description of one that bears no resemblance at all to reality. Jean asks whether the reader will not be put off by the lack of verisimilitude. "Possibly," says Jacques. "What do I care? I shall be read a half century hence" (p. 128). Fifty years or so after 1895 brings us to the beginning of the New Novel.

As more characters escape from novels—one of them "born" at age forty with an unfaithful wife—the fun becomes less literary, more like vaudeville. There is always room for plays on words, however:

ICARE

In my day, it wasn't the young ladies who made declarations of love to the young men.

ADELAIDE

One reads about it in modern novels.

ICARE

Oh, as for me, I'm more read than a reader. (p. 214)

Isolated quotations sound a little labored; one has to read the whole book at a sitting to get into the proper mood for its "airy" nonsense.

Queneau gave *Zazie dans le métro* an epigraph in Greek from Aristotle: *"Ho plasas ēphanisen."* It means, roughly, "He who created it razed it to the ground," and it refers to a wall mentioned by Homer which Aristotle did not believe had ever existed (Fragment No. 173, a quotation from Strabo). This epigraph could also have been prefixed to *Le Chiendent*, to *Pierrot mon ami*, and to several other novels by Queneau. They remind us of those notoriously elaborate pieces of contemporary "sculpture" in the Dadaist tradition that, when set in motion, more or less efficiently destroy themselves. Claude Simonnet has quoted a significant sentence from Valentinus the Gnostic in connection with this tendency of Queneau's: "When you dissolve the world without being dissolved yourselves, you are masters of the creation and of all corruption." Simonnet has also reproduced in his book the Gnostic symbol of a serpent swallowing its own tail, which casts a significant light on Queneau's taste for circular and self-destructive novels. Later in this book we shall examine many other New Novels which are circular and/or self-destructive, from Robbe-Grillet's *The Erasers* to Simon's *The Flanders Road* and Pinget's *The Inquisitory*. All such works embody an anxious search for reality and a profound skepticism about the existence of the object of their search. But the priority in time belongs indisputably to Queneau; although Joyce had conceived *Finnegans Wake* in 1923, he did not publish it in final form until 1939, six years after *Le Chiendent*. Simonnet's *Queneau déchiffré* ("Queneau Deciphered"), which bears the subtitle *Notes sur "le Chiendent"* ("Notes on *le Chiendent*"), might well be the forerunner of a series of studies dealing with Queneau's first book, though these are unlikely ever to rival the avalanche of criticism that has surrounded Joyce's last one.

3

Nathalie Sarraute

FROM JANE AUSTEN TO DOSTOEVSKY

In this chapter, contrary to my practice elsewhere in this book, I find it necessary to make frequent use of the first person singular. It seems that my view of the work of Nathalie Sarraute is itself singular, at least in part: nothing that has been written about her work either by herself or by other critics entirely corresponds with my estimate of it.

Not that I think her novels have been overpraised—except by fanatical admirers of the New Novel or of whatever happens to be regarded as the very latest thing. Rather, they have been praised for the wrong reasons. Intention has too often been confused with achievement, so that the critic fails to see what is actually on the page before him.

"Subtlety" or a synonym thereof is probably the one word that occurs—and recurs—in every discussion of the art of Nathalie Sarraute. Now, it is true that as a psychological novelist she seeks to reproduce modifications of feeling so subtle and so elusive that in everyday life we are never fully conscious of them. In French she calls these modifications *mouvements*, a word that Maria Jolas habitually translates as "movements." This does not seem to me a very happy rendering, as *mouvement* in this sort of context can very often be translated into English simply by the word "emotion" or—

more subtly—by the phrase "emotional stirring" or "stirring of emotion."

In the Foreword[1] to *Tropisms* (New York, 1967), Madame Sarraute gives the most concise statement both of the nature of these stirrings and of the method she uses to render them in her books:

> These movements, of which we are hardly cognizant, slip through us on the frontiers of consciousness in the form of undefinable, extremely rapid sensations. They hide behind our gestures, beneath the words we speak, the feelings we manifest, are aware of experiencing, and able to define. They seemed, and still seem to me to constitute the secret source of our existence, in what might be called its nascent state. (p. vi)

"Undefinable" and "extremely rapid" as these sensations are, it is the novelist's task to define them and to slow them down so that the reader may take cognizance of them.

> And since, while we are performing them, no words express them, not even those of the interior monologue—for they develop and pass through us very rapidly in the form of frequently very sharp, brief sensations, without our perceiving clearly what they are—it was not possible to communicate them to the reader otherwise than by means of equivalent images that would make him experience analogous sensations. It was also necessary to make them break up and spread out in the consciousness of the reader the way a slow-motion film does. Time was no longer the time of real life, but of a hugely amplified present. (pp. vi–vii)

It is her choice of "equivalent images" that makes Nathalie Sarraute's work so much less subtle—at least in its immediate effect—than it is alleged to be. Let me cite a few examples, not from the brief sketches of *Tropisms* but from her first full-length novel, *Portrait of a Man Unknown* (New York, 1958).

[1] This Foreword apparently did not appear in any French edition. It is a shortened version of that prefixed to the London edition of *Tropisms and The Age of Suspicion* in one volume (John Calder, 1963) and dated "Paris, 1962." The phrase "these articles" in the third paragraph refers to *The Age of Suspicion*.

First, here is the title character as seen by the timid male narrator:

> With his subtle flair he scents vaguely something in me, a frightened little animal that trembles and cowers deep down inside. He feels around, the way one pokes with the tip of an iron rod in order to rout out a crab from its hole in the rock; to begin with, perhaps, a bit at random: "Well, well, still making plans this year? Traveling? Corsica? Italy? Eh?" He feels something moving, he comes closer, presses hard. (p. 38)

Next, a scene at the old man's house, a luncheon party:

> Now the conversation had a different sound for me; it had lost its apparently banal, harmless aspect, and I sensed that certain words that were being spoken gave on to vast craters, immense precipices, visible only to initiates, who were leaning, restraining themselves. . . . I was leaning with them, restraining myself, trembling and attracted as they were—over the abyss. (p. 139)

Finally, at what is admittedly the crisis—whether "real" or imagined by the narrator—of the novel, we find images like these describing the old man and his daughter:

> They were standing firmly, brow to brow, heavy and awkward, in their rigid carapaces, their heavy armor—two giant insects, two enormous dung beetles. . . . He felt his rage boiling up, a desire to take her and shake her, to tear off her mask too, that silly, flat face she makes, to crack that carapace she thinks she's so safe in, behind which she dares to defy him, to drag her out into the open, gasping and naked. . . .
>
> The trap door was lifted, they had lifted the trap door, the ground had opened up under their feet, they swayed on the brink of the abyss, they were about to fall in. . . . (pp. 174–5)

In the last passage quoted, I have omitted the dialogue, and I defy anyone to guess what all this grappling of monsters on the edge of abysses is about. In fact, the daughter is asking her father for a fairly large but not unreasonable sum of money to pay for some massage therapy that she feels she urgently needs. We all know that family quarrels are prone to escalate, especially when one party feels that the other is stingy, while the other feels that the first is extravagant. But no unforgivable words have been spoken. Even those that make them actually fall into the "abyss" are harmless enough: "Six thousand francs! For massage! That's all!" (p. 176).

These passages have not been selected at random, but I do not believe they misrepresent the texture of Madame Sarraute's work as a whole. On almost every page one will find a contrast—slight enough at times but very often breathtaking—between the banal conversation or action and the imagery used to define the underlying "movements" or "subconversation." One is particularly struck in the earlier books by the large amount of marine or submarine imagery, such as the crab in my first example. Here, for instance, is an image applied to an innocent young girl in No. XIV of *Tropisms*:

> . . . they saw her sitting silent in the lamplight, looking like some frail, gentle underseas plant, entirely lined with mobile suckers. . . . (pp. 36–7)

Anyone who reads all of Nathalie Sarraute will become extremely familiar with these "suckers" (*ventouses*) and with the "tentacles" (*tentacules*) on which they are usually to be found. She conceives of human relations at this subconscious —not necessarily unconscious—level as furtive yet prehensile, and she believes that all Dostoevsky's characters exemplify the same urge: what Katherine Mansfield called "this terrible desire to establish contact."[2]

Only if we bear in mind that Madame Sarraute regards this urge as the "source" of all Dostoevsky's work can we accept her insistence—in an interview recorded for a German periodical[3]—that the Russian novelist has been the greatest influence on all her writing. Otherwise, there would seem to be no possible point of comparison between his work and hers. His novels are long and crowded with unforgettable characters

---

[2] These words are quoted in English in the French edition.

[3] Mimica Cranaki and Yvon Belaval, *Nathalie Sarraute* (Paris: Gallimard, 1965), pp. 213–22. Referred to hereinafter as "Cranaki." See pp. 13–18 for a valuable chronology of Nathalie Sarraute's life and writings. Much of the same information can be found in English in *The New York Times Book Review*, February 9, 1964, pp. 4, 5, 36, 37.

who kill, rave, fight, make love, give birth, and die; hers are usually short and sparsely inhabited by a handful of anonymous humans who stand aloof from "birth and copulation and death," to use T. S. Eliot's phrase. The most crucial overt act performed by a Sarraute character is likely to be the buying of a house or a piece of furniture, though we are rarely allowed to observe him in the act of earning his living; he is seldom short of money, however, for—in sharp contrast to the wide range of social classes explored by Dostoevsky—he always belongs to the middle classes or to the non-bohemian part of the literary world.

In her essay "Conversation and Sub-conversation" in *The Age of Suspicion* (New York, 1963), Madame Sarraute has implicitly defended the absence of action and the narrowness of social reference in her novels:

> Frequently, doubts and scruples slacken his [the psychological novelist's] endeavors. For where is he to find and be able to examine these secret recesses that attract him, if not in himself, or in the persons in his immediate circle whom he feels he knows well and whom he imagines he resembles? And the tiny, evanescent movements they conceal blossom out preferably in immobility and withdrawal. The din of actions accomplished in broad daylight either drowns or checks them. (p. 82)

In the same essay we are reminded that a tumultuous, Dostoevskian activity does occur in her novels, at least in metaphor if not in fact, at the subconscious level; she writes of

> . . . these inner dramas composed of attacks, triumphs, recoils, defeats, caresses, bites, rapes, murders, generous renunciations or humble submissions. . . . (pp. 93-4)

In the long run, then, her subject matter often resembles that of the most romantic storyteller—but a displacement has occurred from "broad daylight" to the "secret recesses."

So much for subtlety. But the sharp contrast between conversation and sub-conversation—between the highly colloquial yet conventional upper-middle-class dialogue and the submarine, eat-and-be-eaten existence that goes on underneath—

is essentially comic. All discrepancies between ideal and reality or illusion and reality are potentially either comic or tragic. When we examine each of Madame Sarraute's novels in turn, we shall see that the ultimate resolution of a potentially tragic situation is benign or, at worst, ironic. Furthermore, if we resolutely swim on the surface of the dialogue, refusing to be dragged into the depths, we can hardly help noticing— especially in *The Planetarium, The Golden Fruits,* and *Between Life and Death,* her last three novels—that on this level her work can most easily be classified as comedy of manners. Her study in *The Golden Fruits* of the passage of a meretricious novel from fashionable acclaim to equally fashionable oblivion has everything in common with the study of the fads and fancies of intellectual Paris presented by Molière in *Les Précieuses ridicules* or *Les Femmes savantes.*

Why has no critic, to my knowledge at least, written an essay on the comic vision of Nathalie Sarraute? Why has she herself, in her splendid essays on the art of the novel, which often glint with irony for pages on end, never even whispered to us that it is permissible to laugh *with,* though not *at,* her writing?

Again contrary to my practice in most of these chapters, I feel it necessary to deal with Nathalie Sarraute's books strictly in the order of their appearance in French. It took her a long time to get fully under way as a writer, but from the beginning there has been a firm logic in her development. Her works of fiction can be viewed in pairs, perhaps: *Tropisms* contains drafts of a number of passages later reworked in *Portrait of a Man Unknown; Martereau* and *The Planetarium* are mature examples of her fiction, satisfying many of the expectations entertained by lovers of the traditional novel; *The Golden Fruits* and *Between Life and Death* are twin tours de force, dealing with the rise and fall of a novel, first from the point of view of its readers and then from that of its author. Yet these pairs will not remain in watertight compartments: *Martereau,* like *Portrait,* is narrated in the first person by a hypersensitive young or youngish man. *The Planetarium* uses "third-person"

stream-of-consciousness technique—I will explain this paradoxical definition later—like its successors, and also deals to a
great extent with the literary life. In short, though I incline to
believe that *The Planetarium* is Madame Sarraute's masterpiece, I feel impelled not to discuss it first but to leave it to its
chronological—and logical—place in her development.

We begin, then, with *Tropismes*, first published in 1939 by
Denoël. In its current French edition, first published by Les
Éditions de Minuit in 1957, it contains twenty-four short texts.
The Foreword to *Tropisms* tells us that this "is a corrected
re-edition [i.e., re-issue] of the 1939 volume, to which have
been added the six last texts, written between 1939 and 1941."
Elsewhere in the Foreword we read:

> I started to write in 1932, when I composed my first
> *Tropism*. At that time, I had no preconceived ideas on the
> subject of literature, and this one, as were those that followed
> it, was written under the impact of an emotion, of a very vivid
> impression. (pp. v–vi)

Another source (Cranaki, p. 16) tells us that the first to be
written was No. II, and that this was followed by No. IX.
Madame Sarraute's explanation and defense of her scientific
title deserve quotation also:

> I gave them this name [*Tropisms*] because of their spontaneous,
> irresistible, instinctive nature, similar to that of the movements
> made by certain living organisms under the influence of out-
> side stimuli, such as light or heat.
> This analogy, however, is limited to the instinctive, irresisti-
> ble nature of the movements, which are produced in us by the
> presence of others, or by objects from the outside world. It
> obviously never occurred to me to compare human beings
> with insects or plants, as I have sometimes been reproached
> with doing. (p. viii)

In this passage we do see the validity of translating *mouvements* by "movements," for the French word contains the
ideas of both motion and emotion. In the first paragraph the
movements are physical; in the second, psychological. One
wonders why Madame Sarraute uses the word "obviously" in

the last sentence of the quotation. However, her point is clear enough when one reflects for a moment: an analogy is not the same as a one-to-one comparison; human beings do indeed respond instinctively to one another, but they also respond on one or more conscious levels, as we assume plants do not. Literature has always taken note of this instinctive response in special cases, whether it be the love-at-first-sight of so many Shakespearean heroes and heroines or the unreasoning repulsion expressed in this famous piece of doggerel:

> I do not love thee, Doctor Fell,
> The reason why I cannot tell;
> But this I know, and know full well,
> I do not love thee, Doctor Fell.

Written by the seventeenth-century versifier Thomas Brown, this is in fact an adaptation of an epigram by the Roman poet Martial, who flourished in the first century A.D. We can all become aware of such irrational, uncontrollable responses when meeting someone for the first time—especially if we have just been reading a Sarraute novel. We can also, when thus sensitized, discover sub-conversation or Claude Mauriac's "interior dialogue" in unlooked-for places: Edith Wharton's *The Age of Innocence*, for example. At the beginning of Chapter 24 of that work we find mention of "moments when saying became the mere accompaniment to long duologues of silence." Again, at the end of Chapter 26 we read a "mute message" from May to her husband, Newland Archer. What she *says* aloud is "The change will do you good . . . and you must be sure to go and see Ellen. . . ." What she silently *means*, Edith Wharton presents in a "speech" some twenty lines long.

This new art form, the "Tropism," is hard to define: it falls somewhere between the prose poem and the short-short story. No. II is the longest item in *Tropisms*, yet it just barely exceeds three pages; the shortest ones run to less than a page. Max Jacob, himself a poet and the author of some haunting prose sketches rather longer than any "Tropism," wrote Nathalie Sarraute an enthusiastic letter, dated January 28, 1939, that hailed her as a poet (Cranaki, photographic facsimile between pp. 96 and 97). Many of Baudelaire's *Little Poems in Prose* run longer than any item in *Tropisms*. Nevertheless, Madame Sarraute's book, although written for the ear as well as the eye, will probably always be classified as prose fiction, if only because of its close relationship to *Portrait of a Man Unknown.*

It may be useful to compare and contrast *Tropisms* with the short prose works that James Joyce called "Epiphanies"; we must remember, however, that nobody knew what Joyce meant by that term until the publication of *Stephen Hero* in 1944, and separate publication of these brief works—some had been inserted without comment by Joyce into *A Portrait of the Artist as a Young Man* and *Ulysses*—did not take place until 1956. Thus there is no shadow of possibility that Madame Sarraute was imitating Joyce.

The theory of the epiphany is expounded on pp. 211–13 of the New Directions editions of *Stephen Hero*, beginning with the following statement:

> By an epiphany he [Stephen] meant a sudden spiritual mani-
> festation, whether in the vulgarity of speech or of gesture
> or in a memorable phase of the mind itself. He believed that it
> was for the man of letters to record these epiphanies with
> extreme care, seeing that they themselves are the most delicate
> and evanescent of moments. (p. 211)

A study of the forty epiphanies published by Robert Scholes and Richard M. Kain in *The Workshop of Daedalus* shows that they are all either tiny "slices of life," recorded as objectively as possible, or else dreams and moods of Joyce's own. Joyce seems to believe that by recording externals with the utmost scrupulosity one can implicitly reveal the spiritual poverty of others. It apparently never occurred to the very young Joyce who recorded these epiphanies that the inner life of others might be as rich as his own, a shortsighted attitude of which Nathalie Sarraute is never guilty. While often capturing externals skillfully, she constantly probes for the feelings underneath. Only No. XVIII has the total objectivity of a Joycean epiphany in its presentation of an English spinster and her cook, though the street scene of No. I barely dips below the surface.

In the Foreword already cited, Madame Sarraute says:

> This first book contains *in nuce* [in a nutshell] all the raw material that I have continued to develop in my later works. (p. viii)

However, before offering detailed confirmation of this statement, let us look at one or two "Tropisms" for their intrinsic interest rather than their prophetic hints.

No. V, for instance, presents a woman, probably young, who has withdrawn as far as possible from her family and the world, but fears fresh contact at every moment:

> . . . it seemed certain that, for as long as possible, she would have to wait, remain motionless like that, do nothing, not move, that the highest degree of comprehension, real intelligence, was that, to undertake nothing, keep as still as possible, do nothing. (p. 13)
> . . . she remained motionless on the edge of her bed, occupying the least possible space, tense, as though waiting for something to burst, to crash down upon her in the threatening silence. (p. 11)

Any move that she undertakes, even going to the bathroom to wash her hands, may disturb the other members of the household, who seem to lie in wait for her behind their closed doors.

> In the suspended silence, the sudden sound of water would be like a signal, like an appeal directed towards them; it would be like some horrible contact, like touching a jellyfish with the end of a stick and then waiting with loathing for it suddenly to shudder, rise up and fall back down again. (p. 12)

One notes here, of course, not a Dostoevskian reaching for contact but a deliberate avoidance of it, accentuated by the submarine image of the jellyfish, whose shuddering response is perhaps a tropism in the scientific sense. The sketch begins with the phrase "On hot July days," and perhaps the nameless woman's hypersensitive shrinking is only temporary and will change with the weather, but meanwhile she cannot escape:

At the most, by being careful not to wake anybody, you could go down without looking at the dark, dead, stairway, and proceed unobtrusively along the pavements, along the walls, just to get a breath, to move about a bit, without knowing where you were going, without wanting to go anywhere, and then come back home, sit down on the edge of the bed and, once more, wait, curled up, motionless. (p. 13)

No. IX, the second to be written, uncompromisingly shows the tropistic behavior of a human being, a man who is totally disconcerted every time he sees a certain apparently harmless young woman:

She was frightening, mild and flat, quite smooth, and only her eyes were bulging. There was something distressing, disquieting about her and her mildness was threatening. (p. 23)

He suspected as usual that an innocuous question about how she was feeling might release the tension:

She should speak, make a move, show her real self, let it come out, let it finally explode—that wouldn't frighten him. (pp. 23-4)

But somehow he never has the strength to ask the question, and instead he starts talking compulsively,

. . . tossing from side to side (like a snake at the sound of music? like birds in the presence of a boa? he no longer knew). . . . (p. 24)

All he knew was that he

. . . must tell it to her, tell her everything, divest himself of everything, give her everything, as long as she remained there, crouching on the corner of the chair, all mild, flat, squirming. (p. 25)

No. XIX presents, in a partly dehumanized atmosphere reminiscent of semi-abstract painting, the "devouring" of a man by two somewhat older women.

He was smooth and flat, two level surfaces—his cheeks which he presented first to one and then to the other, and upon which, with their pursed lips, they pressed a kiss.

> They took him and they crunched him, turned him over and
> over, stamped on him, rolled, wallowed on him. They made
> him go round and round, there, and there, and there, they
> showed him disquieting painted scenery with blind doors and
> windows, towards which he walked credulously, and against
> which he bumped and hurt himself. (p. 46)

They possess him entirely, and yet he never tries to escape,
even when they let him loose for a while.

> He had developed a taste for this devouring in childhood—
> he tendered himself, relished their bittersweet odor, offered
> himself. (pp. 46–7)

In her essays on the novel, Madame Sarraute hankers after
the freedom enjoyed by the abstract painter, but she has never,
in fact, enjoyed greater freedom than in her first book. All her
sketches are plotless, all her human figures are anonymous and
to a considerable extent characterless; her urban and rural
landscapes are unidentifiable except in Nos. III and XVIII;
indications of epoch and season hardly appear except in Nos.
V and XX. Yet she does not seem to have relished this freedom
sufficiently to keep from writing novels—in which plot,
characters, place, and time are difficult to keep at arm's length.

As has been suggested, *Tropisms* most clearly foreshadows
Portrait of a Man Unknown. No. XII, however, is a somewhat
malicious caricature of a popular lecturer at the Collège de
France, who "explains" Rimbaud and Proust in Freudian
terms.

> "They should not upset you. Look, in my hands they are
> like trembling, nude little children, and I am holding them up
> to you in the hollow of my hand, as though I were their creator,
> their father, I have emptied them for you of their power and
> their mystery. I have tracked down, harried what was miracu-
> lous about them." (pp. 31–2)

This anticipates the essays in *The Age of Suspicion* and also
the novels about literary coteries. So does No. XI, a caricature
of a literary snob who seems repellent to "them," yet "they"
are just as snobbish in their own way:

> Hide it from her—quick—before she scents it, carries it away,
> preserve it from her degrading contact . . . But she foiled
> them, because she knew everything. The Chartres Cathedral
> could not be hidden from her. She knew all about it. She had
> read what Péguy had thought of it. (p. 29)

What is good taste? Who possess it? Is their taste natural or
acquired? These are vital questions in *The Golden Fruits*, as
in the passage just quoted.

But at least half of the items in *Tropisms*—Nos. II, IV, V,
VII, VIII, IX, XIV, XV, XVII, XX, XXII, XXIII—suggest one
or more of the three main characters in *Portrait of a Man
Unknown*: the domineering old man, his shrinking daughter,
the hypersensitive younger man. The most striking parallel of
all can be drawn between No. XV and pp. 131–3 of the New
York edition of *Portrait*. In both passages a young girl is
teased by an old man who is not her father. In *Tropisms* we
have the young girl's point of view; in the novel we see the
scene from a third person's viewpoint. In *Tropisms* the young
girl mentions that she is going back to England for another
visit and is overwhelmed by a barrage of questions:

> "Dover, Dover, Dover? Eh? Eh? Dover? Thackeray? Eng-
> land? Dickens? Shakespeare? Eh? Eh? Dover?" (p. 40)

In *Portrait* the scene is more generalized, so that the rapid fire
of place names varies with the background of the girl:

> "Biarritz? eh? eh? Ustarritz? Do you know what that is? You
> know that? Ustarritz?" He rolls his r's heavily. "Biarritz? La
> Bidassoa? Eh? Eh? Chocoa?" or else, depending upon the in-
> dividual in question: "Perros-Guirec? Eh? Eh? Ploermel?
> Plougastel? Pancakes? Custard pies? Eh? Pont-Aven? La
> Pointe du Raz?" (p. 132)

The other parallels are all much less specific, but nobody who
reads *Tropisms* and *Portrait* in quick succession can fail to be
struck by numerous similarities. We do not know, of course,
whether each time a young woman appears in *Tropisms* she
is *meant* to be the *same* young woman, as no names are used;
the same is true of each appearance of an old man or a younger

one. But since it is a cardinal Sarraute tenet that every human being is more like other human beings than he is different from them, we are free to telescope all the young women into one young woman, and so on.

Tropisms is such a seminal work that I have given it more space than will be allocated on the average to each of the novels. But in order to keep our sense of proportion, let us remember that the New York edition of *Tropisms* is only fifty-nine pages long, exclusive of the Foreword. And the original eighteen items take up only forty-five pages. It is hardly surprising, then, that few readers in 1939 recognized the potential importance of *Tropismes* or that the book received only one review—not in Paris but in a Belgian paper, *La Gazette de Liège.*

It had taken nearly two years to get *Tropismes* published; finished in 1937, it was not brought out by Denoël until February 1939—seven years from commencement to publication of so slender a volume. Nathalie Sarraute's next book, the novel *Portrait d'un inconnu,* was again seven years in the making. Begun in 1941 and finished in 1946 or 1947, it was published in 1948 by Robert Marin. Even with the prestige of a preface by Jean-Paul Sartre, whom Nathalie Sarraute had come to know during the 1940's, *Portrait* sold only four hundred copies in its first edition and the remaining copies were pulped. Reissued by Gallimard in 1956 after the relative success of *Martereau,* *Portrait d'un inconnu* finally began to attract some favorable attention. As *Portrait of a Man Unknown* (1958) it was the first book by Madame Sarraute to be published in the United States.

Portrait shows no sign of the troubled times during which it was written. Being Jewish—although her husband, Raymond Sarraute, is not—Madame Sarraute had to hide from the Germans soon after the defeat of France in 1940. During 1943–44, using the name Nicole Sauvage, she posed as the governess of her own three daughters under the courageous protection of Madame Robert Dieudonné, whose home she was sharing (Cranaki, p. 17).

Sartre called *Portrait of a Man Unknown* "this difficult, excellent book," and difficult it certainly is. Even the title is ambiguous, for the *inconnu*, the unknown man, may be either the old father or the younger narrator, or neither of them. Twice in the novel the narrator tells of a painting that haunts him: a portrait of an unknown man by an unknown artist, it hangs in a Dutch museum. The whole painting, except for the eyes, has an unfinished, fragmentary look:

> The lines of the face, the lace jabot and waistcoat, as also the hands, seemed to present the kind of fragmentary, uncertain outlines that the hesitant fingers of a blind man might come upon haltingly, feeling his way. It was as though all effort, all doubt, all anxiety had been overtaken by a sudden catastrophe, and had remained congealed in action. . . . The eyes alone seemed to have escaped the catastrophe and achieved fulfill-ment. It was as though they had attracted and concentrated in themselves all the intensity, all the life that was lacking in the still formless, dislocated features. (p. 84)

These eyes, with their "distressing, insistent entreaty," virtually forced the narrator to return to the quest he had abandoned, his search for the "secret" of the old man and his daughter.

Later this painting is invoked as the narrator's artistic ideal; reading between the lines, one suspects that it also symbolizes Madame Sarraute's ideal for this novel. The narrator and the daughter are viewing a Manet exhibition; she halts in front of one painting, obviously impressed, and invites his opinion; with many pauses, he gives it as follows:

> "Yes, . . . of course. I must admit, however, that it leaves me rather cold. . . . Undoubtedly, it is extremely good, but it's not what I like best. . . ." I felt myself blushing., . . . "It lacks disquiet . . . a certain . . . I mean to say . . . tremor . . . one feels in it too much assurance . . . too much satisfied certainty . . . or . . . perhaps . . . complacency. . . . I believe that rather than the most perfectly finished works I prefer those in which complete mastery has not been attained . . . in which one still feels, just beneath the surface, a sort of anxious groping . . . a certain doubt . . . a mental anguish . . ." I was beginning to splutter more and more . . . "before the immensity . . . the

elusiveness of the material world . . . that escapes us just when
we think we have got hold of it . . . the goal that's never
attained . . . the insufficiency of the means at our disposal. . . ."
(p. 201)[4]

He then cites, among other examples of the kind of paintings
he means, the portrait of a man unknown. We begin to see
that Madame Sarraute's novel, which shares its title with the
painting, has or aims to have some of the same vital incompleteness, the same anxious groping. Only dead creatures, dead
works of art, are "perfectly finished." The imaginary novel
that gives its name to *The Golden Fruits* is a finished, dead
work of art, as its partly metallic title suggests. Furthermore,
characters in the traditional novel—as Nathalie Sarraute never
tires of stressing in her criticism—tend to show the same
completeness; some live human beings, on the other hand,
show the elusiveness of which the narrator is so conscious in
the old man and his daughter. Unhappily, too many supposedly live humans are so stereotyped that they seem, like
the people in *Tropisms* No. XXIII, to have stepped out of the
pages of famous novels.

Sartre in his preface reads the entire book as the narrator's
futile quest for "an intangible authenticity"—futile because,
in the end, the father and daughter are "a perfectly ordinary
couple" and inhabit, like everyone else except possibly the
narrator, "the reassuring, dreary world of the inauthentic."
Sartre is using this last word in a technical, philosophical sense.
Those who do not see the world existentially are trapped by
the inauthentic.

In the first chapter of *Portrait*—it is divided into eleven
unnumbered chapters of widely differing lengths—we can see
that there are two classes of inauthentic people, those who
don't understand what the narrator sees in his two "subjects"
and those who do. The former, when he asked "if occasionally
they hadn't sensed something queer, a vague something that
emanated from her and clung to them . . ." (p. 17), seemed

---

[4] Madame Sarraute employs the ellipsis (. . .) so frequently that the
reader can safely assume that most uses of it, except at the beginnings
and ends of quotations, are hers.

deliberately to misunderstand. The most they would concede was "Yes, she seems to set great store by people's affection. . . ." (p. 18). Only when they didn't know that this "outsider" was listening would they express their real opinions to each other:

> "He's a selfish old man," they're saying, "I always said so, selfish and close-fisted, people like that shouldn't be allowed to have children. As for her, she's just a crank. She doesn't know what she's doing. In my opinion she's more to be pitied than anything else, poor thing." (p. 19)

This brutal common-sense judgment stuns the narrator temporarily, for it is one of which a hypersensitive person like himself is incapable.

But he goes off to discuss her with "the others, with the people in whose company I feel warmth and intimacy. . . ." (p. 20). Now his problem is inverted: these people take up his hints too eagerly.

> They laugh delightedly, with growing excitement seizing upon bits of stupid gossip, recollections of old news items, thick "slices of life" painted in raw, too crude colors, absolutely unworthy of them and of me. . . . (p. 24)

They speak of the old man's getting up at night: ". . . he is always suspecting her of something. . . ." This idea is later taken up by the narrator in his imaginings: the old man goes down to the kitchen at dead of night; he examines the bar of soap: "She had cut off a large piece, almost a good third" (p. 126). But his friends' other suggestions ludicrously go too far:

> ". . . in fact, his wife died from neglect. . . . It seems he made his children wear black underclothes . . . to save laundry." (p. 24)

In the second chapter the narrator presents the daughter fairly thoroughly but deals with the father more perfunctorily. He suspects that both father and daughter are as much interested in observing him as he them, and that they often tease him. At the beginning of the chapter, he is trying to learn "the other view"—the ordinary, common-sense one—

and shake off his obsession, but he suddenly catches sight of
the daughter in the street, overtakes her, and tries to chat
naturally as if he hadn't deliberately sought to take her by
surprise. She shakes him off, but he follows her in imagination
into her father's study and sketches briefly a quarrel between
them:

> She must be asking for something, he refuses, she insists. It's
> almost sure to be a question of money. . . . (p. 36)

The daughter is, the narrator thinks, one of a large class of
women:

> . . . grandmothers who are not allowed to see their grand-
> children as often as they should, daughters who go to see their
> old fathers at least twice a week, all kinds of neglected women,
> maltreated women, who have come to explain their case.
> (p. 41)

He goes to meet an old school friend who admires him and
has always loved to listen to him gossip. They have an en-
joyable talk, but the friend warns him against his new "discovery" and against categorizing in general. With a cheerful
"Whom are you slandering now?" the daughter surprises
them at their café table. Afterwards, the narrator walks her
home and inquires about her father; to his disgust, she fits
neatly into the cliché category he has framed for her; she
weeps in self-pity as she says,

> "Oh! yes, you really think I'm right, that it's natural and
> normal for me to suffer this way, for me to miss him as I do,
> for me, still, even at my age, to have such need of him . . . ?
> (pp. 56–7)

In a brief third chapter the narrator imagines the old man's
face becoming an immobile mask the very first time he saw
his daughter as a newborn baby. Already she was putting forth
"a tenuous, clinging thread, delicate little suckers . . ." to
ensnare him; in sheer self-defense against the intensity of his
emotion he instinctively assumed this mask, which has hardened with the years and slips on whenever he meets her. Only
on his deathbed will he lay it aside, perhaps.

The fourth chapter, also brief, depicts the narrator's interview with a psychiatrist, whom he tells all about his obsession
with the pair. The doctor professes not to be surprised:

"That's a very usual thing," he says, "nervous people, sensitive
as they are to what you call 'effluvia' or 'currents,' always seek
out one another. These people of yours are highly nervous
individuals. To be convinced of this fact, one has only to
consider the predominant role played, in their case, by 'scenes.'
And also by the clichés you describe and which, as you say,
they affect in order to confront each other, to legitimize their
clashes." (p. 73)

(The clichés mentioned here are those the pair think in when
they confront each other: "I am the Father, the Daughter,
my Rights" [p. 47].)

The psychiatrist has advised him to take a trip and enjoy
himself, so the narrator goes to Holland and pays his favorite
painting a visit. After communing with it in the fifth chapter,
he feels liberated; in the sixth he proceeds to enjoy the build-
ings, the landscapes, even individual stones and fragments of
walls that he is peculiarly fitted to appreciate. Suddenly a
challenge reaches him from Paris: a woman friend whom he
has met by accident tells him how the old man suddenly
exploded in rage about his daughter's traveling, about the expensive trip she had wanted to take in Spain. When his friends
showed surprise at his indignation, he became incoherent:

"That will do! Be quiet! I know them. They're like that.
That's how it is. There's never enough to please them. They're
never satisfied. All alike. I know them. There's never enough.
The moon . . . China. . . ." (pp. 96–7)

In response to the old man's "outcry, the challenge he had
hurled at me," the narrator hurries home, comforted by the
feeling that "The Unknown Man shared my torment. I was
no longer alone" (p. 100). In the long seventh chapter, the
narrator fills out his and our picture of the old man in a
series of quite vivid scenes: visiting the suburb where he used
to live and being chivalrous to the wife of an old friend who
has not fared too well in life; reading an arithmetic primer

in his study; walking and talking about life and death with a man friend and the man's son; waking up at night and examining the bar of soap; teasing young girls, in the passage quoted above.

By this point in the book, the characters of the two antagonists have been firmly established; the moment has surely come for their supreme confrontation—or pseudo-confrontation. But this is delayed until the tenth chapter; the two intervening chapters add little, appearing to contain no more than a few further examples of inauthenticity. The eighth chapter presents two unrelated passages: the first indicates the daughter's capacity for embarrassing other people by ostentatiously pretending not to notice the shabbiness of their clothes, etc.; the second is the luncheon scene quoted from, in which craters seemed to be opened up by the conversation. In the latter passage, the volcanic eruption that the initiates are expecting fails to take place, just as it fails in *Tropisms* No. VII. Even the suggestion that his daughter take up the expensive, newfangled game of golf only amuses the old man.

The main theme of the ninth chapter is the avoidance of another awkward moment by the old man; this time he is in danger not of exploding in wrath but of slipping into authenticity or at least into the metaphysical anguish out of which authenticity is born. Luckily for him—or unluckily, depending on one's philosophical orientation—their old servant comes to his study at that dangerous moment of the afternoon when metaphysical gulfs yawn and informs him that a pipe is leaking in the bathroom wall. It is as though he had drawn her to him at that precise moment by electromagnetic force.

There follows an interesting digression by the narrator on the subject of these "dangerous moments" in the early afternoon:

> This is the hour given over to the "siesta," to rest; the moment, after the excitement of the midday meal, when those who stay behind alone in the silent rooms, suddenly experience a sensation of cold; their heart in their mouth, they are seized with a dizziness, an impression that the earth has suddenly fallen out from under their feet and that they are slipping,

without being able to restrain themselves, into the void.
(p. 149)

In a passage like this, although the matter is idiosyncratically
her own, we can see the debt that Madame Sarraute's manner
owes to Proust.

The ideal escape from such moments is to go out into the
busy streets and look at the things on display in the store
windows, perhaps even buy something.

> Between them and a formless, strange, threatening uni-
> verse, the world of things has interposed itself like a screen,
> to protect them. (p. 150)

Wherever they go, things reassure them. Venice, London,
Moscow, Madrid, Fez—each city is associated with a particular kind of merchandise that is better and cheaper there
than anywhere else. The whole passage on pp. 150–1 is a de-
tachable "Tropism," but when we have separated it from the
novel, we see that it belongs to a different French tradition
altogether: it would hardly be out of place in the pages of
Jean de La Bruyère, the seventeenth-century moralist.

The old man inspects the leak and the damaged wall; he
explodes in fury against all those whose negligence may or
may not have caused the damage. Eventually the old servant
calms him down and convinces him that no real harm has
been done, though for a while the crack in the wall through
which the water oozed had taken on a symbolic significance:

> . . . the threat would be averted . . . he wouldn't be able to
> see the crack anymore, the crack through which . . . his very
> life, it seemed to him, was ebbing away. . . . (pp. 159–60)

The episode has displayed both humorous and pathetic aspects.

Finally in the tenth chapter we come to the climactic quarrel
between father and daughter, to the grappling of "two enormous dung beetles" that has already been quoted at length.
It must be remembered that the narrator could not actually
have been present at such an encounter; perhaps he is making
it all up, but it carries conviction. We are reminded of what
has led up to this struggle over money: all those women—the

entire female sex, it would seem—who have chided the father
for being harsh to his daughter, whereas he is conscious only
of the danger of spoiling her. Ever since she was tiny, he has
taught her prudence and has warned her against what is to
the bourgeois the crime of crimes, "Offhandedness" (p. 180).
The expression, capitalized in the French, is *La Désinvolture,*
for which a somewhat better translation might be "Free-and-
easy-ness," or simply "Letting go."

The old man accuses her of wanting to bring him to a
pauper's grave (*tu me ferais crever sur la paille*) and of having
saved up money secretly. Eventually he stoops lower still:
what she needs to support her extravagance is a rich husband,
but of course she's too unattractive to find one.

> . . . he was going down, he was sinking as though from dizzi-
> ness, drawn further and further down, to the depths of a
> strange voluptuousness, a funny sort of voluptuousness that
> resembled suffering: "Ah! it's because she's too homely, if you
> must know . . . she's too homely . . . and it's probably I too,
> I who forced you . . . I who am responsible for your looks. . . ."
> (p. 187)

Stung by this and other, even more cruel remarks, she blurts
out that she *does* have a suitor, one who doesn't even demand
a dowry. This only enrages him further, and he strikes her,
pushes her out, locks the door of his study.

Can we believe all this? At any rate, she is perfectly calm a
few minutes later when she goes to the Manet exhibition with
the narrator. And when he puts forward his view of what art
should be, she rebukes him, saying, "Watch out, that's very
unhealthy . . ." (p. 203). Either she has changed, then, or, as
the narrator begins to suspect, he has been wrong about her
all along—she has never shared his hypersensitivity. It is
significant that Nathalie Sarraute has withheld until this
episode all physical description of the narrator as well as any
clear indication of his age—although there is a hint on page
28 that he may be thirty-five. Now, as he walks to the art
museum with the daughter, he sees himself in mirrors along
the way:

. . . the fellow "beyond his prime," with the bedraggled air
and short legs, balding and slightly pot-bellied. . . .

She, too, saw it in the mirror, that reflection with the flabby,
somewhat sloppy lines—the unwholesome fruit of obscure
occupations and dubious ruminations, what, in fact, did he do
all day? what did he do with his time? she must have wondered
vaguely. (pp. 198–9)

He is seeing himself through her eyes and already beginning
to realize that she belongs to the common-sense world, as he
does not. Now that we know he is middle-aged, or nearly so,
we find his exacerbated sensitivity less tolerable than we
would in a younger man.

All this prepares us somewhat for the quietly humorous
anticlimax of the eleventh and last chapter. Most of it consists
of a scene in a restaurant where the narrator meets by accident with the father, the daughter, and her future husband,
Monsieur Louis Dumontet. It is no accident that this is the
only one of the characters to whom Madame Sarraute attaches
a name. Here is a man who has never left the common-sense
world, who is thoroughly at home in it. His name is like the
label on a château-bottled wine—a guarantee of the contents.
No possibility of ambiguity—or growth—here. Like Martereau, the only person with a name in Nathalie Sarraute's
next novel, he is what he has always been:

Extremely sure of himself. Unperturbed. Imposing. A rock. A
cliff that has resisted all the onslaughts of the ocean. Unassail-
able. A compact block. All smooth and hard. (p. 209)

The conversation, after the narrator has been introduced, is
all very specific: about a house Dumontet has bought in the
country and is going to modernize; about the local fishing;
about adding a bathroom; about the value of the place as an
investment; about the use of the land around the house; about
the varieties of apple tree to be planted:

Cider apples. Winter apples. St. Laurence apples. Red Roller
apples. Goose-foot apples. . . . Not a sound now. Not the
slightest spark between them, or between them and me. Not a
trace of a current. Dumontet had us all well in leash and was
leading us with a sure hand. (p. 217)

When the narrator says goodbye to him, Dumontet's last words are perfectly in character: "You'll see: trolling is the only way to catch pike" (p. 218).

The narrator is left alone with the old man, who quite happily burbles clichés about his daughter's match and about life in general. The narrator agrees with everything he says. He has changed sides himself:

> The women with the rather faded, slightly washed-out faces, who air themselves in the doorways of the big apartment houses with the blighted façades, or else in the wan little squares, will not grow silent now when they see me coming. They will know right away—they are never wrong—that they need distrust me no longer, that I am one of them. (p. 222)

There is just one slight handicap attendant on his adoption of "the other view": what will happen to vitality now that he has accepted completeness?

> Little by little everything will grow calm. The world will take on a smooth, clean, purified aspect. Somewhat akin to the air of serene purity that the faces of people are always said to assume after death.
> After death . . . ? But that, too, that is nothing, either. Even that rather strange look, as though things were petrified, that slightly lifeless look, will disappear in time. Everything will be all right. . . . It will be nothing. . . . Just one more step to be taken. (p. 223)

End of novel. End of narrator? It seems almost as though the entire book has melted away in the acid bath of irony that is its last chapter.

Another five years passed before the publication of *Martereau* (1953), the first of Nathalie Sarraute's novels to be accepted by Gallimard. This was not in itself a guarantee of success, of course, but it gave Madame Sarraute the assurance —after twenty-one years—that she was regarded as a professional writer.

The year 1953 was a significant one in French literature: Samuel Beckett's *En attendant Godot* was first performed in

Paris in January; *L'Innommable*, the third in his trilogy of
French novels, was first published later in the year; Alain
Robbe-Grillet's *Les Gommes*, inexplicably hailed by some
critics as the first example of *le nouveau roman*, also appeared
that year. One might say that by publishing *Martereau*
Madame Sarraute was joining the movement, but it would be
truer to say that the movement was joining her, since *Portrait*,
her most radical break with the traditional novel, was already
five years behind her. She in turn had been preceded by the
even more experimental novels of Raymond Queneau—but it
is doubtful whether she knew *Le Chiendent* or the early versions of *Saint Glinglin*. Even if she had known them, they
could not have offered any guidance to one who was seeking
to renovate the psychological novel.

Be that as it may, *Martereau* shows us a writer in full control of her innovative technique as well as of her subject
matter. In *Portrait* she had shown that the subject matter of
Tropisms could be developed into a full-length novel. What
she had not fully mastered was the point of view from which
the novel is narrated. If only because the author is a woman,
one might reasonably have expected *Portrait* to be narrated
from the daughter's point of view. On the other hand, one is
impelled to assume that a novel written with such intensity
does contain an autobiographical element, so that the relatively uninvolved male narrator becomes a device necessary
to supply objectivity and "distancing." Madame Sarraute's
parents were divorced when she was two and—after some
complicated shuttling between father and mother and between
Russia and France—she settled permanently in Paris with her
father at the age of eight. There was a stepmother, but she
seems to have played a minor part in Nathalie's upbringing.
The tie between father and daughter until his death in 1949
must have been a strong one, though their emotions doubtless
displayed the love/hate ambivalence that Freud discovered
in all parent-child relationships. I hasten to add that Madame
Sarraute was by no means "homely" in her youth, if photographs are to be relied upon, and that she was no more than

twenty-five when she became the wife of Raymond Sarraute, and partner in his law firm.

Then again, while objectivity may be valuable in some types of novel, Madame Sarraute has chosen to explore the psychological depths, of whose existence we can only be subjectively aware; we can assume their existence in others, but we may utterly misread their "movements," at any rate in the short run. The assumption—crucial to Madame Sarraute's psychological theory—that in the long run one human being's emotions are statistically almost identical with another's cannot be proved or disproved in the present state of scientific knowledge.

So we find that the supposedly "objective" narrator is in fact wildly "subjective," to the point where he may have invented the greater part of the emotional relationship between the daughter and the father. If the reader resents being faced with this uncertainty, he is confusing art and life and denying the novelist her full artistic freedom. But he is perhaps entitled to complain that in *Portrait* Madame Sarraute has not reminded him sufficiently often of the narrator's unreliability. There are a number of scenes at which the narrator could not have been present; some at least of these are narrated with impersonal omniscience: there are no first-personal pronouns to remind us that these scenes may only be taking place in the narrator's imagination.

This problem of point of view is much more skillfully handled in *Martereau*. The narrator, male and hypersensitive as before but younger, is much more involved in the action of the novel than the narrator of *Portrait* was. He is present at every scene that he chooses to narrate to us; if, occasionally, he imagines a scene that did not take place, such as the conversation with his cousin on pp. 203–6 of the translation (New York, 1959), we know from the beginning that it is hypothetical.

There is one exception to this rule, a scene in which we observe Monsieur and Madame Martereau just after the narrator's uncle has visited them; they are alone together, the

narrator definitely is not present. Yet the alert reader comes
to the realization that the scene is in fact being reconstructed
by the narrator—for we are given in succession four different
and somewhat conflicting versions of the same scene. (For
the four versions, see the New York edition, pp. 175–202; the
second begins on p. 183, the third on p. 188, the fourth on
p. 197.) Either by coincidence or because both were imitating
a model unknown to me, Robbe-Grillet occasionally uses multiple versions of the same scene in *The Erasers*. There, the
explanation seems to be that a detective is mentally reconstructing a crime and we are privileged to watch the different
versions of the scene that he imagines. Before World War II,
I remember seeing a farcical murder play, *Who Killed the
Count?*, in which each of several characters, for various flimsy
motives, "confessed" in turn to committing the crime, whereupon his version was reenacted as a flashback on the stage.
Madame Sarraute's use of the device does not resemble that
of the play closely, but Robbe-Grillet's does. In his later novels
and screenplays, Robbe-Grillet has used this device increasingly, to the point where it has almost entirely ousted more
familiar and less ambiguous narrative methods.

Martereau can be viewed as a mirror image of *Portrait*.
Whereas Dumontet, the named character in *Portrait*, appears
only at the very end, his counterpart, Martereau, comes on the
stage relatively close to the beginning of *Martereau* and virtually dominates the rest of that novel. Furthermore, whereas
the narrator of *Portrait* despises Dumontet and values only
those who are complicated, elusive, and hypersensitive, the
narrator of the second novel idealizes Martereau and despises
all those who, like himself, are constantly changing in response
to every psychological current. But if Martereau does not
change, the narrator, being so volatile himself, keeps changing
his opinion of him: can anyone possibly be so solid, trustworthy, and all-of-a-piece as Martereau seems? If it were not
for the narrator's vacillating estimate of Martereau, there
could be no suspense, no story, no novel. As it is, the "real"
Martereau remains the same from beginning to end: the only
inner "movements" we seem to detect in him may be attribut-

able entirely to the imagination of the narrator—not only on pp. 175–202 but elsewhere. Yet we are never sure: after all, in theory everybody has these movements, though only sensitive people pay much attention to them. Is Martereau so insensitive, such a vegetable? Even if he is, is his outer behavior so consistently honorable and trustworthy after all? It seems certain that he did not cheat the narrator's uncle in the affair of the house, but the suspicion that Martereau has been having a love affair with the narrator's aunt is never refuted or corroborated.

The narrator, a young man in delicate health who cannot support himself on his earnings as an interior decorator, lives in Paris with his wealthy uncle and his uncle's wife and teenage daughter. The uncle has risen from small beginnings by sheer business ability; his wife is much younger than he and from a much better family background; like the nephew, she prides herself on her taste in the arts; the daughter is spoiled and unintellectual. The long opening chapter of the book, pp. 1–69—again the chapters are not numbered—establishes, insofar as anything so volatile can be established, the relationships between the narrator and his uncle, aunt, and cousin. By and large, the uncle is the dominant figure in the family group, the stimulus that provokes their tropisms—though of course he responds to them too. At times, however, the aunt proves more than a match for him. A scientific metaphor is used later in the book to describe this phenomenon, but in essence the aunt's technique differs little from that of Shakespeare's Cleopatra:

> . . . there exists between them a system of compensation: that of vessels connected by "U" tubes.[5] When the level lowers in one, you'll see it rise right away in the other. As he becomes more and more depressed, she becomes at once cheerful and full of life, chats with us, shows off. He then becomes gloomier and gloomier. . . . Occasionally, it's he—but very rarely, in such cases he is much the weaker of the two—who, one fine

[5] It should be noted that the "U" tubes do not appear in the original French, which has a less overtly "scientific" flavor: *Il y a entre eux un système de compensation: celui des vases communicants* (p. 144).

day, comes into the dining room, lively as anything, rubbing
his hands together. . . . She immediately assumes her set expression. . . . She now resorts to drastic measures and sets
what I call her pumping system into action: her silence becomes denser, more ponderous, it attracts us more strongly, our
words are caught up by it. . . . (pp. 121–2)

In the second chapter Martereau is introduced as the perfect
foil to this family. He is not only *dur et pur* (hard and pure)
himself, but he confers a certain stability on the narrator
whenever they are together:

His hearty, cordial hand-shake, his tap on my shoulder: "Well,
how goes it, young fellow?" have an immediate effect on me.
This is the laying on of hands, exorcism, the sign of the cross,
that causes the evil One to flee. All at once, as though by
enchantment, they disappear, all the crawlings, tremblings and
shudderings, all the blemishes and wounds left on me by their
unhealthy contact, their ambiguous caresses, their bites. Everything grows smooth, hardens, assumes clear outlines, an aspect
that is well-cleaned, orderly and shining. The bad dream, the
spell, vanish: I see clearly, like everybody else, I know where
I am and who I am. "How goes it, young fellow?" Underneath
these words, in back of his eyes, cleaving to them closely,
without the slightest crack through which anything whatsoever
that was suspicious might seep, nothing but sincere solicitude,
the frankest sort of good-heartedness. . . . (pp. 75–6)

The repetition here of "How goes it, young fellow?" draws
attention to a growing tendency in Madame Sarraute's style.
We shall come across more and more passages of several
pages in length that are punctuated and to some extent unified
by the repetition of a banal remark in which the hearer finds
hidden significance and over which he broods. But, alerted by
this repetition of a remark, let us look for other repetitions in
the passage just quoted. It now becomes apparent that many a
detail is repeated, at least once and often twice, in slightly
different words or imagery. True, "hearty, cordial" is more of
a tautology than the *forte et cordiale* of the French; it can also
be argued that the tap on the shoulder is necessary to complete
the impression begun by the handshake. But how can one

justify the triad of "the laying on of hands, exorcism, the sign of the cross . . ."? One might suggest that it is a mannerism of the over-effusive narrator—but, alas, it has become a mannerism of his creator. I open her next book, *The Planetarium*, absolutely at random and set down the first four lines of page 181:

> . . . way that the end of a bit of horse hair sticks out of a *smooth, well-stuffed* mattress, it sticks out from the *firm, smooth, creaseless* sentence, upon which she has rested a second, lulled by its *harmony, its soothing cadence.* . . .
> [Italics mine]

After this digression on manner, we can return to the matter of the book, which does not, in fact, require too close an examination from this point on. Martereau and the uncle are old friends, but Martereau has not been very successful in a materialistic sense: he is something of a jack-of-all-trades, though he knows the construction business best. The nephew urges the uncle to renew his old friendship with Martereau. Characteristically, the uncle soon finds a use for his friend: Martereau will buy a house in his own name with money supplied by the uncle, who would otherwise be liable to heavy taxes on the sum he wishes to invest in real estate. Martereau agrees and finds a suitable house. The nephew and his girl cousin are then sent to Martereau with the entire purchase price in cash. It never occurs to them to ask him for a receipt. The uncle returns from the long business trip which has prevented him from bringing the money to Martereau himself, and promptly asks the youngsters for the receipt. One suspects that he doesn't really feel the need for one—it might be an awkward piece of evidence against him in the eyes of a tax investigator—but he is scoring a point in the game of all against all that this family constantly plays. The narrator's opinion begins to waver, particularly as Martereau refuses to give a receipt when asked: his integrity has been questioned and he is indignant that such legalistic matters as receipts should have been thrust into an arrangement between friends. The narrator suspects that Martereau realizes he is being made use of as a "front man" (*un homme de paille*) and is planning revenge. Having bought the house, Martereau next moves into it with his wife—claiming that this is the easiest way to supervise repairs. The uncle seems to believe that Martereau is cheating him, but this is probably only a pretense to enable him to score further points against his nephew. In the end, the repairs are completed, Martereau moves out again, all the bills presented for the repair work are scrupulously exact. The book ends with a last glimpse of Martereau, imperturbable and inviolable as ever, preparing his fishhooks with meticulous care.

There remains the odd suspicion that Martereau, who is very attractive to women—no doubt precisely because of his solidity—has been having an affair with the aunt while giving at home the impression of being an utterly devoted husband. The narrator imagines meetings between Martereau and the aunt, but all he has to go on is the belief that one day, while drowsily awaiting his turn in an overheated waiting room for an X-ray, he saw Martereau saying goodbye to the aunt at the doctor's garden gate. But the whole scene is dreamlike, and even as he "observes" it, he asks "Am I dreaming" (p. 214). Madame Sarraute, I am sure, does not want us to make up our minds one way or the other. For the book to achieve its full effect, the various ambiguities should never be resolved. The experience of each one of us probably contains one or many people about whom we cannot make up our minds. So the argument from verisimilitude—that obsession of most novel-readers and novel-critics—can be used to justify ambiguity. A better argument possibly would be that ambiguity is, if not essential to art, at least congenial to it. A psychological case history pretends to certainty for pragmatic reasons; the artist is under no such pressure to rob his characters of mystery. Besides, if our uncertainty were removed, along with it would go a great deal of the book's quiet humor.[6]

[6] Let me just add that the most humorous episode in the book, and one of the most humorous in all of Nathalie Sarraute, does not concern Martereau at all. It is the third chapter (pp. 86–101 of the New York edition), and might be titled, in Victorian fashion, "Chapter Three: In Which the Family Does Not Buy a House in the Country."

1956 was a memorable year for Nathalie Sarraute the writer. Early in it, Gallimard published *L'Ère du soupçon*, a volume containing four substantial essays on the novel. This appeared in the United States some years later as *The Age of Suspicion* (New York, 1963). Toward the end of the year, Gallimard issued a new edition of *Portrait d'un inconnu*, which had fared so badly eight years before. In 1957 came the publication, by Les Éditions de Minuit, of the revised and augmented edition of *Tropismes*. Suddenly, four books by Madame Sarraute— her entire literary output, in fact—were in print simultaneously. But she had suffered a personal loss: her mother, who had settled permanently in Paris in 1921, died in 1956; her father had died in Paris in 1949. Madame Sarraute may have been more attached to her father, an industrial chemist who owned a dye-manufacturing plant, but she probably owes her literary gift to her mother, who published a good deal of fiction in Russian under a masculine pseudonym (Cranaki, p. 14).

The Age of Suspicion need not detain us long, for it has often been referred to implicitly when Madame Sarraute's theory of fiction was under discussion, and I have quoted explicitly twice from the longest and most important essay. The four essays in the volume are printed in the order in which they were written. "From Dostoievski [*sic*] to Kafka," first published in Sartre's periodical, *Temps modernes*, for October 1947, defends the psychological novel as written by Dostoevsky against the novel of the absurd, such as Camus's *L'Étranger* (known in the United States as *The Stranger* and in England as *The Outsider*), purportedly deriving from Kafka's works. Madame Sarraute goes on to show that in fact neither Camus's novel nor the novels and stories of Kafka are devoid of psychological analysis. As we have already seen, she finds at the center of all Dostoevsky's characters "this terrible desire to establish contact" (p. 33).

> Crime itself, assassination . . . is merely . . . the supreme embrace, and the only definitive break. But even this supreme break may yet be repaired thanks to public confession, by

> means of which the criminal deposits his crime in the common
> patrimony. (p. 37)

Kafka's protagonists too, in *The Castle* and *The Trial*, share

> . . . this same passionate, anxious desire to establish contact
> that runs like a guiding thread through Dostoievski's entire
> work. (p. 41)

But whereas Dostoevsky's characters "seek a sort of inter-
penetration, a total and ever possible fusion of souls" with
their fellow man, and sometimes even achieve this, Kafka's
heroes do not attain even the very limited form of contact
that they are in search of:

> . . . to be able to appear and justify themselves before un-
> known, unapproachable accusers, or to seek to safeguard,
> despite all obstacles, some paltry semblance of a relationship
> with those closest to them. (p. 42)

Kafka, she felt, had reached the limit along this line of development—we must remember that none of the works in
which Beckett carried the novel beyond that "limit" had yet
been published. The essay ends with these words:

> To remain at the point where he [Kafka] left off, or to
> attempt to go on from there, are equally impossible. Those
> who live in a world of human beings can only retrace their
> steps. (p. 50)

This was in fact what she herself had already done. As *Portrait*
was to demonstrate in the following year, the way back led to
Dostoevsky and the psychological novel.

"The Age of Suspicion," the next, much briefer essay, appeared in *Temps modernes* for February 1950. Its main theme
is that, whatever the critics may say about the importance of
creating "unforgettable" characters, "not only has the novelist
practically ceased to believe in his characters, but the reader,
too, is unable to believe in them. . . ." (p. 54) One reason for
his disbelief is the discovery of the unconscious, especially
the collective unconscious, which, in Jung's view, belongs to
all human beings alike. The reader, Nathalie Sarraute thinks,
no longer believes in individuality:

He has watched the watertight partitions that used to separate
the characters from one another give way, and the hero become an arbitrary limitation, a conventional figure cut from
the common woof that each of us contains in its entirety, and
which captures and holds within its meshes the entire uni-
verse. (p. 62)

Madame Sarraute felt, and still feels, that this is how things
ought to be: in *The Golden Fruits*, no human being remains
in focus long enough for us to get to know him or her. In any
case, fiction cannot compete with fact and should give up
trying to.

> Where is the invented story that could compete with that
> of Gide's *Séquestrée de Poitiers* [the story of a victim of life-
> long illegal confinement who begs to be allowed to return to
> the unbelievably filthy room from which she has been rescued],
> or with those of the concentration camps, or the Battle of
> Stalingrad? And how many novels . . . would be needed to
> furnish the reader with a subject matter equal in richness and
> subtlety to that offered for our curiosity and reflection by
> almost any well-constructed monograph? (p. 64)

One might expect at this point a plea for sheer fantasy, for
pure invention totally unrelated to the world of fact, but instead the novelist is urged toward introspection: the "complex,
tenuous states that he is attempting to portray," or that
Nathalie Sarraute is at any rate,

> . . . these states resemble certain phenomena of modern
> physics, which are so delicate and minute that even a ray of
> light falling on them disturbs and deforms them. Conse-
> quently, whenever the novelist seeks to describe them without
> revealing his own presence, he seems to hear the reader . . .
> stop and ask: "Who said that?" (pp. 65–6)

Most of the rest of the essay is devoted to extolling the use of
first-person narrative, but we are never quite sure whether the
aim is really to undeceive the reader or to deceive him more
completely than ever. It appears that the "I" is not to be the
novelist but his leading character. Now it is debatable whether
the narrator is in fact the leading character of either *Portrait*

or *Martereau*; besides, as we have seen, Madame Sarraute has not reminded us often enough that there *is* a narrator and that he *is* unreliable. What she could not have known when she wrote this essay but must have suspected by the time she republished it was the fact that *Martereau* would be her last first-person novel.

The thesis of the next and longest essay, "Conversation and Sub-conversation," has already been introduced through quotations from it or from the Foreword to *Tropisms*. The essay was first published in the *Nouvelle nouvelle revue française* for January–February 1956. This is the most brilliant of Madame Sarraute's defenses of the psychological novel as defined by herself, but the hasty reader may easily be misled by the irony of the opening pages into thinking that it is an attack on what it so skillfully defends.[7] No doubt Madame Sarraute was not entirely satisfied with the achievements of Proust, Joyce, and Virginia Woolf, but she was certain that the French novelists of 1956 had not yet learned the lessons taught by this trio well enough to go beyond them. The newness of the New Novel, one may say, lies in the attempt of its authors to begin where these three great experimenters had left off, instead of reverting to the classical tradition of the French novel or following what Madame Sarraute calls the "behaviorist" approach of American novelists like Hemingway. It is interesting to find this essay concluding with a tribute to Ivy Compton-Burnett, who, instead of serving up the "sub-conversation" separately, manages to incorporate it into her highly stylized dialogue, according to Madame Sarraute. The last words of the essay express a philosophical optimism:

> Quite obviously, one day in the near future, this technique, along with all the others, will seem incapable of describing anything but appearances. And nothing could be more cheering and more stimulating than this thought. It will be the sign

[7] In her Foreword to the London edition of *Tropisms and The Age of Suspicion* she wrote: ". . . I should like to stress the fact that when I spoke of the old-fashioned nature of the works of Joyce and Proust, or the *naïveté* of Virginia Woolf's ideas on the subject of the novel, it was quite obviously to poke fun at those who had expressed themselves in this manner about these writers" (p. 10).

that all is for the best, that life goes on, and that we must not turn back, but strive to go farther forward. (p. 117)

The fourth essay, "What Birds See," was written in January 1956 and first published in the volume. Its title refers to the folk tale told about the Greek painter Zeuxis, among others, that one of his paintings was so realistic that birds flew down to eat the grapes in it, mistaking them for real ones. As one might expect, the essay denounces *trompe-l'oeil* realism in the novel. One passage outlines the subject afterwards treated at length in *The Golden Fruits*:

> Every now and then we see our most influential critics in the grip of a kind of dizziness, which is comprehensible of course in persons who are so busy reading. But then they suddenly begin to pronounce a masterpiece and praise to the skies, a work that is devoid of all literary value, as will be proven, some time later, by the indifference, then the oblivion, into which its weakness will inevitably let it slip. (pp. 123–4)

The essay goes on to denounce all conventional realism, whether bourgeois-oriented or so-called "socialist realism." Nathalie Sarraute points out that the latter is ultimately bad in its effect not only on literature but on the revolution it professes to serve. The last few pages of the essay, indeed, read as if they were written primarily with the Communist world in mind—this passage, for example:

> Here and there, by drawing upon a sincere, living experience whose roots go deep into the unconscious source from which all creative effort springs, completely shattering the old, sclerosed forms, writers have discovered and are still discovering the aspect of reality that can render direct and effective service to the propagation and victory of revolutionary ideas. But it can also happen . . . that isolated, maladjusted, lonely individuals, morbidly attached to their childhood, withdrawn into themselves and cultivating a more or less conscious taste for a certain form of defeat, by giving in to an apparently useless obsession, succeed in digging up and laying bare a fragment of reality that is still unknown. (pp. 145–6)

Perhaps Nathalie Sarraute includes among these "lonely individuals" Proust, Joyce, and Virginia Woolf: perhaps, who knows, herself. At any rate, this passage helps to vindicate her choice of narrators for her first two novels.

Le Planétarium (Gallimard, 1959), translated as *The Planetarium* in 1960, is the least difficult of Nathalie Sarraute's novels: many of the characters, for instance, possess both first and last names. Its most difficult feature, perhaps, is its title—at any rate to those who have read the book right through. Actually, this title was originally devised for a second collection of short texts which would have been the immediate successor to *Tropismes* (Cranaki, p. 16). In an interview with François Bondy, published in German in *Der Monat* (March 1963), Madame Sarraute gave a full explanation of the title:

> The Planetarium is not the real sky but an artificial one. And these characters and what they are seeking—for instance, to live in a handsome apartment or to become well known or whatever—make up the surface under which occur the impulses, properly speaking, the minute real dramas, which have nothing to do with the apparent content. (Cranaki, p. 216; my translation)

Another difficulty, one that diminishes as the reader penetrates deeper into the book, is presented by the narrative technique. Madame Sarraute has abandoned the first-person narrator for good, and instead we find what I have called "third-person stream of consciousness." Here is an example of what I mean, from the opening chapter:

> . . . it was stupid of her to have been so afraid, this door had nothing in common—what an idea even to have imagined it, but she had begun to see oval doors everywhere, she had never seen so many, it's enough to think about a thing for you to begin to see nothing but that—nothing in common, absolutely nothing, with the oval doors she had seen in suburban bungalows, in country houses, hotels, even at her hairdresser's. . . . No, she has no need to worry, the whole thing is in perfect taste, quiet, distinguished . . . she feels like running . . . now

is the moment, she can go home, they've had ample time to finish . . . everything must be ready . . . (pp. 10–11)

It is fairly easy to grasp what is going on after reading a page or two of this: only slight changes are needed to turn it into pure interior monologue:

. . . it was stupid of *me* to have been so afraid, this door *has* nothing in common. . . .

Further along in the passage, one doesn't even need to change the tense, only the person:

No, *I have* no need to worry, the whole thing is in perfect taste. . . .

When both tense and person are changed, we have an equivalent of indirect speech, replacing the direct speech that seems appropriate to interior monologue. It is as though Madame Sarraute had written, "*She said to herself that* . . . it was stupid of her . . ." and then decided to leave out the italicized words. What is the effect of this shift from direct to indirect speech? Essentially it reminds the reader that he has before him a *narrative*; he is being told a story, even though narrative phrases such as "She said to herself that . . ." have been left out. Nathalie Sarraute is trying to play fair with him, but very soon he is unconsciously "translating" into direct speech and feels that he is by turns within the minds of all those whose interior monologues are being presented.

Just a word about terminology here: in my usage, "interior monologue" applies to all those passages in which a character seems to be talking mentally to himself; "stream of consciousness" is a more inclusive term that refers to passages in which the character is aware not only of his own interior monologue but of sights and sounds from the external world—and especially of spoken dialogue. The entire opening chapter consists of Aunt Berthe's stream of consciousness: at first we notice only interior monologue, but then, as she talks to the workmen, we see her awareness broaden.

"But it don't look bad . . . that's just an idea of yours, come on, now, it's just a matter of habit, you'll get used to it, you'll

see . . . it's very nice, it's real pretty . . . just leave everything the way it is . . ." That protective tone of theirs, that
familiar manner . . . they are already settling in like con-
querors, making themselves at home, their drunken soldiery,
their hardened troopers are patting her cheek, pinching her
chin . . . There now, that's better, getting a little easier to
handle ain't you, my girl, she's beginning to come round,
beginning to listen to reason . . . Come on, now, you'll get
used to it . . . Serves her right. It's her punishment for being
so cowardly . . . How could she have fallen so low as to place
herself àt their mercy, accept their rule, ask them for aid and
protection, offer to cooperate with these ignorant creatures
who are ravaging, disfiguring the entire countryside, who destroy works of art, tear down charming old homes which they
replace with those cement blocks. . . . (p. 17)

Clearly, much of this is never put into words by the old lady:
she hears the workmen's soothing words, becomes indignant
at their patronage of her, imagines their thoughts; no doubt
medieval images of conquering hordes of barbarians float in
her mind's eye, mingled with modern images of barbarians in
the building industry.

In the second chapter we are present at a social occasion
and move from consciousness to consciousness. It begins with
a few lines of direct speech, but the consciousness that registers
them is (we eventually discover) that of Alain Guimiez,
nephew of Aunt Berthe. His mother-in-law is urging him to
tell her guests about his aunt and about her qualms concerning the oval door. Alain rather resents being pounced on like
this. We then shift into the mother-in-law's consciousness:

But how glum he looks suddenly, what a wry face he's
making . . . What has come over him? . . . The dry little tone
with which, all at once, he refuses, and that derisive glance
. . . Usually, he's more accommodating, less timorous . . . But
you never know with him . . . It's enough for him to feel that
she is very keen . . . Or else it's a lack of confidence in himself
all of a sudden, unsociability, laziness . . . How complicated,
how difficult to get along with people are, she can't understand
it . . . he needs a good shaking up . . . "Come on now, don't be

ridiculous, don't make us beg you . . . you're keeping us on
tenterhooks . . . come on, be nice . . . tell it . . ." (pp. 23–4)

Henceforward, this will be Madame Sarraute's technique for
presenting a scene with a number of participants. The
chapter will consist of a number of divisions, each made up
of one or more paragraphs and separated from the divisions
which precede and follow it by a space equivalent to two lines
of text. Typically, these divisions will resemble the one just
quoted in full: first we have the sub-conversation and then the
conversation, the dialogue spoken aloud.

Once the reader has familiarized himself with its technique,
The Planetarium becomes an extremely entertaining comedy
of manners: its surface reminds me most of Jane Austen,
though its depths are Proustian; we must not forget, though,
that much of Proust's work is itself comedy of manners.

Alain Guimiez, the protagonist, reminds us strongly of the
narrators in the two earlier novels, but he is less introverted
and, unlike them, he is married. His wife, Gisèle, comes from a
family perhaps a little more conventionally bourgeois than
his own, but there is not much to choose between their backgrounds. Alain, however, is torn between his love of comfort
and status on the one hand and a hankering after scholarly
and literary success on the other. Still in his twenties, he is
working on a doctoral dissertation in art history and making
slow progress—in part because he is subject to sudden obsessions that absorb most of his energies. The objects of his
three obsessions in the course of the novel may seem wildly
disparate, but the successive emotions they arouse in him are
basically the same. The first of these obsessions that we become aware of concerns an antique *bergère*, which he feels
he must have, though his in-laws think it would be much more
sensible to spend the money they are giving the young couple
on a pair of "sensible" leather armchairs.

When his wife seems to be veering toward her parents' view,
there is a bitter quarrel. Alain stomps out of their small apartment, and we then learn of his second obsession, for his anger
gives him the courage to telephone the great woman writer

Germaine Lemaire, whose approval and friendship he desperately wishes to gain. She has a little court of admirers, male and female, younger than herself, to whom she is perfectly willing to add Alain.

It is Germaine (known to her intimates as Maine) who supplies Alain with his third obsession. He happens to tell her that his aunt once, half jokingly, offered him her apartment— larger, pleasanter, in a much better neighborhood than his and Gisèle's cramped quarters. But he, with the soul of an artist, has no intention of accepting any such thing. Whereupon Germaine says:

> "But personally, I believe, on the contrary that, if I were in your place, I should accept. Only too delighted. I mean it. They ought to be of some use at least, all those people. So take what you want. It's darned pleasant not to live in cramped quarters. And it will take more than that to make a slave of you." (p. 104) [8]

Having thus been given absolution by his goddess, Alain embarks on a relentless pursuit of Aunt Berthe's apartment. Housing is so scarce in Paris that a triple exchange has to be arranged, because it would be altogether impossible to persuade Aunt Berthe to move into Alain's hole-in-the-wall. However, by now the aunt has regretted ever making the offer, and diplomatic moves are initiated. Gisèle goes to coax Alain's father, and he in turn approaches his sister, Berthe. The opportunities for sub-conversation in both these interviews are fully exploited, but M. Guimiez hasn't the heart to press his sister. Then Alain comes and threatens his aunt: legally she has no right to so many rooms, because of the postwar housing shortage. Ironically, both Alain's father and the aunt feel that he is so greedy and demanding chiefly because his aunt spoiled him after his mother's death, passing on

[8] It has been remarked by reviewers, myself included, that Madame Maria Jolas's translations, though remarkably faithful, are not colloquial enough. Admittedly, her dialogue aims at English rather than American idiom, but she has lived too long in Paris to write spoken English with the fidelity of ear that Nathalie Sarraute brings to spoken French. The above quotation illustrates this point.

to him her love of luxury and her tendency to obsession—as in the case of the oval door.

After Alain's appalling cruelty to his widowed aunt, M. Guimiez visits her again; Madame Sarraute thinks it worthwhile to devote two successive chapters to this scene: the first (pp. 234–52) presents it from Berthe's point of view; the second (pp. 253–68), from her brother Pierre's. The two views differ, of course, but not too drastically: tragedy or the profound irony that resembles tragedy is too devoid of nuances to appeal to Nathalie Sarraute. Pierre tells his sister what she wants to hear—that Alain really loves her—and her mood becomes more and more buoyant as the scene progresses; he, on the other hand, grows steadily more depressed: Alain has turned out exactly as Pierre had always feared he would. Still, there is some comfort in the thought that Berthe will leave the securities she has inherited from her dead husband to Alain— his future is assured. Pierre can stop worrying about his son. Brother and sister end the interview calm and affectionate.

Meanwhile, Alain's relationship with Germaine has had its ups and downs. With his father he meets her by accident in a bookstore, and she treats them both very brusquely, perhaps because she senses his father's poor opinion of her. Alain doesn't dare get in touch with her again until a mutual friend tells him she has been inquiring about him. He confides to the friend, René, his fears about her having dropped him.

A few evenings later, René visits Germaine, who is in a despondent mood; she has just read a headline in a literary journal: "Isn't Mme. Germaine Lemaire our Madame Tussaud?" She is shocked by this suggestion that her works have no more life than wax figures, but when she picks up one of her own books and rereads a favorite passage, it all seems dead. René tells of meeting Alain and of Alain's odd idea that M. Guimiez had in some way offended her. As a matter of fact, he had.

> She had suddenly felt herself exposed, blushing, trembling before this gaze from which there poured on to her, covering her, the cold spite, the contempt, of a man who has been pampered, gratified, for many years, with grace, youth and

beauty, the distaste of a fastidious connoisseur for a woman . . . but she didn't look like a woman, she was a shapeless, unnamable something, a frightful monster, hair all disheveled, a few forlorn locks, she was aware of them, hanging down in back. . . . (p. 190)

At that moment she had hated both Pierre and Alain, "the man-cub. . . ." Her expression of disgust reveals all too clearly what her feeling had been, but René reassures her: "That lad is very attached to you. . . ." Eventually, filled with a sense of relief, she answers René, her conversation sharply contradicting the sub-conversation:

"Not at all, what's got into the boy, I didn't think anything at all. I can't say that I found his father exciting . . . but more than anything else, I had no time, I was in a hurry . . . People imagine that you can always be at their beck and call, they're really funny . . ." (p. 191)

Impulsively, she suggests that they all go over at once to visit Alain (still in the old apartment). This is almost too much happiness for Alain; when he first hears her voice on the telephone, he thinks it is an old friend of his, mimicking her, and says, "Who? Germaine Lemaire? . . . Why not the Pope?" To his delight, she at once notices and admires the Louis XV *bergère* about which there had been so much fuss.

Eventually the tenuous threads of the plot converge at their destined end in the last chapter: Germaine comes to visit Alain and Gisèle in Aunt Berthe's old apartment, where they are now comfortably at home. Alain has everything he wanted—the *bergère*, the apartment, the friendship of Germaine Lemaire. But he is not his aunt's nephew for nothing: just as she began to have doubts about her oval door the moment it was installed, so he now begins to have doubts about Germaine Lemaire. Her taste doesn't seem quite impeccable: she approves too easily of the oval door; she would prefer "a good comfortable easy-chair" in front of a certain window instead of the old church bench that he and Gisèle have chosen; she has no doubts about the authenticity of a medieval statuette that he feels may have been clumsily "restored."

> She stares fixedly at the shoulder, the arm, she swallows them stolidly, her strong stomach digests them easily, her eyes maintain the calm indifferent expression of a cow's eyes . . . Surprise, disappointment mingle in him with a sensation of relief . . . something changes place . . . there is a breach, a sudden cleavage . . . he feels that he is out of his element . . . the oval door is floating, uncertain, suspended in limbo . . . massive old convent door or that of a cheap bungalow . . . And the bench? . . . He would like to look away, to pretend that he has seen nothing, that he has not detected this embarrassing thing about her, like a ridiculous defect, a secret infirmity . . . (p. 290)

These doubts had been implanted in him during a scene in the previous chapter: Adrien Lebat, a former classmate—whom Alain greatly admires for his brains, his integrity, his hard work, his indifference to fame—had spoken slightingly of Germaine, especially of her vanity. Alain had fortunately been able to dismiss these charges against his idol when Lebat suddenly revealed a very human streak of vanity himself. But now Germaine begins to speak of her immense admiration for Lebat and arouses Alain's jealousy. He tells her of the chink in Lebat's armor:

> "I had spoken to him of an article that had appeared about him . . . he had hardly listened, of course, he had an air of complete detachment, and I was like you . . . quite . . . quite . . . awe-struck . . . Then, afterwards—we had already left each other—he ran to catch up with me, all out of breath: 'Hey, there, Guimiez, about that article, tell me, who wrote it? what's the date?' "
> She doesn't move. She plunges a hard gaze deep into his eyes: "Oh, that, really . . ." Everything in him, everything about him is coming apart . . . "You're very severe . . . I think we're all of us, really, a bit like that." (pp. 295–6; I have supplied some missing quotation marks)

Again we have an ambiguous ending which leaves us uncertain about virtually everything and especially about the worth, whether moral or artistic, of Alain Guimiez and Germaine Lemaire. Once more, too, this ambiguity is comic—perhaps even more so than before. The greatest gift of the humorist is the capacity to laugh at himself: I keep wondering to what extent Germaine Lemaire is intended as a mocking self-portrait of Nathalie Sarraute.

Les Fruits d'or (Paris, 1963) was the first of Nathalie Sarraute's books to receive official recognition from the literary world, being awarded the Prix International de Littérature for 1964, in which year it was also published in New York as *The Golden Fruits*. A writer rarely attains international recognition until his or her best work has been completed for some time: *The Planetarium* will seem to many readers more deserving of an award than *The Golden Fruits*, but undoubtedly the latter is Madame Sarraute's most original work. It presents a logical stage in the line of development established by her previous novels, yet to reach that stage required an adventurous leap forward by a woman already in her sixties.

In *The Golden Fruits* Madame Sarraute at last achieves the novelistic ideal adumbrated in her critical essays: no characters, no plot. At least there are no *human* characters, but it would be possible to argue that the imaginary novel "The Golden Fruits" by Bréhier is the central "character" of Madame Sarraute's book and that the plot—or at any rate the story—concerns the rise, triumph, and fall of Bréhier's novel.

Although there are no human characters in *The Golden Fruits*, there are human beings, most of whom have either a first or a last name and sometimes both. But each of them appears only for a page or a few pages, says his say or feels his mute feelings about the imaginary novel, and drops out of sight for good. In the title essay of *The Age of Suspicion*, Madame Sarraute complained about a bad habit possessed by "even the most experienced reader":

> Like Pavlov's dog, in whom the tinkle of a bell stimulates the
> secretion of saliva, he creates characters at the slightest pos-
> sible suggestion. As in the game of "statues," each one he
> touches turns to stone. They merely serve to swell in his

memory the vast collection of inanimate figures to which, day in, day out, he is constantly adding and which, since he first learned to read, has been regularly growing as a result of the countless novels he has absorbed. (pp. 67–8)

Even the most keen-eared and ravenous among my fellow dogs are not going to catch more than the faintest tinkle from this novel. One of us might well wonder whether the Jean-Pierre who is so late about climbing on the band wagon (New York edition, p. 102) is not the same Jean-Pierre who belittles Bréhier as a person when the hue and cry against the latter's book has finally begun (p. 157). It might be appropriate if he were, but the name Jean-Pierre is so common in France that one cannot be sure.

Besides the common first names that pepper the book, there are a number of uncommon last names—usually assigned to critics or novelists—that may well have been chosen with a certain malice. They seem like the names one finds in satiric works, and there are certain passages in *The Golden Fruits* which cross the boundary between stylized realism and carica-ture, between comedy of manners and satire.

I may have become too suspicious myself in this "age of suspicion," but out of the twenty fictional last names in the book, at least the following ten are disturbing: Bréhier sounds very much like *brayer*, "truss"; Bernier could be from *berner*, "to hoax"; the Spanish-looking Ramon could come from *ramoner*, "to sweep chimneys"; Brulé is pronounced exactly like *brûlé*, "burnt"; Legris suggests *le gris*, "the gray"; Orthil is presumably pronounced like *ortie*, "nettle"; Pithuit suggests *pituite*, "mucus"; Boully looks like *bouillie*, "pap, baby food"; Mettetal suggests English "metal" rather than French *métal*, but Madame Sarraute studied for a year at Oxford; finally, the English-speaking reader will know what to think of a critic named Parrot, though the French name for the bird is *perro-quet*.

A further question naturally arises: is this book a *roman à clef*—do most of the critics and novelists mentioned have recognizable living counterparts? So far as I know, no French critic has suggested the possibility. Indeed, the accepted view

of Nathalie Sarraute as an ultra-serious writer seems to preclude the mere asking of such a question. Again, I am suspicious. I have already used the word "caricature": in one
passage in particular I see a lampoon either on two living
critics or on two imagined exponents of recent trends in
French "highbrow" criticism. Other critics and the salon amateurs in the book employ the traditional vocabulary of literary
appreciation in France, but this pair engage in a dialogue
that seems well rehearsed, using the vocabulary of the new
"structural criticism":

> "This book, I believe, establishes in literature a privileged
> language which succeeds in investing [à cerner] a corre-
> spondence that is its own structure. It is a very new and very
> perfect appropriation of rhythmic signs that transcend by
> their tension the inessential in all semantics. The inessential
> character that you, my dear friend, have described so well."
> The other, opposite him, writhes briefly, as though traversed
> by a sudden, short gust of wind, then immediately becomes
> calm and bows his head slowly: "Yes. Undoubtedly. We have
> here a takeoff [envol] that abolishes the invisible by blending
> it with the ambiguity of what is signified."
> —We agree absolutely. Thus, an a-temporal dimension is
> dissolved here in the becoming of a thematic. Because of this
> fact, this work, down to its most structured strata, is a poem.
> —I would go even farther. In my opinion, it is by appre-
> hending the inexpressed simultaneously, in different modes,
> that this book avoids the petrification of what is structured.
> In this way, it deploys—and how magnificently!—gratifying,
> literally, our every exigence. (p. 73)

I have indicated two places where I am dubious about
Madame Maria Jolas's translation, but in either French or
English the meaning of this duet must be opaque, except
possibly to convinced "structuralists." Now that existentialism
has gone out of fashion, structuralism is the all-purpose password in French intellectual circles.

The response of the uninitiated seekers of enlightenment to
this duet is hilariously rendered by Madame Sarraute:

> Those who, during a brief moment, had entertained a hope of settling in the smiling lands they had glimpsed, resume their trek, dreary captive band dragging their chains, banished to heaven knows what marshy vastnesses, what endless stretches of icy tundras. (pp. 73–4)

Entertaining in a different way is the discomfiture of the unfortunately named Parrot. It marks the beginning of the end of the vogue for Bréhier's novel. Parrot has been inveigled into a trap by his interlocutor's flattery: ". . . Brulé told me: do read Parrot's article. It's really excellent. You'll be convinced" (p. 121). And the speaker has read the article and in general he *is* convinced, so he says, but the article lacked examples. Luckily he has a copy of the novel with him; will Parrot point out "Just one passage . . . so I can tell . . . a few lines chosen by you, to show me . . ."? (p. 122). Parrot hasn't the heart to refuse this innocent inquirer after knowledge. "Everything about The Golden Fruits is excellent . . . just any part . . ." (p. 124). But somehow, as he turns over the pages, the silent expectancy of his audience

> . . . drains all the sap from the words he is reading, pumps off their blood, they are empty . . . little withered things . . . (p. 125)

Eventually, after turning a number of pages without seeing anything that looks right, he reads aloud more or less at random. Even he feels that the words are falling flat; at the end, dead silence from the audience would have been preferable to the polite murmurs of "It's very fine." He answers apologetically:

> "No, I think that is an overstatement. At the very most, this passage is pretty well done. One reading, like that, a bit haphazardly, can never be very effective. And after all, I may be wrong . . ." (p. 128)

There is a certain traditional narrative continuity linking the first three chapters—unnumbered as usual. In the first, a woman is scolding a man for handing her a Courbet repro-

duction without even looking at it; he must have mortally
offended the man who had produced it from his pocket after
extolling the beauties of the original. The scolded man finally
retorts that she wasn't very tactful herself when, to soothe
the Courbet fancier, she asked what he thought of "The
Golden Fruits."

> It was a scream to see his icy look when he said that, with
> that forced manner: "Yes. Certainly. It's very good." What did
> you expect? Isn't it the latest rage? Didn't Bernier write an
> article? Didn't Ramon? What else could he say?
>   —Oh, it's not that . . . You can't understand . . . I had
> hoped that there would be a discussion . . . I couldn't bear
> for all the bridges to be down . . . (p. 16)

This expresses vividly the social value of aesthetic "crazes"
for Courbet or for a book like "The Golden Fruits." They
establish an "in group," satisfy the need for "a sense of belonging." Nathalie Sarraute would have made a fine social
psychologist had she not become a novelist.

In the second chapter, the disgruntled Courbet fancier
visits a critic friend of his to complain about the philistinism
of many of the people he feels obliged to meet socially. The
rejection of Courbet does not rankle as much as the hypocritical offering of "The Golden Fruits." On this point the
critic—probably Brulé—reassures him. Why, he himself is at
work on an article about the book. It's "superb" (p. 29). The
visitor has his doubts, looks at the copy on his friend's desk,
becomes convinced. In the third chapter the critic sits down
to continue his article and starts to pile on the praise with a
trowel. We begin to suspect that Nathalie Sarraute herself
does not intend us to like Bréhier's novel when we see some
of the things the critic thinks and says about it. He delights in
"this written language that . . . hardens what should endure."
Madame Sarraute prefers spoken French to written French as
a literary medium and associates hardness with artistic death.

The critic becomes more and more exalted with his own
appreciation of the book:

"Superb . . ." Higher . . . "A pure work of art . . ." Higher . . .
"Nothing comparable in our literature . . ." Higher, higher
still . . . "The best thing that has been written . . ." still higher,
the tall branches brush the sky . . . "The best thing that has
been written since Stendhal . . . Since Benjamin Constant . . ."
(p. 37)

Now we *know* what we're supposed to think. Madame Sarraute
complained in "What Birds See" that "if a novel is written in a
style that recalls the classics," critics usually make compari-
sons between it and Benjamin Constant's *Adolphe* or Madame
de La Fayette's *La Princesse de Clèves*, regardless of the
poverty of the subject matter covered by this stylistic *pastiche*.
The long fourth chapter takes place at a big social gathering.
The discussion of "The Golden Fruits" begins with a reference
to Brulé's article on it: "Absolutely first class. Perfect." It is
clear that literary traditionalists predominate in the group;
everybody must come into line behind Bréhier's novel:

Real values are triumphant. Decent people can breathe freely.
No doubt about it, we had a close call. Yelping hordes had
invaded everything, ignorant plebeians, overrunning everything, slashed sacred images, profaned holy places. Just any
barbarian, sprung up from heaven knows where, held forth
with the most insane declarations. People had borne it all in
silence. Day after day, they had been obliged to watch their
closest friends go over basely to the side of those in power.
Stench and sweat. Low guttural speech. Scurrilous language.
We were obliged to put up with all that. To observe, power-
less, all the debaucheries, festerings, swarmings, amorphous
magmas, somber muddles, nights traversed by sinister lights.
And suddenly, this miracle. This little thing with its modest,
tame appearance. The Maid in her shepherdess robe. All at
once, the forces of evil are swept away. Order reigns at last.
(pp. 38–9)

Nathalie Sarraute must have taken ironic pleasure in writing
this, which includes some oblique denunciation of herself and
the other New Novelists; a similar passage denouncing "pro-
fundities" and "obscure processes" will be found on pp. 48–9.
The comparison of the book to St. Joan is delightful.

As this long chapter goes on, we are thrown a name here and there to which a speech can be attached, but more and more the participants become anonymous. The two super-critics already quoted do not have one name between them. The man and the woman who at the end of the evening re-main the only skeptics are not clearly identifiable either.

There follow two brief chapters devoted to individual critics: Orthil, painter and poet, clowns his way through a self-contradictory panegyric of "The Golden Fruits"; then Mettetal announces that he "was struck by Bréhier's great talent at the very beginning . . ." only to be reminded by one of his hearers that in fact his review of Bréhier's first book was unkind—but she in turn is silenced by Mettetal's eager listeners.

In the next short chapter the novel has achieved its apothe-osis: it is all things to all men:

> What humor . . . Savage humor. Grim. Grim and ingenuous. A sort of innocence. Clear. Dark. Biting. Confident. Smiling. Human. Pitiless. Dry. Moist. Icy. Burning. It transports me into an unreal world. It's the realm of dreams. It's the realest of all worlds. The Golden Fruits is all that. (p. 99)

The book marks an epoch:

> "There will be those who came before and those who came after The Golden Fruits. And we'll be those who came after." (p. 103)

As usual, having brought her novel to its crisis, Madame Sarraute lingers for a superfluous chapter or two before moving to the inevitable conclusion. The Parrot chapter al-ready quoted justifies its inclusion, but two other chapters read like critical essays by the author herself, turned into dialogue form. One of these demolishes the argument "that that banal, platitudinous side you speak of, is precisely what Bréhier was after, he did it on purpose" (p. 107). The demoli-tion applies not only to this particular book and author but to all uses of the "done on purpose" argument. The two dis-putants in this chapter later get into another argument, about the merits of a poet named Varanger. Madame Sarraute here permits herself a wild parody, two lines by this alleged poet. The first is *Furtive silexes of lingering day sealing the amphorae of sky*, and the other, *And fire and azure flay my night* (p. 118). Comment on these ought to be unnecessary. Another, briefer chapter discusses "certain extraordinary changes of attitude . . . like collective hallucinations," such as the one provoked by "The Golden Fruits" (p. 130).

After this point the didactic note disappears again, and in the final four chapters Bréhier's novel plunges rapidly to oblivion—whether permanent or not, nobody knows. First comes the triumph of the "hold-outs," Jacques and his doting wife, who had refused to succumb to "The Golden Fruits" and now feel the euphoria of those who have survived a reign of terror. Jacques, she tells her listeners, duped a critic by producing, in a few minutes at his typewriter, a page that he claimed Bréhier had omitted from "The Golden Fruits." Her friends want to know what that proves, and she embarrasses Jacques by suggesting that it proves he is a better writer than Bréhier.

In the next chapter the defeat of Bréhier becomes a rout; only one man present still defends "The Golden Fruits." The supposedly irrefutable answer to him is: "It's easy to see that you don't know Bréhier." The author as well as the book is now fair game. In the second-last chapter Bréhier has to defend himself, without success, against his critics' charges of plagiarism.

In the last chapter we meet the one person who still cares for the book, who still believes that in time it will come back into favor. The reader, of course, has no assurance that this one man may not be right. Madame Sarraute has rather stacked the cards against "The Golden Fruits," but she has taken care not to rob this book of all the ambiguity that gave piquancy to its predecessors. The last word, however, is left with the triumphant horde: "*Vous en êtes encore . . . aux Fruits d'Or?*" I would translate this as "You still haven't gotten over . . . The Golden Fruits?"

Before leaving this novel, I should like to emphasize the

constant presence and subtle variety of the sub-conversation, especially in the long fourth chapter: the sufferings of the successful novelist Robert Hunier, for instance, as his treacherous followers defect to the new leader, Bréhier. More interesting still, in its mingling of literary criticism and novelistic cliché with "real" life, is the reaction of a young wife to the discussion. Someone has been praising a scene in "The Golden Fruits"—clearly of the utmost banality—in which Gilbert rises without a word and goes to fetch Estelle's scarf:

> . . . in a few words, everything is told . . . We witness the dawn of love . . . (p. 50)

Suddenly, in her mind's eye, one listener sees again something that had failed to arouse her suspicions when it occurred:

> The movement of the arm that spreads out the folded coat across the back of the car, across the folds of the lowered hood [top of a convertible], behind the thin shoulders, which are heaving . . . the head leans back, the nape drops onto the soft folds . . . tenderness, silent acquiescence distend this movement, it vibrates, carrier of vows, of secret pacts, covertly concluded between them, in her presence, before her very eyes . . . (p. 52)

Suddenly she, "so timid, always so silent," has lost her head; not only has she intervened in the discussion but she is shouting:

> "It's false. I tell you it is. More than false. That's what's meant by the false truth of novels. That gesture of putting a scarf about the shoulders of a woman who feels cold can mean any number of things . . . or nothing. Mere courtesy, and nothing more . . . Take Pierre, my husband, why, it's a thing he does quite naturally, for just anybody. . . ." (pp. 52–3)

The implications of Madame Sarraute's little scene are subtle indeed: in the first place, the young woman is saying exactly the opposite of what, in her heart of hearts, she now believes. In the second place, there can be some truth to life even in so specious and artificial a novel as Bréhier's. In the third place—and don't let us suppose that Nathalie Sarraute has forgotten the fact for a moment—the apparently real-life reaction of the young wife to a fictional scene itself occurs within a work of fiction, more authentic perhaps than Bréhier's but still open to the gravest suspicion.

Entre la vie et la mort, Madame Sarraute's latest novel, was published by Gallimard in 1968 and appeared in New York the next year as *Between Life and Death*. In 1967 Madame Sarraute had published with Gallimard a volume containing two one-act plays, *Le Silence* ("Silence") and *Le Mensonge* ("The Lie"), neither of which has been translated into English. Both were originally written for broadcasting. The first had its radio première in German translation in 1964; the second made its debut simultaneously on French, Belgian, and German television in 1966. Both were staged for the first time under the direction of Jean-Louis Barrault in 1967.

Looking back at *The Golden Fruits* from the vantage point of *Between Life and Death*, we see that a major theme of the former novel was salvation through literature: everyone in it except Bréhier was seeking that modern savior, a truly great writer. To read his work in the proper spirit would be a sacramental act, a means of attaining grace (in the theological sense). But in order to be saved, the would-be "faithful" must learn to distinguish between the true messiah and the impostors; as we have seen, their task is by no means easy. That the messiah happens to be a false one need not prevent the temporary establishment of a "church militant" among his followers or the persecution of those "heretics" who refuse to believe in him. Bréhier, the false messiah, escapes crucifixion in the literal sense, but his ego undergoes a thorough scourging and humiliation before his erstwhile followers consent to forget him.

What is it like to become one of these temporary messiahs? Since we are never permitted to see inside the mind of Bréhier, *The Golden Fruits* fails to answer this question, but *Between Life and Death* concerns itself with very little else. In it we share the viewpoint of the unnamed author of an unnamed book, catching glimpses of his childhood, the writing

of the book, its acceptance by a publisher, its reception by
the literary world, and the adulation of the author by at least
some of his readers. We do not experience his downfall; while
his first book is still a success, he embarks upon a second, and
Nathalie Sarraute leaves him at that point.

In the opening chapter the protagonist is still one of the
worshipping many—the consumers not only of literature but
of its by-products—listening to an author who has already
"arrived" bewail the sufferings of authorship, which he proudly
wears like stigmata: "I tear out the page. . . . I throw it away.
I take another sheet. I write. . . . I reread. . . ." Before the
novel is over, the protagonist in turn will be exposing his
wounds to an admiring audience, using practically identical
words. But he must undergo some ordeals first, and we find
him in the second chapter being put in his place by a woman
writer who shows him sympathy but makes it quite clear that
he is not yet "one of those who tear out, crumple and throw
away. . . ."

In the third chapter the protagonist's memory brings us
back to his childhood; he is traveling in a train with his mother
and, instead of watching the scenery, he is murmuring to himself a series of words of similar sound. The chapter begins thus:

> *Hérault, héraut, héros, aire haut, erre haut, R. O.*, in rhythm
> with the sound of the wheels, rolling across the flat white
> plains. (New York ed., p. 16)

These words evoke images "from his collection." Hérault, the
name of a "department" (one of the territorial divisions of
France), conjures up its shape and color on a familiar map.
Héraut ("herald") and *héros* ("hero") are traditionally evocative. *Aire* is a word of many meanings, but in combination
with *haut* ("high") the obvious reference is to an eagle's
eyrie. *Erre haut* ("wanders high") suggests a monk walking on
a mountain top. The letter "R" in French is pronounced
rather as a Scotsman would pronounce the name of the town
of Ayr, but the future writer sees an image suggested by its
shape:

R, on its wide-spread bulldog paws, is waiting. O, we've come
full circle. Everything closes and we start over again . . .
Hérault. . . . (p. 17)

When his mother asks him what he is saying to himself, he
at first replies, "It's just words." But she is not deceived and
begins to recite her equivalent of the *Magnificat*:

Just words . . . that that should happen to her . . . All the
hope, all the premonitions while she was carrying him, the
foreknowledge, the pride when they showed him to her, when
they laid him in her arms . . . It had seemed insanity . . .
But who was it who said that madmen always win? There
was not the slightest reason to believe that she, of all women,
would one day receive a visitation. (pp. 23–4)

Up to this point we can accept her thoughts with a certain
solemnity, in spite of patronizing reflections to the effect that
every mother of a first-born son must have such premonitions.
But Nathalie Sarraute's irony breaks loose, and the mother's
thoughts continue as follows:

There had been of course, in the family, a great-uncle who
played the violin, a grandmother who had kept a diary during
a trip to India . . . extracts of which had been published in
La Gazette du Poitou . . . But from that to thinking . . . That
was lunacy. And now it's happened . . . is it possible? . . .
Just words . . . (p. 24)

The reference to the provincial newspaper reduces the whole
passage to caricature. While the tone of *Between Life and
Death* as a whole is less satirical than that of *The Golden
Fruits*, it juggles the sacred and the profane together more
daringly.

In case we should miss the implication of "Just words," the
chapter ends with someone offering to the delighted mother
this resounding cliché,

". . . a poet, this has been said before and it's true, is the man
who knows how to make a poem out of words." (p. 26)

Still, now that the protagonist is an adult, he does not
share his mother's confidence in his predestined mission, and

for the next four chapters his uncertainties are explored. He shows a not entirely attractive talent for mimicry, a gift that in *Portrait* Madame Sarraute already associated with the potential novelist. Finally, stung by the remark, "But why don't you write? All you do is talk about it," he sets to work.

The eighth chapter, a longish one, attempts to convey in the abstract what it is like to write fiction. There are no direct quotations or specific clues to the content—just a series of emotions, conveyed to us in a series of images such as the following:

> From the soft substance with the insipid smell there trickled a sort of vapor, steam . . . it is condensing . . . the little drops of words mount in a thin jet, they shove one another, then fall down again. Others mount, and others still . . . (p. 63)

The whole passage, with its astonishing repertoire of metaphors for the workings of inspiration, needs to be read very carefully, for it cannot be summarized. All irony has disappeared from Madame Sarraute's tone. Eventually the protagonist "must become two persons. One-half of me becomes detached from the other: a witness. A judge . . ." (p. 68). The dialogue between creator and critic begins within him, the latter being very plain-spoken indeed: "But between ourselves two words suffice. As coarse as these two: it's dead. It's alive" (p. 69). This remark at least partially explains the rather ominous title, *Between Life and Death.*

After this moving chapter, which contains only an occasional glint of irony, we find ourselves back in the comic everyday world again, enduring with the protagonist the normal "whips and scorns" of submitting a book to a publisher, getting it accepted after some revision, and then getting oneself accepted as "one of us." There is the anxious time during which it seems that everyone is deliberately ignoring the book or refraining from mentioning it because they have nothing good to say. Eventually, the approving remarks begin. Then along comes the first professional critic, finding things in the book that the author had no idea were there: "Symbolism. Surrealism. Impressionism. Close-ups. Pan-shots. Structure.

Spiral. Rotation movement" (p. 99). The critic treats it as if he were a magician and it were a top hat. Eventually he produces a scene that the author, chagrined, quite definitely knows isn't there. But the critic retrieves himself ingeniously.

More trying in the long run than the professional readers are the amateurs, especially the numerous friends of the author who see themselves or their friends in the book. Still more knowing friends see the author himself there: "Your entire childhood. I saw it . . . camouflaged, of course, but there it is, it's about that, don't deny it . . ." (p. 110).

Hardest of all to cope with are stern Father and adoring Mother. Father's opening gambit is: "How much did they take to publish that?" (p. 115). Brutal but frank, it is easier to overcome than the more subtle sneers that follow. Mother, on the other hand, has "always *known*." Yet she worries that the book will not be properly appreciated by others. Also, her loyal certainty, impervious to evidence, does not gratify her son as much as a more reasoned and reasonable admiration would have; even if the book "stank," she would still love it, he fears.

And now total strangers come to visit the Master, seeking a charismatic experience. At first they wonder if they have not followed a false messiah yet again:

> One wonders in the face of such conformity, such banality, even of behavior, in his haircut, his clothes, if they haven't made a mistake, if they are really going to be the first to have entered where, later, people will stand in line to get in. . . . (pp. 134–5)

But eventually these first pilgrims to the shrine are cheered by something, he is not quite sure what. Later he learns from a mutual friend that they were convinced by his way of making tea. They insisted that he used a samovar, although he does not own one: ". . . they sensed that there was a ritual they would have to submit to . . . You made it in their presence . . ." (p. 133). I do not wish to stress the savior analogy unduly, but this episode has overtones of a communion rite, of a Last Supper, however ironically presented.

Soon there comes the scene that reproduces the one in the first chapter—only this time with our protagonist in the leading role. He feels that he is indeed enacting a role, that his own will counts for nothing:

> His arm stretches out, folds, his head is swaying from side to side . . . he doesn't know very well what is happening to him . . . it's not he, he is not capable of it, who is making these movements all alone.
> It's those people, gathered together around him, who are forcing him to make them. . . . (p. 145)

Very soon he finds himself saying,

> "Well . . . I don't know . . . his voice is unsure, still a bit hoarse, it could be the voice of someone else . . . It's very hard for me . . . I keep starting over again . . . He folds his arm . . . He clenches his fist . . . I tear it out . . . He stretches his arm . . . I take another sheet. . . ." (p. 145)

Once again we see exemplified the Sarraute doctrine of the undifferentiated unity of human nature, as expounded in the essay "The Age of Suspicion." In fact, the whole novel preaches it. Every man or woman whose environment makes it possible for him or her to become a moderately successful novelist will have the same experiences and play the same roles. The very anonymity of the protagonist in *Between Life and Death* enables us to identify with him and assures us that we would be he under the same circumstances.

Eventually he becomes intoxicated with his power over the "faithful" and cries out in truly messianic manner, "The dead shall rise again!" It doesn't matter what he says:

> Everything that comes from me, in any form, everything must be taken. Who turns away? Who refuses? You can either take it or leave it. And who would dare leave it? Who here would have the courage to take the risk?
> Nobody. They've been brought to heel. Trained. (p. 150)

And why not? What is the writer, the creative artist, in the secular religion of today? Or rather, what is he not?

> Countless titles uphold his power. He is a magus. A wise
> man. A prophet. A sphinx. A sorcerer. A dowser. A natural
> force. A prism. A catalyzer. A conductor traversed by the
> strongest, the weakest currents. He is the precious vessel in
> which, from time immemorial, the great myths have come
> down to us. He is the founder of an order. The creator who
> only complies with his own laws. (pp. 150–1)

He seems to be not only God the Son, the "precious vessel,"
but also God the Father, the Creator. But all this is a pose
that he strikes for the faithful, the consumers, the non-writers.
Let him become conscious of the presence of a fellow writer,
especially one of less recent vintage than himself, and his
seeming megalomania shrivels. He still feels very insecure on
the other side of the curtain veiling the Holy of Holies, not at
all at ease in Zion.

Eventually there comes the anguished moment, long post-
poned, when he must start writing again. The whole last
chapter is devoted to this experience, treated with the same
seriousness as the writing of his first book in the eighth
chapter. Things do not go well at first; the creative and critical
selves bicker about the value of what has been written. Is it
alive or dead? Alive, somewhere:

> Follow it wherever it will . . . It, the unnameable . . . what
> I feel . . . I alone . . . this untouched, living thing . . . I don't
> know what it is. All I know is that nothing in the world can
> make me doubt its presence. (pp. 181–2)

And so we reach the concluding words of *Between Life and
Death*, in which the critical self is called on to bear witness
that life is not yet extinct:

> . . . you my double, my witness . . . there, lean over with
> me . . . let's look together . . . does it emit, deposit . . . as
> on the mirror we hold before the mouth of the dying . . . a
> fine mist? (p. 183)

One feels, here as elsewhere, that the true function of the
writer/savior is not so much to create life as to raise Lazarus
from the dead.

In following the development of Nathalie Sarraute as a novelist, we have seen her begin with an ambition to rival Dostoevsky in his exploration of the obscure depths of human motivation. Then, as she gained mastery of her craft, her feminine humor and acute observation of the surface of upper-middle-class life seemed to be taking her out of the Dostoevskian depths into that well-lit drawing room where Jane Austen presides over the comedy of manners. But in her latest book, even as her humor and irony play over the contradictions and absurdities of the literary life, we see her filling her lungs and readying herself for the plunge. Suddenly, she is down below with Dostoevsky again, searching in the murky depths for those authentic yet unidentifiable impulses toward truth that redeem, even when they cannot excuse, all the petty vanities of the creative writer.

4

Alain Robbe-Grillet

DESCRIPTION AND NARRATION

In *Jealousy* (New York, 1959), we find the following description of a presumably imaginary song sung by a "native" driver:

> Because of the peculiar nature of this kind of melody, it is difficult to determine if the song is interrupted for some fortuitous reason . . . or whether the tune has come to its natural conclusion.
>
> Similarly, when it begins again, it is just as sudden, as abrupt, starting on notes which hardly seem to constitute a beginning, or a reprise.
>
> At other places, however, something seems about to end; everything indicates this: a gradual cadence, tranquillity regained, the feeling that nothing remains to be said; but after the note which should be the last comes another one, without the least break in continuity, with the same ease, then another, and others following, and the hearer supposes himself transported into the heart of the poem . . . when at that point everything stops without warning.
>
> . . . the song resumes, from the direction of the sheds.
>
> It is doubtless the same poem continuing. If the themes sometimes blur, they only recur somewhat later, all the more clearly, virtually identical. Yet these repetitions, these tiny variations, halts, regressions, can give rise to modifications—

though barely perceptible—eventually moving quite far from the point of departure. (J, pp. 66–7; TN, pp. 83–4)[1]

Almost all this description could be applied to the novel by Alain Robbe-Grillet in which it occurs. *Jealousy* (published in French as *La Jalousie* in 1957) gives an extraordinary impression of arbitrariness to the unprepared reader at first encounter, yet it is probably, on further acquaintance, the author's most appealing book for general reader and critic alike. At any rate, it is undoubtedly the classic example to date of Robbe-Grillet's characteristic narrative technique. His two earlier novels, *The Erasers* and *The Voyeur*, show that technique in process of development; his two later novels, *In the Labyrinth* and *La Maison de Rendez-vous*, largely adhere to the technique already developed in *Jealousy*, while adding some refinements.

Although the description of the song vividly suggests the baffling complexity of the structure of *Jealousy*, it gives no notion of the strangeness of the book's texture. In his previous novel, *The Voyeur*, Robbe-Grillet had laid great stress on what his protagonist Mathias sees, but the reader was also allowed to know some part at least of what the character thinks and a little of what he feels. In *Jealousy*, however, we are confined almost entirely to what the protagonist sees. True, his observations are put into words, and the choice of words will sometimes hint at his attitude toward what he sees, but he never comments directly on it. Not only do we never learn his name, but he never even refers to himself as "I." Both the title of the book and his constant preoccupation with

[1] Key to abbreviations:

E:	*The Erasers* (New York, 1964)
FNN:	*For a New Novel* (New York, 1965)
IL:	*In the Labyrinth* (New York, 1960)
J:	*Jealousy* (New York, 1959)
LYM:	*Last Year at Marienbad* (New York, 1962)
MR:	*La Maison de Rendez-vous* (New York, 1966)
TN:	*Two Novels by Robbe-Grillet: Jealousy & In the Labyrinth* (New York, 1965)
V:	*The Voyeur* (New York, 1958)

All the above were translated by Richard Howard and published by Grove Press.

the behavior of a woman named A... and a man named Franck—who lives with his wife, Christiane, on a neighboring banana plantation—suggest that the observer is the jealous husband of A.... The observer, needless to say, knows who he is and what his relationship is to A... and Franck: consequently, he doesn't have to tell himself these things. If we want to know what goes on behind his eyes, we have to construct it, imagine it, for ourselves. In the process, we may come gradually to identify ourselves with him, in a more intimate way than we are accustomed to identify with much more appealing fictional heroes.

In applying the verb "to see" to the protagonists of both *The Voyeur* and *Jealousy*, one becomes guilty of ambiguity. Both these characters, like all of us, see not only what is objectively present to the open eye but what memory, dream, imagination, or even hallucination present to the "mind's eye." To that extent, we are allowed to penetrate the mind of the jealous husband, but we can never be entirely sure just which scenes are observed by his outer eye and which by the inner eye, since both types of vision are treated as identical. Furthermore, everything that either "eye" sees is described in the present tense, so that we cannot distinguish what is happening "now" from what is being remembered from the past or anticipated in the future.

In effect, Robbe-Grillet is transferring to the novel a technique that is more appropriate to the cinema. In the Introduction to *Last Year at Marienbad* (New York, 1962), he points out that "on the screen verbs are always in the present tense. . . ." He then discusses the consequences of this fact in detail: nobody in a movie audience, for example, feels at all disoriented by a flashback, even when he sees supposedly past events happening "now" before his eyes.

> Having granted memory, the spectator can also readily grant the imaginary, nor do we hear protests, even in neighborhood movie theaters, against those courtroom scenes in a detective story when we *see* a hypothesis concerning the circumstances of a crime, a hypothesis that can just as well be false as true, made mentally or verbally by the examining

magistrate; and we then see, in the same way, during the
testimony of various witnesses, some of whom are lying, other
fragments of scenes that are more or less contradictory, more
or less likely, but which are all presented with the same kind
of image, the same realism, the same presentness, the same
objectivity. And this is equally true if we are shown a scene
in the future imagined by one of the characters, etc. (LYM,
p. 13)

All the justification needed for the adaptation of this cinematic technique to the novel is supplied in the next paragraph
of the Introduction.

> What are these images, actually? They are imaginings; an
> imagining, if it is vivid enough, is always in the present. The
> memories one "sees again," the remote places, the future
> meetings, or even the episodes of the past we each mentally
> rearrange to suit our convenience are something like an interior
> film continually projected in our own minds, as soon as we
> stop paying attention to what is happening around us. But at
> other moments, on the contrary, all our senses are registering
> this exterior world that is certainly there. Hence the total
> cinema of our mind admits both in alternation and to the same
> degree the present fragments of reality proposed by sight and
> hearing, and past fragments, or future fragments, or frag-
> ments that are completely phantasmagoric. (LYM, p. 13)

To speak of an "exterior" world at all, let alone to say that it
"is certainly there," is to make a big philosophical assumption
that fortunately need not be examined closely here. By and
large, Robbe-Grillet takes the common-sense view about the
existence of the external world, but he is forced to admit, as
we shall see, that some of his descriptive and narrative techniques call that existence in question. One such technique is
of course the refusal, so noticeable in *Jealousy*, to make any
overt distinction between the "interior film" and the registering
of the external world. The commercial cinema has certain
conventions for making such distinctions: "a few blurry
seconds, for instance, are enough to warn [the spectator] of a
shift to memory . . ." (LYM, p. 12). In *Last Year at Marienbad*
and in the films he has directed himself, Robbe-Grillet has

employed a variety of techniques to indicate shifts in time, in authenticity, etc. Changes in lighting or in camera speed and the use of still shots are examples. But in *Jealousy* the reader is granted the pleasure—some feel it a chore—of deciding for himself whether a shift has been made or not.

What does the husband/observer see? Naturally, he sees his wife and Franck together often—and not always when they are physically present. He sees his wife alone a great deal too. But most of the time he is looking at objects, at things rather than people. Robbe-Grillet has received a great deal of both praise and blame for this feature of his work, sometimes called *chosisme* ("thingism") and sometimes confused with objectivity. He finds it easy enough to defend this practice against its detractors. In an interview with André Bourin (*Les Nouvelles littéraires*, January 22, 1959), he set forth his defense thus:

> "There aren't only objects in my books, as people so readily repeat. However, objects do play a large part in them, as indeed they do in our daily lives. We live in a world of objects; even where feelings are involved, passion, anguish, there are almost always material objects present to support them. . . . Do you think that fear, at the moment when we live it, is anything other than a material presence to us: a door that opens, a shadow that moves forward . . . ? And is jealousy, anything but the sight of two armchairs too close to one another, or the movement of a hand?" [My translation]

It has not been nearly so easy for Robbe-Grillet to defend himself against those of his admirers who praise him for his objectivity. He took up this point in an essay, "New Novel, New Man," first published in 1961 and reprinted in his *For a New Novel* (New York, 1965). At best, he showed, the term "objectivity" was ambiguous; when applied to his own novels or those of the other New Novelists, it was meaningful only

> . . . in a very special sense: oriented toward the object. Taken in its habitual sense—neutral, cold, impartial—the word became an absurdity. Not only is it *a man* who, in my novels for instance, describes everything, but it is the least neutral, the least impartial of men: *always* engaged, on the contrary, in an

emotional adventure of the most obsessive kind, to the point of often distorting his vision and of producing imaginings close to delirium. (FNN, p. 138)

In *Jealousy* we see the world through the eyes of the jealous husband and are thus at his mercy, in terms not only of the external phenomena that he selectively chooses to observe, but even more of the involuntary mental visions that he cannot choose *not* to see. (Mathias in *The Voyeur*, who has a sadistic obsession with immature girls, is an observer still more riddled by subjectivity.) Yet the husband's observations often are as outwardly dispassionate and "scientific" as the following:

> The space between A . . .'s left hand and Franck's right hand is approximately two inches. (J, p. 16; TN, p. 49)

We have to supply his emotional reaction to this verifiable fact for ourselves, or else assume that he remains unconscious of any such reaction; perhaps his response is visceral only.

In pondering the descriptive passages of *Jealousy*, one tends to recall the more bizarre examples, such as the geometrical and arithmetical description of the banana plantation that surrounds the house. There will be something to say about that particular one later, but let us look at a more conventionally evocative description, that of A . . . brushing her hair.

> The brush descends the length of the loose hair with a faint noise somewhere between the sound of a breath and a crackle. No sooner has it reached the bottom than it quickly rises again toward the head, where the whole surface of its bristles sinks in before gliding down over the black mass again. The brush is a bone-colored oval whose short handle disappears almost entirely in the hand firmly gripping it.
>
> Half of the hair hangs down the back, the other hand pulls the other half over one shoulder. The head leans to the right, offering the hair more readily to the brush. Each time the latter lands at the top of its cycle behind the nape of the neck, the head leans farther to the right and then rises again with an effort, while the right hand, holding the brush, moves away in the opposite direction. The left hand, which loosely confines the hair between the wrist, the palm and the fingers, releases it for a second and then closes on it again, gathering the

strands together with a firm, mechanical gesture, while the brush continues its course to the extreme tips of the hair. (J, pp. 40–1; TN, p. 66)

This quotation, slightly more than half the complete passage, deserves careful reading. The more closely we look at it, the more clearly we see that while the *situation*—a woman brushing her long hair—is indeed "conventionally evocative," the description itself is anything but that. If we did not already know that Robbe-Grillet was an agronomist by profession before he took up writing, we would still feel that the author of this passage must be either a scientist or an engineer. It has all the precision of a time-and-motion study. If one had never watched with emotion while a woman—mother, wife, lover, or actress of stage or screen—brushed her hair, one might well not feel the slightest emotion on reading this description. But its precise account of the movements of the head and hands, which seem hardly to vary at all from woman to woman, brings the archetypal ritual to life before the mind's eye.

Turn now to a description of an inanimate object—a venetian blind. The French word for this is *jalousie*, which also means "jealousy." As a result, the French title of the book, *La Jalousie*, can be translated as either *Jealousy* or *The Venetian Blind*. The possibility has occurred to some critics that the latter translation is the correct one, for the observer often spies on A . . . through the slats of a blind. Perhaps his jealousy exists only in the minds of us, his sentimental readers?

Once the bedroom is empty, there is no reason not to open the blinds [*jalousies*], which fill all three windows instead of glass panes. The three windows are similar, each divided into four equal rectangles, that is, four series of slats, each window-frame comprising two sets hung one on top of another. The twelve series are identical: sixteen slats of wood manipulated by a cord attached at the side to the outer frame.

The sixteen slats of a series are continuously parallel. When the series is closed, they are pressed one against the other at the edge, overlapping by about half an inch. By pulling the

cord down, the pitch of the slats is reduced, thus creating a
series of openings whose width progressively increases.

When the blinds are open to the maximum, the slats are
almost horizontal and show their edges. Then the opposite
slope of the valley appears in successive, superimposed strips
separated by slightly narrower strips. In the opening at eye
level appears a clump of trees. . . . (J, pp. 122–3; TN, pp.
119–20)

This text, like many another descriptive passage in Robbe-
Grillet's works, could serve to illustrate his contention that
his kind of novelistic description and cinematic description
stand at opposite poles.

> . . . when the [novelistic] description comes to an end, we
> realize that it has left nothing behind it: it has instituted a
> double movement of creation and destruction which, moreover,
> we also find in the book on all levels and in particular in its
> total structure—whence the *disappointment* inherent in many
> works of today.
>
> The concern for precision which sometimes borders on the
> delirious (those notions so nonvisual as "right" and "left,"
> those calculations, those measurements, those geometric points
> of reference) does not manage to keep the world from moving
> even in its most material aspects, and even at the heart of its
> apparent immobility. It is no longer a question here of time
> passing, since gestures paradoxically are on the contrary
> shown only frozen in the moment. It is matter itself which is
> both solid and unstable, both present and imagined, alien to
> man and constantly being invented in man's mind. The entire
> interest of the descriptive pages—that is, man's place in these
> pages—is therefore no longer in the thing described, but in
> the very movement of the description. (FNN, p. 148)

The whole essay, "Time and Description in Fiction Today"
(1963), is perhaps the most profound of all Robbe-Grillet's
theoretical writings.

Looking back at the description of the venetian blind, we
can see that it makes us very much aware of how the world
looks when seen through such a blind. In a very short article
with a very long title, *"Notes sur la localisation et les déplace-*

ments du point de vue dans la description romanesque,"[2]
Robbe-Grillet has pointed out the importance of the location
of the observer in his descriptions. He freely acknowledges
the possible influence of the cinema on the New Novelist's
concern with such questions as "Where is this object seen
from? At what angle? From what distance? Under what
illumination? Does the glance rest on it for long or does it
pass on without insisting? Does it move or remain fixed?" The
net effect of this concern is to reject the "perpetually omniscient and omnipresent novelist. It is no longer God who
describes the world, it is man, *a* man. Even if it is not a
character, it is in any case *a man's eye*." At one point in
Jealousy, the husband, outside, watches A... move about her
bedroom; when she halts in certain parts of the room, he
cannot see what she is doing, because she is "masked" by
part of a wall or a piece of furniture.

God is absent from Robbe-Grillet's work not only as omniscient observer but also as immanent presence in nature.
Robbe-Grillet has written an essay on the subject, "Nature,
Humanism, Tragedy," in which he finds even Camus and
Sartre guilty at times of anthropomorphism. "Metaphor," he
writes, ". . . is never an innocent figure of speech" (FNN, p.
53). Alerted by this statement, we come to realize the paucity
of even "dead" metaphors in his own writing. After reading
"Nature, Humanism, Tragedy," we begin to grasp the real
novelty of the notorious description of the banana plantation
in *Jealousy* (J, pp. 18–22; TN, pp. 50–3). The landscape presented there neither sympathizes with man nor influences his
emotions. In spite of being man-made to the extent that it has
been cleared and planted, it remains alien to man. Furthermore, it is impossible to gauge the mood of the observer by
his description, from which the following is a characteristic
excerpt:

> Without bothering with the order in which the actually
> visible banana trees and the cut banana trees occur, the sixth

[2] "Notes on Localization and Shifts of Viewpoint in Novelistic Description," *Revue des lettres modernes*, V (Summer 1958), 256–8. The
passages quoted below from this article are translated by me.

row gives the following numbers: twenty-two, twenty-one, twenty, nineteen—which represent respectively the rectangle, the true trapezoid, the trapezoid with a curved edge, and the same after subtracting the boles cut for the harvest.

And for the following rows: twenty-three, twenty-one, twenty-one, twenty-one. Twenty-two, twenty-one, twenty, twenty. Twenty-three, twenty-one, twenty, nineteen, etc. . . . (J, p. 21; TN, p. 52)

Does the "concern for precision" shown here "border on the delirious," or is the husband merely looking at the new plantings with a neutral, professional eye, or—a third possibility— is he trying to hypnotize himself into a calmer mood by a procedure akin to counting sheep? Each reader will have to decide among these three possibilities on his own. Making such choices constitutes one of the lesser but real pleasures in reading the New Novelists.

"All these pages about description!" the disgruntled reader begins to mutter. "When is this stupid critic going to say anything about narration?" Let us bring M. Robbe-Grillet to the witness stand to answer that question. In the "old" novel, he says,

The reader overly concerned to know the story could even consider himself justified in skipping the descriptions: they involved only a frame, which moreover happened to have a meaning identical to that of the picture it was to contain.

Obviously, when this same reader skips the descriptions in our books, he is in danger of finding himself, having turned all the pages one after the other with a rapid forefinger, at the end of the volume whose contents will have escaped him altogether; imagining he has been dealing hitherto with nothing but the frame, he will still be looking for the picture. (FNN, p. 147)

Of no New Novel will this be more true than of *Jealousy*, which contains virtually no narration, its place being supplied by a montage of descriptions and snatches of conversation. Many of these apparent film sequences or excerpts from a sound track are repeated one or more times in the course of the book, usually with slight variations at each repetition.

These repetitions suggest flashbacks to an earlier period in a time sequence. Another device reminiscent of the cinema is the "dissolve" of one description into another without transition. (An example will be given later.)

Inevitably, the conscientious reader will attempt to construct a chronological sequence for himself: he will use as a measure of time, for instance, the point A... has reached in a novel about Africa that she is reading and discussing with Franck, who apparently has already read it. Or he will date something as occurring before, during, or after the journey that A... and Franck make together to the only town in the unnamed tropical country where the book is set. Unfortunately, Robbe-Grillet himself assures us that

> The narrative was . . . made in such a way that any attempt to reconstruct an external chronology would lead, sooner or later, to a series of contradictions, hence to an impasse. And this not with the stupid intention of disconcerting the Academy, but precisely because there existed for me no possible order outside that of the book. (FNN, p. 154)

Perhaps in compensation for this fluidity and expansiveness of time, there is an extraordinary, almost claustrophobic rigidity and limitation of space. All American editions of Richard Howard's translation that I have seen contain a detailed plan of the house and its surroundings, including the location of many of the pieces of furniture in the house. Such a diagram does not form an integral part of any French edition, so far as I know, but I assume it was the work of Robbe-Grillet himself.

No reader who does not skim or skip need fail to separate from each other the brief scenes, descriptions, and dialogues of which the book consists, or to recognize them when they are repeated. They are like musical themes—to be developed, dropped, given a reprise, at the will of the composer. As far as one can see, the resulting structure is neither completely random nor completely in accordance with a preordained plan. The book is divided into nine unnumbered chapters, each identified by its opening phrase. Unfortunately, neither of the American editions gives the table of contents correctly; each contains a different mistake, the net effect of which is to list eight chapters instead of nine. A correct table of contents in English would read:

> Now the shadow of the column . . .
> Now the shadow of the southwest column . . .
> The brush descends the length . . .
> In the hollow of the valley . . .
> Now the voice of the second driver . . .
> Now the house is empty . . .
> The whole house is empty . . .
> Between the remaining gray paint . . .
> Now the shadow of the column . . .

In this table both symmetry and asymmetry, likeness and difference, are clearly to be seen. The openings of the first and last chapters are identical. Five chapters begin with "Now," two pairs of them being successive chapters; three chapters, two of them successive, begin "Now the shadow . . ."; two successive chapters begin with references to the emptiness of the house. Like the description of the native song with which we began, the table of contents gives us clues to the relative proportions of continuity and discontinuity in the structure of the novel. But the novel differs sharply from the song in one respect: we correctly deduce that the end is coming, not only because the opening of the first chapter is repeated but because in the last chapter we find "tranquillity regained."

Something has been said earlier of the repetition-with-slight-variations which seems a basic device in *Jealousy*. The question now arises: why the variations? Is the author varying the wording to avoid monotony? Most unlikely! Does the variation indicate that an imperfect memory of the original scene is being presented? Very likely. Is life on the banana plantation so monotonous that the characters do the same things day after day with only minimal variations? Equally likely.

At least one of these repetitions with variations, however,

differs so sharply in content from the original scene, yet remains so similar in form, that it constitutes not only a verbal but in some sense a visual pun. The most violent action that occurs in *Jealousy* is the killing of a centipede, a large one, of a species common in the tropics. Franck kills it one evening at dinner to reassure A..., who detests the creatures. The crucial moment is presented thus:

> Franck, who has said nothing, is looking at A... again. Then he stands up, noiselessly, holding his napkin in his hand. He wads it into a ball and approaches the wall. (J, pp. 39–40; TN, p. 65)

He kills the insect, and the moment is given added drama by the fact that the husband has done nothing except make a joke at the expense of A...'s timidity. The killing of this—or perhaps another—centipede recurs more than once. When left alone in the house during the absence of A... and Franck in town, the husband either kills or imagines he is killing a similar insect. A... and Franck had not intended to spend the night in town, or at any rate attributed their being delayed to the breakdown of Franck's car. The husband suspects that they are spending the night together. Once again, as he prowls the empty house, he "sees" Franck kill a centipede:

> Franck, without saying a word, stands up, wads his napkin into a ball as he cautiously approaches, and squashes the creature against the wall. Then, with his foot, he squashes it against the bedroom floor. (J, p. 112; TN, p. 113)

Unfortunately, the verbal pun does not come through in English translation. The word translated "napkin" in both passages quoted is *serviette*, which can mean both "table napkin" and "towel," though in the latter sense it is an abbreviation for *serviette de toilette*. The next paragraph of the bedroom scene reads thus in English:

> Then he comes back toward the bed and in passing hangs the towel [*serviette de toilette*] on its metal rack near the washbowl. (J, p. 112; TN, p. 113)

In the French, therefore, the pun is driven home by this paragraph. Furthermore, in one version of the dinner-table scene A...'s reaction is described thus:

> The hand with tapering fingers has clenched into a fist on the white cloth. (J, p. 64; TN, p. 89)

In the imagined bedroom scene, we read:

> The hand with the tapering fingers has clenched into a fist on the white sheet. (J, p. 113; TN, p. 113)

Here, what I have called a visual pun is more striking than the verbal similarity. In comparing these passages, we begin to grasp the full significance of what is said about the native song in our very first quotation: ". . . these repetitions, these tiny variations, halts, regressions, can give rise to modifications . . . eventually moving quite far from the point of departure."

One more example of these verbal/visual subtleties must suffice: it will illustrate the "dissolving" of one description into another that has already been mentioned. The husband is spying on A... and Franck; after opening and closing the door of the master bedroom as though he had gone in there, he slips into his office, through the venetian blinds of which he can catch a glimpse of them sitting with their drinks on the veranda. On the corner of his desk (not of the "dressing-table," as Howard translates *bureau* here) is a framed photograph of A..., taken at an outdoor café in Europe:

> She has turned slightly to smile at the photographer, as if to authorize him to take this candid shot. Her bare arm, at the same moment, has not changed the gesture it was making to set the glass down on the table beside her.
>
> But it was not to put ice in it, for she does not reach for the ice bucket of shiny metal which is immediately frosted over.
>
> Motionless, she stares at the valley in front of them. She says nothing. Franck, invisible to her left, also says nothing. Perhaps she has heard some abnormal sound behind her and is about to make some movement without discernible preparation, which would permit her to look toward the blind quite by chance. (J, p. 50; TN, p. 72)

Here the scene in the photograph dissolves into that on the veranda almost without transition. The gesture of putting the glass on the table belongs to the photo, but the ice bucket is part of the drinking ritual in the tropics. This device, sparingly used in *Jealousy*, becomes a compulsive mannerism in the two later novels. In *In the Labyrinth*, the etching of the tavern scene entitled "The Defeat of Reichenfels" plays the role of the photograph of A...; in *La Maison de Rendez-vous*, the same function is filled by several illustrations from Chinese magazines.

What exactly *does* happen in *Jealousy*? Well, it depends on what one means by "happen." The devotee of action-filled plots would say that exactly nothing happens. On the other hand, one is forced to conclude that a good deal happens *to* the emotions of the jealous husband, while much else happens *in* his imagination. He really sees only three tiny incidents that might be considered suspect: the moment (or moments?) when the couple's chairs and therefore hands are placed so near each other; one (or two?) occasions when A... has just got out of Franck's car and puts her head back in through the window; an occasion (or two?) when, after he has seen A... write a letter on blue notepaper of a readily available brand, folded sheets of similar blue paper appear in Franck's shirt pocket. What he really hears, or thinks he hears, is equally innocuous or ambiguous: A...'s and Franck's half-intimate chatter about the African novel that he, the husband, has not read; a joke between them about Franck's not being much of a mechanic. This latter appears after the night that Franck and A... had to spend in town. Some of the context is worth quoting to illustrate Robbe-Grillet's skill in devising ambiguous dialogue and in showing its effect on the husband:

> The sentences [of Franck's last speech] followed one another, each in its place, connecting logically. The measured, uniform pace was like that of a witness offering testimony, or a recitation.
> "Even so," A... says, "you thought you could fix it yourself, at first. At least you tried. But you're not much of a mechanic, are you?"

She smiles as she says these last words. They look at each other. He smiles too. Then, slowly, his smile becomes a kind of grimace. She, on the other hand, keeps her look of amused serenity.

Yet Franck can't be unused to makeshift repairs, since his truck is always having engine trouble . . . [This is the gist of what the husband says, obviously, but his remarks are never given in direct speech.]

"Yes," he says, "I'm beginning to know *that* motor pretty well. But the car hasn't given me trouble very often."

As a matter of fact, [the husband again] there has never been another incident with the big blue sedan, which is almost new, moreover.

"There has to be a first time for everything," Franck answers. Then, after a pause: "It was just my unlucky day . . ."
(J, p. 56; TN, p. 76)

Is A. . . twitting Franck with his poor performance in bed, and is Franck's last speech a covert apology? Neither the husband nor the reader will ever know for sure.

Not all of the novel remains on this light-comedy level. The writer of back-cover copy for the first Evergreen paperback edition of *Jealousy* said: "Murder lies at the heart of the story, and the reader, groping towards it as he looks out of the murderer's mind, discovers its obsessive, frightening presence in the haunted plantation house behind the banana trees." One expects him to continue, "Watch for the film version of this palpitating drama at your local drive-in!" While one need not accept the view that the jealous husband becomes a murderer, there are certainly moments when he has murder in his heart—or at least a wish that Franck and perhaps even A. . . might meet with accidental death:

In his haste to reach his goal, Franck increases his speed. . . . In the darkness, he has not seen the hole running halfway across the road. The car makes a leap, skids. . . . On this bad road the driver cannot straighten out in time. The blue sedan is going to crash into a roadside tree whose rigid foliage scarcely shivers under the impact, despite its violence.

The car immediately bursts into flames. The whole brush is illuminated by the crackling, spreading fire. It is the sound the centipede makes, motionless again on the wall, in the center of the panel.

Listening to it more carefully, this sound is more like a breath than a crackling: the brush is now moving down the loosened hair. (J, p. 113; TN, pp. 113–14)

The word "crackling" (*crépitement* in the French) unites the sounds of the fire, the centipede, and the hairbrush. It should be noted, however, that the word "brush" in the English does duty for two similar but not identical French words, *brousse*, meaning "underbrush," and *brosse*, meaning "hairbrush"; a pun may not have been intended here by Robbe-Grillet. The scene of the car wreck seems entirely a product of the husband's imagination.

The sixth and seventh chapters, covering the twenty-four hours that the husband spends alone in the house while A... and Franck are at the port town, contain some of the most evocative writing in twentieth-century French literature. The night scenes in particular, when the house is lit by a single kerosene lamp that the husband carries from empty room to empty room, compel the reader to visualize them with amazing clarity. The descriptions of the insects buzzing round the lamp on the veranda and of the moment when the lamp suddenly goes out in the husband's hand are perhaps the most effective. After the light goes out, the husband feels his way in the dark to a drawer in the bedroom. Out of it he takes *une touffe de soies, ou de crins très fins, qui ressemblent à des cheveux*, for which Howard's "a skein of fine silk threads like hair" (J, p. 117; TN, p. 116) is an inadequate translation. Apparently this is a switch of artificial hair that A... sometimes wears. A little further on, the husband's fingers tease it. Howard renders this as: "Like this shapeless darkness, the silky hair flows between the curving fingers." The French (*Pareille à cette nuit sans contours, la chevelure de soie coule entre les doigts crispés*) could be translated: "Like this boundless night, the hair piece of silk flows between the clenched fingers." The husband fails to return it to the drawer, where A... looks for it vainly at another time. Even though the fingers are clenched or contracted, there seems to be no hostility toward A... in this stroking of the substitute hair, which may continue throughout the hours of darkness.

Apart from the imagined accident, there are perhaps two hints of lethal violence—intended rather than carried out, in any case. One of these occurs in the second-last chapter. A... is in the master bedroom; the husband is watching her from the veranda:

> The room now looks as if it were empty. A... may have noiselessly opened the hall door [i.e., the door from the bedroom into the hallway] and gone out; but it is more likely that she is still there, outside the field of vision, in the blank area between this door, the large wardrobe and the corner of the table. . . . Still, the concealed exit by which it communicates with the hall, the living room, the courtyard, and the highway multiplies to infinity her possibilities of escape. (J, pp. 127–8; TN, p. 123)

Why should she try to escape, unless there is someone it would be wise to run from? In the next paragraph, however, she reappears at a window of the bedroom.

The second hint is even more tenuous: in describing the veranda outside the bedroom window at some unspecified date, the observer notes:

> From one corner of the window, a dark liquid has flowed down over the wood, crossing the boards one after another from ridge to ridge, then the concrete substructure, making an increasingly narrow streak which finally dwindles to a thread and reaches the veranda floor in the middle of a flagstone, ending there in a little round spot. (J, p. 109; TN, p. 111)

In the final chapter, the "dark liquid" is spoken of as "reddish" or "red," suggesting blood. But immediately after two paragraphs of this sinister description of the streak on the wall, we read,

> The spot has always been there, on the wall. For the moment there is no question of repainting anything but the blinds and the balustrade—the latter a bright yellow. That is what A... has decided. (J, p. 144; TN, p. 135)

Is a "spot" the same as a long "streak"? The French word *tache* can be translated "spot," but here I suggest it means "stain" and does refer to the sinister "reddish streak."

Like almost everything else in the final chapter, the paragraph just quoted is reassuring and suggests "tranquillity regained." We have, as always, no sure way of telling where the evening scene of this chapter is to be fitted into the chronological sequence—if any existed! A novel about Africa is being discussed, but in such vague terms that we have no idea whether it is the one previously mentioned or another with a similar African setting. What impresses one about the chapter is the tolerant mood of the observer. When A... sits in the bedroom to write a letter, he seems ready to believe that she is answering one received from Europe. Finally, note the approving tone of this paragraph:

> Franck, at this point, begins to tell an anecdote about a truck of his with engine trouble. A..., as politeness demands, asks for details to prove the attention she is paying to her guest, who soon stands up and takes his leave, in order to return to his own plantation, a little farther east. (J, p. 148; TN, p. 137)

Is this the end of the affair, or is it the beginning, or was there never any affair at all? As Franck says more than once in regard to the African novel, "It's all mental, things like that." In any case, what we have just finished reading is a work of fiction, so that the final, seemingly neutral, words of the book are as false—or as true—as everything else in it:

> It is six-thirty.
> Now the dark night and the deafening racket of the crickets again engulf the garden and the veranda, all around the house.

A reader is entitled to protest that, although he has never confused events in a novel with events in real life, he has always thought of the novel as a prose *narrative*; furthermore, his definition of a narrative requires the presence of a chronological sequence, whether stated or merely implied. As far as he is concerned, *Jealousy* is closer to being a lyric poem or a musical composition than a novel. To which this would be the only possible reply: if one concedes that the movie camera "narrates" in an eternal present tense, then *Jealousy* too is a narrative; if one denies that premise, then *Jealousy* is not a narrative and consequently not a novel, by definition.

Having so minutely examined Robbe-Grillet's method as demonstrated in *Jealousy*, we can deal with his other books more rapidly. It is an extraordinary fact that, given the intensely literary nature of French culture, Alain Robbe-Grillet's education was about as non-literary as a Frenchman's can be. Having taken a degree from the Institut National Agronomique, he worked as a biologist, specializing in the diseases of the banana plant, until 1951, when he was nearly thirty. He practiced his specialty first in Africa, then in the French West Indies, so that his working experience parallels that of the husband/observer in *Jealousy*.[3] It was only a short time before he abandoned his original profession that he began to write, having apparently had no youthful aspirations in that direction at all. Clearly, his lack of early literary ambition and training made it relatively easy for him to let fresh air into the stifling hothouse of the conventional French novel.

Robbe-Grillet began by writing a complete novel, *Un Régicide* ("A Regicide"), that has never been published. He followed this with his first published novel, *Les Gommes* (Paris, 1953), which did not appear in English translation as *The Erasers* until 1964. It was his second novel, *Le Voyeur* (Paris, 1955), translated into English as *The Voyeur* (New York, 1958), that established his reputation with American readers. Robbe-Grillet has mentioned "the reproachful half-silence" that met his first book in France and "the massive and violent rejection meted out by the newspapers" to his second (FNN, p. 7), but the fact remains that he was hailed as the leader of a new literary school, in a very influential article by the critic Roland Barthes, when he had published

[3] See "Robbe-Grillet," *The New Yorker*, January 9, 1965, pp. 24–5.

only one novel and the brief sketches called in translation
"Three Reflected Visions." A translation of this article will be
found in *Two Novels by Robbe-Grillet* (New York, 1965),
pp. 11–25. It first appeared in the French periodical *Critique*,
in the issue for July–August 1954, under the title *"Littérature
objective: Alain Robbe-Grillet."* The objectivity of the article
itself might have been easier to credit if it had appeared
elsewhere, for *Critique* is published by Les Éditions de Minuit,
who have been Robbe-Grillet's publishers from the beginning.

In the same periodical are to be found two book reviews
that may be the earliest critical studies written by Robbe-
Grillet: at any rate, they both cast a prophetic light on *The
Erasers* and on much of his later work. In the issue of *Critique*
for November 1951—note the early date—Robbe-Grillet reviews a detective story, *La Loutre*, by Jean-Charles Pichon,
and takes the opportunity to make some striking generalizations about the genre. He sees the detective story taking over
the place formerly held in fiction by the love story, and the
"couple" of murderer and victim replacing that of lover and
mistress:

> . . . the "act" *par excellence* is no longer the possession of a
> body but its destruction. Middle-class morality yields its role
> to the penal code—more serious, perhaps, or less decrepit?
> Reality, nonetheless, does not take on the too reassuring ap-
> pearance of a police report, and the margin for error with
> which the truth likes to surround itself remains intact: it is
> no longer a matter of lies told by the unfaithful one or suppo-
> sitions made by the jealous man, but of frame-ups, alibis, false
> testimony . . . As for time—the principal character in every
> novel, so they say—it is honed to a keener edge than ever
> before, each second becoming in the hands of the judge a piece
> of evidence that can furnish proof of innocence or guilt.
> (*Critique*, VII, 1002–3; my translation)

The other review, published in February 1953, concerns a
piece of science fiction translated from the Spanish of Adolfo
Bioy Casares under the title *L'Invention de Morel* ("Morel's
Invention") and published in 1952. The novel carried a short
preface by that wizard in the manipulation of time, Jorge

Luis Borges, whom Robbe-Grillet has read with profit. Actually, Borges is here concerned less with time than with downgrading the emphasis laid on psychology by critics of fiction and with defending the value of pure storytelling. The aspect of *L'Invention de Morel* that Robbe-Grillet most admired, however, was its discovery of the "modifiable past." Whereas the hero is able actually to change the past by means of "Morel's invention," Robbe-Grillet's characters, and especially the hero of *Last Year at Marienbad*, change the past only in their imaginations.

It is possible, however, to say of the extraordinarily ingenious plot and manipulation of time in *The Erasers* that they do succeed in altering the past after the fact. One conceivable meaning of the novel's title is that an error made in the past is erased retrospectively and the "correct" result inserted, just as a cheating schoolboy might "correct" his math homework after the answers have been given out—always provided that he has the right type of eraser, such as Wallas, the protagonist of Robbe-Grillet's novel, seeks vainly in stationery store after stationery store.

Wallas, the bumbling detective in what from one angle can be considered a parody of a detective story, comes to an unnamed northern European city from "the capital" to investigate a murder that has not in fact taken place. A mysterious band of assassins with vaguely hinted political aims have been killing a designated victim every evening at exactly 7:30 p.m. Garinati, the man appointed to kill a prominent citizen named Daniel Dupont, fails to follow strictly enough the instructions given him by a certain Jean Bonaventure or "Bona," apparently the "mastermind" of the murder organization. As a result, Garinati merely wounds his intended victim, who hides and has a doctor friend spread the news that he has died and his body has been sent to the capital for a post-mortem. The government, hoping to entrap its enemies, does not even inform its own police of what has really happened. Wallas, left in ignorance, wanders about the city, rather like a Kafka hero, following up a number of false trails. Eventually, exactly twenty-four hours after the original murder attempt,

Wallas is in Dupont's study when Dupont arrives to pick up some important papers before leaving for the capital. Wallas sees a gun in Dupont's hand and shoots him dead: the victim is the same, but the detective is now the killer. The victim, the would-be murderer, and the would-be detective all show varying degrees of incompetence in their appointed roles, but at least the victim enacts his part correctly when given a second chance. This is a basic travesty of the detective-story convention; in addition, those familiar with the genre will find many of its less essential aspects imitated and made ridiculous.

But the detective story has a lineage that runs back at least to *Oedipus Rex*. On the title page of *The Erasers* will be found a quotation from Sophocles: "Time that sees all has found you out against your will." As Bruce Morrissette has shown,[4] the text of the novel contains a number of seemingly insignificant details which offer parallels with the story of King Oedipus: a drunkard asks what is in effect the riddle of the Sphinx; a favorite textile design in the city of the murder shows a ewe suckling a human baby; the eraser Wallas is trying to match has "di" as the middle syllable of its brand name, etc. We are never told for certain that Daniel Dupont is Wallas's father, but the detective does remember dimly being in this city as a child to visit his father. The only woman who attracts Wallas during the day is too young to be his mother, but she is the estranged wife of Dupont.

The Erasers has a number of meticulous descriptions, but these are—to use Robbe-Grillet's own terminology—the frame for the picture rather than the picture itself. Also, the chronological scheme that Robbe-Grillet was to mock and deliberately confuse in later books is indispensable here. *The Erasers* begins with a Prologue that contains a flashback (E, pp. 16–22) describing the murder attempt as Garinati remembers it, but the book otherwise moves forward chronologically from 6:30 a.m. on the morning after the murder attempt to a little after 7:30 p.m. the same evening. The Epilogue then presents

[4] Bruce Morrissette, "Oedipus and Existentialism: *Les Gommes* of Robbe-Grillet," *Wisconsin Studies in Contemporary Literature*, I (1960), 43–73.

a brief period of time beginning at 6:30 a.m. the following morning. One curious quirk occurs in the time scheme, however: Wallas's watch stops for exactly twenty-four hours, beginning at 7:30 p.m. on the day of the unsuccessful attempt and ending when he fires the fatal shot. As far as the watch is concerned, then, the murder occurred exactly when it was supposed to, and Wallas's wanderings throughout the day take place outside of time. For twenty-four hours, all the members of the murder organization except Garinati have believed that Dupont is dead, and, as it turns out, he might as well have been. Their designated victim for the second day, Alfred Dupont, is killed at exactly the same moment as his namesake Daniel.

In addition to this major example of the "modifiable past," there is a minor example which anticipates much of the narrative technique of *Jealousy*. Chapter 3 begins with a rather startling and precise description of Daniel Dupont's suicide (E, pp. 133–5); it is not until we read "Here Laurent stops . . ." that we realize the local police inspector, Laurent, is trying out a new hypothesis in his "mental cinema." Wallas in his turn (E, pp. 163–5) tries out a couple of further hypotheses. Then Laurent tries again (E, pp. 194–6). In all these cases, as in watching the type of film referred to by Robbe-Grillet in his Introduction to *Last Year at Marienbad*, we see hypothetical actions pass before our eyes as if they were actually taking place.

Something even more curious happens during the interview between Garinati and Bonaventure at the beginning of Chapter 2 (E, pp. 93–100). We are given two slightly different accounts of Garinati's apology for not killing Dupont and Bonaventure's attempt to convince him, by showing him the newspapers, that Dupont is in fact dead. This looks like a "modifiable present" rather than a "modifiable past," but perhaps the explanation is that the dull but truthful Garinati has to be told everything twice before he understands what Bonaventure means—and even then he is not convinced. Or perhaps Garinati goes over the whole scene in memory again to try and convince himself that such an incredible interview ever took place. Because of his limited intelligence, Garinati's consciousness—his very existence, even—can at times be reduced to his sense impressions alone. Section 7 of Chapter 4 (E, pp. 208–13), containing the reader's last glimpses of Garinati, thus becomes the most "objective" passage in the whole book.

Before leaving *The Erasers*, let me stress that it is the most amusing of Robbe-Grillet's novels. The author told me himself that there are pages in his books which make him laugh uncontrollably (*me donnent le fou rire*, to quote his exact words) when he rereads them. Many of these pages must occur in *The Erasers*, though there is some "deadpan" humor in *Jealousy* too. The husband's pedantic attempt to verify whether A... has had her soup when he cannot quite remember seeing her put a spoon to her lips (J, p. 12; TN, p. 46) is a memorable example, as is the conversation about Franck's skill as a "mechanic," partly quoted above. Robbe-Grillet exploits the comic convention that all jealous men— and particularly all jealous husbands—make themselves butts for humor by their very humorlessness. Similarly, Wallas's superior, Fabius, may or may not be a fabulous detective: he is certainly a humorless bureaucrat. No detective with a forehead—a "frontal surface"—measuring less than fifty square centimeters is really acceptable to Fabius; Wallas's measures only forty-nine, so that he is hired merely on probation. Besides watching for absurdities of this kind, the reader who wants to extract the fullest enjoyment from *The Erasers* should be alert for loose ends in the plot—surely left untied deliberately? For instance, by a series of accidents Wallas manages to intercept a message from Bona to a certain "André WS." This letter seems to concern the murder of the second Dupont, Alfred. How, then, is Alfred's murder successfully accomplished if the murderer who was to replace the inefficient Garinati has not received his orders?

The Voyeur, appropriately enough, stands about halfway between *The Erasers* and *Jealousy* in Robbe-Grillet's technical development. Like *Jealousy*, it is narrated in the third person from the viewpoint of a single character, Mathias, who is also the protagonist. *The Erasers,* on the other hand, while usually narrated from the viewpoint of one character at a time—Garinati, Daniel Dupont, Wallas, Laurent, or another—sometimes falls into the type of omniscient, eye-of-God narration that Robbe-Grillet was to condemn later. Furthermore, Robbe-Grillet has become much more at home with the device of treating the "inner film"—whether it be the flashback of memory or the leap forward of the imagination—as identical in quality with the perception of the outside world. Even a reader trained on *Jealousy* may find himself temporarily disoriented by the leaps in time and space made by Mathias's consciousness in the earlier book, particularly during the opening pages.

On the other hand, the treatment of time in *The Voyeur* is perhaps *less* sophisticated than in *The Erasers.* Basically, chronological time is followed in both books: as we turn the pages in numerical order, the hours and days in the story pass by in numerical order also. True, mental or "human" time flashes back or forward upon occasion, but the reader never wonders which direction is which; he does not get hopelessly disoriented as does a reader of *Jealousy.* In one respect, however, *The Voyeur* handles time in a more old-fashioned way than *The Erasers*: almost everything that happens in *The Voyeur* is related in the past tense, whereas *The Erasers* uses the present tense as consistently as does *Jealousy,* so that everything is always happening cinematically right before one's eyes.

There is just one aspect of the handling of time in *The Voyeur* that disturbs and confuses the reader in a more radical way than does the behavior of Wallas's watch. Virtually every moment of Mathias's first day on an island off the coast of France is accounted for, at least from the time when his ferryboat begins its approach to the island landing slip to the moment when he just misses the same boat returning to the mainland six hours later. Yet nearly an hour of that time is not directly narrated in its chronological order. It is during that gap of time that Mathias tortures and murders a thirteen-year-old girl named Jacqueline who was minding her sheep in an isolated part of the island. We learn later what has happened to the girl, partly through Mathias's memories and partly through the reports of those who found Jacqueline's body in the sea, already marked in tender places, it seems, by the bites of sea creatures. Actually these marks are cigarette burns made by Mathias, who had stripped Jacqueline naked, tied her to some of the pickets used to tether the sheep, gagged and tortured her, and then flung her over a cliff into the sea.

Because of the gap in the narrative, it is possible to imagine either that Mathias committed the murder during a mental blackout or that he imagined the whole murder and torture scene; the actual murderer, then, would be one of the precociously promiscuous girl's male or female enemies. However, it seems unlikely that Robbe-Grillet wants the reader to believe either of these hypotheses. When the narrative resumes, Mathias is busy trying to concoct an alibi, so that he must have committed the murder consciously if he committed it at all. On the other hand, if all his supposed memories of the sadistic act are hallucinations, why do the objective facts corroborate his memories so precisely?

No, these hypotheses will not work. Whether we read novels in the naïve spirit displayed by A... and Franck, "speaking . . . of the scenes, events, and characters as if they were real . . ." (J, pp. 53-4, TN, p. 74), or whether we remember always that they are works of fiction, the sole responsibility for the gap in the narrative lies with the author himself. His primary motive, one might guess, was the preservation of decorum; murders must not take place "on-stage," whether the author be Racine or Robbe-Grillet. *The Voyeur* was bound to shock many readers in any case because the murderer neither displays remorse nor is punished for his crime; it was better not to defy public opinion any more than was necessary in the interests of realism. Anybody but a practicing sadist would be happy to be spared a fully lit, blow-by-blow view of the crime, while gaining a subtle aesthetic pleasure from reconstructing the deed on the basis of hints and glimpses from Mathias's memory.

Mathias visits his native island, which he has not seen since he was a child, for the purpose of selling wrist watches. He proposes to cover the entire area by bicycle within the six hours of the ferryboat's stay, but a number of apparently fortuitous events conspire to arouse his sadistic tendencies. These seem to have manifested themselves at least once before, in a crime recorded in a newspaper clipping that he carries in his wallet—though perhaps the clipping merely recounts a crime he would have liked to commit. At any rate, the victim's name seems to have been Violet, for he keeps calling Jacqueline that.

He first hears of Jacqueline from her brother, who is a deck hand for the ferryboat line. Before catching the ferry, he has glimpsed from the street, early in the morning, a man striking a woman in a ground-floor bedroom—at least, he thinks so. On the ferry itself he picks up a neatly coiled hank of cord in the form of a figure eight, sees a girl child leaning back in a suggestive pose, and observes two iron rings—suitable for tying wrists to, no doubt—set near each other in the wall of the ferry slip. Soon afterwards, ashore, he learns from Jacqueline's mother where she is tending sheep. Part I of the novel ends as he turns his bicycle off the main road toward where the girl is.

At the beginning of Part II we find him back on the main road, where he meets an old family friend, Madame Marek. She presents him with a near-perfect alibi, assuming that he has just been to visit her house and apologizing to him because he must have found no one at home. Shortly afterwards, a fisherman who recognizes him and calls him "Matt," although Mathias cannot remember ever having met him, invites him home to lunch. The fisherman's wife or woman is also present. Mathias erroneously thinks that his host's name is Jean Robin. Later Mathias desperately tries to cover his planned sales route on the island but has little success in selling watches because he hurries his clients too much. Then the bicycle breaks down and he just misses the ferry. Thus ends Part II.

In Part III Mathias has to remain on the island from Tuesday to Friday, the next time the boat comes. He manages to find lodging in what may very well have been his boyhood home.

Jacqueline's body is discovered, but nobody seems anxious to have her death inquired into. There are too many possible suspects for comfort, though the island people do not include Mathias among them. The girl's mother seems almost relieved that Jacqueline has died in what might conceivably have been an accident—even though her body was naked when found. Far greater scandals would surely have occurred if the girl had lived much longer.

Mathias does some very foolish things while trying to destroy clues and tighten his alibi. He revisits the scene of the crime, hoping to find the half-smoked cigarettes—admittedly of the most popular brand—that he had thrown away. There he meets the woman of "Jean Robin"—whose real first name turns out to be Pierre—a close friend of Jacqueline's, who was with her until shortly before she was murdered. Pierre's woman does not suspect Mathias, however, being convinced that Pierre is guilty; in fact, she has found one of the half-smoked cigarettes and regards it as conclusive evidence against Pierre. She does not intend to inform the police, however.

When Mathias revisits the Mareks, he finds that they suspect their rather dull-witted teenage son Julian of killing Jacqueline. Julian insists that he was at the farm at the time of the murder and supports his alibi by asserting that he saw Mathias waiting about outside the farmhouse. Mathias knows this is a lie, though it confirms his own false alibi. What is Julian's motive?

As Mathias rethinks his alibi, we recall Robbe-Grillet's dictum that "each second [becomes] in the hands of the judge a piece of evidence . . ." Mathias decides that there is still "a hole in his schedule," just as there is a "hole" in the narrative of the novel between Parts I and II:

> The abnormal, excessive, suspicious, inexplicable time amounted to forty minutes—if not fifty. It was more than enough to account for the two successive detours: the trip to the farm and back—including the minor repair to the gearshift in front of the closed door—and the trip to the cliff and

back—including. . . . Mathias would merely have had to hurry
a little. (V, pp. 173–4)

Mathias again makes the mistake of returning to the scene
of the crime and finds that Jacqueline's sweater did not fall
into the sea along with the rest of her clothes. At some risk to
his life, Mathias climbs down to where the sweater is and
makes sure that this time it goes into the sea. Suddenly he
realizes that Julian Marek has been silently watching him.
Julian tells him that Jacqueline's sweater was in the same
place yesterday and shows him one of Mathias's gumdrop
wrappers that had been left at the scene of the crime. It
occurs to Mathias that Julian might have watched the entire
crime, and for a moment he feels ready to throw the boy over
the cliff. Recoiling, he goes on talking to Julian and eventually becomes convinced that the boy knows everything and
will accuse him to the police later that day. A chance turns
up to leave the island by fishing boat at once, but Mathias
feels that flight is useless. In the end he leaves the island by
the regular ferry on Friday without any charge having been
brought against him.

Critics have been greatly exercised by the presence of figure
eights in the book: the hank of cord, the pattern traced by the
principal roads on the island, and several others. Are these
patterns symbolic? Those who think they are should explain to
us just exactly what they symbolize. The views expressed in
"Nature, Humanism, Tragedy" seem to preclude allegory and
symbolism as well as metaphor. Surely the intelligent view is
to regard these various figure eights as a recurring structural
and/or decorative motif? That, at any rate, is the view which
I will continue to take of them.

In a prefatory note, the reader of *In the Labyrinth* (New
York, 1960), which had appeared in French as *Dans le
labyrinthe* only a year before, was specifically urged not to
attempt an allegorical interpretation of Robbe-Grillet's fourth
novel:

This narrative is not a true account, but fiction. It describes a reality not necessarily the same as the one the reader has experienced: for example, in the French army, infantrymen do not wear their serial numbers on their coat collars. Similarly, the recent history of Western Europe has not recorded an important battle at Reichenfels or in the vicinity. Yet the reality in question is a strictly material one; that is, it is subject to no allegorical interpretation. The reader is therefore requested to see in it only the objects, actions, words, and events which are described, without attempting to give them either more or less meaning than in his own life, or his own death. A. R.–G.

The note, quoted above in full, cannot of course be regarded as anything but an expression of intention on the part of the author: it is for the reader or the critic to say whether the narrative is in fact "subject" to an allegorical interpretation. The last sentence of the note is particularly ambiguous, for many men give a symbolic or allegoric interpretation to their own lives and deaths—not to mention those of their national or cultural heroes.

Nevertheless, it is a salutary if irksome discipline to read this dreamlike narrative of a soldier's last days and hours as if it were a piece of reporting. The narrative makes clear to us that the soldier is exhausted, demoralized by defeat, feverish from some infection, afraid of both the enemy and his own military authorities, wandering in the streets of an unfamiliar city. No wonder his waking experiences are dreamlike and disoriented, especially as the streets of the city are so often empty and the houses kept dark and shut up through fear of the approaching enemy. Add to this that the soldier has forgotten just where or when he was to meet his dead comrade's father (if it was his father) and deliver to him the package that he carries under his arm.

Many readers, after even this brief summary, will be only too ready to diagnose yet another allegory of the plight of modern man—or man without the adjective—a novelistic version of, say, *Waiting for Godot*. Or one might draw a parallel with Kafka, interpreting *In the Labyrinth* as a version of the search for recognition and acceptance seen in *The*

Castle—only transferred from a rural setting to the urban landscape of *The Trial.* One factor sharply differentiates Robbe-Grillet's novel from Kafka's, however: the anonymous soldier accepts his fate without a murmur, whereas Kafka's protagonists are full of anguish about their plight and passionately eager to state their claims to justice or toleration. It is as though his debilitating experiences—mental, moral, and physical—had left the soldier with only one purpose, one link to life: the delivery of the package. At one point he thinks of dropping it into a sewer, but he cannot bring himself to do so. Indirectly, the package brings about his death at the hands of enemy soldiers; it becomes possible, *without* allegorizing, to see the package objectively as the equivalent of his personal fate. In the long run, the package with its banal contents— exposed to us at the end of the book—becomes almost the protagonist of the novel. Until the contents are exposed, we may feel that the package contains more mystery than the unprepossessing soldier himself.

The empathetic reader who succeeds in avoiding the temptation to allegorize will be repaid by a sense of the reality and immediacy of the soldier's plight that verges on the inexplicable. Up to now, the account of *In the Labyrinth* presented here has deliberately, even perversely, ignored an aspect of the book that confronts the reader in the very first sentence and in the very first word, which is "I." Although the first person singular does not occur again until the final unnumbered chapter or section of the novel (IL, pp. 199–207; TN, pp. 266–72), it is clear that the story is narrated or reconstructed imaginatively by someone who is not the soldier but rather a non-practicing medical man—or at any rate someone with medical knowledge and access to drugs—the same person who lives in the room with red curtains described so meticulously in the opening chapter (IL, pp. 7–21; TN, pp. 141–9).

The final chapter, besides listing the contents of the box— mainly letters to the dead comrade, Henri Martin, from his fiancée—seems to clear up many details about the soldier and about the people in whose apartment he died: a man who

pretends to be a cripple, a youngish woman, and a boy of
about ten who appears to be the woman's son but insists that
the "cripple" is not his father. Yet all this seemingly factual
detail is vitiated by the narrator's slipping into a confusion
that has bewildered the reader throughout the novel. Once
again, for the last time (IL, pp. 204–6; TN, pp. 270–1), the
soldier, the young woman, and the child are identified with a
soldier, the lone waitress, and the only child to be seen in an
etching that hangs on the narrator's wall. This picture is described in great detail at the beginning of the second chapter
of the book (IL, pp. 21–6; TN, pp. 150–3). It depicts a
crowded tavern or café scene and bears a rather puzzling title,
"The Defeat of Reichenfels." Every figure in the picture is a
civilian except three weary soldiers sitting at a table, only
one of whom is seen full-face. The only woman in the picture
is a waitress carrying a tray. The only child is a boy sitting on
the floor in the foreground.

Over and over again throughout the book the soldier who
wanders with the package appears in the café scene of the
picture, or the soldier who appears full-face in the picture
steps out of the café into the labyrinthine streets of the unfamiliar city. Over and over again the boy and the soldier—
or at any rate *a* boy and *a* soldier—meet in the street or the
café. Eventually the boy, by his curiosity, attracts the attention of some enemy soldiers, who give the protagonist his fatal
bullet wound. The soldier dies in the apartment of the boy's
family, where on an earlier occasion the mother had given
him food and wine.

What is the reader to make of this constant "dissolving" in
and out of the picture, which reminds us of the more sparing
use of the device in *Jealousy*? (There, A... in the snapshot
becomes identified with A... in "real" life just once; on
another occasion a port scene, depicted on a calendar in a
color photograph, also "comes to life.") Either the narrator
is using the picture as an aid to his imagination in trying to
fill the gaps in his knowledge of a real soldier, or he is a
professional novelist like Robbe-Grillet, inventing the whole
story with the help of a picture on the wall and a box of old

letters and odds and ends that he emptied on his desk and
then put back in the box before settling down to write. If
he were a novelist, he would have to be an extremely good
one to write the fascinating and moving work that we have
just been examining—*In the Labyrinth*.

It may seem like hindsight to say now that it was inevitable
that Robbe-Grillet should turn to the cinema, but anybody who
read his article "A Future for the Novel" when it first appeared
in French in 1956[5] must have felt that its author would not
be happy until he tried his hand at films, whether as writer or
director or both. Robbe-Grillet is discussing the difference
between the "countless movie versions of novels that encumber
our screens" and the novels on which they are based:

> Anyone can perceive the nature of the change that has
> occurred. In the initial novel, the objects and gestures form-
> ing the very fabric of the plot disappeared completely, leaving
> behind only their *significations*: the empty chair became only
> absence or expectation, the hand placed on a shoulder became
> a sign of friendliness, the bars on the window became only
> the impossibility of leaving. . . . But in the cinema, one *sees*
> the chair, the movement of the hand, the shape of the bars.
> What they signify remains obvious, but instead of monopo-
> lizing our attention, it becomes something added, even some-
> thing in excess, because what affects us, what persists in our
> memory, what appears as essential and irreducible to vague
> intellectual concepts are the gestures themselves, the objects,
> the movements, and the outlines, to which the image has
> suddenly (and unintentionally) restored their *reality*. (FNN,
> p. 20)

When Robbe-Grillet did make his début in the film world,
it was under the best possible auspices. Alain Resnais, the
director of *Last Year at Marienbad*, had won several prizes
with his first feature-length film, *Hiroshima mon amour*, completed in 1959. The script for it was written by Marguerite
Duras, often included among the New Novelists. In his earlier,
shorter films, Resnais had shown a propensity for shooting

[5] "*Une Voie pour le roman futur*," NNRF, IV (July 1956), 77–84.

original scripts by writers linked to the New Novel, such as Raymond Queneau and Jean Cayrol. The script for Resnais's third feature-length film, *Muriel*, was also provided by Cayrol. Reasonably enough, for his second major film Resnais turned to Robbe-Grillet. The masterpiece that resulted marked an epoch in the art of the cinema and was acclaimed as the best film shown at the Venice Festival in 1961. The same year *L'Année dernière a Marienbad* was published in book form as a *ciné-roman* or "film novel," illustrated with forty-eight "stills" from the film. In his Introduction, Robbe-Grillet wrote that the text of the book was "in principle the one given to Resnais before the shooting began, made somewhat more accessible by a slightly different presentation. . . ." There were of course

> . . . discrepancies between this account of a film and the actual film as seen. These slight changes have either been dictated by material considerations . . . or else imposed on the director by his own sensibility. But it is not to dissociate myself from Alain Resnais' mediations that I present my initial text here, for on the contrary that text has only been reinforced, as I have indicated above; the only reason is one of probity, since the text is published under my signature alone. (LYM, p. 15)

In response to the world-wide success of the film, an English translation of the *ciné-roman* appeared in New York in 1962, even more copiously illustrated than the French edition. It would be sheer insanity for a literary critic to attempt to summarize the film in any words but those of Robbe-Grillet himself, as given in his Introduction. The story of the film is so similar in form and mood to *Jealousy* that it could not possibly have been used

> . . . as the basis for a film in traditional form, I mean a linear narrative with "logical" developments. The whole film, as a matter of fact, is the story of a persuasion: it deals with a reality which the hero creates out of his own vision, out of his own words. And if his persistence, his secret conviction, finally prevail, they do so among a perfect labyrinth [*dédale*] of false trails, variants, failures and repetitions! (LYM, p. 10)

The last two sentences, with only slight changes, could be used to describe both *Jealousy* and *In the Labyrinth*. Although a different French word for "labyrinth" happens to be used, the last sentence casts a new light on the choice of title for the latter novel, which on first acquaintance seems to refer mainly to the labyrinthine streets of the city where the soldier wanders.

Robbe-Grillet's synopsis begins with a description of the setting of the film, "an enormous hotel, a kind of international palace, huge, baroque, opulent but icy. . . ." He then describes the formal, dreamlike behavior of the guests and the stifling psychological atmosphere, from which it seems impossible to escape. He focuses on the wanderings of a stranger through this hotel.

> His ears register snatches of phrases, chance words. His eyes shift from one nameless face to another. But he keeps returning to the face of a young woman, a beautiful perhaps still living prisoner of this golden cage. And so he offers her the impossible, what seems most impossible in this labyrinth where time is apparently abolished: he offers her a past, a future, and freedom. He tells her that he and she have already met the year before, that they had fallen in love, that he has now come to a rendezvous she herself had arranged, and that he is going to take her away with him.
>
> Is the stranger a mere seducer? Is he a madman? Or is he simply confusing two faces? (LYM, p. 11)

At first the young woman treats the whole thing as a joke, but the man "insists, offers proof." She begins to be convinced, then takes fright.

> She doesn't want to leave this false but reassuring world of hers which she is used to and which is symbolized for her by another man, solicitous, disillusioned and remote, who watches over her and who may in fact be her husband. But the story the stranger is telling assumes ever greater reality, becomes more and more coherent, increasingly present and irresistibly true. Present and past, finally, are intermingled, while the growing tension between the three protagonists creates fantasies of tragedy in the heroine's mind: rape, murder, suicide. . . .

Then, suddenly, she is ready to yield. . . . She already has
yielded, in fact, long since. After a final attempt to resist, to
offer her guardian a last chance of winning her back, she seems
to accept the identity the stranger offers her, and agrees to go
with him toward something, something unnamed, something
other: love, poetry, freedom . . . or maybe death. . . . (LYM,
pp. 11–12)

The conclusion of this summary is curious indeed, especially if one turns from it to reread "Nature, Humanism,
Tragedy," with its repudiation of the "old myths of depth."
Robbe-Grillet's synopsis of *Last Year at Marienbad* makes
the film sound somewhat more tragic than it appeared to me
when I saw it. Indeed, Robbe-Grillet's account of the three
main characters—A, the heroine; M, the "husband"; X, the
stranger—in the next paragraph seems to deny their capacity
for tragedy.

They are nothing but what we see them as: guests in a huge
resort hotel, cut off from the outside world as effectively as if
they were in a prison. What do they do when they are elsewhere? We are tempted to answer: nothing! Elsewhere, they
don't exist. As for the past the hero introduces by force into
this sealed, empty world, we sense he is making it up as he
goes along. There is no last year, and Marienbad is no longer
to be found on any map. This past, too, has no reality beyond
the moment it is evoked with sufficient force, and when it
finally triumphs, it has merely become the present, as if it had
never ceased to be so. (LYM, p. 12)

We have not learned anything really new about Robbe-Grillet's
narrative technique from reading his Introduction to this film
novel, but anybody who has seen and enjoyed the film *Last
Year at Marienbad* will very likely find it less difficult in the
future to understand and appreciate Robbe-Grillet's novels.

Let us deviate from chronological order just a little to deal
here with Robbe-Grillet's only other published *ciné-roman*,
L'Immortelle (Paris, 1963). I greatly regret not having seen
this basically simple and beautiful film—the text is illustrated
by forty stills—shot on location in Istanbul (alias Constanti-

nople, alias Byzantium). The book has not been translated into English, and the title is hard to render in a language that has no inflection for the gender of nouns and adjectives. One might translate it as "The Immortal One," remembering that "One" is emphatically feminine. Both the heroine of the film and the immortal city of Constantine are without doubt referred to in the title.

L'Immortelle fully vindicates the Robbe-Grillet technique of refusing to distinguish between what is seen by the outer eye and what is seen by the eye of memory. The hero, N, loses the heroine, L, twice: once by her absence, and then, after he has found her again, by her death. When she is no longer present in the flesh for one reason or the other, he searches for her and continues to see her among the poignant landscapes and seascapes of Istanbul that she had acquainted him with for the first time; either that, or he sees her in his own apartment, where they acted out their love for each other. In the end, he cannot endure the separation of death and commits suicide by smashing her automobile into the same tree that killed her. Such is the strong, simple story line, though it is crossed by more than Robbe-Grillet's usual number of false trails. There is an atmosphere of mystery about L that is never dispelled: we are never even sure what her first name is—Leïla, Lale, or something else beginning with "L"? Is she French or Turkish? Why does she disappear? What is her relationship, if any, with M, the man in dark glasses with the two big dogs? We don't know and, what's more, we don't care. Any creaking piece of stage machinery will serve, so long as it keeps the lovers apart and brings them to a tragic end, though we sometimes wish Robbe-Grillet would not take such pleasure in introducing all the old clichés of the suspense film so that he can parody them. Often, too, he seems not to know where to draw the line between a mystery and a *mystification*—French for a hoax.

One particularly flagrant example occurs when L has made an appointment to meet N in the courtyard of a mosque. N waits alone for some time, then asks an old Turk who is selling postcards and religious objects whether he has seen a woman waiting there. The old man says he has not, in halting French. Eventually N goes into the mosque and finds L there; she seems pleased but not surprised to see him. As they leave the mosque, N pauses to put on his shoes, but L, with her shoes still in her hand, walks on until she is standing in front of the old man. The following exchange then takes place:

> OLD MAN: [In French] *Very fine mosque . . . Old . . . Very old . . . Very old ceramics . . . Very old . . .* [Then in Turkish] *The stranger waited nearly twenty minutes. He waited in the courtyard, in the sun, and he looked at his watch often. Then he came to me and asked if I had seen a woman. I answered: I've seen no one.*
>
> The young woman has looked at the old man during his entire speech, apparently attentive, smiling. Then she makes a little gesture of thanks and holds out to him a folded note [*billet*] that she has taken from her handbag, a tip, no doubt; she starts walking again, accompanied by N, who has just caught up with her again. (pp. 63–4, my translation)

Is she trying to avoid N or to test his patience and fidelity? Or does Robbe-Grillet simply want us to plague ourselves with stupid questions like these to which there can be no verifiable answer in relation to a work of fiction? Even if we change the form of the question and ask what Robbe-Grillet intended her motives to be, he can supply an evasive or misleading answer, or he can say, "I intended absolutely nothing except to have L do precisely what she *has* done in the film. It is up to the audience to attempt to divine her motivation, if they think the task worthwhile. As for me, I have set down only the 'facts.'" There are many other scenes in the film that seem designed to confuse us—and amuse us too, no doubt, though the French word *amuser* has overtones of distraction and deception.

Another distracting aspect of this film novel is the way in which the dialogue fights against the visual image. To judge by the illustrations, Robbe-Grillet and his cameramen have exploited to the full the glamour, especially when a product of decay, that is present everywhere in modern Istanbul. Yet L in particular always insists that the glamour and the

seeming antiquity are false. For instance, just after she and N
leave the old man in the scene just quoted, she says:

> L: *All that is false, naturally.*
> N: *All what?*
> L: *What he was saying. It isn't old at all, it's been recon-*
> *structed since the war.*
> N: *Still, it's written up in all the guide books.* (p. 64, my
> translation)

The persistent cynicism of L's dialogue, far from undercutting
the glamour of the pictorial image and the near-sentimentality
of the plot, seems to enhance them. This conflict between
cynicism and exoticism, realism and romanticism, is to be
found everywhere in the creative work of Robbe-Grillet.
Reading his critical essays, one thinks of him as an icy-brained
rationalist, a logician and technician of the novel, but just try
to summarize a Robbe-Grillet film or novel in a single paragraph without making the plot or situation sound melodramatic!

According to Joseph Morgenstern's brilliant *Newsweek* review of a more recent film written and directed by Robbe-
Grillet, this artistic schizophrenia has reached what may be
its limit in *Trans-Europ-Express*:

> From the outset we know the story is a figment of Robbe-
> Grillet's imagination. We see him sitting with a producer and
> script girl in a compartment of the Trans-Europ-Express be-
> tween Paris and Antwerp, toying with the idea of a movie that
> might be made on or around the train. Jean-Louis Trintignant
> sits down in the compartment just long enough to give Robbe-
> Grillet his inspiration for an atrociously lurid melodrama about
> a dope runner (Trintignant) on his first international run.
> "But is there really a Paris-Antwerp drug traffic?" asks the
> producer. "Of course," Robbe-Grillet replies, "since Trintignant
> is in it."
>
> While producer and script girl keep insisting that the de-
> tails must make sense, Robbe-Grillet insists that they need not.
> (*Newsweek*, May 27, 1968, p. 95)

We have already seen that the details in *L'Immortelle* very
often do not make sense either, but it is comforting to have

Robbe-Grillet's word for this in the later film and to learn that he has at last been able to give full play to his effervescent sense of the ridiculous.

Morgenstern goes on to make some very shrewd comments about the comportment of the "hero" in *Trans-Europ-Express*:

> Trintignant does seem to suspect that the whole thing is a put-up job on the part of some unseen god of a writer-director. As the non-plot thickens, as he follows his fetishes, encounters a devious prostitute (Marie-France Plisier) and slinks through the complications of someone else's imagination, he never cracks a smile—he can't afford not to be taken seriously, since he barely exists to begin with.

Robbe-Grillet makes clear in his preliminary notes to *L'Immortelle* that the male protagonist, N, is deliberately intended to appear disoriented in pretty much the way described by Morgenstern in speaking of Trintignant:

> Why an N? Doubtless in order to indicate his very special position in the story, which is a little comparable to that of the *narrator* in a modern novel: narrator who "tells" nothing, but through whose eyes everything is seen, through whose ears everything is heard, or through whose mind everything is imagined. That is what gives him, when he is present on the screen, his appearance of being at once empty and awkward, evidently an inappropriate one for a movie "hero." (p. 9)

It is hard to understand why the narrator should be represented as empty and clumsy; perhaps Robbe-Grillet's point is that N is not supposed to be seen at all: we should be seeing through his eyes, not seeing *him*. It's like having the camera itself appear on the screen. On the other hand, nothing would be technically easier than to make the narrator the camera—one that sees and speaks but isn't seen at all. Still, we cannot deny that if the "narrator" or observer of *Jealousy* did ever step before our eyes, he would cut a strange, awkward figure indeed.

Robbe-Grillet assures us not only that Istanbul is a real city but that L and the other people whom N meets are real too.

But the moment they pass inside someone's head, they instantly become *imaginary*, properly speaking. That is the reason why the young woman will "freeze" sometimes like a wax figure from the Musée Grévin, or like a goddess, a stereotyped prostitute, or even an erotic photograph in the most naïvely traditional style.

The same goes for the city. Thoroughly contaminated in the man's mind by a medley of Pierre Loti, the Blue Guide and the Arabian Nights, the city will shuttle constantly between its tourist-postcard aspect and the blatant "symbolism" of iron chains and barred windows, but without ceasing for all that to be full of the living hum and bustle of boats, ports and crowds. (pp. 9–10)

In examining these films of Robbe-Grillet's and what he says about them, we have undoubtedly learned to understand certain aspects of his novels. I have the uneasy feeling, however, that *La Maison de rendez-vous* (Paris, 1965; English translation with same title, 1966), Robbe-Grillet's last novel to date, has been "contaminated" by his film experience. On the screen, the details need not make sense, for they "are there," as Robbe-Grillet insisted in the essay "A Future for the Novel." We have prima-facie evidence for their truth, they keep our eyes and ears momentarily entertained, and then they are gone forever—or at least until the next showing of the movie that we happen to see. But a novel is there in our hands; we can puzzle over an inconsistent detail for hours if we wish; we can also, if we wish, take the book firmly in one hand and throw it in the wastepaper basket. If *La Maison de rendez-vous* were made into a film, we might, to quote Joseph Morgenstern's words about *Trans-Europ-Express*,

. . . find ourselves following, often doggedly but sometimes with surprising relish, the details of a story we know has no depth, reality or significance. (*Newsweek*, May 27, 1968, p. 95)

As it is, though, I for one have failed to find in *La Maison* either the amusement or the intense emotion of the other four novels.

Before looking at the final work, let us note two other publications that complete the Robbe-Grillet canon. In 1962 he published *Instantanés* (translated by Bruce Morrissette as *Snapshots*, New York, 1968). Although described as "stories" on the cover of the New York paperback edition, these are in fact no more than brief prose descriptions or sketches. "Three Reflected Visions" and "The Way Back" date from 1954; "Scene" from 1955; "The Shore" from 1956; the three sketches, "In the Corridors of the Métro," from 1959; and "The Secret Room" from 1962. This last sketch is dedicated to Gustave Moreau (1826–98), the Symbolist painter so much admired by Joris-Karl Huysmans: Robbe-Grillet does not tell us whether it is based on a picture with the same title. It contains the most explicit manifestation to date of that rather fetishistic sadism which crops up in so many of Robbe-Grillet's novels and films. Chains and iron rings are favorite fetishes; we remember the latter in *The Voyeur* especially, and L in *L'Immortelle* always wears a chain somewhere about her: the illustration to Shot No. 304 is the most sadistic in implication. Now, in "The Secret Room," a voluptuously formed naked woman, lying on thick cushions and Oriental rugs, has her ankles attached by chains to two iron rings set in the floor and her wrists ringed by iron bracelets which are attached by chains to two pillars. When we first see her, she is dead, her left nipple destroyed by a stab wound from which blood has trickled in various directions. The man who presumably has killed her is near the top of the staircase leading out of the dungeon. But as though time or a camera were run in reverse, we next see him near the bottom of the staircase, and then stabbing the living, writhing body. At the end of the description, time has moved forward again and the room is empty. From what one knows of Moreau, the opening murkily lit scene is based on his picture, if any. The more explicit and more brightly lit scenes presumably come from Robbe-Grillet's overheated imagination. Some of his readers, at least, will feel that the female breast can be put to better uses.

Nothing could provide a sharper contrast with the brief work just described than the collection of essays entitled *Pour un nouveau roman* (Paris, 1963), translated as *For a New Novel: Essays on Fiction* (New York, 1965). This book has been quoted from so frequently in these pages that it seems pointless to do more than draw attention to the book reviews grouped under the heading "Elements of a Modern Anthology." These deal with some writers particularly admired by the New Novelists: Raymond Roussel, Italo Svevo, Samuel Beckett (here considered only as a playwright, with reference to *Waiting for Godot* and *Endgame*). The work of the paraplegic poet Joë Bousquet, paralyzed by a war wound, is also discussed, as is an early work by Pinget, *Mahu*, described as "A Novel That Invents Itself." One further point about *For a New Novel*: these essays, written at different times and in different contexts, do not present a monolithic attitude to the writing of novels. As Robbe-Grillet himself says, it is not surprising

> . . . that there should be developments from one essay to another, among those that follow. Not, of course, the crude repudiations mistakenly denounced by readers who have been a little too careless—or ill-disposed—but reconsiderations on a different level, re-examinations, another side of the same idea, or its complement, and in some cases simply a warning against an error of interpretation. (FNN, pp. 12–13)

The subtitle "A Novel That Invents Itself" might be applied to *La Maison de Rendez-vous*, but a better explanation of the book's peculiarities is that it is a novel in process of composition. The author—not necessarily to be identified with Robbe-Grillet—may be mentally running over a series of groups of alternative scenes. In each group he can choose only one of the alternative actions or motivations. Each of these will then have to be made logically and chronologically consistent with the choices made from the other groups. Consequently, the book as we read it contains such notations as these:

> If Manneret has already just been murdered, this scene takes place earlier, of course. (MR, p. 130)
> Then comes the scene of the shopwindow. . . . However, it

must not take place precisely at this point, where it would not be understandable. . . . (MR, p. 42)

But meanwhile there has been the episode of the broken glass. . . . (MR, p. 41)

Afterward, there is the opium den, already described. . . . [Robbe-Grillet has not in fact previously described it, as far as this long-suffering reader can recall.] (MR, p. 140)

Some inconsistencies remain in the foregoing; it has none-theless happened, in every point, in this manner. The rest has already been reported. (MR, p. 113)

At times the "author" has set down a list of adjectives, some of which are mutually incompatible: "her huge, green, burn-ing, intense, icy, irrational eyes . . ." (MR, p. 58). Presumably he will later decide whether the eyes are to be "icy" or "burning," and then strike out the irreconcilable adjectives.

At certain points, so long as the required result is obtained, the details (all clichés in any case) don't really matter:

> The door of the apartment is ajar, the apartment door is wide open, despite the late hour, the apartment door is closed—what does it matter?—and Manneret himself comes to open it; or else it is a Chinese servant girl or a sleepy young Eurasian girl whom the bell, whom the insistent electric buzzer, whom the thumps of fists against the door have finally roused from her bed. What does all that matter? What does it matter? Edouard Manneret has not yet gone to bed, in any case. He never goes to bed. He sleeps fully dressed in his rocking chair. He hasn't managed to sleep in a long time, the strongest soporifics having ceased to have the slightest effect on him. He is sound asleep in his bed, but Johnson insists that he be wakened, he waits for him in the living room, he shoves aside the terrified servants and enters the bedroom by force; all this comes to the same thing. Manneret first takes Johnson for his son, he takes him for Georges Marchat or Marchant, he takes him for Mr. Chang, he takes him for Sir Ralph, he takes him for King Boris. It comes down to the same thing, since ultimately he refuses. (MR, p. 151)

Manneret will not give Johnson the money he wants, so John-son kills him. But we have already had several other versions of Manneret's death. This happens to be the last one in the book, but we do not know whether it is more reliable than any of the others. It is clearly impossible to summarize the plot of this novel, for it has no single plot. Yet to summarize all the possible plots might take hundreds of pages, for it is a mathematical truth that each time we are confronted by a choice among two or more mutually exclusive developments, we must *multiply* the plot possibilities by two or more. A novel consisting of ten episodes, in which a single alternative is posed for each episode except the first, will proliferate into two-to-the-ninth-power (that is, 512) different versions!

There is another category of passages which, like the picture of "The Defeat of Reichenfels," may be regarded as the sources—humble enough—of the "author's" inspiration. Important among these is the description of the cover of a Chinese picture magazine (*un illustré chinois*).[6]

> Under a horizontal heading in large, square-cornered ideograms . . . a crude drawing represents a huge European salon whose walls, elaborately decorated with mirrors and stucco, must be meant to suggest great luxury; some men in dark clothes or cream or ivory dinner jackets are standing here and there, chatting in little groups; in the middle distance, to the left . . . a waiter . . . is about to serve a glass of champagne, on a silver tray, to a fat important-looking man who, his arm already extended to take his glass, is talking to another guest much taller than himself . . . ; in the background . . . a large double door has just opened, letting in three soldiers in battle dress. . . . (MR, p. 19)

This may well be the origin of the scene at the Blue Villa, owned by Lady Ava, in which three Hong Kong police raid the night club/brothel.

In what is perhaps a copy of the same illustrated paper, overleaf from the cover, we are shown "three stylized drawings" of a young woman on a bed which have much to do with the view given of the relations between Manneret and a Eurasian girl named Kim. The description of these drawings (MR, pp. 51–2) is too long to quote, but they seem sadistically

---

[6] Richard Howard translates *illustré* as "tabloid," but *Time, Newsweek*, or a Sunday magazine supplement could be described as *un illustré*.

pornographic until we are told that the captions in Chinese affixed to the three pictures mean, respectively,

"Drugs are a Disloyal Friend," "Drugs are an Enslaving Tyrant," "Drugs are a Deadly Poison." Unfortunately the sweeper [who has picked up the magazine in the gutter] cannot read. As for the short fat man with the red face and bald head who is telling the story, he does not understand Chinese; at the bottom of the last picture, he has only been able to make out some very tiny Western letters and numbers: "S.W.N. Tel.: 1-234-567." A far [from] scrupulous narrator, who seems to be unaware of the meaning of the three initials (Society for the War on Narcotics) and who insists, on the contrary, on the attraction of the illustrations to a specialist, he declares to his interlocutor—who is quite incredulous, moreover—that the drawings are an advertisement for some clandestine establishment in the lower part of the city, where habitués are offered forbidden and monstrous pleasures which are not those of morphine and opium alone. (MR, p. 53)

This passage, incidentally, illustrates the curious "Chinese-box" or "Hall-of-Mirrors" effect created by much of *La Maison de Rendez-vous.* The fat man who develops an elaborate fantasy about these drawings may be none other than the fat man of the garish cover of the magazine, who has somehow become a reader of the same magazine! The worthy-seeming advertisement may in fact be what he claims it is, for Lady Ava later says, "Our telephone number's been changed. Now it's one, two hundred thirty-four, five hundred sixty-seven." (M, p. 98) This same fat man wears a Chinese seal ring on which is carved a young woman on a bed in a posture similar to that in the first of the drawings.

But, then again, the source of the book may be "the same fat, red-faced man . . . talking in a loud voice about life in Hong Kong . . ." (p. 4). As "Eve, Eva, Eva Bergmann, Lady Ava, Lady Ava, Lady Ava" (p. 133) lies on her deathbed, she tells the "I" of the novel—always assuming that the first person singular stands for the same individual throughout the book rather than for several different people!—

. . . that her name is neither Ava nor Eve, but Jacqueline, that she has not married an English lord, that she has never gone to China: the fancy brothel, in Hong Kong, is merely a story people have told her. In fact she wonders now if it wasn't actually in Shanghai, a huge baroque palace with gaming rooms, prostitutes of all kinds, fine restaurants, theaters with erotic performances and opium dens. It was called "Le Grand Monde" . . . or something of the sort. . . . Her face is so blank, her gaze so remote, that I wonder if she is still quite conscious, if she is not already a little delirious. . . . She has also been told that meat was so rare there and children so numerous, that little girls who didn't find a protector or a husband soon enough were eaten. But Lady Ava does not believe that this detail is true. "It's all stories," she says, "invented by travelers." (MR, p. 134)

These last sentences refer to a particularly loathsome story about the fate of a little Japanese girl, Kito, who took part in some of Lady Ava's erotic theatrical performances, was sold to "Sir Ralph" Johnson, and had tested upon her one of the potions developed by Edouard Manneret and sold commercially by Johnson. Manneret

. . . was addicted . . . to both vampirism and necrophilia, so that the death of Kito, on whom the new product proved its efficacy by the absolute mastery it left to the beneficiary, must soon have passed into the losses and gains of the association [between Manneret and Johnson]. (MR, p. 119)

Much of what follows hovers on the borderline between "black humor" and sadism—a line one would prefer not to have to draw:

Her bloodless body . . . was sold to be served with various sauces in a well-known . . . restaurant. The Chinese cuisine has the advantage of making its contents unrecognizable. It is obvious, nonetheless, that the meat's origin was revealed— with proofs to support the matter—to certain customers of either sex with depraved tastes, who consented to pay high prices in order to consume this kind of meat; prepared with particular care, it was served to them in the course of ritual banquets whose setting, as well as the various excesses to

which these celebrations gave rise, necessitated a private
dining room located apart from the regular rooms. The fat
man with the red face describes with delighted precision some
of the perversions committed under such circumstances, then
continues his story. (MR, p. 119)

This story of his, "a classic story of white-slave traffic," began
as far back as page 7.

Perhaps, after studying the passage just quoted, the reader
will agree that although Robbe-Grillet has made a very ingenious attempt to show us a novel in process of composition,
if the novel were in fact completed it would be a piece of
trash not worth reading. Whereas *Jealousy, In the Labyrinth,*
and even *The Voyeur*—not to mention, of course, the two
great films, *Last Year at Marienbad* and *L'Immortelle*—forced
us to undergo experiences that enlarged our imaginations and
therefore made us more aware of certain aspects of reality,
both *The Erasers* and *La Maison de Rendez-vous*—and doubtless *Trans-Europ-Express* too—are tiresome bits of trickery.
Why? Because they are mere pastiche or parody of mass-
appeal (and mass-produced) "literature." They may to some
extent expose to ridicule the falsities of kitsch and thus
obliquely illuminate the truth, but they never confront the
reader with authentic experience as Robbe-Grillet's best novels
and films do. *Jealousy* admittedly is a tissue of illusions, but
then the "truth" about this peculiarly human emotion—as
Shakespeare knew—is that it feeds on illusion and deliberate
falsehood.

In his essay "On Several Obsolete Notions," Robbe-Grillet
has denied that form and content can be separated and that
content is the more important of the two:

> We thus see the absurdity of that favorite expression of our
> traditional criticism: "X has something to say and says it well."
> Might we not advance on the contrary that the genuine writer
> has nothing to say? He has only a way of speaking. He must
> create a world, but starting from nothing, from the dust. . . .
> (FNN, p. 45)

I would assert rather that any writer with something genuinely new to say finds a new form in which to say it; also, as

Butor contends, to create a new form is to make a tool for
the discovery of new content. I think that Robbe-Grillet has
done this over and over again in the novels and films just
cited with approval. In *La Maison de Rendez-vous*, however,
he has developed the method of *Jealousy* to a point of no
return. He has evolved a form, a tool, so refined that it altogether fails to get a purchase on reality. Paradoxically, this
avant-garde instrument fastens instead upon those most phil-
istine, traditional, and formula-ridden of artistic manifestations, the works that cater to the fantasies of the common man.
The great writers, on the other hand, like Robbe-Grillet at his
best, are "masters of reality." No doubt we may expect fine
novels and/or fine films from his fertile imagination in years
to come, but in the unlikely event that he has exhausted his
talent, Robbe-Grillet created once for all in *Jealousy* a narra-
tive/descriptive method that novelists will be making use of
for at least the next generation.

5
Michel Butor

THE SCHEMA AND THE MYTH

MICHEL BUTOR occupies a paradoxical situation in what we may call the hierarchy of the *nouveau roman*. On the one hand, he has written four novels of unquestionable though uneven merit, one of which justifiably became a best seller in his native France; as a result, his eminence among the school of novelists we are examining has been taken for granted by a growing body of critics; yet he has not published a novel since 1960, and it seems quite possible that he will never write another. On the other hand, he has published a series of brilliant articles on the theory of the novel, to be found in his volumes of criticism, *Répertoire* and *Répertoire II*, which have made him at least as important an expounder of the newness of the New Novel as Alain Robbe-Grillet or Nathalie Sarraute; yet it can be shown that all his novels except the last break very little new ground and owe much of their success primarily to Butor's mastery of those old-fashioned components, plot and characterization.

Naturally, this mastery appears most strikingly in Butor's most popular novel, *La Modification* (*A Change of Heart*), which was first published in 1957 and won the Théophraste Renaudot Prize, second only in prestige to the Goncourt Prize, for that year. As a result, it sold over a hundred thousand copies in France and was translated into at least thirteen languages. One might attribute its success to the bourgeois moral that it seems to inculcate: a husband wavers mentally between wife and mistress but ends by deciding to stay with his wife. This theme, however, is treated with classical astringency rather than sentimental sweetness, and it is possible to conclude that the real moral of the story is anti-bourgeois. At any rate, the critic may well "rejoice to concur with the common reader" in viewing this as the masterpiece among Butor's novels.

The scope of the novel is restricted to one man's reflections, memories, dreams, and perceptions during a railroad journey between Paris and Rome which lasts not quite twenty-four hours (21 hours, 35 minutes, to be exact). Within this larger restriction an even narrower one is imposed, for we are not allowed to share this one man's experience directly except when he is occupying a third-class compartment that seats eight passengers when full. Each of the nine chapters in the book begins with his entering this compartment and ends with his leaving it—whether to eat in the dining car, to go to the toilet, to stand in the corridor, to walk on the platform at a stop, or finally to leave the train at his destination. What he does in these intervals outside the compartment is made known to us only by anticipation or by memory, if he happens to remember.

As a result, the reader shares much of the protagonist's claustrophobic reaction to his confinement: his awareness of the changing complement of passengers, of their luggage in the racks, of the typical railroad-car décor (including banal photographs of tourist landmarks in Paris), and even of the litter that accumulates on the floor. A rather simple grammatical device intensifies the reader's identification with the protagonist: the whole experience is narrated in the second person. Thus the book opens, in Jean Stewart's translation, with these words:

> Standing with your left foot on the grooved brass sill, you try in vain with your right shoulder to push the sliding door a little wider open.[1]

[1] *A Change of Heart* (New York, 1959), p. 1.

It should be noted that in the French the polite second person plural, *vous*, is used, rather than the more intimate singular, *tu*. It is therefore clear that the narrator is in some sense addressing the reader and not merely himself. Presumably the narrator and the protagonist are one. In the passage just quoted, he seems to be narrating everything simultaneously with its occurrence, and this impression is kept up throughout the book. Thus a stream-of-consciousness technique is employed, yet we are always conscious of a narrator, no matter how much we identify with him.

Just who is this narrator/protagonist? Since he is perfectly aware of his own name and is telling his story in the first instance for and to himself, we have to wait a long time (until page 96 in the New York edition) to find out that his full name is Léon Delmont. In all likelihood the reader will promptly forget the name again, since it seems not to be given in full throughout the rest of the novel. It is best that the narrator *should* remain semi-anonymous in this way, so that we can the more readily identify with him—though it will obviously be easier for men than for women to do so.

By eavesdropping on Léon's stream of consciousness, we gradually piece together all the necessary information about him. It must, unfortunately, be presented in summary here, all in one block, thus completely falsifying one of the book's most realistic effects.

Léon Delmont is a successful business executive, head of the French sales organization of an Italian typewriter firm, Scabelli, whose principal office is in Rome. He owns a car and lives with his wife, Henriette, and four children in an expensive Paris apartment at 15 Place du Panthéon. As part of his job, he has been in the habit of making regular monthly train journeys from Paris to Rome for meetings. About two years earlier he met Cécile Darcella, of French birth and the widow of an Italian engineer, who works at the French Embassy in Rome. At the time, she was returning to Rome by train from a visit to her native Paris. They have since become lovers, and one of their great delights is to explore Rome together. Cécile has paid one rather unsatisfactory visit to Paris in the

meantime, during which she met Henriette and got on rather
well with her. Cécile is sufficiently in love with Léon to want
to move to Paris permanently and have him live with her there
without divorcing his wife. Léon, who reluctantly "celebrated"
his forty-fifth birthday on Wednesday, November 13, 1955,
just two days before his train journey begins, is some fifteen
years older than Cécile and at heart much more settled and
conventional. Inevitably, though, his middle-aged love affair
has made him feel younger and ready for daring resolutions:
after months of procrastination, he has at last found a job for
Cécile in Paris and a possible apartment for them to live in.
On an impulse, he has decided to be himself the bearer of
these good tidings, taking a brief vacation from his job,
Friday to Tuesday, though of course he does not tell his employers that he plans to go to Rome. Henriette thinks, or at
any rate is supposed to think, that he has gone to Rome on
urgent business, although he had just returned on the Monday
from one of his regular monthly trips. Cécile does not know
that he is coming, for he wants to surprise her with the long-
awaited good news.

Obviously, although Delmont thinks he has already made
his decision, he has in fact established an "open-ended"
situation: he has not yet told Cécile of his "decisive" steps;
he has not even told her that he will be in Rome. These two
omissions underlie the classical division of the original French
edition into three "parts" of three chapters each. (It is most
unfortunate that this tripartite division has been dropped from
the New York translation.) Chapters 1–3 contain the exposition of the original plan and the anticipation of Cécile's joy
at hearing about it. In Chapters 4–6 (Part II of the French),
Delmont comes to realize that he lacks the courage to go
through with the plan, particularly the break involved in
leaving Henriette and the children and moving in with Cécile.
How is he going to behave toward Henriette next Tuesday,
even, after he has told all his plans to Cécile? We are given
four different anticipatory versions of his approach to Henriette in a poignant passage (pp. 136–8, New York edition).
But, besides his cowardice, a basic fallacy vitiates his plan:

Cécile and his love for her are associated exclusively with
Rome; their love is bound to fade in Paris; unpleasant memories of Cécile's one visit to Paris since they became lovers
flood in upon him to confirm this impression. Thus by the end
of Chapter 6 he has decided to let things go on as they are
and not to tell Cécile the "good news." Chapters 7–9 (Part III
of the French) force upon him the logical conclusion that he
had better not let Cécile know about his trip at all, since he
cannot tell her why he originally started out on it. Instead of
staying, as he had planned, in a vacant room sublet from
Cécile's landlady, he must find a hotel: it cannot be the one
where he stays on business trips, since he is not supposed to
be in Rome; symbolically, he decides to stay in the hotel where
Henriette and he spent their honeymoon before World War II,
and where they also stayed during a disappointing visit to
Rome three years ago. He becomes convinced that in the end
he and Cécile will cease to be lovers, although for the present
he will continue to see her on his monthly visits to Rome.
Henriette and he will eventually become reconciled:

> You say, I promise you, Henriette, as soon as we can, we'll
> come back to Rome together, as soon as the waves of this
> perturbation have died down, as soon as you've forgiven me;
> we won't be so very old. (p. 248)

Almost the concluding paragraph of the novel, this passage is
certainly open to an accusation of sentimentality, but the
words "we won't be so very old" are charged with irony.
Obviously Léon feels too old already to make a fresh start in
life.

The family may have triumphed, but Léon feels little besides a sense of defeat; his one hope of snatching victory from
this defeat is to write a book which "should show the part
Rome can play in the life of a man in Paris; the two cities
might be imagined one above the other, one of them lying
underground below the other, with communicating trap doors
which only a few would know . . ." (pp. 243–4). Paris is the
Ego, Rome the Id?

The extent of his defeat is measured by the harshness of

the judgment that he feels will be passed upon him by Cécile. Although she is not presented entirely without irony, Léon feels that her anti-Catholic, anti-bourgeois attitude is freer and nobler than his own hypocritical and fearful deference to Church and State. (Cécile is made a little ridiculous by her refusal to set foot inside the Vatican; this means that she can never see the Sistine Chapel frescoes, for instance.) His whole love affair has been a masquerade, in which he has pretended to be younger and more emancipated than in fact he is:

> . . . your eyes fill with tears of disappointment; you wonder, How can I ever make her understand and forgive me for the lie that our love has been, except perhaps by means of this book in which she would appear in her full beauty, adorned with the glory of Rome which is so perfectly reflected in her. (p. 246)

One of the most interesting and "realistic" features of *A Change of Heart* is the materialistic influence that prompts this spiritual defeat. Because he is traveling at his own expense, Léon has chosen to travel third-class rather than first. The discomfort of his seat and the overcrowding in the compartment make it impossible for him to read the book he has just bought or to sleep in peace. His fitful sleep is haunted by a continuous nightmare, while his waking hours are filled by uncomfortable memories. Cécile's unsatisfactory journey to Paris and back was undertaken in his company in third class (thanks to the same bourgeois stinginess that has prompted the economizing on his present trip). Furthermore, on their honeymoon trip Henriette and he traveled third-class, because in those days he could afford no better. As an added turn of the screw, his compartment is shared throughout the present journey by a honeymoon couple on their way to Sicily. Léon is trapped in a vicious cycle: his bourgeois conditioning is reinforced by the discomfort of the journey, but without this conditioning he would never have bought a third-class ticket in the first place.

Inevitably, this summary has made the novel seem much

more straightforward than it is. Actually, its structure, especially in relation to time, is extremely complex. In a series of
interviews with Georges Charbonnier broadcast in France
during January and February 1967, Butor explained his need
for a logical schema to underpin each of his novels.[2] The
basic structural element in *A Change of Heart* is, quite simply,
a timetable, a train schedule, "Edition of October 2, 1955,
winter service, valid until June 2, 1956, inclusive . . ." (p. 18).
Like every such timetable, it translates time into space and
space into time: "This train will stop at Dijon and leave again
at 11:18, it will pass through Bourg at 1:20 p.m., leave Aix-
les-Bains at 2:41 . . ." (p. 21). The schedule provides Butor
with more than the timetable for a one-way journey, Paris–
Rome: it also contains the timetable of the express train that
Léon takes when he travels first-class (it includes no third-
class cars). Furthermore, every outward-bound trip implies
a return journey, so that every station on the line can suggest to Léon some past or future journey from Rome to Paris,
in first or third class, and the time of day at which he usually
passes that station when homeward bound.

But this set of fourfold possibilities does not reveal the full
complexity of the skein of Léon's memories. Besides the
routine monthly journeys, which have become blurred into
one general impression, he is aware of at least eight significant
trips on this line—past, present, *and* future. Let us tabulate
them:

> *Past:* 1. Pre-war honeymoon trip *to* Rome with Henriette.
> (The return trip is hardly recalled at all.)
> 2. Three years ago, the return trip with Henriette
> *from* an unsatisfactory winter visit to Rome. (The
> outward-bound trip seems to have been com-
> pletely forgotten.)
> 3. Two years ago, the trip *to* Rome during which he
> met Cécile in the dining car and traveled with
> her in her third-class compartment the rest of
> the way.

[2] Georges Charbonnier, *Entretiens avec Michel Butor* (Paris: Gallimard, 1967), pp. 16–17, 50, and *passim*.

4. One year ago, the trip *from* Rome to Paris with Cécile.

5. The disillusioned trip *to* Rome after Cécile's Paris visit.

6. Earlier this week, his return trip in first class *from* the latest of his monthly visits to Cécile and Rome.

Present: 7. The current trip *to* Rome.

Future: 8. The return *from* Rome on Monday next.

When he is not occupied in observing his surroundings, Léon is usually remembering or anticipating one of these journeys. Often the association of a memory with a particular station will cause his mind to leap from one journey to another. No doubt Butor could have compiled an arbitrary numerical series dictating the order in which memories of the different journeys would recur to his protagonist, though it does not appear that he has done so. In his fourth novel, *Degrees*, some readers may suspect the functioning of just such a mechanism.

In a curious passage in *A Change of Heart*, Léon uses the metaphor of a "mental machine" to describe the processes at work in his mind during the journey:

> You say to yourself, if there hadn't been these people, if there hadn't been these objects, these images onto which my thoughts fastened, so that, during a journey unlike my other journeys, cut off from the habitual sequence of my days and actions, a kind of mental machine was set up, making the various regions of my being go sliding one over the other, tearing me apart,
>
> if there hadn't been this set of circumstances, if the cards had not been dealt this way, perhaps this yawning fissure in my being would not have appeared during the course of this night, perhaps my illusions might have held for a little longer. . . . (p. 240)

These "regions of my being" (*régions de mon existence*) are presumably first of all Paris and Rome; then his home life with Henriette, his business life, and his "holiday" life with Cécile; then the various periods of his past and future evoked by this journey: at any rate it was as the result of remembering all those different rail journeys that the destructive mental machine set to work.

In each of Butor's three other novels we shall find a schema —usually in some sense a timetable—by which time and place are intimately related. The characteristically punning title of his second novel, *L'Emploi du Temps* (*Passing Time*, in English), means "timetable" as well as "daily routine" and, most literally, "use of (one's) time."

In every Butor novel, however, alongside this logical, mechanistic, workaday schema, we can trace a totally different type of structural device: intuitive, artistic, nocturnal. Dreams, myths, rituals, works of art (real or imaginary) are used separately or in combination as analogues of the characters' experience in what we may call the objective or materialistic or daylight world.

In *A Change of Heart* this nocturnal element consists mainly of a continuous dream which Léon takes up at the point where he had left off, each time he falls briefly asleep during his uncomfortable and exhausting night on the train. This dream or nightmare contains elements of a *rite de passage* or initiation ritual: Léon is undergoing an ordeal, but more and more he begins to feel that he is on trial; the dream becomes toward the end a vision of judgment. It is easy to trace some of the motifs from waking experience that have been incorporated into this dream. While he thinks of the train passing the Forest of Fontainebleau, Léon remembers the legend of *le grand veneur* (The Great Huntsman), a giant figure who stops wanderers in the forest and asks them, "*M'entendez-vous?* Do you hear me?" (p. 95). As Léon struggles with himself, he imagines the Huntsman putting more and more embarrassing questions, such as "*Qu'attendez-vous?* What are you waiting for?" (p. 114). Eventually he realizes, as he remembers his honeymoon journey, that it was probably Henriette who first told him of the legend:

> the Forest of Fontainebleau full of young green shoots (and
> wasn't it she who told you, at that point, how she used to

walk there as a child with her sisters, terrified as soon as
dusk fell of meeting the Great Huntsman, who would challenge them and carry them off?). . . . (p. 198)

No wonder the imagined questions become more and more
reproachful!

It is hard to say precisely where the dream begins, since
at first Léon seems to be imagining the contents of a book—
either the one he has bought in Paris and keeps by him
throughout the journey without opening it or even glancing
at the title, or else one that he will buy in Rome to read on
the return journey—"a book . . . which ought to be about a
man lost in a forest that keeps closing up behind him, so
that he can't make up his mind which way he ought to go. . . ."
At first we see parallels to the Great Huntsman legend, but
soon (pp. 184-5) the lost man has become Aeneas in Book VI
of Virgil's *Aeneid*, seeking the way to the Underworld. Charon
(p. 189) asks the same questions as the Great Huntsman. The
road through Hades eventually leads to the outskirts of Rome,
to a statue of Janus, the two-faced god, and to the she-wolf
that suckled Romulus and Remus. For a time the nightmare
takes on a more modern, Kafkaesque quality. A newcomer to
the compartment seems to ask all the unanswerable questions:

> "Who are you? Where are you going? What are you
> seeking? Whom do you love? What do you want? What are
> you waiting for? What are you feeling? Can you see me? Can
> you hear me?" (p. 219)

Eventually the dream reaches its climax in confrontations with
the Pope, with the prophets and sibyls and the King of the
Last Judgment from Michelangelo's Sistine Chapel, and with
a procession of the gods of ancient Rome, culminating in
Venus.

Waking up for the last time, Léon remembers how he and
Henriette visited the Temple of Venus and Rome during their
honeymoon:

> Suddenly, sitting on the bench, in the heady evening air, she
> asked you, "Why Venus and Rome? What's the connection
> between the two?" (p. 234)

This is perhaps the most unanswerable question of all, at least for Anglo-Saxons who are accustomed to associate Venus and her pleasures with Paris rather than Rome. But Léon understands that he is a victim of the myth of Rome as the center of the known world: center of the Empire first, then of the Church. Our world now lacks a center, but the prestige of Rome, which has cast its glamour around Cécile, is also paradoxically forcing Léon and Cécile apart, insofar as in France the Roman Catholic Church still provides the ultimate sanction for family life.

In examining the division of the novel into three parts, we have sufficiently observed the logical development of the plot, which many an "old" novelist might see fit to envy. Something ought to be said in conclusion, however, about the extremely penetrating—and, for that very reason, extremely old-fashioned—character analysis in *A Change of Heart*. True, Henriette is a dim figure and Cécile an over-idealized one, but this is because we see them only through Léon's eyes. His estimate of them is one of the touches which contribute to an extremely lifelike portrait of a man of forty-five whose neck is being chafed by the marriage yoke. Butor works very contentedly within the French classical tradition of character drawing, presenting Léon as at one and the same time an individual and a type. Without intervening to comment in his own person, Butor can still make us aware of the detached irony with which he often views his protagonist. One longish passage will have to stand for many others in the same vein:

> At that time you intended to settle everything by letter and not to see Cécile again until your next monthly trip, for the annual meeting of the directors of Scabelli's foreign branches, and it was only on Wednesday that things came to a head, and that, no doubt, because it was November 13 and consequently your birthday, and because Henriette, who still clung to these ridiculous family ceremonies, had laid particular stress on it this year, being suspicious of you, with even more justification than she knew, and hoping to hold you, to ensnare you in this net of petty rites, not out of love of course, all that came to an end between you long ago (and if

there had been some sort of youthful passion once, it had never been anything comparable to that feeling of release and enchantment that Cécile brought you), but from her dread, increasing daily (how she was aging!), of seeing any alteration in the order of things to which she was accustomed, not really out of jealousy but out of the haunting fear that some rash step on your part or some violent disagreement might ruin her comfort and the children's. . . . (p. 25)

The comments in parentheses imply a damning complacency on Léon's part. In what sense has he been granted "release," if he is capable of imputing such shabby motives to his wife? And is he really aging any less rapidly than she? A critic in his early fifties can only salute with admiration the insight of a novelist who wrote this passage when barely thirty.

A *Change of Heart*, then, has a great deal in common with the traditional novel. What links it and Butor's other novels most closely with *le nouveau roman* as a school is the almost obsessive concern with structure, though this seems unnecessary in a work that is already held tightly together by a logical plot. It is plotless novels that need to be given form by the use of schemas or myths.

Other characteristics of the New Novel to be found in *A Change of Heart* are the readiness to make unheralded shifts from one level of time to another and the interest in "point of view" that leads to the experiment of writing an entire novel in the second person. The employment of stream-of-consciousness technique is peculiarly appropriate in a story whose main action is internal, psychological. The very first novel to use this technique, Édouard Dujardin's *Les Lauriers sont coupés* (*We'll to the Woods No More*, first published 1887), dealt with a young man's vacillation between two attitudes toward his beloved. (Valéry Larbaud, in a conscious attempt to imitate Dujardin, wrote a short novel in the same manner dealing with a young man's mental vacillation between two women during a train journey: *Mon plus secret conseil.* . . .)

Passage de Milan (1954, not yet translated into English) compresses into its punning title the *locale*, the catastrophe,

and one of the myths with which it deals. 15 Passage de Milan
is a seven-story apartment building (with a basement, naturally) in Paris. The little street on which it stands is presumably
named after the Italian city, but the French word *milan*, as we
are reminded on page 8, can mean "kite" in the sense of a bird
of prey:

> *Dans le haut de l'air, ailes déployées, si ce n'est un avion*
> *c'est un milan.* (High in the air, wings spread, if it isn't a
> plane it's a kite.)[3]

As we shall see, one of the young male visitors to the building
has the rapacity of a kite and does even more damage than he
intended. Furthermore, as Butor explained to Georges Charbonnier (*Entretiens avec Michel Butor*, p. 51), the kite in
ancient Egypt was the god Horus. (English-language authorities usually identify Horus with the falcon, but this is irrelevant to the interpretation of Butor.) Two of the tenants in
the building are keenly interested in Egyptian archaeology.

There will be more to say about the myth of Horus later
and about the ritual and works of art which also parallel the
action. For the moment, we had better examine the schema,
which bulks as large in this novel as in the other three. Briefly,
it consists of the multiple levels of the apartment building,
the channels of communication between them, and the timetable of the movements of all the occupants and their visitors
from floor to floor and in and out of the building. It will help
the reader greatly to understand from the beginning that each
of the twelve chapters into which the book is divided corresponds to an hour on the clock, from seven in the evening
until seven in the morning, the hour which rings out from the
clock tower of the neighboring convent in the last sentence of
the book.

The internal organization of the apartment building is
probably very common in Paris, but it takes a non-French
reader some little time to map it out for himself. Basically,
there are three lines of vertical communication: the main stair-

[3] The reader unfamiliar with French needs to be told that the French
word for "kite" in the sense of a child's toy is *cerf-volant*.

case, the elevator, and the service staircase. The main staircase begins on the ground floor, where the concierge and his wife live, and runs only as far as the fifth floor. There is only one apartment on each floor from the first through the fifth. The elevator, like the main staircase, runs only to the fifth floor, but, unlike the staircase, it descends to the basement. The only line of communication that runs all the way from the basement to the sixth floor is the service staircase. The kitchen doors of all the apartments open onto the latter, just as all the front doors open onto the main staircase.

Although there are windows between the main staircase and the service staircase to light the latter, there are no communicating doors between them. Some of the grim hide-and-seek that goes on during the later stages of the novel is incomprehensible unless these aids and barriers to communication are fully understood.

We can now proceed to list the inhabitants of the various floors, beginning at the top, in order to help the reader to visualize the layered arrangement of the building:

Sixth Floor. This is a rabbit warren of small bedrooms. All the servants, male and female, sleep here, as do the older boys from the families below. Two spare rooms are occupied by a senile, retired servant, Elisabeth Mercadier, and a salesgirl, Liliane Fraisin.

Fifth Floor. The painter Martin de Vere lives here with his wife, Lucie; his baby daughter, Miette; and two small sons. Part of the apartment is sublet to Gaston Mourre.

Fourth Floor. Here live a wealthy couple, Léon and Lydie Vertigues, who are giving a party in honor of the twentieth birthday of their only daughter, Angèle, on the night we are privileged to observe. Gertrude is their maid.

Third Floor. Samuel Léonard, a wealthy Jewish businessman and amateur Egyptologist, lives here with his supposed niece (actually his illegitimate daughter), Henriette Ledu. He has two servants, Mme Phyllis and a young Egyptian named Ahmed, with whom he carries on a homosexual relationship. Léonard is also an amateur writer of science fiction and has

invited in a group of professionals in this genre on the night
of the novel.

Second Floor. Here lives the large, three-generation family of
Frédéric and Julie Mogne. The three boys—Vincent, Gérard,
and Félix—sleep on the sixth floor, but the two younger
daughters, Martine and Viola, sleep in the apartment, as do
their parents; their paternal grandfather, Paul Mogne; and
their maternal grandmother, Marie Mérédat. Their married
sister, Jeanne, comes to dinner with her husband, Henri (not
to be confused with the rapacious Henri Delétang).

First Floor. The widowed Mme Virginie Ralon lives here with
her two sons, both Roman Catholic priests. The Abbé Jean
is an Egyptologist by profession, while the Abbé Alexis is the
chaplain in a secondary school. Mme Ralon's nephew, Louis
Lécuyer, has a room on the sixth floor, but he has been invited
to dinner this evening. Mme Charlotte Tenant, the family's
widowed cook, was one of the late M. Ralon's numerous
mistresses.

Ground Floor. The concierge (superintendent) and his wife,
Godefroy and Eléonore Poulet, live here.

Once again, as well as an elaborate schema, we have a plot:
in this case, one that leads up to and away from a distinctly
melodramatic catastrophe. We even have a "villain" who provokes the catastrophe, but it is not until page 166 (in a novel
286 pages long) that we learn of his criminal (or perhaps
psychotic) aims. Up to that point, the main trend of the book
is descriptive rather than narrative. Butor told Charbonnier
that *Passage de Milan* was begun in Egypt and that he felt a
need to re-create life in Paris (*Entretiens*, pp. 49–50). Consequently, the family dinner of the Mognes is described with
particularly loving care, tinged with irony. The Ralons' dinner
is also viewed, though in less detail. We learn more about
Angèle's party than about any of the other social activities:
we watch the young people arrive, chat, drink, dance, eat
and dance some more; we even learn a good deal about the
various dances—fox trot, waltz, rumba, tango—and the recorded music to which they are danced. The discussion of the
theory and practice of *romans d'anticipation* (science fiction)

at Samuel Léonard's is also presented in somewhat excessive detail. Finally, so that all five apartment floors may be represented, we are treated to an impromptu discussion of painting at the de Veres'. Some of the painter's friends arrive to accompany him and his wife to a film at about the same time as two of Angèle's guests, Bénédicte and Gustave; the latter are persuaded by a mutual friend to visit the painter before joining the party.

Before the villain, Henri Delétang, has been unveiled to us by the simple device of exposing his interior monologue, we have detected only one valid strand of plot, the potential jealousy of Louis Lécuyer. He has agreed to squire Henriette Ledu to the party, but he is obsessed by Angèle's loveliness. The two elder Mogne boys, Vincent and Gérard, virtually monopolize their hostess, however, so that Louis becomes more and more deeply chagrined.

Henri Delétang gives the impression of having wandered into Butor's novelistic world by mistake out of a book by Gide —*Lafcadio's Adventures* or *The Counterfeiters*. He is determined to steal something of value from the Vertigues family, which he will then conceal in the pockets of his schoolfellow Denis Petitpaté next day (p. 201). He has already made a similar theft from the Petitpaté home (p. 169). The motive for these thefts is never made fully clear, but the three fathers are business associates, whether in fact they make up the firm of "Petitpaté, Delétang, Vertigues et Cie," (p. 202) or not. Henri feels that Angèle's parents would not have invited him if it were not for this business association, but his hostility seems chiefly directed against his own father: "Never will I pardon him the stigma that he has bequeathed me along with his name" (p. 202).

Henri has come to the party with a girl named Clara Grumeaux, who is even less socially acceptable than he; unknown to him, she is the mistress of the de Veres' tenant, Gaston Mourre. There is a comic moment at the end of the party when Henri and Clara each try to shake the other off so that they can slip back into the building after ostentatiously leaving it. They both succeed in doing so. Henri has stolen

Léon Vertigues's keys and thus is able to let himself into the
apartment. Contrary to his calculations, Angèle is still awake
and in the living room, daydreaming about the party and her
future wedding; her white evening gown is already almost a
wedding dress. She screams when she sees Henri entering.
Louis, who cannot sleep and has been prowling the house,
hears her and breaks through a window from the service staircase into the main staircase. He enters the apartment through
the front door, left open by Henri:

> And sees the terrified Angèle being kissed on the mouth by
> Delétang; hurls a candlestick.
> Flight. Fall.
> She has struck the sharp edge of the marble table with her
> temple. (p. 246)

Henri makes good his escape, but Louis stays in the apartment, in hiding, until the de Veres find Angèle dead. Then, in
despair at the unlikelihood that even the Ralons will believe his
story, Louis runs to hide in the basement. There he is discovered by Samuel Léonard, who arranges his escape to Egypt.
Why? Presumably because Léonard thinks that Louis was the
young man he surprised in Ahmed's bedroom a little earlier
and could not at the time identify. Actually, that young man
was Vincent Mogne. As the book ends, the fêted Angèle is
dead, Henri Delétang has escaped scot-free, and Louis, the
orphan, has become the exiled scapegoat. No poetic justice
here.

As Butor pointed out to Charbonnier, almost all the inhabitants of the building have been brought into contact with
each other through their awareness of the party on the fourth
floor. And this party was of a special kind, a festival cele-
brating the passage from adolescence to adulthood. Butor went
on to say:

> . . . in this book, Egypt appears as a sort of sounding board.
> There is in this building an abbé who is an Egyptologist. There
> happens to be there too a gentleman who has come back from
> Egypt. With an Egyptian, a young Egyptian man, in his
> service. He has come back from Egypt and has in his apart-

ment a collection of Egyptian objects. At the end of the book a young man will be driven out of Paris and go to try his luck in Egypt. All these elements supply a sort of frame of reference, a point of comparison. The Paris building appears in the guise of a fact of civilization that can be put in relationship to other facts of civilization. (*Entretiens*, p. 54)

And so, when "this festival ends in a death, a death due to chance," the Western view of death as "something that disturbs us terribly, that embarrasses us terribly, that happens always as something unforeseen" (p. 55) can be contrasted with the Egyptian view of death as something always to be foreseen and almost looked forward to. Butor says of his characters: "All these people who were put in contact with each other by a joyful festival, all these people find themselves harshly confronted with each other in face of the intrusion of death" (p. 54). Actually, when this confrontation occurs, nothing significant comes of it except Samuel Léonard's doubtful kindness toward Louis Lécuyer. Everybody goes through the expected motions mechanically, and no social fusion or private change of heart takes place.

Before concluding with a brief analysis of the "mythic" elements, we must examine in some detail the narrative technique which permits these and the schematic elements to achieve a sort of unity, however imperfect. As Butor admitted to Charbonnier, "I found myself, in doing this book, with an extremely mobile narrator, whose mobility I did not truly control. I have tried, in the books that followed, to control the mobility of the narrator" (*Entretiens*, p. 48).

Actually, during a large part of the book, one is not conscious of the presence of a narrator at all. The frequent passages of third-person, past-tense narration presuppose the telling of a story by *someone, after* the events. But this kind of impersonal, omniscient narration is too familiar to attract our attention. Hardly more disturbing is the still more frequent use of present-tense narration in the third person; this of course brings us much closer to the events than the past-tense narration with which it alternates—without, one feels, very compelling reasons for the shifts back and forth. Occasionally, however, we are made very conscious of a narrator who is inviting us to stand by him and observe what is happening: "Station yourself at the door, you will have the closed window in front of you, with its drapes which frame it, and, standing out against the reflections in the panes, the black hair of Félix . . ." (p. 53). This passage occurs in the account of dinner at the apartment of the Mognes. The circulation of the serving dishes about the table is presented with conscious humor: "At first the trajectories reproduce the preceding ones, but attentive minds will already have noticed that the change in circumstances is going to bring about a remarkable complication. To wit: the two dishes, which were interchangeable just before, are now clearly differentiated and must of necessity be passed to every one of the diners" (pp. 63–4).

Mingling with these different types of third-person narration are numerous paragraphs in stream-of-consciousness style, some presenting the thoughts and others the dreams of various characters. Butor, like Claude Mauriac in some novels written a few years later, usually gives us no "stage direction" to indicate who is thinking or dreaming. We thus have to discover the identity of the character for ourselves on the basis of internal evidence. The only exception to this rule is provided by Chapter 6 (pp. 164–80), where each stream of consciousness is identified by its owner's name in the margin. The young people at the party are eating their midnight supper, so that conversation is at a minimum, but the principal reason for identifying their thoughts relates to the plot. We might be unable to decide which of the numerous characters present at the party was planning larceny if he were not explicitly identified as Henri Delétang.

The fluidity of modern narrative techniques can be demonstrated by a comparison between Zola's *Pot-Bouille*, the first famous novel about a Paris apartment building, and *Passage de Milan*. With Zola, each chapter is devoted to a single family in a single apartment. With Butor, as we have seen, each chapter corresponds to an hour, so that he must try to keep us abreast of events on all seven floors (and in the basement when necessary) more or less simultaneously. At first, of course, all the characters are awake and need to be kept in touch with. In Chapter 6, between midnight and one o'clock, the author can assume that everybody is asleep except those at Angèle's party and those at Samuel Léonard's. In the next chapter, between one and two, some of the sleeping characters are beginning to dream. As the book proceeds, the author shows less and less anxiety to warn us of a shift from floor to floor, but early on he feels obliged not only to signal such changes but to remind us of the relative positions of his characters on a vertical scale. For instance, *Montons* ("Let's go upstairs," p. 11) brings us from the Ralons' floor to the Mognes'. Later, M. Mogne "unties his shoelaces" (p. 13). In the next paragraph we read, "Alexis had just done the same thing a few meters below him, separated by the planks, the beams, the laths, and the plaster which forms the ceiling of his dark bedroom. . . ." We are back on the first floor again. Devices of this kind quickly grow tedious, and Butor shows discretion in dropping them fairly quickly. Throughout the night, however, he continues to note the passing of each Métro train underground as it shakes the whole house.

And now let us examine a ritual, some works of art, and three dreams. We have already noted Butor's reminder that Angèle's twentieth birthday party is *une fête de passage*, a festival of passage from youth to adulthood. This recalls to us the word *Passage* in the title, but we now know that for Angèle the party was a ritual of passage into death and the other world rather than into adulthood. Henri Delétang's kiss was the kiss of death for her.

The discussion of science fiction in the apartment of Samuel Léonard refers to various imaginary examples of that art, already written or projected. Not all science fiction is in question, but only those *romans d'anticipation* ("novels of anticipation") which attempt to predict the shape of a future world. (Readers of French may be interested in turning to Butor's philosophical essay on Jules Verne, dating from 1949, which appears in *Répertoire*.) It does not seem that any of these imaginary novels bears any direct resemblance to the action or structure of *Passage de Milan*. Rather, the function of this discussion, set against the background of Léonard's collection of Egyptian *objets d'art*, is to contrast Western modes of thought, oriented toward the future, with Egyptian and Eastern modes of thought in general.

More specifically relevant is a fascinating series of paragraphs (intermingled with other material on pp. 112–21) in which the painter Martin de Vere explains a new series of sketches that he has been doing, based in theory upon the art of Ancient Egypt:

> "You know, in the Egyptian rooms of the Louvre, that little tomb one goes into, covered with bas-reliefs lit up behind glass. Look here—it's a book on Saqqarah—look at these groups of birds turning their heads in opposite directions, the bodies of the sailors in boats that follow one another, and the women carrying offerings, like living bars dividing a stave into measures, between which there are played melodies of ducks, flowers and baskets. The artist of Beni-Hassan makes us pass from one dancing girl or one warrior to another by the continuation of the same movement, but in the great friezes of wrestlers, each time a red one and a black one, he has mixed up the successive snapshots of various bouts, in such a way that the series of figures become enlaced in a vast counterpoint." (p. 112)

Some of this description of Egyptian art surely presents analogies with Butor's novel, which shows us the inhabitants of floor after floor grouped in friezes one above the other, and in which each paragraph is likely to be a snapshot of a single character at a single moment.

De Vere's sketches based on these Egyptian principles began by being very abstract; then he took to incorporating letters of the alphabet in his designs; finally he traveled backwards in time from the letter to the hieroglyph and introduced into his paintings groups of representations of objects. On his easel there is the beginning of an oil painting, divided into twelve colored rectangles arranged in three horizontal rows of four; these he is going to fill with playing-card designs:

> "You see, my house has only twelve rooms, but the ordinary deck contains 52 cards. The division doesn't come out without

a remainder. Therefore in the middle row I'm going to superimpose five figures instead of four." (p. 119)

He proceeds to show his friends sketches of various arrange-
ments of cards, some of which seem prophetic of Angèle's
party, as Bénédicte later perceives (p. 170). The most significant parts of Martin's commentary on his sketches run as
follows:

> "Yes, you have the queen [*dame*] of hearts on the left and
> the knave [*valet*] of clubs facing her, separated by the ace of
> spades and one of the little knaves; the six others surround
> the scene. . . ." (p. 120)
>
> "I like this central king," he says, as if talking to himself,
> "bigger than the two knaves, this contrast with the neighboring
> scene, where this ace that I wanted to look like an eagle in full
> flight corresponds to him. Now what to do with this tiresome
> queen? She could be placed horizontally?" (p. 121)

Here, surely, we see Angèle and her suitors, Henri as the bird
of prey (Horus again?), and finally the stricken Angèle as the
horizontal queen. Again prophetically, the two sketches just
described are blown by a draft against an electric radiator
during the night, catch fire, and float against the canvas with
the twelve rectangles, "whose fresh paint grows dirty and
melts at the center" (p. 180).

Finally, let us look at the dreams of Félix, the youngest
Mogne boy, and the two brothers Ralon. Félix's dream, dispersed over pp. 220–33, shows him climbing an edifice similar
to the Eiffel Tower, in company with his grandfather, Paul
Mogne, with whom he has a warm relationship in his waking
hours. The old man is in splendid fettle to begin with, but he
tires as they climb higher, and Félix begins to lose touch with
him in a fog as they mount higher still. Turning in his bed to
look for him, Félix wakes up. Is this climb a journey toward
death, the death of the grandfather, whom Félix must lose as
he advances in life? At any rate, as he mounts from level to
level of the tower, Félix is enacting a series of rites of passage.

Alexis Ralon is chaplain at the *lycée* attended by his
nephew, Louis. Because of this new professional relationship,

their old intimacy has suffered, a situation which in some respects anticipates that in Butor's fourth novel, *Degrees*. Louis
does not feel that he can turn to Alexis for help after the
catastrophe. Alexis too is in dire need of sympathy but has no
one to turn to. Restless and passionate like his father, he has
missed the opportunity to enter the foreign-mission field. He
seems also to be a latent homosexual, haunted by the faces
of his students. He fears that, when he has succeeded in falling
asleep, his dreams will be "neither peaceful nor chaste" (p.
185). It becomes more and more clear (pp. 196–7) that he has
lost his religious vocation. He hears a murmur of voices saying,
"Alexis, Alexis," and this enables the reader to trace his dream
(pp. 211–26). He wakes up to the sound of his mother's voice
saying, "Alexis, Alexis." Martin and Lucie de Vere have found
the body of Angèle and want the priest to inform Angèle's
still sleeping parents of their loss. The dream is once again of
a passage toward death, it would seem. Alexis is lying on the
bottom of an open boat at night in a Breton port; the boat
leaves its mooring and floats out to sea, where it begins to
sink. "And I cannot tell the color of the bird that has just
closed its talons [*ses serres*] on my hand" (p. 221). Once
again we have met a bird of prey, no doubt the god Horus.
The dream ends:

> Beyond the phosphorescence of the clotted twigs, while the
> pieces of my boat sink and scatter about me, that tide of faces
> that is only too familiar to me, and the lips of Louis, who is
> easily distinguishable on the sandy bottom, articulate silently:
> "Alexis, Alexis." (p. 226)

The Abbé Jean Ralon, the elder brother, whose specialty is
Egyptology, has a longer and more complex dream than anybody else, but it takes careful reading to distinguish where his
dream begins and ends. It can easily be confused with his
mother's memories, which also contain allusions to the Middle
East, where her husband traveled frequently. It can, even
more easily, be confused with the unhappy musings of Ahmed,
who yearns for his native Egypt and fears that he will never
be able to return there if his jealous master dismisses him

after surprising him with Vincent. The recurrent phrase which enables one to recognize Ahmed's stream of consciousness is "*dans ces maisons*" ("in these houses," pp. 237–45). The kite appears in Ahmed's thoughts too: "It was on leaving Alexandria that I saw the last kites [*les derniers milans*]" (p. 239).

In Abbé Jean's dream (dispersed over pp. 204–20), his bed turns into an Egyptian boat steered by his "guardian," who looks like Ahmed but is decidedly bigger. Jean sees himself at first lying prone, wearing a soutane, with his hands crossed on his breast holding a crucifix. But his journey is definitely into the supernatural world of the Egyptians, where he is upbraided for not recognizing one of the ancient gods (p. 209) but is also told that he does not have to undergo trial; he may escape the gravest dangers (p. 220).

The full significance of the dream is revealed when Jean awakens:

> I missed everything, the sparrow-hawk, phoenix of hell, who rises above the serpent scarab, leaving the green body of his shade, the gods who employ stars to sing their hymns and bring to the sun, in his barge of state, his new face, and the great company of hours and heavenly bodies which accompany him in his ascent from the waters. Blinded, abandoned, excluded from the light by the closing of the door, I mingled my tears and my terror with those of all the inhabitants of these marshes of naphtha. (pp. 282–3)

Soon, however, Jean is mortified to realize how unfaithful he has been to Christ. He imagines the Savior addressing him from the crucifix as he celebrates Mass:

> ". . . your dreams are more sincere than your prayers; go then to those gods which torment you and no longer perpetuate this lie of consecrating my body and my blood with words which come only from the surface of your heart." (p. 283)

Jean in turn upbraids Christ for allowing him to fall a prey to "these old enchanters who laugh at my ignorance" (p. 284).

Thus it is not entirely true to say that the night just over has brought no revelation to any of the characters. Yet Jean's moment of insight into himself bears no direct relationship to

the catastrophe: it would appear that he has not yet learned
of the death of Angèle, which would give added meaning to
his dream.

L'Emploi du Temps (1956), Butor's second novel, the
ambiguities of whose title we have already explored, is a less
ambitious, less experimental work than *Passage de Milan.* The
events are recounted in the first person and past and present
tenses by a single, clearly identified narrator. Although these
events take place in the course of a year rather than a single
night, they involve no more than eight or ten major characters
whom the reader can recall as individuals, as compared with
two or three times that number in the earlier book. Because
of one's constant, even oppressive awareness of the presence
of a narrator, there is never any doubt as to who is speaking
or thinking. Paradoxically, however, just because we are
limited to a single viewpoint, we can never be sure of the trust-
worthiness of the narrator's reports of events or his interpretation of them; we have been robbed of the illusion that we are
able to see and judge events for ourselves.

Butor has exploited the basic untrustworthiness of all one-
sided narration as brilliantly as any novelist before him. One
cannot deny that *Passing Time* (to use the English title)[4] has
a plot, but one is tempted to add that it has two: a subjective
one and an objective one. The narrator, Jacques Revel,
imagines two love stories, in each of which he is the hero, and
a murder attempt for which he is in his own mind indirectly
responsible. Objectively, one recognizes the two love stories,
but their heroes turn out to be two other people, Lucien Blaise
and James Jenkins. As for the supposed murder attempt, it
was probably a mere accident, although the unknown driver
of the car involved did commit a crime by not stopping after
he had knocked down a pedestrian, George William Burton.
Since the guilty driver was never apprehended, that part of
the plot remains a mystery without a solution; it is possible
also that some of the mysterious fires which occurred in

[4] New York, 1960.

Bleston during the year were set by an arsonist. If so, who was he? Horace Buck, who loathes Bleston? Jacques Revel himself, who also hates the city of his exile and is perhaps concealing something crucial from his reader (or even, pathologically, from himself)? Burton, the accident victim and detective-story writer, who has expressed his detestation of Bleston in a book, *The Bleston Murder*, written under the pseudonym of J. C. Hamilton? We are not permitted to know the answer.

It will be best to give the complete plot in outline at this point. Jacques Revel, a young French business employee, arrives in the English city of Bleston on October 1. He is to work for the firm of Matthews and Sons for exactly a year. At first, his experiences resemble those of the protagonist of Kafka's *The Castle*. Arriving by the wrong train, he finds no one to meet him and cannot even remember the address of the hotel where he was to stay. Only one of his office colleagues, James Jenkins, shows him any true friendliness. His hotel room is utterly depressing, but he cannot find any better place to stay at a price he can afford. The first person to invite him into his home in Bleston is a Negro, Horace Buck. Later, Horace also finds him a decent room. Jenkins eventually invites Jacques to his home also and introduces him to Mrs. Jenkins, his mother. Through Jenkins, Jacques meets a sales-girl in a stationery store, Ann Bailey. Jacques and Ann become quite close friends, and he meets her mother and her younger, prettier sister, Rose. Rose is studying French at Bleston University, so that, for the first time since he arrived, Jacques can speak freely with someone in his own language. He forsakes Ann for Rose, who is glad to have someone with whom to practice French for her forthcoming examination. In March, Jacques meets a compatriot, Lucien Blaise, a hotel employee, and introduces him to the Bailey girls. To Jacques's utter surprise, Lucien and Rose become engaged just before Lucien's return to France on August 3. Jacques then makes a vain attempt to reestablish himself on the old footing with Ann during the two remaining months of his stay in England, but some unconscious obstacle prevents him from speaking his mind, and he learns on August 30 that Ann has become engaged to James Jenkins. Jacques goes back to France alone on September 30.

As for the "murder" plot, quite early in his stay Jacques finds a copy of *The Bleston Murder* in a bookstore and uses it as a sort of guide to Bleston. He has it beside him on a restaurant table one day when Burton notices it and strikes up a conversation. Without admitting that he is J. C. Hamilton, Burton soon reveals that he and his wife, Harriet, both write detective stories. He invites first Jacques and then Jacques and Lucien to his home. Eventually they persuade him to admit that he is the author of *The Bleston Murder*.

Soon afterwards, on June 1, Ann gives back to Jacques his first copy of *The Bleston Murder*, which he thought he had lost but which in fact he had lent her in December or January. She had in turn lent it to her cousin Henry, who had been struck by the fact that, in this novel of fratricide, the house in which the two brothers lived bore a close resemblance to the house of his friend Richard Tenn. Now, Tenn had lost a brother in an automobile accident three years ago, two years before the publication of the detective story. Had Burton based the novel on fact—or supposed fact? (Jacques never actually puts this question to Burton.) At any rate, Henry lent the book to Richard before at long last returning it. Jacques rather foolishly boasts that he knows the author of the detective story, and when Rose in her best French asks him for the man's name, he blurts it out. When Burton is run over, apparently deliberately, by a black Morris car on July 11, Jacques is convinced that Tenn has learned the identity of J. C. Hamilton and attempted murder. Later Jacques discovers that Tenn's Morris is not black, and his suspicions fall instead on James Jenkins, who, as Butor's reader is well aware by this time, drives a black Morris belonging to Matthews and Sons. Why should Jenkins wish to kill Burton, whose photograph Jacques had once pointed out to him? Because *The Bleston Murder* speaks slightingly of the New Cathedral in Bleston, on which his maternal grandfather, E. C. Douglas, was the principal sculptor employed.[5] It seems a flimsy enough motive for even an act of sudden impulse, in spite of the fierce family pride that James's mother obviously carries in her heart. We do not know whether James is exonerated or incriminated by the nightmare which he relates to Jacques (New York edition, p. 292). On the very evening of the accident James had dreamed that he ran down a man on Brown Street at the rush hour. When he awoke, he realized that the man was Burton. Learning later of the accident, he had carefully retraced his own movements on that evening: "It was practically impossible for me to have been on Brown Street at the time of the accident" (p. 293). Since Jacques had not told James of his suspicions, it would seem unlikely that James should tell him of the dream unless it were true. For some days, however, Burton too was convinced that his being knocked down was deliberate; later, he decided that he had let his professional imagination run away with his reason.

So much for the rather abortive plot, which is not quite so self-canceling as some of Raymond Queneau's, but certainly belongs in their tradition. Once again, in *Passing Time*, we can trace a schema and a myth—two myths, in fact—as well as a plot. And once again the schema involves both time and place.

The time element is the more significant of the two, for the book is in essence a *recherche du temps perdu*. Jacques sits down at his table on May 1 to begin what he hopes will be a chronological account of his experiences since he arrived in Bleston. His feelings have reached such a pitch of animosity against the city—symbolized by his burning the street map of Bleston which he had bought from Ann at their first meeting— that he thinks he must explore their origins by writing this narrative or else go mad. At first he sticks·fairly closely to his plan of dealing with the past only, but as time goes on, current happenings related to past events seem too important to be passed over. Instead of the past forcing its way into the

---

[5] The sculpture in the New Cathedral (pp. 130–1) provides a striking example of the imaginary works of art we shall be examining a little further on.

present, as in Proust, we find the present forcing its way into a narrative concerned with the past. Eventually, Jacques begins to reread the earlier part of his narrative and to remember the time when he wrote it as well as the time he was writing about. He thus begins to juggle three "times" (distant past, recent past, and present) instead of two (past and present). The running heads to the pages of both French and American editions keep constantly before us this multiple time scheme. Here are the running heads from a few typical consecutive pages (192–7) of the New York edition; italics indicate the month in which Jacques is writing and capitals the month or months he is writing about: "*July*: DECEMBER; *July*: MAY; *July*: MAY; *July*: MAY, JULY; *July*: JULY; *July*: JULY, DECEMBER."[6]

The following chronological table, with page numbers from the New York edition, will give some idea of the way in which Jacques's intended straightforward narrative becomes increasingly complicated by the pressure of events:

May 1. J. starts writing about the events of seven months before (p. 3).

May 19. J. ends account of first week in October; life in Bleston has become routine for him, hence "my real research begins" (p. 34).

June 2. The present begins to bulk larger than the past, after Ann returns his first copy of *The Bleston Murder* (p. 59).

June 24. "The fact is that the present (including these last few days) now absorbs my mind so entirely that I have spent a whole evening trying to thrust it aside . . ." (p. 123).

July 1. J. feels "compelled to interrupt the pattern I had been following for the past month in my narrative, mingling regularly, week by week, notes on current happenings with recollections of last November. . . ." He reverts to May 31 (p. 139).

July 15. This is a crucial date, being the one on which he

---

[6] Butor pointed out to Charbonnier that *Passing Time* is constructed like a musical canon: "In the first part one month is narrated, in the second part two months, in the third part three months, in the fourth part four months and in the fifth part five months" (*Entretiens*, p. 106). He also notes that the events of certain months are related in chronological order and those of others in *reverse* chronological order (p. 107).

learns of Burton's accident. This event and its antecedents
tend to dominate the rest of July (p. 169).

July 28. J. begins to reread what he has written (p. 194).

August 4. J. does his rereading more systematically, now that
he has learned of Rose's betrothal; he is trying to find out
where he went wrong (p. 202).

September 1. J. writes: "I listened to the mutter of all those
days in March and February which I had not yet tackled,
the big two-months' gap in the very middle of my re-
cension . . ." p. 266).

September 30. As his train moves out of Bleston, J. is scribbling
frantically, trying to fit in important bits of February and
March (pp. 309–10).

Poor Jacques has set himself a comically impossible task, that
of narrating a whole year's events in the five months left of
his Bleston stay. The narrator of *Degrees* will find his similar
self-imposed task tragically impossible. Another similarity
between Jacques Revel and Pierre Vernier is that their literature interferes with their lives. As Jacques writes,

> . . . during the whole of May, the clue to my behavior is not
> only the fact that I had those conversations with George
> Burton . . . but also that I used to spend every weekday
> evening writing, and consequently had far less time to see
> Ann and Rose, or James Jenkins (outside office hours), or
> Lucien, or Horace. (p. 193)

Thus, as he attempts to come to terms with Bleston on the
plane of art by writing about it, Bleston is defeating him on
the plane of life by allowing James and Lucien to rob him of
both Ann and Rose, his Ariadne and his Phaedra.

The spatial element of the schema is well exemplified by
the sketch map of Bleston which faces the opening page of
both the French and the American editions. On this we can
trace Jacques's movements among what are for him the principal landmarks of the imaginary city. In one aspect, at any
rate, this map translates time into space: we can find on it the
eight fairgrounds encircling the city center; each month the
fair moves clockwise to another of the eight. This fair becomes
to some extent a place of escape from Bleston for Jacques,

Horace, and even James, but some of the mysterious fires occur in the fair and there are other sinister manifestations associated with it.

Jacques never learns to do without his diagram of the Bleston bus routes or his street map of the city. Having burned the old map, he has to buy a new one from Ann, to her mystification. At the same time he buys the ream of paper on which to write his narrative. In one sense the map is his Ariadne's thread, guiding him through the spatial labyrinth of Bleston; in another sense his writing is the thread, guiding him, he hopes, through the temporal "labyrinth of my days in Bleston, incomparably more bewildering than that of the Cretan palace, since it grows and alters even while I explore it" (p. 195).

Such references to Ariadne introduce the more important of the myths used by Butor, that of Theseus. This is embodied in a series of what one assumes to be imaginary works of art, reminding one of the paintings of Martin de Vere in *Passage de Milan*. (After *Passing Time*, Butor, who has written an essay on the imaginary works of art in Proust, continues to describe works of art in his novels—and even more in his non-fiction—but they are all known masterpieces rather than creations of his imagination.) The legend of Theseus is portrayed in the Harvey tapestries, on display in the Bleston Museum. These eighteen scenes, woven in France in the eighteenth century, are listed on page 161 of *Passing Time* and described in detail on the following pages.[7] Jacques imagines himself as Theseus and Ann as Ariadne, whom he deserts for Rose/Phaedra. In fact, it is Lucien who turns out to be Theseus, although Jacques had cast him in the role of Pirithoüs and, later, in that of the god Dionysus who rescues the forsaken Ariadne. All these identifications with the myth are made explicitly by Jacques (p. 180). Ironically, when the role of Theseus has been filled by Lucien and Jacques has cast himself as Dionysus instead, James in his turn snatches that

[7] Through a typographical error, the American edition lists only seventeen scenes; the fourth scene, the slaying of Cercyon, has been omitted.

role away. Usually, when a mythical parallel is used in a modern novel (as in Joyce's *Ulysses*), its existence is only hinted at and the reader is left to work out the parallel himself. By making the parallel explicit but erroneous, Butor creates an ironic flavor unique in such use of myth.

The second myth, that of Cain and Abel, finds its parallel not in *Passing Time*, properly speaking, but in the plot of *The Bleston Murder*, another imaginary work of art. But the inspiration for the Cain-and-Abel plot of the detective story is drawn from still another imaginary work of art, the so-called "Murderer's Window" in Bleston Old Cathedral, which shows Cain, "dressed like Theseus," killing Abel (p. 71). The careful reader will not identify either Jacques or Lucien—or Richard Tenn or James Jenkins, for that matter—with Cain, but will remember that Cain was the first man to build a city as well as the first murderer, a significant correlation for one who hates a city as cordially as Jacques hates Bleston. Furthermore, the mid-sixteenth-century stained-glass artist "took as model [for Cain's city] the city then spread before him, the Bleston of those days . . ." (p. 74). (Similarly, the burning city of Athens in the last of the Theseus tapestries reminds us of Bleston with its many fires.) But we must not forget the ironic fact that "The artist paid tribute to Cain as being the father of all the arts" (p. 75).

The Old Cathedral once possessed other windows devoted to cities: the New Jerusalem, Babel, Sodom and Gomorrah, Babylon, Rome. Only fragments of Babel, Sodom, and Babylon have survived, however, suggesting the decadence of city life exemplified by Bleston. Jacques believes not only that Bleston is fated to be destroyed by fire like Sodom and Gomorrah but that it desires its own destruction. The whole of Part V (the book is divided into five parts, each corresponding to one of the five months, May to September, in which Jacques writes his narrative) resounds with apocalyptic accents. Poor defeated Jacques, having lost his Ann, overcompensates by prophesying the downfall of the wicked city that has overcome him:

And so I thank you, Bleston, for taking such cruel and blatant revenge on me [by depriving him of Ann]; I shall have gone from you in less than a month, but I shall still be prince over you since, by acknowledging my defeat, I have managed to survive (as you secretly wished me to) the fate you had in store for me, I have not been engulfed; and now, having endured the ordeal of your fury, I have become invulnerable, like a ghost; I have won from you this offer of a pact, which I accept. (p. 272)

It is hard to grasp from Jacques's ravings—at times there is no other word to describe them—just what the terms of this mysterious "pact" are. In essence, probably, Bleston has agreed to let him escape back to France if he will express in his writing the city's repressed death wish. Ann and Rose must read his manuscript (though Ann knows no French),

. . . so that through the eyes of these two sisters you yourself, Bleston, may begin to interpret this interpretation of yourself which I have begun and which I shall carry on till I leave, striving to abide faithfully by the rules of that obscure pact to which I could not but subscribe, striving to satisfy that dormant, muzzled, buried desire within you, aroused by the wound I dealt you, that desire for death and for deliverance, for light and for fire. . . . (pp. 278–9)

As his train gets ready to leave, on the last page of the book, he writes of "*Bleston, l'agonisante, Bleston toute pleine de braises que j'attise.* . . ." Jean Stewart's translation of these words, "Bleston, as you lie dying, Bleston, whose dying embers I have fanned" (p. 310), is misleading. Read rather "all full of *glowing* embers that I *am stirring up.*"

The style which Butor has devised for the neurotic, almost psychotic, Jacques is obsessive nearly everywhere that it is not apocalyptic. Sentences several paragraphs in length are held together by the repetition of key phrases, often containing a relative pronoun. Jacques seems tremendously concerned that we should realize that he has had *two* copies of the Bleston street map and *three* copies of *The Bleston Murder*. Passages like the following undoubtedly reinforce our sense of Jacques's compulsively neurotic personality, but they also tend to bore and irritate the reader, who has read several of them already and will read many more:

> With what relief, on the morning of Sunday, November 18, did I stuff into my one and only suitcase the few articles I had taken out of it, the few articles I had bought in Bleston, the map of Bleston like the one now lying folded on the left-hand corner of my table, the map I had bought from Ann Bailey, the bus-route plan, of which I had not needed to buy a second copy, and the novel by J. C. Hamilton (whose real name I had not yet discovered), *The Bleston Murder*, which was still in my possession that day (for I only lent it to James, I remember quite clearly, the day after our first visit together to Pleasance Gardens), that copy of *The Bleston Murder* which must now still be at the Baileys' house, which their cousin had returned to them (it was Ann who had let him take it, it was to her I had entrusted it; Rose would not have forgotten, would not have pretended she had already given it back to me) after lending it to that unknown friend of his, that Richard Tenn whose house, so he told them, bore so strange a resemblance to the house where the two brothers lived, the murderer and his victim—that copy I had thought lost, identical in text with the one I now possess, only, at that time, a trifle cleaner-looking. (p. 115)

To see this compulsively associative style at its peak, however, we must turn to the passages in which Jacques apostrophizes, first Rose, then Ann, after he has lost them. The entry for Friday, August 8, for example, beginning "Rose, whom . . . ," is a three-page sentence fragment divided up into twelve "paragraphs," all of which except the last begin with "Rose" followed by a relative clause and end with a comma instead of a period (pp. 214–17). We find a similar but briefer lamentation over Ann on pp. 275–6. The device is a traditional poetic one, and these passages do have a certain poetic quality, but it tends to be vitiated by sentimentality. Here is the conclusion of the lament over Ann:

> Ann, whose gray eyes that looked so kindly at me last winter now haunt me, now are closed to me, those eyes to which, despite all our estrangement, something bitter like the mist of those days still binds me indissolubly. (p. 276)

Butor uses this kind of prose poetry, these paragraph-long clauses, much more sparingly in *La Modification*, but an outstanding characteristic of Butor's prose throughout his novels is this reaching after a sustained melody, usually elegiac in tone. The proliferating relative clauses, often strung together in chains, create a feeling of free association—each memory that surges up begets another, which recalls another, which prompts a fourth, which leads to a fifth, which . . . and so on.

Before turning from *Passing Time* to *Degrees*, Butor's fourth and last novel, let us consider the former as if it were a detective story, for Jacques Revel and Pierre Vernier, the narrator of *Degrees*, share some of the attitudes (and even methods) of the traditional detective. Burton, the detective-story writer, expounds an elaborate theory of his craft (pp. 152–4, 178–9) of which only the essentials can be quoted here:

> "A major part of the relations existing between the partici-pants in the drama were maintained only through the errors, ignorance and lies which he [the detective] abolishes; the actors group themselves in a new pattern from which one member of the former grouping is automatically excluded." (p. 153)

Furthermore, the time scheme of Jacques's manuscript resembles that of the detective story, where, according to Burton, "the narrative gradually explores events anterior to the event with which it begins . . ." (p. 178). The event with which *Passing Time* really begins, although it takes us some time to learn this, is the burning of the map. At any rate, it cannot be denied that both Burton's typical detective story and Jacques's manuscript superimpose "two temporal sequences, the days of the inquiry which start at the crime, and the days of the drama which lead up to it . . ." (p. 179).

But who is the detective and who is the criminal in *Passing Time*? Jacques in the end makes it clear to us that he is both. He writes, after learning of Ann's engagement, an event that "abolishes" a quantity of "errors, ignorance and lies": "The pattern is complete, and I am left out of it . . ." (p. 268).

Degrés (*Degrees*, first published in French, 1960) is Butor's most recent novel and, for me, his most ambitious and original work in the genre—yet, at the same time, because of its very ambition and originality, an artistic failure. Although it does in fact come to an end in less than four hundred pages, it seems—and in one sense actually is—interminable. In an interview with F. C. St. Aubyn (in French, *French Review*, XXXVI, 12–22), Butor has admitted this:

> In *Degrees* there is set in motion a sort of descriptive machinery. This machinery is fundamentally incomplete. It cannot come to an end. One can continue indefinitely to enlarge the contexts methodically, but then the book would turn out to have thousands of pages, millions of pages. (p. 20)

The only solution Butor finds to the problem of bringing the machinery to a stop is to kill off his narrator, or rather to have his narrator collapse under the magnitude of his self-imposed task, as Jacques Revel almost did. This device seems an abdication, on the part of the novelist, of his artistic function. The death of Angèle in *Passage de Milan* can be excused, particularly in view of the mythical context—Horus, the kite, and so on. But in *Degrees* it would surely have been better to let the finite part merely suggest the infinite whole or else to adopt the circular form, so dear to Joyce, Beckett, and Queneau, that implies an infinite repetition.

To translate the title *Degrés* by the English word "degrees" alone is to be content with an approximation at best. In an academic context—the novel centers on a *lycée*—one's first association in English might well be with academic degrees. In French, however, this would be among the last associations to arise. The primary meaning of *degré* in French is "step," referring to a staircase or ladder; obviously this meaning opens the way to a wide range of rather trite metaphoric references. Another meaning that operates very effectively in the particular context is "degree of relationship," since the narrator compiles his document for the benefit of his nephew; he might not have started work at all if he had not been struck by the unusual number of blood relationships between teachers and students in his *lycée*. But, most significantly, the narrator specializes in the teaching of history and geography. The class hour upon which the whole book pivots is concerned with the discovery of America, and another class is devoted to the explanation of latitude and longitude. Both these last, of course, are measured in degrees, and this perhaps gives us the clue to the unique structure of this novel. The narrator constantly harks backward in time and follows a character forward from his summer holidays until his life intersects with those of his classmates/colleagues and teachers/students during the fall term, the intersection being accompanied by the passing of one or more "landmark" dates on the calendar. It is as if the story Pierre Vernier is trying to tell were the surface of a sphere—or at any rate a segment of one—which he tries to catch in a net of lines of latitude and longitude. One might think of each individual's "story line" as moving east to west along a line of latitude and each date as a line of longitude intersecting all these parallel lines.

On this matter of titles and names, it is worth adding that Pierre Vernier was also the name of the French mathematician (1580–1637) who invented the vernier, or vernier scale, a device for indicating fractional parts of divisions (such as degrees); it forms an essential part of the sextant, as well as of other navigational and surveying instruments. The reader will think it negligent on Butor's part to give Vernier, the uncle, and Eller, the nephew, the same first name. Actually, wherever this ambiguity occurs in Butor, it is deliberate; he admires Faulkner's use of the same device: see the essay on "Family Relationships in William Faulkner's *The Bear*," in *Répertoire*, obviously of the greatest relevance to *Degrees*.

The fictional Vernier's discussion of "projection," the ways in which the spherical surface of the earth may be represented on a flat map, is relevant also, both to this book and to the whole problem of narration in general, the conversion of life into literature:

> I was trying to explain that it is impossible to represent the earth exactly without distorting it, just as it is impossible to represent reality in speech without using a certain kind of

projection, a system of points of reference whose shape and organization depend on what you are trying to show, and, as a corollary, on what you need to know

(this latter, obviously, I didn't tell you in class, it's an idea that came to me as I was writing),

and that our habitual representation of what is happening in the contemporary world, and of universal history, is constantly distorted by the primacy, in our minds, of the cylindrical projection, the so-called Mercator projection. . . . (New York ed., 1961, pp. 48–9)

The passage just cited reads like an invitation to examine the familiar problem of "point of view" as it affects *Degrees*, but in the long run it will be more convenient to summarize the plot now and leave discussion of the more technical problem until a little later.

Pierre Vernier, who teaches at the Lycée Taine in the Latin Quarter (Butor himself is an alumnus of the Lycée Louis le Grand) of Paris, has for some time had the idea of describing a class, students in the same grade (*seconde A*, corresponding roughly to tenth-grade college preparatory) who take his history and geography courses together. There are thirty-one students, and they take courses with eleven teachers in all, including the art and physical-education teachers and the chaplain, who teaches religion to any Roman Catholic who wishes to attend his classes. Since "class" is such an ambiguous word in American usage, it must be made clear that it is the *group* of boys and their masters which Vernier wishes to describe, and not just a particular *class hour*, although one such hour, on Pierre Eller's fifteenth birthday, October 12, 1954, is made the inaugural point of the whole project. During this class hour Vernier lectures on the discovery and conquest of the American continent.

Vernier has undertaken the whole project because Eller, his namesake and favorite nephew, has now become his pupil for the first time, and is at the same time studying French, Latin, and Greek with another uncle, Henri Jouret. Several other boys in the class are related to teachers, and this will help Vernier to learn more about his pupils, but he relies above all upon the information supplied him by Eller, to whom he confides his project on that memorable October 12 (Columbus Day).

Besides confiding in his relative by marriage, Henri Jouret, Vernier also confides in his woman friend, Micheline Pavin, whom he met in Greece during the summer vacation. Vernier's thirty-fifth birthday occurs soon after Eller's fifteenth, and it is high time that he married and settled down instead of living with the Ellers, his sister and her husband. However, Pierre feels that he cannot embark on his self-chosen task unless Micheline, like a damsel of the Middle Ages, commands him to. She does so, and he decides he cannot marry her until his deed of knighthood has been completed. Micheline is presented as a young woman with a certain sense of humor; why she would consent to this quixotic plan devised by the humorless Pierre passes the reader's understanding.

Very soon young Eller, who at first is excited by the confidence reposed in him by his uncle, becomes profoundly uneasy about the role of informer that has been thrust upon him. He feels that he is violating his Boy Scout oath and begins to identify with the boy werewolf that he has read about in a science-fiction magazine. When a classmate of his, Michel Daval, makes a shrewd guess at the pact between uncle and nephew, Eller breaks with Vernier, who finds the atmosphere so strained that he has to move out of the Ellers' apartment. He falls ill, recovers, falls ill again, and is at the point of death soon after the beginning of the new school year. Before he dies, he is at least assured of Pierre Eller's forgiveness, as is only just, for Vernier undertook his whole project for the benefit of Eller and the younger generation generally, more than as a token of his love for Micheline.

There are several minor plots within the major one. M. Bailly, the English teacher, and his wife, English teacher in a girls' school, decide to get a divorce, since they are both having extramarital affairs. M. Bonnini, the Italian teacher, loses his wife as the result of an operation. M. Hubert's wife has her first baby. Henri Jouret and his wife Rose, with their children, present a model of contented, uneventful family life.

Of the family life of the Ellers we learn suprisingly little.
Some of the students have moments of drama in their lives,
but these hardly amount to plots.

The reader will naturally wonder how the private lives of
the Bailly family belong in what is supposed to be a documentary study, since it is impossible that Vernier should have
witnessed, say, a scene in their bedroom, and improbable that
Bailly should have reported it to him. The only answer we
receive to this objection is the following:

> . . . to describe the space in which these facts occur, and
> without which it is impossible to make them appear, it is
> necessary to imagine a quantity of other events impossible to
> verify. . . . (New York ed., p. 46)

The context in which Vernier makes this statment actually
concerns the weighty problem of whether a student named
Alain Mouron climbed the rope in gym class on a certain day
or worked out on the parallel bars. It is impossible for Vernier
to discover which he did. It should be far more difficult still
for a character as lacking in insight and imagination as Vernier
is to picture with any verisimilitude just what M. and Mme
Bailly did or said in the privacy of their bedroom. Actually,
the personality of Vernier, the "viewpoint character," constitutes the crux of the whole book. Only an obsessed, humorless
figure would embark on such a preposterous project to begin
with; what value can the reports of such a man have either as
scientific fact or as literature? Furthermore, if we are not
interested in him as a human being, how can his end really
be tragic? The height of absurdity is perhaps reached when,
in his effort to keep up with all the work of Pierre Eller's class
as well as with the preparation he has to do for his own
courses throughout the school, Vernier decides that he ought
to learn German and Spanish. Micheline remarks (mockingly,
one hopes): "That might take you quite some time . . ." (p.
221). But, by and large, we find little of the irony that seemed
evident in *A Change of Heart*. One feels that Butor, like his
narrator, had made up his mind to write this book, and so
gritted his teeth and went through with it. But Vernier, of

course, does not write a book. He always refers, not to "this book," but to "these notes":

> . . . these notes about our class, which are meant for you, Pierre, though not as you are today—not only because you would probably be unable to read them and be interested in them, but also because they are not yet in condition to be read, because you must wait until they are completed, corrected, which may take quite a long time— (p. 46)

As this and other passages already quoted suggest, *Degrees*, like its immediate predecessor, *A Change of Heart*, is written in the second person. But this time the intimate second person singular, *tu*, is used throughout, whether the uncle, Pierre Vernier, is addressing his nephew, Pierre Eller, as in Part I; or whether the nephew is supposed to be addressing the uncle, as in Part II; or whether the boy's other uncle who teaches at the *lycée*, Henri Jouret, is supposed to be addressing his nephew, as in the greater portion of Part III. In order to clarify this rather baffling statement, we turn to Butor himself:

> In *Degrees* there are different narrators, at least at first sight. If we look at things more closely, we see that there is only one narrator but that this single narrator is incarnated in at least two different characters. Now, in *Degrees* there are three parts in which the first person changes, but in the second part it is the first narrator who puts words in his nephew's mouth, and this in such an absolutely clear fashion that there cannot be any possible doubt about the matter. In the third part things are a little bit more complicated. We can't always stay at the elementary level. In the third part it's the first narrator who puts words in the mouth of one of his colleagues, but in the course of this third part the first narrator fades out, so that at the end of the book it is in fact the colleague who ends the narration, the account. At that moment we are in fact confronted by two different narrators, two characters who follow one another in the composition of a book. Only, this character who is going to take the place of the first narrator does nothing to add another point of view. He subordinates himself entirely to the plan of the first narrator. He's not even going to try to continue the book. For him it's a matter simply

of ending the book in its incompleteness, of showing that it
ends at a certain point. (*French Review*, XXXVI, 13–14)

The shift in viewpoint from Part I to Part II should permit
us to see school life through a student's eyes instead of a
teacher's, but since Vernier is really still the narrator and
since he has relied on information supplied by his nephew in
Part I, we are not conscious of much change of perspective.
Indeed, most of the unhappy relationship of M. and Mme
Bailly is recounted in Part II. All the most dramatic moments
in the book are deliberately held back until Part III: Michel
Daval's accusation (pp. 343–4), Pierre Eller's hysterical outburst in his Uncle Pierre's class (p. 345), Vernier's illness (pp.
302–3), his pathetic letters (pp. 327–9), the reconciliation of
uncle and nephew (p. 346). Yet most of these events have
occurred before the writing of Part II has been completed. It
is left to Henri Jouret, who has taken over as the *actual*
rather than the *supposed* narrator on page 330, to recount
many of these significant events.

Now, when Vernier apologizes for "these notes" on the
ground that they are incomplete and uncorrected, we would
be foolish to mistake this apology by the narrator for an
apology by the author who created him. Novelists since Sterne,
if not earlier, have been using this trick to conceal a deliberate
pattern behind an apparent confusion. The whole disorganized
appearance of the narrative, and especially the failure to
mention so many important events until the very end, was
unquestionably planned by Butor. Beneath the appearance
of disorder lie all kinds of patterns. In his interview with F. C.
St. Aubyn, Butor revealed one important and precise schema,
that for the detailed treatment of the forty-two school characters (thirty-one students and eleven teachers):

In the first part [the novel is divided into three parts, as
already indicated] there are seven divisions. In each division
three new characters appear, making 21 characters in all who
have come on the stage, eleven teachers and ten students. In
the second part there will be two new characters who come
on the stage in each of the seven divisions, which makes

fourteen more students who have entered the novel in the
second part. In the third part, in each division there is a new
character, a new student, who appears. Consequently there
will be seven divisions. Thus we have all the students appearing at least once by the end of the book. (*French Review*,
XXXVI, 21)

One quick way of confirming this statement is to turn to the
first division of each part, which is very short, less than a
page. In Part I, although in fact nine names are called by
Vernier from his roll, the significant characters are "I,"
"you . . . , Pierre," and "your uncle Henri Jouret, on the other
side of the wall . . ." (p. 7). At the beginning of Part II,
although three other names are briefly mentioned, Philippe
Guillaume and Bruno Verger are drawn to our attention for a
longer moment (p. 109). At the beginning of Part III, we note
the name of Denis Régnier, who has received a lot of attention
already, but the remark "Bernard de Loups is scratching his
auburn hair" constitutes, if memory serves, all the information
we are vouchsafed about Bernard besides his name and the
position of his seat in class (p. 257). In the slightly longer
second division of Part III, which chiefly concerns Michel
Daval, an important character among the boys, we eventually
find three other boys' names, those of Alain Mouron, Maurice
Tangala, and Jacques Estier. Now Mouron is another important character, and Tangala, the Negro in the class, has
been dealt with in Part I, but we have not really heard anything of Estier up to now: we find that he "plans to be an
engineer" (p. 261).

In Part I, where the characters are taken together in threes,
Vernier himself makes clear the principle underlying these
groupings:

> Up to now, I have been able to deal with these characters
> in triads, two teachers and one student: you, your Uncle
> Henri, me; Monsieur Bonnini, Monsieur Hubert, Denis Ré-
> gnier; Monsieur du Marnet, Monsieur Tavera, Hubert Jourdan;
> or else two students and one professor: Alain Mouron, Michel
> Daval, Monsieur Bailly; Francis Hutter, Jean-Pierre Cormier,

Monsieur Hutter, because of the degrees of relationship unit-
ing them. (p. 78)

It should be noted that the grouping together of du Marnet,
Tavera, and Jourdan is based on physical resemblance rather
than any known relationship (pp. 54–5).
  Vernier continues:

> After these five groups, I have constituted a sixth one, within
> which these relationships—despite that snare, the identity of
> two surnames—are of an indefinite degree, equivalent, as far
> as I know, to those that might exist between any two students
> taken at random and one of their teachers in any class of any
> lycée: Jean-Claude Fage, Henri Fage, Monsieur Martin. . . .
> (p. 78)

Finally, having two teachers left over—the physical-education
instructor, M. Moret, and the chaplain, Abbé Gollier—he pairs
them with a student to whom they are more than normally
unlikely to be related, the Negro boy, Maurice Tangala. Thus
there is a certain logic about the groupings in Part I, and in
each of its seven divisions the degree of kinship between the
members of each triad becomes progressively more remote. In
Part II, what links the pairs together, Butor told St. Aubyn, is
proximity in space. Those who live near each other or sit near
each other in class are grouped together. In Part III, as the
students are taken singly, no group relationships are possible.
  Behind this schema lies still another—a more objective one:
a timetable, or, rather, two timetables. The first is the schedule
that Vernier establishes for himself in order to fit in his class
hours, his class preparation, his study of the textbooks used by
his colleagues to teach his nephew, his compilation of the
notes we are reading, and his private life—if any. More important and vaster is the master schedule of all the class hours
and room assignments of all the teachers in the Lycée Taine
on all the floors of the building. And behind this looms the
whole centrally organized system of secondary education in
France, a byword for standardization since the days of Napoleon I. In moving thus from schema to schema, we are follow-

ing the process which Butor, one remembers, called "enlarging the contexts methodically."

And behind this last schema lies another schema—call it Culture or Education with a capital letter—that is so vast and indefinite as to rejoin the world of myth. In Butor's other novels we could draw a hard-and-fast boundary line between the schemas and the myths, but in *Degrees* we can no longer do so. This notion of a culture that can be transmitted to the next generation, of a standardized education that can be imposed upon the individual, is the underlying myth of *Degrees*, a very different sense of the word "myth" than that used in my discussion of the myth of Theseus in *Passing Time*. Nevertheless, as we read passage after passage describing what secondary education actually consists of in the classroom, we feel that we are watching the enactment of inexplicable rites, sanctioned by a body of myth that everybody takes on trust. In the literature courses, much of the material studied is in fact mythical: Homer's *Odyssey* in Greek; Virgil's *Aeneid* in Latin; Dante's *Divine Comedy* in Italian; Rabelais's *Gargantua and Pantagruel* (expurgated, of course) in French. Occasionally a bewildered boy wonders what the text is all about, but no one seems to wonder why the text is being read in the first place. This is what you do in secondary school in order to graduate—and in France, failure to pass the dreaded *bachot* or baccalaureate examination at the end of the *lycée* course is tantamount to failure in life as a whole, for members of the middle class at any rate.

Often the factual material transmitted in non-literary courses raises even more baffling questions. Take, for example, the following geography quiz:

1: What is an isotherm?
2: What are the hottest and coldest points of the globe, and why?
3: What is an inversion of temperature? (p. 162)

Vernier sets this; Eller answers the first two questions and gives up on the third after looking at his neighbors' papers and finding they don't know the answer either. Neither asks himself why it is deemed necessary for a non-specialist to know the answers to these questions in order to be called a cultured or educated person. Vernier does realize at one point that he has forgotten most of what he learned or was supposed to have learned in tenth grade. Perhaps the real reason why his task overwhelms him is that he fails to grasp the educational process as a meaningful whole. Who could succeed when the process is such a patchwork of examined and unexamined tradition, intelligent innovation, and wrong-headed change for change's sake? It is just as well that the students resist the process in all the traditional ways: cheating, loafing, swapping stamps, or reading science fiction in class, and so on.

Scattered through the text of *Degrees* we find a large number of quotations from the European literature that is being studied—chiefly by Eller's class, but also by other classes. Butor himself speaks of the "stylistic color" (texture) that these quotations impart to what might otherwise be too monochromatic a text (*Entretiens*, p. 149). Besides quotations from the authors mentioned, there are quotations from Montaigne, Racine, the Duc de Saint-Simon, Montesquieu, Marco Polo, Shakespeare, Coleridge, and several more. One cannot help feeling that a James Joyce would have chosen the quotations so craftily that each would be a comment on some event or idea described in the novel. Butor would probably object to such a practice as too pat, but from time to time his quotations are very apposite. A chapter heading from Rabelais, for instance—"How Gargantua was so disciplined by Ponocrates that he did not waste an Hour of the Day" (p. 203)—reminds us keenly of poor Vernier's self-imposed schedule. On page 338 there are two quotations which bear the utmost relevance to Pierre Eller's situation:

> ". . . after which Gargantua with his tutor briefly reviewed in the manner of the Pythagoreans all that he had read, seen, learnt, done and heard in the course of the whole day . . ."

This, from Rabelais, recalls the nightly meetings during which the boy reports to his uncle. Here is another:

". . . of great valor, strong feeling and frankness, the
ordinary qualities of a young man. He was fifteen years of
age, and it was said that he was very intelligent, whether this
was the truth or whether his misfortunes made this appear to
be true without his having been able to give such evi-
dences . . ."

A surprising number of French people would recognize that
as a quotation from the second prose preface to Racine's
verse tragedy *Britannicus*; it is a description of the historical
Britannicus. A little earlier, Eller, who is beginning to identify
himself with the werewolf boy, has read with a sense of ill
omen the famous passage about the young Nero from the
same preface:

". . . He has not yet killed his mother, his wife, his tutors,
but he has within him the seed of all these crimes; he is
beginning to desire to shake off his yoke. He hides his hate
under false caresses. In a word, he is here a nascent
monster . . ." (p. 336)

After all, then, culture has its validity: the words of a
seventeenth-century French classic author about a Roman
emperor and his first victim can be applied to a crisis in the
life of a twentieth-century French schoolboy. But it is only
in Part III, close to the end of the book, that we find such
frequent relevance in the quotations.

Nevertheless, in spite of all the ingenuity that has gone to
the building up of this mosaic, this television picture made up
of tiny dots of light, "this book in facets" (as Butor himself
has called it), it takes an enormous supply of good will to
carry one through a fairly typical page, such as the following
(p. 325, New York ed.):

On All Saints' Day, Monsieur Bailly took his children to the
Montparnasse cemetery.

On All Souls' Day, Denis Régnier went with his mother and
his sister to the Père-Lachaise cemetery.

On Wednesday your uncle, recovered, went back to the
lycée,
the maritime peoples: Cretans, Phoenicians, early Greeks . . .
And you, also recovered, went back to school the following

Saturday, and you had to take the written history quiz like
the rest, since it had already been announced for the preceding
Saturday and hadn't been given then on account of your
uncle's grippe:

the discovery of America, Philip II, Cromwell,

lesson on Louis XIII: Marie de Médicis and her foster sister,
Léonora Galigaï, the fowler Albert de Luynes, the murder of
Concini, his wife, Léonora, burned as a witch . . .

and on Richelieu: the proscription of duels, the siege of La
Rochelle, Samuel Champlain in Canada, sugar cane in the
Antilles, the slave trade, the spice trade . . .

On Sunday, the whole Bailly family went to visit the
Davals' new apartment.

On Monday, Denis Régnier, in bed since the Saturday before, grippe again, got up for lunch but had to go back to bed
because of a rise in temperature.

> *"Caesar, to the soothsayer:*
> The ides of March are come.
> *Soothsayer:*
> Aye, Caesar, but not gone . . .";

it was Hubert Jourdan whom you accompanied to his métro
stop, then, passing a newspaper kiosk, you bought the November issue of *Fiction*.

Your Uncle Pierre went to call for Micheline Pavin outside
her office and brought her to your apartment for dinner; it
was more or less her official introduction to the family.

Denis Régnier, still in bed, found great solace in the notion
that he had just missed an hour of gym and that he was at this
moment avoiding an hour of geography.

On Thursday, your uncle continued, in *Sixteenth Century
French Authors*, with the study and annotation of the selections
we had discussed . . .

After all, we have encountered the two holy days before,
though we can't remember just how often; presumably we
weren't told before which cemeteries the Bailly and Régnier
families visited, but we can't remember and don't much care.
The trouble is that Butor, who works out his books so meticulously[8] in numerous drafts, *does* remember. Furthermore, he

[8] In this context it is worth noting, however, that in *Passing Time* he
makes the mistake of thinking that All Saints' Day is a public holiday in
England. There are other similar errors in that novel.

probably has a plan to tell him exactly how many times he *must* turn back to All Saints' Day 1954 in order to complete his net of narrative threads. One wishes that the visits to the cemetery and a number of other details on the page quoted had fallen through the net and perished.

Again, look at the chapter or division of Part III from which this page comes. It is arranged chronologically, and presumably it introduces one student who has never been mentioned before. But what other principle or principles of arrangement are at work to decide which of the forty-one other characters will be mentioned and what new facts (as well as old ones) will be supplied about them? Neither Butor nor Vernier condescends to explain to us. The chapter begins: "In September 1954, the Huberts left their Savoie village rather early, because the baby was expected at the end of November, and they wanted to be back in Paris in time" (p. 304). For some pages the narrative shuttles back and forth among the Huberts, Michel Daval, and the Eller family, then turns to Alain Mouron, to Vernier and Micheline Pavin, back to Eller, back to Vernier, and eventually begins to flood us with fragments of information like those on the page quoted. The chapter ends with the fall term of 1955 already well under way and Vernier in the hospital (p. 330).

Degrees resembles *Passage de Milan* more than it does the two intervening novels. Although not all of the later novel takes place in the school building, we do see parallels between the many-storied *lycée* and the apartment building. In both books, Butor is trying to handle the relationships of a large number of characters in space and time. In both, the portrayal of individual character is subordinated to the achievement of an overall effect and an overall structure, though the characters in the earlier book are considerably more interesting and more successful in arousing our sympathy. In both books there is still a plot, but the catastrophe, which is inadequately prepared for, completely overshadows the other elements of the plot.

In *Degrees* Butor has created a doctrinaire example of the

New Novel in which everything else has been subordinated to an essentially arbitrary structure that bears little relation to the rudimentary plot. This structure is, as he has said, a sort of descriptive machine—and furthermore a machine that, like some of Queneau's novelistic structures and some examples of contemporary "sculpture," destroys itself. Butor himself has spoken (*Entretiens*, p. 135) of "*Cette organisation fixe en train de se détruire, d'exploser dans un livre comme* Degrés . . ." ("This rigid structure in process of destroying itself, of exploding, in a book like *Degrees* . . .")[9] Yet the machine *has* succeeded in describing in a unique way—though not the only possible one—that immense and growing area of Western society that we call "Education."

In all of Butor's novels we find a determined attempt to adapt form to content. In a number of critical articles and in the series of interviews with Charbonnier, Butor has insisted that new literary techniques make possible the discovery of new subject matter and, conversely, that the discovery of a new subject matter demands the evolution of a new technique to deal with it. Also, his seemingly rigid schemas are instruments of discovery which serve to "provoke inspiration" (*Entretiens*, p. 113). It is curious that, in the whole course of his interviews with Charbonnier, Butor never once makes direct reference to his own use of myth. In a sense, a myth too is a schema, a structure borrowed from the past instead of the present, but it is a less rigid structure than the true schema—open to all sorts of interpretations and containing many ambiguities. The dialectic established between the schemas and the myths, especially in *Passing Time*, is Butor's most original contribution to the practice of the novel and provokes some of his most evocative writing.

Of Butor's later career, during which he has striven to revolutionize—among other things—the form of the travel book (*Mobile: Study for a Representation of the United States*), the architectural guidebook (*Description de San*

---

[9] A strangely prophetic remark in the light of the French student revolt in 1968.

Marco), and the opera libretto (*Votre Faust*), there is no space to speak here. In many ways, however, it is more dazzlingly revolutionary than his relatively brief period of preoccupation with the novel.

6

Claude Simon

ORDER AND DISORDER,
MEMORY AND DESIRE

CLAUDE SIMON is plainly the most "impure" artist among our
seven novelists, in the sense that he excludes no aspect of life
from his purview: "birth and copulation and death," politics,
economics, science, the arts. In his crowded, turbulent books
we find scenes of war, crime, revolution, and imprisonment;
details of farming and the care of horses; the lure of alcohol,
fast cars, and gambling; the technicalities of sport, dress, and
interior decoration. Even in Pinget, the most "inclusive" of
our novelists after Simon, we find almost no mention of war
and revolution, which play so large a part in *The Flanders
Road* and *The Palace*. Queneau, whose wide range of experience includes first-hand contact with war and revolutionary
movements, shows the typical urban intellectual's ignorance
and mistrust of sport (except boxing) and agriculture. Claude
Mauriac, whose preoccupation with sexuality is greater even
than Simon's, shares Queneau's urban and intellectual preju-
dices. Butor, though keenly aware of history in the widest
sense, views it at second hand through its manifestations in
the fine arts and literature; sexuality, too, he sees in its cultural
and intellectual rather than its physical aspects; as for the
average man's preoccupations with money, sport, food, and

drink, he seems largely indifferent to them. Those of our writers—Mme Sarraute, Robbe-Grillet—who abstract from life to an even greater degree than Butor inevitably seem to have very little in common with Simon, who has said of himself, "I am not an intellectual, but a sensory."

If we are tempted to regard Simon as an impure artist because of his great concern with the minutiae of life, we run the risk of classifying him as impure in another, related, way by attributing to him an insufficient concern with form. Such a judgment would be a gross error, whether it referred to Simon's intention or to his achievement. Far from being unconcerned with form, Simon consciously strives for it, as his apprenticeship to painting presumably trained him to do. His less successful novels—notably *The Palace*—suffer from too great rigidity of structure rather than too little. As epigraph to *The Wind* he quotes a dictum of Paul Valéry: "The world is incessantly threatened by two dangers: order and disorder." Simon himself, as a novelist, is threatened by these twin dangers, but in his best work to date, *The Flanders Road*,[1] he triumphantly passes between Scylla and Charybdis, creating a precarious balance between order and disorder. Paradoxically, though life is meaningless to Simon as a man, to Simon as an artist it is never entirely formless. This concern with form, even more than his skepticism about the possibility of knowing anything for certain about the stream of phenomena, classifies him indisputably as a New Novelist.

Two other characteristics of many of the New Novelists have become increasingly important in Simon's work. One is the passion for minute description which has led some critics to name the New Novelists *l'école du regard* ("the school of the gaze"), though Robbe-Grillet has pointed out that much of his own description is more abstractly geometrical than truly visual. As a result, "things *are there*" in Simon's novels, often endowed with an intrinsic importance unrelated to their symbolic value for the human mind that perceives them. The other characteristic, ultimately of more importance, is the

[1] *La Route des Flandres* (Paris, 1960; tr. Richard Howard, New York, 1961).

attempt to convert the novel from an art of time to an art of space, so that when we have read a book through—probably not for the first time, however—we can get the impression of "seeing it all at once," just as we do a painting or a map. Toward the end of *The Flanders Road*, Simon uses the image of a battle map, reminding us that on it, when the movements of an army over a period of days are traced by arrows, we do in fact see time translated into terms of space. To do the same thing with words on pages that have to be turned instead of with lines on a single sheet is obviously extremely difficult. Nevertheless, as Joseph Frank and other critics have shown, a number of twentieth-century novelists have tried to do just this.

In an interview with André Bourin which appeared in *Les Nouvelles littéraires* (December 29, 1960), Simon revealed how he hit upon a "spatial" design for *The Flanders Road*. He had thought about this novel, based on his experiences as a cavalryman during the French defeat of 1940, for almost twenty years:

> At last I set to work on it, and to begin with I worked for eight months in the dark. I couldn't *see* this book at all. I perceived only simultaneous emotions arising in my mind; everything presented itself at the same time. Only later did its composition appear to me as I thought about the form of the ace of clubs which cannot be drawn without lifting pencil from paper except by passing three times through the same point. That point, in *The Flanders Road*, is the dead horse toward which the cavalrymen return three times in their wandering. [My translation]

This novel, not only Simon's best but his most characteristic, will be examined here in considerable detail. Although the reader cannot know this when he first opens the book, everything in it not only revolves about the fixed point represented by the dead horse but is remembered by one man from a fixed point in time. Simon has been deeply influenced by Proust, and all his later novels are "remembrance of things past." This use of memory first appears in the third part of *Le Sacre du printemps* (1954); the narrator of the next novel, *The Wind*, re-creates the story of Montès from his own and others' memories; *The Grass* seems to be unfolding in the present but is eventually seen as being remembered later, with varying degrees of clarity, by Louise, the protagonist; the events of *The Palace*, set during the Spanish Civil War, are remembered by its protagonist on his return to Barcelona fifteen years later; *Histoire* is a tissue of memories and mementos. It must always be kept in mind, too, as Simon told Bourin, that "memory never restores to us more than fragments of our past." In fact, Simon once thought of calling *The Flanders Road* "A Fragmentary Description of a Disaster."

Georges Thomas (whose last name we know only because of his previous appearance in *The Grass*) is remembering his experiences of war in 1939–40 and of prison camp thereafter during a single night in 1946—the one that he spends in bed with Corinne, the widow of his former captain in the French cavalry, de Reixach. In the first two parts of the novel, we are made conscious of Corinne's presence only fleetingly and infrequently (pp. 42, 96–8, 189 of the New York edition, corresponding to pp. 42, 95–6, 187 of the French). But in the third and final part we are constantly aware of her until she dresses and leaves the hotel room in a fury.

To understand Georges's obsession with Corinne, we have to bear in mind the years he spent in a German prison camp thinking of her and talking of her with two other men from his unit, a young Jew named Blum and an older man named Iglésia, de Reixach's orderly. The taciturn Iglésia, who in peacetime had been trainer and jockey for de Reixach's stable of race horses (a whim of Corinne's), was coaxed and needled by the two younger men into admitting (or inventing) a sexual relationship with Corinne which had lasted for years, an affair of hurried copulations in the stables. De Reixach, a stoical aristocrat twice Corinne's age, had seemed not to notice anything, but Iglésia was convinced that he suspected the worst, especially because on one occasion de Reixach had insisted on taking Iglésia's place as jockey and riding a favorite filly in a steeplechase, over the bitter protests of Corinne. It seemed to Georges and the ironic Blum that the master had hoped, by taking the servant's place, to regain his place with Corinne too, but he was symbolically beaten into second position in the race, whereas Iglésia would undoubtedly have won. Corinne had burst into tears, partly of rage, at her husband's defeat, but her liaison with Iglésia, himself twice her age and of almost repellent ugliness (as well as of inferior social status), remained unaffected. Georges became convinced that de Reixach's death in battle, because of the negligent way in which he walked his horse into an ambush, was a discreet form of suicide.

In seeking out Corinne after the war and—three months later—becoming her lover, Georges is not only satisfying the desire that has accumulated in him through years of sexual deprivation but also seeking for the truth about her relationship with Iglésia and about de Reixach's supposed suicide. All he learns is that she has married again and has made no attempt to see Iglésia; the last pages of the book are filled with the refrain *mais comment savoir, comment savoir* ("but how can you tell, how can you tell?"). By becoming her lover, with brutal completeness and finality, Georges has sought to reconquer the past—and, through the memories which surge up within him, he has in a sense succeeded—but ultimate truth eludes him. He cannot even be sure about his true feeling for Corinne: is he passionately in love with her, or is she—as Corinne insists with growing fury—only a "thing" for him, a vulva, one of those half-abstract obscenities, unattached to any face or personality, that soldiers draw on toilet walls? Certainly, during their night of love-making, he is never conscious of her face; at best she is for him a goddess (not a fertility goddess, since she has never borne a child), neither *a* woman nor *the* woman but Woman.

De Reixach too has become, if not a mythological figure, at any rate a legendary one, by virtue of his identification in Georges's mind with a de Reixach who lived a century and a half earlier and was also supposed to have committed suicide. As we learn at the very outset of the novel, Georges himself has de Reixach blood through his mother (the garrulous,

tragicomic Sabine of *The Grass*), who inherited, almost by
accident, the de Reixach family mansion and ancestral portraits. As a child, Georges was terrified and fascinated by the
portrait of that earlier de Reixach, which the years had defaced
in such a manner that it looked as if part of the head had been
shot away; by coincidence, the original had indeed shot himself in the head. There were two versions of the motive for
that earlier suicide: one, that de Reixach, having become a
traitor to his class and espoused the French Revolution, had
been overwhelmed with shame and remorse after a defeat of
the French forces by Spanish guerrillas; the other, that he too
had become aware of his young wife's infidelity with a servant.
Two portraits of the wife exist, one painted before her husband's death and the other afterwards. In the first she looks
prudish enough but holds in her lap a carnival mask with a
long nose oddly reminiscent of Iglésia's; in the second she
appears a very merry widow indeed. The identification of
descendant with ancestor made explicit in Georges's discussion
of these portraits with Blum is profoundly Proustian.

If the central "triangle" of the novel is mirrored by these de
Reixachs of the portraits, it finds yet another reflection in an
incident during the first autumn of the war. De Reixach's
squadron was being billeted in a French farm when a furious
quarrel broke out between the farmer and the mayor's assessor,
who had charge of the billeting. The farmer, a lame man re-
jected by the army, threatened to shoot the assessor if he
entered the farmhouse; apparently the assessor had seduced
the farmer's sister-in-law while her husband was away at the
war. De Reixach calmly placed himself between the two men
and eventually quieted the farmer; Georges, who had seen
the brother's wife for a fleeting moment after milking time,
her skin as white as the milk itself, became obsessed with this
woman and tried to worm the whole story out of the neighbors,
thus anticipating his later behavior with regard to Corinne.
The peacock worked on the lace curtain of the farm wife's
bedroom becomes symbolic to Georges of her proud, pale
beauty. It was in the barn of this billet, too, that Georges saw
a horse die, apparently aware of its approaching death and

seeing clearly the nothingness that awaited it. The other horse, killed in battle, that Georges later passes—not three times but four, of course, since he *returns* to it three times—recalls this nothingness. (Simon told Bourin that he agreed with Robbe-Grillet about the meaninglessness of the world, but he also said, "If I were not naturally an atheist, I would see God's face everywhere: in a stone, in a tree, on a child's face.")

We have viewed the central emotional tangle of *The Flanders Road* from more than one vantage point, but we have not yet reconstituted the chronological sequence of events from which Georges's memory picks here a fragment and there a fragment, according to his personal association of ideas. Setting aside Georges's childhood memories of the legendary de Reixach, which date from at least ten years—or, if you wish, 150 years—before the war, we obtain the following rough outline:

1936: Marriage of de Reixach and Corinne.

1936–9: Horse racing and adultery (narrated by Iglésia in prison camp). During this period Georges catches his only pre-war glimpse of Corinne, at a horse show.

Fall 1939: Movement of the squadron in the rain to the billet where the lame farmer and his sister-in-law live. The unit spends a day or two there in continuous rain.

Winter 1939–40: De Reixach tells Georges that he has received a letter from Sabine and acknowledges their relationship. The ground is frozen hard.

May 1940: After ten days of maneuvering in glorious spring weather, the squadron is wiped out in two ambushes, the second killing Captain de Reixach and his lieutenant. Georges and Iglésia wander about, trying to escape the Germans.

June (?) 1940: Georges, huddled in a cattle car with countless other prisoners on their way to Germany, meets Blum again in the dark.

1940–5: Prison camp in Germany, where Blum and Georges are reunited with Iglésia.

Fall 1941: Georges attempts to escape.

1943: Blum, ill with tuberculosis, is removed from the camp and presumably dies or is killed.

Summer 1946: Georges meets Corinne.
Fall 1946: They become lovers for one night.

Lest this outline should suggest a greater continuity than
actually exists, it should be stressed that Georges's memory—
like Iglésia's, for that matter—recaptures only certain days and
nights. Iglésia remembers with particular vividness the day
de Reixach rode in the steeplechase. Georges remembers only
certain moments and conversations from prison camp: a day,
for example, when the three surreptitiously bake a loaf from
stolen flour; a day when he and Blum are shoveling coal;
the day he attempts to escape while picking up fallen acorns
for food, only to be recaptured by some civilians out for a
day's hunting.

Much of the difficulty experienced at a first reading of the
novel arises from the way in which Georges's mind shuttles
to and fro among his memories. As he lies beside Corinne in
the dark, this night can become any night of the past: the
night of the rain in the billet while the horse was dying; the
night after de Reixach's death, which Georges and Iglésia
spent in a farmhouse, dead drunk; the night Georges met
Blum in the overcrowded cattle car—the weight of Corinne's
body on his becoming confused with that of his fellow
prisoners. A word or an image will trigger an associated idea,
transporting Georges instantaneously from one moment of his
past to another quite remote, or from the present moment
with Corinne to a quite different one in the past. Memory is
conceived of as operating in a fashion analogous to dreaming,
so that a shift in time may be prompted by a Freudian pun.
One such has been omitted entirely from the American translation (p. 296). In the French (p. 290), the word *gland* (meaning *"glans penis"*) reminds Georges of the other meaning of
gland ("acorn"); suddenly he is no longer with Corinne but
under the oak trees on the day of his attempted escape, pretending to pick up acorns as he watches the German sentry.
Similarly, a natural analogy between grass and pubic hair
brings him back to Corinne from a moment when he lay with
his face in the grass before being captured; then he is snatched

away from her again by the memory of a night when he slept on the grass among a crowd of other prisoners, head to foot. Each posture adopted by Georges and Corinne for the sexual act provokes its own analogies, and her body becomes the terrain of his battle experience.

Inevitably, the day of the squadron's annihilation and de Reixach's death—together with the night and day which followed it—occupies Georges's memory more than any other period. Having hardly slept at all during the whole preceding week, he spent that day in a state between sleeping and waking; hence it comes back to him easily as he lies between sleeping and waking in the hotel bed, with or without Corinne. The ambush early in the day, which reduced the squadron to four men—de Reixach, the second lieutenant, Iglésia, and Georges—is remembered at a significant moment: Georges is visualizing the steeplechase, ridden by de Reixach and narrated by Iglésia, when suddenly the cavalcade of jockeys and race horses is replaced by a vision of the advancing squadron; after the reader has experienced the confusion of the rout as seen and felt by Georges, we return to the conclusion of the race; one of de Reixach's gallant defeats is paralleled by the other.

As for de Reixach's final catastrophe, when he is shot from his horse as he pulls his saber from the scabbard and falls brandishing it futilely in the air, we approach it twice, first at the beginning of the book and again at the end. Here the "ace-of-clubs" or clover-leaf structure of the main narrative becomes particularly significant. If one draws an ace of clubs without lifting pencil from paper, in the way suggested by Simon to Bourin, and begins with a short vertical stem, the figure is evidently not complete until the fixed point has been reached for the fourth time. Hence the dead horse appears in the book four times. Georges first noticed it a short time before de Reixach's death; he and Iglésia found themselves beside it again after escaping from that second ambush; they then took refuge in a neighboring farmhouse, so that Georges saw the horse twice more before leaving the area, because on the first of these two occasions their flight was prevented by the

presence of a German soldier. Now, if one's pencil passes the
fixed point for the fourth time, it is natural for it to travel
again over one of the loops or leaves already drawn. (The
book is divided into three parts, corresponding to the three
loops.) Thus in the last half dozen pages of the novel, after
the final glimpse of the dead horse, we find ourselves riding
once more with Georges behind the erect figure of de Reixach
toward the captain's final disaster or triumph.

Disastrous blunder or triumphant suicide—"how can you
tell?" Georges began his night of memories with the virtual
certainty that it was suicide, but now, after Corinne's questioning of his own motives, he is no longer sure of anything.
Both his own life and de Reixach's had seemed to reveal a
pattern, of which Corinne in each case was an integral element, a fixed point. Now the patterns lie shattered. Perhaps
de Reixach had led them into danger so slowly only because,
with his characteristic sympathy for beast rather than man, he
wanted to give the horses a rest. After his long night of remembering, Georges is left with only one certainty, defined
in the novel's final phrase, "the incoherent, casual, impersonal
and destructive work of time." (Note that the final word of
The Flanders Road, as of Proust's *Remembrance of Things
Past*, is *temps*, "time.")

Yet, if the pattern of these lives is shattered, the pattern
of Simon's book remains, raising its triune symbol of order
triumphantly above the fragmentary disorder of history and
time. And hand in hand with order, as always, goes beauty,
not merely the sort of beauty one can find in Goya's terrifying
series of etchings, *The Disasters of War*, but also a more
familiar kind that gains poignancy from Simon's oppressive
awareness of its transience: the beauty of young women, of
jockeys' silks and thoroughbred horses, of a cavalry squadron
before battle, of the French landscape not yet defaced and
eroded by the tide of war, of the archaic ideals upheld by a
dying aristocracy. Life may be meaningless for Simon, but he
cannot persuade either us or himself that it is not good. Thus
a book like *The Flanders Road* is not merely a work of art, it
is a means to knowledge—of ourselves and of the world. As

Simon said to Bourin, "Art, like science, is a means of knowledge [*un moyen de connaissance*]; it rests upon the establishment of 'relationships.' Art in itself has a profound value; but let us not confuse the moralist with the creative writer."

Before we leave *The Flanders Road*, something ought to be said about its style and that of Simon's later novels in general. Naturally there are variations in style from passage to passage and from book to book, but the reader cannot go very far without noticing the enormous length of many sentences—in the manner of Proust or the later Faulkner—and the numerous parentheses—sometimes set one within the other—that are partly responsible for their length. If he knows anything about grammar at all, he can hardly fail to notice also the frequent recurrence of the present participle. Consider, for example, this passage in the account of the race ridden by de Reixach (p. 150 of the New York edition), in which the present participles have been italicized for the purpose of illustration:

> Then they reached the gate, he tossed the sponge behind him without looking, and the chestnut leaped ahead like a spring, *starting* at a gallop, *pulling* as hard as she could at the bridle, neck turned slightly to one side, one shoulder forward, her long tail *whipping* the air, *bounding* as if she had been a rubber ball, de Reixach inseparable from her, almost *standing* in the stirrups, his chest forward, the pink spot of the silk quickly *diminishing* from bound to bound, silently, Iglésia *standing* there against the white barrier, *watching* them diminish disappear scarcely *rising* as they took the little hedge before the turn, after which he saw nothing but the black cap and the silk no longer *diminishing*, *moving* now—*rising* and *falling* —above the hedge and to the right, and *disappearing* behind the little woods: then *leaving* the bucket and sponge there and as fast as his legs allowed (that is, the way a jockey can run, that is, almost the way a horse runs when you've cut off its legs at the knees) *heading* toward the grandstand, *butting* into people, head raised, *looking* for Corinne, *passing* the place, finally *discovering* her, *turning* back, *climbing* the stairs and as soon as he was beside her suddenly motionless, turned toward the little woods. . . .

Another writer might have used the first fourteen participles,
as far as the colon, to give an instantaneous picture of the start
of the race, which after all lasts only a few seconds; but surely
it would then be natural to continue:

> . . . he *left* the bucket . . . *headed* toward the grandstand . . .
> *looked* for Corinne, *passed* the place, finally *discovered* her,
> *turned* back, *climbed* the stairs. . . .

Clearly, what Simon is attempting by the use of this syntactical
device is to telescope time so that we *see everything at once*
instead of in succession, to convert narration in time into a
picture in space. Often his use of parentheses has a similar
effect, enabling him to show more than one thing happening
at the same time and thus achieve simultaneity as well as
instantaneity. Another device, borrowed from Faulkner, that
Simon uses to compress time is the omission of verbs of saying:

> and she Oh you know I never pay any attention to uniforms
> and I Good God (p. 211)

This helps give the impression that a whole conversation is
remembered in an instant, especially when all punctuation is
also omitted.

Curiously, Simon borrows another device from Faulkner—it
can also be found in Proust—which has the opposite effect of
slowing down the narration: the practice of offering alterna-
tives or stressing the tentativeness of a judgment or description
by the use of "perhaps," "as if." The following description of
the crowd at the race track (pp. 152–3, New York edition) is
a classic example (italics mine):

> a species *or* class *or* race whose fathers *or* grandfathers *or*
> great-grandfathers *or* great-great-grandfathers had one day
> found a means, by violence, trickery *or* constraint exercised in
> a *more or less* legal fashion (and *probably* more than less, con-
> sidering that right, law is always only the consecration of a
> state of force) of amassing the fortunes they were now spend-
> ing but which, by a *sort of* coincidence, a curse attached to
> the violence and the trickery, condemned them to find growing
> round them only that fauna which is also trying to acquire (*or*

to profit by) those very fortunes (*or* merely fortune) by violence *or* trickery, and whom the former managed to jostle
(breathing the same air, trampling the same dusty gravel, *as if*
they had been assembled in the same salon) without even
seeming to notice their presence, nor even—*perhaps*—to see
them. . . .

When Georges is analyzing the motives of another character
who is an enigma to him—de Reixach, Iglésia, or Corinne—
this tentativeness has great virtue; it is part of the New
Novelists' rigorous effort to avoid the assertive, inauthentic
omniscience of earlier novelists. In the passage quoted, however, it has degenerated into a trick of style, for, even with all
the tentativeness of "or" and "probably" and "perhaps," the
passage remains a piece of dogmatic generalization—whether
we characterize the dogma as Marxist or Nietzschean or
Rousseauist. The views expressed in it are certainly in keeping with Georges's character, but similar passages in other
novels by Simon cannot always be assigned to a particular
character; they suggest that the author, perhaps because of
his admiration for Proust, has not always made such a sharp
distinction between the moralist and the creative writer as he
did in the interview with Bourin. Generally speaking, such
moralizing passages exude a pessimism almost as trite as any
optimism could be.

Besides its Proustian and Faulknerian overtones, the style
of *The Flanders Road* sometimes reveals a Joycean influence
also. For instance, in the first of many references to the feminine sex organ (pp. 41–2 in the French), we read of

cette chose au nom de bête, de terme d'histoire naturelle—
moule poulpe pulpe vulve—faisant penser à ces organismes
marins et carnivores aveugles mais pourvus de lèvres, de
cils. . . .

Richard Howard (New York edition, p. 41) translates as best
he can:

that thing with an animal's name, a term of natural history—
mussel sponge valve vulva—suggesting those deep-sea and
blind carnivorous organisms still furnished with lips, with
hair. . . .

Inevitably, Howard misses most of the assonance, conso-
nance, and play of meaning in the original series, *moule poulpe
pulpe vulve*. *Moule* can mean both "mussel" and "mold"; the
second meaning, by which the vulva becomes the mold into
which Man is pressed and from which he issues, is played on a
few lines later. Other reminiscences of the technique of *Finnegans Wake* will be found elsewhere, such as the list of place
names which Howard has done his best to translate on pp.
303–4 of the American edition. Finally, the dry, impersonal,
almost scientific description of the four cavalrymen riding
once more into the second ambush (pp. 304–12, New York
edition) recalls the technique of the second-last ("Ithaca")
episode of Joyce's *Ulysses*:

> . . . and armed that is all four provided with a curved saber
> about a yard long and weighing two kilograms the blade care-
> fully sheathed in a metal scabbard itself protected in a brown
> cloth case, saber and scabbard held by two straps called
> pommel strap and saber strap. . . . (p. 306)

As the style in *Ulysses* reflects the exhaustion of Stephen and
Bloom after their long day, so the style here reflects Georges's
exhaustion after his long night with Corinne and provides the
ideal vehicle for his disillusionment:

> . . . since subsequently—that is, when the war was over—she
> [Corinne] refused to admit that she could have maintained
> personal relations with him [Iglésia] at one moment or another,
> not even attempting to learn what had become of him, not
> attempting to see him again (and he not attempting to see
> her either), so that there was perhaps nothing real in all this
> save vague rumors and gossip and the boasting which two
> captive young men [Blum and Georges], imaginative and de-
> prived of women, encouraged him to make or rather which
> they extracted from him. . . . (p. 310)

In spite of its identifiable sources, then, and regardless of the
generalizations that can be made about it, Simon's later style
is a flexible instrument which he adapts to the mood and
subject of his narration, dialogue, and description.

Simon's other novels will be examined more briefly in the order of their publication—with one exception. It has not been possible to obtain a copy of his first novel, *Le Tricheur* ("The Cheat," never translated). Simon himself insists that he does not possess a copy and is too dissatisfied with the book to permit its republication. It was completed in 1941, after Simon's escape, in November 1940, from a German prisoner-of-war camp, but not published until 1946, when the well-known critic Maurice Nadeau compared it favorably with Camus's *L'Étranger*. At the time he wrote *Le Tricheur*, Simon still thought of himself as a painter. It is not quite clear when he wrote his curious autobiographical work, *La Corde raide* ("The Tightrope," not translated), which was published in 1947; at any rate, in this book too he speaks as a painter: "A guy paints because he has in him the need to paint, just as a guy talks if he's talkative by nature . . ." (p. 69, my translation). He has a great deal to say about Cézanne and a certain amount about Picasso. All this is mingled in a confusing way with reminiscences of the Spanish Civil War, a visit to Russia after his return from Spain, and his experiences as a cavalryman and prisoner during 1939–40. These reminiscences will be discussed later in connection with the autobiographical novel *Histoire*. Suffice it to say now that *La Corde raide* is an unsatisfactory, poorly ordered book, but in the five years between its publication and that of his next book, *Gulliver*, Simon had made himself a professional writer.

Gulliver (Paris, 1952, never translated), which can hardly be considered a New Novel, was written before Simon had developed his mature style. It contains no long sentences, no stream-of-consciousness passages, no sudden shifts in time and space prompted by the association of ideas. Instead of being seen through the memory of one or more characters, it is narrated in the third person by an omniscient author, and, with one exception, its chapters are arranged in chronological order, although there is some overlapping of time among several of them. As in most New Novels, however, its action takes place within a very short period—two days and two nights.

Gulliver approaches the New Novel more closely in its presentation of character than in its narrative technique. The
motivation of none of the characters, with the possible exception of Bert and Herzog, is ever made clear to us. Not only do
they have little or no conscious insight into why they behave
as they do, but Simon makes no attempt to reveal their unconscious motivation, as a Freudian novelist would. The
quotation from Lichtenberg on the title page—*Non cogitant,
ergo sunt* ("They do not think, therefore they are")—sums
up the author's view of his main characters. He presents them
almost entirely through their words and actions, which he
does not attempt to explain or judge.

The whole book is a dismaying vision of disorder, unpalliated by the imposition of any compensating order, either
moral or artistic. Yet the reader, because of the compulsive
power with which the story is told, watches with fascination
rather than disgust what he can only regard as the triumph of
evil. He is even tempted into wondering whether the categories of good and evil are applicable to such thoughtless
monsters as the de Chavannes twins, who seem like giant
children rather than mature, responsible men.

The center of the disorder in the book is the de Chavannes
family, consisting now of the twins, Jo and Loulou; their sister,
Eliane; their dipsomaniac uncle; and their grandmother, the
only one who clings to the aristocratic values of the family's
past. But "values" is perhaps the wrong word, for she preserves
the form rather than the content of aristocracy; like de
Reixach, all she is concerned with is keeping up appearances,
and though she knows how corrupt her two grandsons are, she
never admits it for a moment. As for Jo and Loulou, the only
check on their behavior is the childish rule that "Grandmother
must never know." A veil of lies and ruses must be thrown
over all disorder, whether moral or physical, in her house and
family. The essential inhumanity of the grandmother comes
out most clearly in her inability ever to forget that Herzog,
her late husband's assistant and the real source of his success
in the academic world, is a Jew.

Around the brink of this vortex of disorder, in imminent

danger of being destroyed by it, circle the other main characters: Max Verdier, Thomas Serres, Herzog, Bobby, Bert, and the family's servants, Joseph and his wife. Ultimately, all of these meet with disaster except Tom, who is saved by his own integrity, and perhaps Herzog, to the extent that he is still able to retain his illusions. The setting is the two neighboring towns of Villeneuve and La Bastide in southwestern France, and the time is approximately that of the Battle of the Bulge, December 1944.

Jo and Loulou are huge, powerful young men, too stupid to be afraid of most dangers but with a streak of cowardice in them nevertheless. A pair of budding Fascists before World War II, they took opposite sides after the French defeat in 1940. Jo went to England and joined the Free French forces, while Loulou joined the hated Vichy *Milice*, a French police force which abetted the Germans in suppressing the Resistance. Jo's record is not much better, since he is believed, when captured by the Germans, to have betrayed the Resistance group to which he had been parachuted. When the book opens, Jo is at home on leave from the Free French Air Force, and Loulou has secretly come home too, although a fugitive under sentence of death, to obtain more money. He gets it by pretending to Herzog that he can arrange the release of Herzog's wife and daughter, who have probably perished long ago in a German extermination camp. Though knowing what a scoundrel Loulou is, Herzog would sooner give him a hundred thousand francs than admit to himself that he has lost all hope of seeing his wife and child again.

Max, the wealthy son of a bourgeois family, still handsome in middle age, is perhaps more truly the Gulliver of the novel's title than either of the two giant brothers. He seems a giant tied down by Lilliputians, a man of great potentialities who has been prevented by his environment from fulfilling them. He grew up hating his parents, perhaps because he felt that they did not love him; at any rate, he himself seems incapable of normal love. As soon as he was old enough, he cut himself off from his parents and would not accept any money from them. Women were attracted to him, but he could never

give them anything more than physical satisfaction, and as a
result one of them committed suicide in his apartment. When
his parents died, he inherited their wealth but remained in
Paris as the patron of a group of avant-garde writers with
left-wing views. Eventually he drifted back to his native place
and became fascinated by the de Chavannes twins; he imitated
their gambling, their love for fast cars and sport. After years
without women, he became Eliane's lover, but she soon
realized that he did not love her and refused to marry him,
even though she bore him a child. When the book opens she
has changed her mind and wants to marry him, because she
feels the child needs a father, but in the meantime Max has
fallen in love for the first time—with Bobby, a lower-class boy,
a rugby player, who had been a hero of the Resistance but is
not above accepting money from Max and taking part in the
black market. Indirectly, the twins have destroyed Max by
their corrupting influence.

Bert, a tragicomic "injustice collector," had formerly been
one of the writers subsidized by Max; he now owns a bookstore and writes slashing anonymous editorials for the local
newspaper. He is in love with Eliane, who does not love him
and finally tells him that Max is the father of her child, adding
to the irrational grievance that he already feels against Max.

Everything comes to a head on the day Loulou returns
home. After a rugby game, which first strikes the keynote of
violence, Bobby makes it clear to Max that he is finished with
him. Then, in a spirit of bravado and against Tom's advice,
he and a friend take two girls to the same roadside inn where
Max and Jo are spending the night before going hunting early
next morning. Tom, as Max's guest, and the foolhardy Loulou
join the hunting party. Before the night of hard drinking is
over, Loulou has killed Bobby, who in a drunken fury had
vowed to kill or capture him. Max is desolate; Jo, who wants
more of Max's money, tricks Eliane into visiting Max, hoping
that she can now win back her former lover. This adds the
last straw to Max's burden; he escapes from them and drives
away; at dawn he commits suicide by driving over a cliff.
Tom, a former prisoner of the Germans and the sole survivor

of the Resistance group supposedly betrayed by Jo, becomes
Eliane's lover that same night; we are led to believe that they
may find happiness together. Bert, who next day tries fren-
ziedly to prove that Max and Tom had murdered Bobby,
learns of Max's suicide and realizes that he has lost all hope
of winning Eliane.

These events, which hold out little hope for anybody except
Tom and Eliane, are set within an even more depressing frame,
supplied by the opening and closing chapters. The former
takes place *after* the main action, serving more as epilogue
than prologue, and reveals that Loulou has escaped scot-free,
at least for the moment, while the anger of former members
of the Resistance has vented itself in the murder of the
servant Joseph, who was only an accessory to Loulou's ex-
tortions from Herzog. In the concluding chapter, Herzog tries
to console his housekeeper, Bobby's mother, and offers to pay
for her son's funeral. Left alone, the woman has nothing to
say except "Dirty Jew! Dirty pig of a Jew!" One feels that
Simon, having devised not one but two unpleasant endings
for his book, decided to make use of both by assigning one to
the first chapter and the other to the last. At the center of the
book stands one of Simon's pitiless sexual episodes: Max
breaks in on Bobby, his friend, and the two whores when the
orgy is at its depth rather than its height. To make everything
still more desolate, Bobby's girl is shown next day to be overwhelmed by his death, having unprofessionally fallen in love
with him. *Gulliver* reminds us in some ways of the novels
of Dostoevsky, another of Simon's idols alongside Faulkner,
Joyce, and Proust. But whereas Dostoevsky's conclusions are
always optimistic—often in seeming disregard of the premises
which he has stated—Simon's pessimism here is so extreme
as to parody itself.

The disorderly form of the book has perhaps been unduly
emphasized so far; as the reader will have noticed for himself,
two elementary formal principles are at work: chronological
order and plot. Indeed, one might object that there is too
much plot, not merely for the purposes of a New Novel but
for those of a traditional novel also. Yet some of the moments

which will remain in the reader's memory, such as the rugby match in the rain, are those where nothing seems to be happening at all and time is standing still. Even when something crucial *is* happening, such as the murder of Bobby, we still get this feeling of time being arrested or at least slowed down, of dramatic action halted and turned into what used to be called a "tableau"—from the French word for "picture." Another painterly quality of many scenes in this book is their chiaroscuro, the strongly marked light and shadow of the descriptive writing, enhanced by the fact that much of the action takes place at night. Some of the book's humor—more akin to Faulkner's than to Dostoevsky's even in the treatment of the masochistic Bert—is also visual, almost slapstick: for instance, when Jo returns to his bedroom to find the air full of feathers, his dogs having torn up the eiderdown quilt. Yet even this ridiculous moment supplies us with another image of disorder.

Simon's next book, *Le Sacre du printemps* ("The Rite of Spring," Paris, 1954; never translated), reveals a new concern with form; no longer content to follow chronological order, he begins to manipulate time. A translation of the table of contents will illustrate this point:

PART ONE
December 10, 1952
December 11, 1952
PART TWO
December 10, 11, and 12, 1936
December 12, 1952

It may be relevant to recall the chapter headings of Faulkner's *The Sound and the Fury*: "April 7, 1928; June 2, 1910; April 6, 1928; April 8, 1928."

The 1952 chapters mainly concern young Bernard, whereas the 1936 chapter relates an adventure of his stepfather, for whom he feels an Oedipal resentment, during the Spanish Civil War. The effect of this juxtaposition of two dissimilar narratives is to point out a parallel between the two men:

each, at about the same age, became involved in a quixotic enterprise which ended in failure and disillusion; each, in the springtime of life, enacted his "rite of spring."

Point of view as well as time is manipulated in this novel: the first chapter is narrated (or experienced) by Bernard in the first person, whereas the second and fourth chapters are narrated in the third person. The third chapter begins in the third person but soon shifts to the first; not until we have almost reached the end of it do we know for certain that the stepfather (whose name we never learn) is recounting his own youthful experience to Bernard's mother.

The style (in the most restricted sense) of this novel also shows a change from that of its predecessor. Simon no longer appears content to emphasize the visual qualities in his writing: we cannot escape the feeling that he has begun to *listen* to his words as he writes them. This practice begets a certain preciosity as well as euphony: note the recurrence of triads of adjectives and, less often, of nouns.

The plot of Bernard's adventures, as developed in the first two chapters, seems banal. A serious undergraduate, whose only luxury is a motorcycle, Bernard is trying to live without women, having discarded his first mistress. His motives are those of Hamlet, for he cannot forgive his mother's remarriage: "Frailty, thy name is woman." When confronted with a damsel in distress, however, he shows astonishing readiness to help. Édith, the daughter of a family friend and the elder sister of a stupid boy whom Bernard is coaching in mathematics, needs money desperately for a purpose which she keeps secret. She has stolen a ring from her mother, and Bernard agrees to sell it for her. Bernard is put in touch with a young "fence" named Jacky, who has a mistress named Josie. Jacky does not seem eager to buy, and Bernard spends a considerable time with Josie, waiting fruitlessly for Jacky to keep an appointment with him. Bernard drinks more than he is accustomed to and accompanies Josie back to her apartment, where she has little difficulty in seducing him. Soon after, Bernard discovers that the ring is missing. He rushes back to the apartment, finds Jacky and Josie in the street before he gets there, pours out his accusations, and has a fist fight with Jacky in which he is ignominiously defeated. For a moment Bernard contemplates suicide, but eventually he tells Édith the story of his failure. She asks him if he knows a doctor, but at first he fails to understand; finally she blurts out that she is pregnant.

In the fourth and final chapter, after Bernard has persuaded his repellent elder brother, Michel, who is an intern, to perform an abortion for the price of Bernard's precious motorcycle, we find that Simon has withheld some essential information from us. The story of Bernard is not quite so banal as it seemed: for about a year he has known that his stepfather is or was in love with Édith—and thus is probably the father of her child. (Later, Bernard learns that his mother has tolerated this escapade.) Having overheard the stepfather making an appointment with Édith, Bernard now arranges things so that he and his mother surprise the pair in a restaurant. This is too much for Édith, who runs away blindly and is knocked down by a car. While waiting for news in the hospital, Bernard and his stepfather have a long conversation in which the stepfather gradually wins Bernard's grudging sympathy. As a result of the accident, Édith has a miscarriage. The stepfather suggests that Bernard might still win Édith if he wishes, but Bernard emphatically refuses. About to burst into tears, the boy fumbles for his handkerchief; as he pulls it from his pocket, there falls out on the floor—the ring. End of novel. The reader realizes, with some chagrin, that what he had mistaken for tragedy is a rather typically French comedy.

The real tragedy of the book is to be found in the stepfather's narrative of gun-running during the Spanish War. The central figure here is an Italian named Ceccaldi, a professional adventurer, whose authenticity makes Bernard's future stepfather ashamed of his own rather Boy Scoutish dabbling in revolution. Ceccaldi is only concerned to make a good job of the gun-running, for which he is being paid, and his seeming indifference to ideology arouses the hostility of Suñer, a Spanish revolutionary. The young Frenchman admires Ceccaldi's assured virility and his ability to turn a relationship with an aging prostitute into a sort of poem of sensuality. Only later does he realize that he has failed Ceccaldi by being insufficiently suspicious of Suñer. The Spaniard, fully aware of what he is doing, surreptitiously unloads Ceccaldi's gun. He then tricks the young man into accompanying him and the cargo of arms to Spain. In their absence, two Franco agents who have been lurking about the French port murder the defenseless Ceccaldi. When the stepfather has finished telling his story, his wife makes a comment.

> "After all," she said, "he was bound to end that way sooner or later, don't you think?"
> "Probably," he said.
> "I imagine, even, that a man like that would have hated to die in his bed."
> "Yes. Yes certainly. It's a hell of a lot better than to end up like me, selling old junk, as your son says."
> "Don't talk nonsense. I'd be so happy if you both managed to get along well with one another. He talks like a child."
> "No," he said, "he's right." (pp. 202–3, my translation)

The stepfather is clearly still a romantic at heart, as his affair with a girl half his age proves. One imagines that Ceccaldi would have split his sides laughing at this comfortably married antique dealer who still wants to have his cake and eat it too. At bottom, the stepfather is as much a comic figure as Bernard, who, like him, will always look back nostalgically on his three days as Don Quixote.

Le Vent (Paris, 1957; translated as The Wind, New York, 1959) presents us with another Don Quixote, in the person of Montès, but this time he has taken on also certain aspects of Prince Myshkin in Dostoevsky's The Idiot. Indeed, the very first words of the novel are "An idiot, that's all," and they refer to Montès.

This is the first of Simon's novels to be narrated entirely from the point of view of a character within it, but it is not the protagonist who tells the story; instead, it is a minor character, a teacher in a lycée and writer on church archi-

tecture, who attempts to reconstruct the events after they have
happened. The French edition bears a subtitle, *Tentative de
restitution d'un retable baroque* ("Attempted Restoration of a
Baroque Altarpiece"), which suggests the effort of reconstruction at the same time that it offers further implications:
Montès seems, as does Dostoevsky's "idiot," a Christ-like
figure, while some of his adventures are baroque almost to
the point of grotesquerie. It may even be possible to identify
the altarpiece within the book itself: in the convent parlor
where Montès visits the two little orphan girls there hangs

> . . . a big dark oil-painting (he didn't have time to look at it,
> he told me that the whole time he stayed with them he was
> vaguely aware of it to his left: something with women in blue
> veils, and nails, and drops of blood carefully painted on the
> pierced feet, and a black sky) . . . (New York ed., p. 245)

As this passage suggests, the narrator is helped in his work
of restoration by the long conversations during which Montès
confides much of his own version of the story to him. Others
give the narrator supplementary information; for instance,
the book opens with a long, contemptuous monologue about
Montès by his former lawyer, as loquacious in his own way
as Faulkner's favorite lawyer-narrator, Gavin Stevens. The
current gossip of the town fills many gaps in the story.

Although the technique of "restoration" would have permitted a different arrangement, the events of *The Wind* are
narrated in roughly chronological order. Antoine Montès returns to the place of his begetting, an unnamed town in
southern France, after the death of his father, whom he has
never seen but whose property he inherits. While Montès's
mother was still carrying him in her womb, she surprised her
husband making love to the maid and left him forever the
same day. Montès has grown up in northern France and knows
nothing of the customs of the south; still less does he know
anything about the cultivation of the vine, yet he insists that
he will try to rehabilitate his father's vineyard rather than
sell it.

Montès's bizarre character and appearance lie at the root

of many of his difficulties, but probably no outsider could
have settled in the town without severe though concealed
opposition—symbolized by the wind of the title, which blows
through the town with invisible but brutal force during eight
or nine months of the year and provides a physical obstacle
to Montès's progress when he first rides his bicycle from town
to the family property. This bicycle is but one of the signs of
his eccentricity, along with his shapeless beret, his long hair,
his shabby clothes, the camera always slung about his neck
and dangling on his chest, his old man's face—although he
is hardly more than thirty-five. His character, a strange mixture
of guilelessness—especially in money matters—passivity, and
stubbornness, is as disconcerting to the average bourgeois as
his unconventional appearance. Like Christ, he exercises an
irresistible attraction upon children and women, though many
men find him baffling or contemptible. Like Christ too, he
brings not peace but a sword,

> . . . no sooner appearing than arousing rebellion, desire, dis-
> cord, anger—a man who, judging by appearances, wanted to
> be, tried to be, *was* the contrary of all this. . . . (p. 12)

Montès exercises his catalytic influence on three families in
particular. The first is that of his late father's bailiff, whose
daughter was the elder Montès's mistress. Montès, with un-
characteristic decisiveness and harshness, dismisses the bailiff
and then goes out to the property before the bailiff has left
it; much to his surprise, the old peasant makes a murderous
attack on him. Then the bailiff refuses to leave, bringing a
successful suit against Montès for breach of contract.

A second family cast into disorder by Montès is that of a
widowed relative, called an uncle by courtesy but in actuality
a cousin. This widower has two daughters: Hélène, the married one, incarnates all the bourgeois virtues and thus inevitably becomes an instrument of Montès's undoing; Cécile,
the unmarried one, falls desperately in love with Montès, who
makes no response. She first breaks off her engagement, then
takes her fiancé back when Montès ignores her, and finally

bullies the bewildered fiancé into taking her maidenhead before she discards him for good.

Most tragic of all is Montès's effect on the family of Rose, the maid at the sleazy hotel where he stays. She is the wife of a gypsy—an ex-boxer and petty thief—who is unfaithful to her with Hélène's former maid. Rose has two daughters, one by another man, and Montès becomes devoted to these children. He and Rose fall in love but do not become lovers. The gypsy is jealous and threatens to murder Rose if she betrays him to the police. Because of the meddling of a petty Judas named Maurice, who resents Montès's integrity as a living reproach to his own inauthenticity, Hélène learns of a robbery committed by the gypsy. She informs the police, hoping to cure Cécile of her attraction toward Montès. When the police come for the gypsy, he fulfills his threat to murder Rose and is himself killed by the police. The public-welfare authorities take Rose's two children, although Montès makes vain efforts to adopt them. For a time he is allowed to visit the girls, who adore him and regard him as their true father, but eventually the authorities remove them to another institution, refusing to tell Montès where they are. In despair, Montès sells his property, just seven months after his arrival, but seemingly cannot make up his mind to leave the town.

Such is the violent, sordid, and grotesque raw material of which this story is composed, but in the telling it is transmuted into a kind of poetry. A passage at the very beginning of the novel prepares us for the indirect and fragmentary way in which the altarpiece will be restored. The narrator is describing the notary telling

> . . . what he knew of the story, or what he imagined, having, in relation to the events which had occurred during the last seven months, like everyone else, *like the heroes of those events*, only that fragmentary, incomplete knowledge consisting of an accretion of sudden images (and those only partially apprehended by the sense of sight) or an accumulation of words (themselves poorly grasped) or a welter of generally ill-defined sensations, and everything—words, images, sensa-

tions—vague, full of gaps, blanks that the imagination and an approximative logic tried to remedy by a series of risky deductions. . . . (p. 10, New York ed.; my italics)

Yet these deductions, though risky, are not necessarily false:

because either everything is only chance and then the thousand and one versions, the thousand and one appearances of a story are also a story, or rather are and constitute *the* story, since that's the way it is and was and remains in the consciousness of the people who lived it, suffered it, endured it, laughed at it; or else reality is endowed with a life of its own, disdainful and independent of our perceptions and consequently of our knowledge and especially of our thirst for logic. . . . (p. 10)

In the latter case, naturally, any quest for reality is doomed to failure, but if a novelist accepts the former alternative, the thousand and one appearances, he has hit upon impressionism. One feels that Simon is recapitulating in his own career the history of the twentieth-century novel: with *The Wind* he has caught up to Ford Madox Ford's *The Good Soldier* (1915) and is in hot pursuit of Proust—overtaken in *The Grass*—and Joyce—overhauled in *The Flanders Road*. However, his mature style is beginning to take shape in *The Wind*; it is significant that this was the first of his novels to be published by Les Éditions de Minuit, a house intimately associated, under the guidance of Robbe-Grillet, with the development of the New Novel.

The passages just quoted indicate that Simon has identified a new source of disorder—the very nature of human consciousness—over and above the moral disorder so effectively presented in *Gulliver* and *Le Sacre du printemps*. We have also been made aware of the paradox that Montès, with his "longing for order and stability," possesses the "catastrophic gift of attracting trouble the way other people attract dogs or money, of communicating, spreading this confusion, this chaos. . . ." One incident shows that Montès hates and fears not merely disorder but even change:

. . . he had suddenly broken off with a girl back there [in northern France] the day he realized how unbearable, how intolerable it would be for him to see her with her hair done in a different way, or even wearing a different dress from the one she had on the day he met her the first time. . . . (p. 77–8)

The gulf between Montès's yearning for order and the disorder that he achieves makes him a comic as well as a tragic figure. He is at one point specifically compared with the great European clown Grock, and many of his misadventures remind us irresistibly of the little tramp created by Charlie Chaplin. Not content with getting himself assaulted by the bailiff, he later invites and receives a knockout blow from the gypsy, Jep. On one occasion, Cécile watches him "engaged . . . in an evidently unequal struggle against the sleeves of the jacket he was trying to get on" and asks angrily, "Is this a circus act?" Yet the two women who love the clownish Montès, Cécile and Rose, both say to him, "What do you think you are, a saint?" and in the mouths of both it becomes at once an accusation and a declaration of love. It is part of the planned disorder of this ironic book that words never mean what they seem to. In what the narrator calls a "strange and nocturnal love duet," presented on pp. 95–107 (New York edition), "the subject of love had not come up once (in words)"; throughout it Montès and Rose remained on a bench in the square outside the hotel, "sitting so they faced in the same direction, with enough room for at least another person in between them. . . ." It was their only love scene.

Having spoken of planned disorder, one must concede that this book is weakened by a too cunningly contrived plot. The ultimate catastrophe which overwhelms Rose and Jep (and, as a consequence, Montès too) is brought about by an overly neat sequence of cause and effect, though the effects are not intended by those peripheral characters, Maurice and Hélène, who set the causes in motion. Montès, naturally, intends no harm to Rose when he rebuffs the offered friendship of the repulsive Maurice; Maurice intends only to blackmail Cécile when he approaches her father and sister; inadvertently, he gives Hélène a piece of information about the gypsy which she correlates with other facts that she already knows; yet she certainly does not will the deaths of Rose and Jep when she goes to the public prosecutor to accuse the gypsy of robbery. Maurice and Hélène are not really necessary to the pictorial grouping of *The Wind* even in their roles as foils for Montès and Cécile, but they are indispensable to the plot. Furthermore, since a plot—a sequence of cause and effect—needs time in which to unfold, it becomes an insurmountable obstacle to the dissolution of time into space. As we have seen, in *The Flanders Road* Simon was to abandon plot almost entirely in favor of exploring, in great detail and from many aspects, an unresolved situation. But his renunciation of the artificial order obtainable from a contrived plot began with the novel immediately preceding *The Flanders Road*, namely *L'Herbe* (*The Grass*).[2]

The title of this novel refers in part to the grass in which Louise Thomas lies with her unnamed lover, in part to the epigraph, from Boris Pasternak: "Nobody makes history, nobody sees it happen, any more than one can see the grass growing." Yet something *does* happen, a situation *is* resolved. Louise makes up her mind—or, rather, her mind is made up in spite of her—not to leave her husband for her lover, though why or when that decision was made will always remain a mystery to her:

> . . . she could see him later the way he [her husband] stood there, and she would wonder then if it wasn't at that moment that she made up her mind, although, she would think bitterly [*avec ironie*], it was about as futile to try to know the moment when a decision was reached and the reasons for that decision as to know the moment (and the reasons why) one catches a cold, the only possible certitude in the one case or the other (the decision or the cold) being when the one or the other reveals itself, and by then they have already been established for a long time. . . . (pp. 127–8, New York ed.)

In *The Grass*, Simon approached from a new direction the problem of achieving instantaneity, of "seeing everything at

[2] Paris, 1958; translated, New York, 1960.

once." Perhaps recognizing that time is inescapable for the
novelist, he chose for treatment one of those periods when
time seems to stand still. The ten days during which Louise's
aunt by marriage, Marie, lies on her deathbed all seem like
one day. In a sense, nothing is happening, all the characters
are simply waiting for the old spinster to die so that they can
resume their lives where they left off. The novel opens with
Louise telling her lover that she cannot leave with him until
the old lady is dead; he fails to understand why. "But she's
not related to you," he says, very reasonably. Nevertheless,
Louise feels an obligation to Marie; she treasures the cheap
ring which the old lady gave her on her marriage far more than
the expensive jewels given her by her husband and his wealthy
parents (she herself comes from a poor family), and she
treasures too the love which Marie has given her, even though
she knows that she is loved not for any intrinsic qualities but
simply because she has become the wife of Marie's only
nephew.

During one of her few conscious moments on her deathbed,
Marie gives Louise another gift—an old tin cookie box which
holds, in a sense, her whole life. Along with her few keepsakes
and her bits of inexpensive jewelry, the box contains some
cheap notebooks forming a sort of lifelong diary. As Louise
turns over pages here and there, she realizes that this is no
private confession but a record of income and expenditure. It
reveals, with a poignancy that no intimate journal could ever
evoke, a lifetime of abnegation: the countless petty economies
by which Marie and her late sister, two country schoolteachers,
the daughters of an illiterate peasant, managed to give their
only brother, Pierre, the education that enabled him to become
a university professor and to marry the wealthy, aristocratic,
and beautiful Sabine de Reixach. And when that task had
been accomplished, the two spinsters did not relax their
efforts but kept up the family farm as best they could and
renovated the farmhouse from top to bottom. Marie, after her
sister's death, fled to her brother in the south during the fall
of France and never returned to the family home, which was
sold after World War II.

Now Marie lies dying, the sound of her labored breathing filling her brother's house and—so it seems to Louise—all the grounds around it. The ten days of her death agony are separated from everything that precedes and follows them by that sound and by the smell of the rotting pears that lie in thousands under the young trees her nephew had bought with the proceeds of the sale of her father's farm.

This nephew, Louise's husband, is none other than Georges, the protagonist of *The Flanders Road*. He is now years older— it is 1952—than he was to be in Simon's next novel, but no wiser. His whole life seems to be a rebellion against the career which his father had planned for him. Having either flunked out of or failed to gain admission to the prestigious École Normale, he refused to continue his education after the war, preferring the life of a farmer, wanting to become as similar as possible to his illiterate grandfather. "I wish I'd never read a book," he tells Louise. Ironically, he has no aptitude for farming either. In disregard of the local farmers' advice, he has planted a great number of pear trees, only to find that all the fruit falls off before it is ripe. His marriage to his lower-class mistress has turned out badly, and he is losing so much money at poker that both Sabine and Louise suspect him of having stolen an emerald from his mother to pay his debts.

Georges's parents are no happier than he is, partly because of their anxiety about him. Pierre, the retired professor, has become monstrously, dangerously obese. He manages to walk each day to the summerhouse in the garden, where he sits most of the day, endlessly writing, but he seems to have lost faith in the value of what he writes. Sabine, who cannot reconcile herself to old age and death, adds to his suffering. At least ten years younger than her husband, and thus hardly more than sixty, she makes herself hideous by using too much make-up and dyeing her hair. She is contemptuous of Marie, who has never been married or borne children, but at least the spinster has grown old with dignity. Sabine has always been obsessed by her husband's (probably imaginary) infidelity. Having been one of his students before she married him, she was always more or less jealous of his female students afterwards. When he was old and retired, she hoped to have him all to herself, but now he wants to sleep in a separate bed, even in a separate room. This gives her the grotesque idea that he is still unfaithful to her, although Pierre is too heavy to be able to walk out of her sight, let alone to desire or attract any other woman. Sabine has taken to nipping brandy secretly out of a perfume bottle; one night Louise overhears a grotesquely comic struggle in their bedroom, which adjoins hers. Pierre tries to take the brandy bottle away from the tipsy Sabine, and both of them fall down three times.

The unconscious Marie remains, as she has always been since her arrival from the north, the happiest member of the household. Curiously, in view of her peasant background, she is an atheist; Sabine adds to her own misery and that of her husband by insisting that Marie should be given the last rites of the Catholic Church, whether she wants them or not. Meanwhile, whenever she looks at the dying woman, Louise gets the strange feeling that Marie is forcing her to stay with Georges. Her lover, who remains a shadowy figure, is being transferred to a new post; Louise keeps promising each night that she will go away with him, but she comes to realize that she will not keep her promise and thus will break with him.

As Louise leafs through Marie's "diary," many of whose pages are reproduced in the text, she finally comes upon a photograph in which Marie is gazing at a young man with frank admiration. The pattern of her self-sacrifice is now complete: for Pierre's sake she must have made a conscious renunciation of marriage and motherhood. The practiced novel-reader has been expecting such a turn of events; Marie's self-sacrifice will surely inspire Louise's own renunciation. But things are not quite so simple, if only because Louise seems to have made up her mind long before, perhaps out of pity for Georges.

One must insist again that *The Grass* has no plot, no explicit linkage of cause and effect. In the last analysis, Louise's break with her lover—and remember that this is left implicit; there is no "farewell scene"—is an effect without a cause. Or if there is a cause, it is the whole atmosphere of the ten days, not any specific event or emotion, that brings about the rupture. The situation is analogous to that in Michel Butor's *La Modification* (*A Change of Heart*), published by Les Éditions de Minuit the year before *L'Herbe*. Butor's protagonist similarly renounces his mistress and decides to stay with his wife, not for any one specific reason, but because of the whole complex of experiences—fatigue included—which makes up his overnight train journey to Rome. The cat which was a silent witness to many of Louise's meetings with her lover plays almost as big a part in her decision as does the dying woman.

Yet in the long run it is Louise's identification with Marie that counts most. There is a curious moment, almost at the end of the book, when Louise is lying on the grass, her nakedness still exposed, her lover standing above her, ready to leave. She thinks, "Now I'm dead . . . Good. I was so tired, so . . ." After the man drives off, she still lies there,

> her lips forming once more the word "Yes," knowing now that she wouldn't go, knowing that he knew she wouldn't go . . . knowing that she had already known it before she came, wondering only how long she had known it, if she hadn't always known it, if all the rest hadn't been just a lie, if all the rest had even existed. . . . (p. 208)

It is as if she has put herself in the place of the dead (or soon-to-be-dead) woman and thus finds renunciation easy.

In the novels previously discussed, we have seen the conflict between order and disorder presented, if at all, in terms of an opposition between art and life: Simon's art imposes order upon his transcription of the disorder of life. At one moment in *The Grass*, Louise's thoughts make this opposition explicit:

> . . . the characteristic property of reality is to seem unreal, incoherent to us, since it presents itself as a perpetual challenge to logic, to common sense, at least as we have grown accustomed to see them predominate in books. . . . (pp. 84–5)

Yet *The Grass* offers a new version of the opposition between order and disorder: for the first time in a novel by Simon, there is a character who not merely aspires after order, like

Montès, but achieves it. Marie's ordered life, symbolized by
"the sloping, regular, and impersonal handwriting with the
carefully formed letters" and the neat columns of figures in the
notebooks, is contrasted with the disorder of her brother's
family. One motive, conscious or not, for Louise's decision is
the attraction which this orderliness has for her. It is also
possible to see memory, in spite of its instantaneous shifts in
time and its seeming capriciousness, as a force working toward
order. At times, when Louise remembers the period of Marie's
death agony, she can see herself "from outside," so to speak,

> . . . with that perspective which remoteness in time affords,
> free from the subjection of the present, watching herself act
> with that kind of half-scornful, half-irritated, slightly envious
> condescension we feel toward ourselves when we see ourselves
> after the fact, as we would watch a child act, unaware of what
> we know, have learned in the light of what has happened
> since, as if knowing the future conferred a superiority upon us,
> whereas all we have gained is perhaps to have a few less illu-
> sions, a little less innocence, so that it has not been a gain at
> all, but a loss. . . . (p. 106)

The wry conclusion of this passage suggests that Louise's decision may in the end have left her no happier, but at least she
has come to share some of the perspective, the ordered vision,
of the artist.

Nevertheless, we must not attribute to memory a greater
precision than it can achieve; no unambiguous chronological
order can be reestablished among the events of the crucial ten
days:

> . . . later, when Louise remembered that period . . . it ap-
> peared to her not like a specific slice of time, measurable and
> limited, but as a vague, criss-crossed interval, composed of a
> succession, an alternation of ups and downs, of darks and
> lights. . . . (pp. 104–5)

Some of the scenes which she "remembers" from that time
may not have occurred at all,

> belonging . . . , perhaps, to that domain of the latent, the
> inexpressed, or—the limit, the line of demarcation between

the formulated and the unformulated consisting only of this porous, clumsy and fragile barrier of words—perhaps not. (p. 126)

Specifically, the scene in which she accuses Georges of stealing the emerald, tells him she is going to leave him, and provokes him into striking her may never have taken place.

Before we leave *The Grass*, the superiority of its narrative technique over that of *The Wind* should be emphasized. Not only has the clumsy device of reconstruction or "restoration" been dispensed with, but the narrator has been eliminated also. Instead of being told a story by an observer, we are experiencing events directly through the consciousness of the protagonist. The fact that as a result Louise's husband and lover become rather vague figures, lacking the sharply objective outline imparted to characters with whom she is not emotionally involved (Pierre and Sabine especially), only heightens the realism. A newcomer to Simon would be well advised to begin with *The Grass*, not only as a useful introduction to the method and some of the characters of that masterpiece *The Flanders Road*, but also as an important novel in its own right. If the inexperienced reader complains afterwards that *The Grass* has a beginning but no ending, one can only refer him to the epigraph. He has shared in the making of history, the growing of the grass, but history never comes to an end and the grass never stops growing.

After the fluidity of *The Grass* and *The Flanders Road*, the rigidity of *The Palace*[3] comes as a shock. Clearly, Simon is attempting a new technique—new for him, at any rate, though long stretches of the book are embarrassingly reminiscent of the work of Robbe-Grillet. I have suggested that Simon is recapitulating in his work the development of the twentieth-century novel; in this book, he has finally begun to assimilate the techniques associated with a founder of the "New Novel school"—in the narrowest sense of that phrase. Simon's readiness to adopt the techniques of other novelists, a feature of his

---

[3] *Le Palace* (Paris, 1962), translated as *The Palace* (New York, 1963).

work referred to frequently in this chapter, may give rise to
serious doubts about his originality. These are surely ill-
founded, for he cannot borrow anything without giving it his
own unmistakable stamp.

The Palace deals with a situation very similar to that in
the third section of *Le Sacre du printemps*. The time is once
again the early days of the Spanish Civil War, but the locale
has been changed to Barcelona, seat of the Republican government. Three or four of the five main characters correspond to
the trio in the earlier book: a French student is virtually in-
distinguishable from the stepfather-to-be; a Spaniard who
looks like a schoolmaster bears a strong similarity to Suñer,
although a second Spaniard, a bald man, shares some of his
characteristics; finally, the role of Ceccaldi is given to a tall,
sardonic American from the Lincoln Brigade. These four men
—the student, the schoolmaster, the bald man, the American—
are thrown together with a fifth, an Italian revolutionary of
limited intelligence who is known as *l'homme-fusil* ("the man-
rifle") or, in Richard Howard's translation, simply as "the
rifle," because of the weapon that he carries with him everywhere as his only baggage. The American's cynical remarks
about the progress of the war and about his certainty that
Commandante Santiago was murdered by the government
police—his comrades in arms—not by the Fifth Column, make
the two Spaniards suspicious of him. We are led to believe
that he was taken away in the middle of the night to suffer
the same fate as Santiago. The student feels, as the stepfather
felt about Ceccaldi, that if he had been more alert he might
have saved the American's life—even though, in typical Simon
fashion, we never know for certain that the American did not,
as the bald man insists, simply go off in the middle of the
night to rejoin his unit at the battle front.

Throughout most of the book, we experience events directly
through the student's consciousness, but we are occasionally
reminded that in fact everything is being remembered by the
same man fifteen years later (i.e., in 1951) on his first visit to
Barcelona since the Civil War. As Wordsworth wrote in
"Tintern Abbey":

> . . . with many recognitions dim and faint
> The picture of the mind revives again.

Barcelona seems to have changed very little from the days before the Spanish Revolution, but of course it looks very different from the days when the former student first knew it. What he misses most is the gun which nearly every man in the street carried at that time. The "Palace" of the title—a former luxury hotel commandeered by the government for offices— has since burned down and been replaced by a bank. One feels that Simon has gained very little by splitting his observer into the student of the past and the mature man of today, except perhaps that he thus finds justification for his epigraph, a definition borrowed from the *Dictionnaire Larousse* which has the effect of a pun:

> *Revolution:* the locus of a moving body which, describing a closed curve, successively passes through the same points.

The ubiquitous pigeons of Barcelona are very much in evidence both then and now, providing one of the associative links which permit the Frenchman's consciousness to slip from present to past and back again.

The novel is divided into five chapters, all but one of which are arranged in chronological order. The title of the first, "Inventory," gives us fair warning that this book is going to be much concerned with "objects" in the special sense of that word employed by Robbe-Grillet. We see at least as much of the room in which the five men are sitting as of the men themselves. It was formerly a palatial hotel bedroom, but all the original furniture and paintings have been removed. In their place we are given an inventory of the new furnishings, described at great length: a refectory table taken from a monastery or some similar institution; "two dining-room chairs in fake German Renaissance style"; "a little desk with stacks of paper and a black typewriter, the trade-mark (REMINGTON) in half-effaced gilt letters"; "a huge couch (apparently moved, this time, not from a convent, but from a deluxe brothel, unless it was from an episcopal palace)"; a varnished wooden rocking chair; a wooden kitchen chair; pictures of Marx and

Stalin tacked to the walls in place of the mildly erotic eighteenth-century prints (reproductions of Boucher paintings, probably) which had been there previously; finally, a plan of the city.

It is true that a careful study of these objects and a sense of those they replaced will give us some awareness not only of the physical manifestations of a revolution but also of its spiritual qualities. Even the headlines of the various Barcelona newspapers scattered on the table, with their very similar comments on the death of Santiago, will, when quoted *verbatim*, impart an ironic flavor to the text. But Simon obviously feels that something is missing, as we discover in the third chapter, "The Funeral of Patroclus." This contains an objective, "camera eye" view of Santiago's funeral procession as seen by the student. Soon, however, we are learning facts about some of the participants in the procession that the student could hardly have known at the time:

> . . . the president (they had even elected a president) walking in the same row with the others . . . with the same dim, fixed, somnambulistic stare . . . the same drained, exhausted expression—not sad, or overwhelmed, or frightened—although the dead man (the one whose body had been found in a suburban empty lot with two bullets in the back of his neck) was his friend and personal adviser whom several of the nineteen others who called themselves the government had asked him to repudiate, which he had refused to do and which had been done for him now, by means that were definitive if not legal, so that he had the privilege, which is not granted to everyone, of being able to follow his own funeral now. . . . (New York ed., pp. 127–8)

Presumably the truth about Santiago's murder had become known to the former student during the succeeding fifteen years, but it seems pointless for Simon to abandon the nineteenth-century convention of authorial omniscience in favor of Robbe-Grillet's objectivity if he is then going to smuggle back the equivalent of editorializing by the author anyway.

Chapter 2, "The Rifle's Story," is a flashback presenting the student's train journey to Barcelona and his first hair-raising

automobile ride through its streets. He has met the Italian
with the rifle on the train, and all through the journey and the
car ride the Italian is giving him a detailed, vivid account of
his assassination of an Italian Fascist leader in an expensive
Paris restaurant. Such objects as a revolving door, a screen,
and the V-shaped shirt front of the maître d'hôtel take on
almost a life of their own in this cinematic presentation, while
the student wonders why he is being told the story.

The most significant part of the fourth chapter, "In the
Night," deals with the time spent by the student in his bedroom, watching the dark window of the American's room
across the courtyard. He refuses to admit to himself why he is
keeping this vigil, but clearly he feels that the American is in
danger. Unable to sleep, he spends a long time staring at the
labels on an empty cigar box; we are treated to a five-page
description of them. Eventually he falls asleep in spite of
himself and awakens to hear footsteps and voices moving
away down the corridor. He stares at the American's window,
which is still dark; suddenly a light goes on and a naked
woman draws the curtain across the window. The student lies
down, "cursing himself and calling himself a fool for the third
time that night. . . ."

In the fifth chapter, "Lost and Found," he wakes up late
for an appointment with the American, who is nowhere to be
seen. Suddenly the boy realizes that the window where he
saw the woman was not the American's at all. He rushes
frantically about, seeking for information from the "schoolmaster," the proprietor of his hotel, the bald man, but he gets
no answer except the bald man's, which he does not believe.
Finally he catches sight of the Italian in the distance and
pursues him to an underground lavatory, only to find that the
man-rifle has killed himself with his rifle, accidentally or on
purpose. Chapter 5, like Chapter 2, is an outstanding example
of Simon's virtuoso skill in presenting hurried action; the
reader participates almost physically in the student's frantic
dashing about, and the young man's emotion, so intense as to
become a physical sensation, is magically communicated. The
dreamlike world of anxiety and frustration familiar to us from

Kafka's novels is here immensely accelerated, as though Orson Welles's film of *The Trial* were being run through a projector at ten times the normal speed. These chapters provide a violent contrast with the static quality of the other three, but all five share the same mechanical quality: accelerating the machine does not make it any the less a machine. The figure of a naked woman which appears fleetingly in this novel, as in every other novel of Simon's, reminds us that his true subject matter was and remains not objects but human flesh and blood.

Simon's second-last novel, *Histoire* (Paris, 1967; translated, with same title, New York, 1968), contains its share of objects meticulously described. Like the contents of Aunt Marie's cookie box in *The Grass*, however, they are mainly objects with deep human associations: the picture postcards that the narrator-protagonist's mother received from her officer fiancé during their long engagement, similar cards exchanged by other members of the family, and an occasional photograph of relatives and/or friends. Not only the foreign or French scenes on the cards but the postage stamps too are described with great care. Early in the book, the cards' chief rivals for such minute attention are bank notes of the current French series, whose materialistic connotations serve as a foil for the romantic associations of the exotic postcards. Ecclesiastical vestments, flowers, and the maneuvers of a water-skier are among the other "objects" claiming attention from the narrator's compulsively observant eye.

But the sufferings of the human spirit and the degradation and decay of the human body bulk much larger in this "story" that is also a "history" (*histoire* has both meanings in French) than anything non-human. Simon has returned to the family history of the Thomas/de Reixach clan and to the South of France in which it has its roots. On the one hand we are aware of the provincial, claustrophobic atmosphere that enclosed *Gulliver*, *The Wind*, and *The Grass*. On the other hand, as in *The Flanders Road*, we are constantly aware of that wider world open to some of these southern aristocrats by virtue of their wealth, their culture, their sense of patriotic duty, or their love of adventure.

Comparable to *The Flanders Road* in richness if not in sheer intensity, *Histoire* is also comparable in narrative technique, for it is once again "remembered by one man from a fixed point in time," as I remarked of the earlier novel. Here, however, the remembering does not take place at night but during the waking hours of a rather trying Friday. The narrator-protagonist (or observer-protagonist) is living alone in his old family home in a small city of southern France (probably Simon's boyhood hometown, Perpignan) and goes about his business in or near that city. The time seems to be the 1960's, and symptoms of the affluent society are all about him, even though he shares but little in its affluence. (He owns a car, for instance, that is almost as run-down as his house.) Indeed, his chief tasks for the day are to arrange a loan from his bank, to sell the antique chest that up to now has held his mother's correspondence, and to obtain a cousin's signature on a document mortgaging part of the family estate. All this he accomplishes, observing the new with distaste and remembering the old with a mixture of distaste and nostalgia. As in *The Flanders Road*, memory is evoked by association of ideas; in daylight the external stimuli to remembrance are more numerous and varied than those encountered by Georges Thomas in the darkness of the hotel bedroom that he shared with Corinne.

The narrator's jaundiced vision is at least partly attributable to the fact that his wife, Hélène, has left him—how recently, we cannot be sure—and he therefore suffers both regret and remorse. He occasionally hints, by mythological allusions, at an inner torment that is too subjective to be made explicit by Simon's objectifying technique: no image from the narrator's past life can represent this all-pervasive anguish; instead, he imagines himself being devoured by the bronze-beaked birds of Lake Stymphalus (p. 27) or wearing the poisoned shirt that Deianira innocently gave to Hercules (pp. 309, 323).

The opening chapter alone is not firmly anchored within the narrator's day. In it he remembers the old ladies who used to come to this house to visit his mother and *her* mother; a Mass

said in his mother's bedroom when she was dying; the enlargement of his dead father's photograph hanging on the wall near
her bed; the postcards from his father already mentioned,
here briefly introduced to us but recurring in various contexts
throughout the day.

From the beginning of the second chapter, when he
awakens, we are taken through the day in chronological order.
No doubt many of its minor events are passed over in silence,
but we are informed of the time at intervals: noon, two o'clock,
five o'clock, nightfall. It is possible to regard the last chapter,
in which nearly all the themes and characters of the book are
briefly reintroduced, as a sort of epilogue or coda outside of
time; it would be equally possible to claim that, like the
second-last chapter, it portrays the narrator's stream of consciousness as he sits in a bar near his home eating a sandwich
and drinking a beer, the supper of a lonely man. Or we may
imagine that he has gone home to bed and is lying sleepless,
like some of those whom he is remembering.

In the course of the day he remembers many of the crucial
moments in his own life and remembers or imagines some of
those in the lives of his closest friends and relatives. His
father, Henri, who was killed in World War I, he cannot remember at all, and he tries to reconstruct him from his photograph, the laconic messages on the postcards, and the foreign
scenes portrayed there, ones which must have been familiar
to the officer. He tries to imagine his mother as a young
woman, but he can only remember her as a living skeleton on
her deathbed or carried downstairs for a musical evening. The
household he grew up in was a strange collection of the
widowed and the orphaned: his maternal grandmother; his
mother; her widowed brother, Charles; Charles's children,
Corinne and her younger brother "Paulou" or Paul; the narrator, himself about Corinne's age.

Corinne is of course the future Baronne de Reixach, already
at fifteen having an affair with a hairdresser who plays the
violin; the narrator from time to time remembers how her
first husband met his death and thinks about the rumors concerning her affair with a jockey. Paulou, a weedy, timid boy,

grows up to be a professional rugby player, built like a wall or a fullback.[4] A mighty fornicator in his football days, he has settled down in a house on the Mediterranean coast with his wife and a little daughter named Corinne; from there he commutes to his successful real-estate business in town. He leaves the office so early on Fridays that the narrator has to pursue him home to get his signature before mailing the document to Corinne.

Another of the narrator's contemporaries whom we see as a boy and again as a successful man of today is Bernard Lambert. Of lower-middle-class background, he was celebrated for his anti-clericalism at the Catholic school he attended; he introduced the narrator, his classmate, to Communism but disapproved of the narrator's supplying guns to the Anarchists of Barcelona during the Spanish Civil War. After nightfall on this Friday, the narrator hears loudspeakers amplifying an anti-Communist speech that Lambert is delivering to a large and enthusiastic audience in City Hall.

Certain scenes from the narrator's life appear in his memory once during the day; others, for whatever reason, more than once. As one would expect, the Mass at his mother's deathbed reappears; the scene at the station when he says goodbye to Hélène for the last time recurs over and over again. A scene in a museum in Greece reappears perhaps because it constituted the first tiff between the narrator and his wife, on their honeymoon. It is not so easy to see why a street scene of an ambush (or imagined ambush) by the Fifth Column in Barcelona should be dwelt on in such detail. One reason why memories of Barcelona surge up so often—and it should be recalled that Barcelona is perhaps closer by land to Perpignan than is Marseilles—is that Hélène's final departure takes place on the Barcelona Express. The earliest memory of Corinne, climbing a cherry tree as blood trickles down her bare leg, also appears more than once.

Curiously, however, there is only one character in the book— besides the narrator—who becomes for the reader a truly be-

---

[4] A fullback (*arrière*) is exactly what he becomes, not a "goalie," as in Richard Howard's translation. There is no goalie in "rugger."

lievable human being: Uncle Charles. This rather ineffectual
man, who leads the life of a literary and artistic dilettante in
Paris for most of the year, does his best to shoulder his re-
sponsibilities as guardian of the narrator and in some sense
both father and mother to his own children. We see him often
in his role as director of the family vineyard, testing the alcohol
and sugar content of the wine and deciding the amount of
fertilizer needed. He is gently sarcastic about the narrator's
halfhearted attempts to learn Latin and his escapades during
the Spanish War, but he does not punish him for "borrowing"
The Golden Ass from his shelves while still a schoolboy. He
gives Corinne the only discipline that willful girl ever receives; we do not observe his relationship with Paulou at all.
With the help of an old photograph showing Uncle Charles
in an artist's studio where a naked model is posing, the narrator reconstructs his uncle's love affair with the model—which
apparently begins when Charles's wife is already fatally ill. It
is very difficult to keep Charles's marital tragedy separate
from the narrator's because, in reconstructing the former,
the narrator borrows from his own experience. We cannot be
sure whether the unhappy couple lying on the bed in the last
chapter are Charles and his sick wife or the narrator and
Hélène: "he" slips into "I" and back again in a subtle and
ambiguous way. Nor are we sure whether the infidelity with
the passionate girl in—or rather out of—a kimono is the
narrator's or the uncle's. We recognize, however, that the narrator has come to identify himself with Uncle Charles, respect-
ing him for his old-fashioned dignity and loving him for his
faults.

That Simon "signature," a nude woman, is abundantly
present in the description of the photograph of Van Velden's
studio (New York edition, pp. 225–39). So is that other trade-
mark, the vulva. Apart from its implicit presence in the studio
scene, it appears in several other passages, notably pp. 101–2.
After reading this last passage, one wonders whether the girl
who has depilated herself is Corinne or Hélène. The writer of
jacket copy for the New York edition of *Histoire* seems convinced not only that Corinne and the narrator have been

lovers but that she has committed suicide: ". . . the suicide of
a cousin adored but somehow betrayed by the narrator,
abandoned by him for the Spanish Civil War to re-enact,
more violently, her mother's mysterious death. . . ." I feel,
however, that the narrator's asking Hélène to imitate the
depilation of classical Greek women is the cause of their
temporary tiff in Greece and that she in the end complies with
his bizarre request. As for Corinne's "suicide," we are told
explicitly that she is living in Nice on the crucial Friday (p.
54), and she is again spoken of as alive on p. 256. As for the
recurring headline, "SHE THROWS HERSELF OUT OF THE FOURTH
FLOOR WINDOW," seen in its most complete form on pp. 93–4,
it is only a sample of what is to be found in Friday's paper;
several other headlines are also quoted, though perhaps not so
frequently. (No apology is offered for this lengthy attempt to
clear up a misconception that is likely to reach many American
readers, at least. It serves as a reminder of the many ambiguities in *Histoire*, some of which continue to baffle me.)

The attempt noted in *The Flanders Road* "to telescope time
so that we *see everything at once* instead of in succession, to
convert narration in time into a picture in space," has become
more difficult in *Histoire* because the narrator is himself in
motion during so much of the day. Nevertheless, the oft-
mentioned postcards do in a sense succeed in cramming a long
stretch of time into a small space in the third drawer of a
chest.[5] One specific passage captures this idea vividly, as the
narrator envisages his mother looking over some of her dog-
eared postcards:

> . . . before or after what did it matter since it was all over now
> present immobilized everything here in the same moment
> forever the images the moments the voices the fragments of
> time of the multiple sumptuous inexhaustible world scattered
> on a dying woman's bed. . . . (p. 326)

Who, it is now high time to ask, can this unnamed narrator
be? Is he the narrator-protagonist of *The Palace*, whose Barce-

---

[5] An inventory of what the narrator clears out of the drawers will be
found on pp. 208–23 of the New York edition.

lona experiences seem very similar to his? He cannot be Georges
Thomas of *The Flanders Road* and *The Grass*, though he must
be a cousin of his. It may have occurred to some readers that
Georges Thomas and Claude Simon are somewhat similar
names—each consisting of a fairly common French first name
and a surname that is in fact equally common as a first name,
both Simon and Thomas being among the Twelve Apostles.
Following up this clue, we find in *La Corde raide* that some of
Simon's war experiences were very similar to those of Georges
Thomas: the death by ambush of Simon's colonel in the
cavalry, for instance; the prison-camp period; and the prisoners'
train journey.

On the other hand, we find from the article by André
Bourin cited earlier that Simon's father was an officer and
that young Claude was brought up by an uncle after his
father's death. The narrator's mother in *Histoire* traveled over-
seas with her husband for the first two years of her married
life; Claude Simon was born at Tananarive (Antananarivo) on
the island of Madagascar in 1913. The Spanish War experiences of the narrator of *The Palace* correspond precisely in
some respects with those narrated in *La Corde raide*; other
details in Simon's autobiography from this period are transferred to the narrator of *Histoire*.

All in all, though it is likely that if Simon had given his
narrator a name, the surname would be Thomas, we can safely
say that *Histoire* is the most autobiographical of all his novels
to date. Another of the New Novelists once gossiped a little
to me about Simon's marital difficulties, but, more to the point,
Simon himself has freely admitted to me that Marie's diary in
The Grass and the postcards in *Histoire* are transcribed directly
from his family's "archives." They resemble the *objets trouvés*
around which much modern sculpture and many collages are
constructed, and there is no doubt that Simon weaves fiction
around his authentic documents. Uncle Charles, for example,
is a more cultured person than the uncle whose last days are
described on pp. 21–7 of *La Corde raide* and of whom it is
there said that "he had never taken much interest in anything
in life except women, wine and tobacco."

Although the first person singular is used freely in *Histoire*, there may be some significance in the fact that the last word of the book is "me" (*moi* in the French). We already noted that the last word of *The Flanders Road* is "time." It would be incorrect to say that Simon has shifted his attention from time to himself: "time and me," the relationship of the individual to time, has provided the focus for his best work, as it did for Proust's. Perhaps this is the true meaning of the ambiguous title *Histoire*: every individual's story has to be related to that vast scale of measurement that may be called either time or history.

Once again, in *Histoire*, we see order being imposed upon disorder, though this time the order is fluid rather than rigid. If the structure of *The Palace* reminds us of architecture by its rigidity, the structure of *Histoire* reminds us of music by its fluidity: themes are stated and either developed or dropped, only to be restated and perhaps more fully developed later—all with what seems to be complete freedom. Yet we can see that ultimately Simon covers all the ground that he needs to as a novelist. His "story," his *histoire*, has been told, if we have the intelligence to read it. We have come to know a great deal about the narrator—not only the events of his life but the heredity, environment, and personalities that have helped to make him what he is today. What we do *not* know about him is, in part, something that we do not know about ourselves either—namely, what he will do next. But we do know what our own goals and hopes are; here Simon does not play fair with us, for this side of his narrator is left completely in the dark.

Let us note in conclusion the final deft touch that completes the structure of *Histoire*: as does Sterne's *Tristram Shandy*, the book ends with its "hero" waiting to be born. A longish excerpt from this concluding passage will give some idea of the texture of Simon's latest novel and show that his style has not changed much in the seven years since *The Flanders Road*, though the punctuation has become even more sparse:

Corinne

go away you hear me leave me alone leave me alone all of
you leave me alone

I stood there a moment in the hall I could hear vague
muffled noises in the pillow she must have been lying on her
bed Once or twice more I tried turning the handle Corinne!
She kept silent I left It was only Maman who could get anything out of her But already too sick by then stuffed with
morphine she slept almost all the time out of reach then having
already endured everything somnambulistic and serene perhaps having reached (or returned to) an eternal felicity among
the curving palm trees interlacing swaying their pendent crests
against the pale sky pale mountainsides ringing a gulf of pale
water a group of figures with black faces dressed in white shirts
and trousers and with broad hats two of them on the right
holding little donkeys by the bridle among the patches of sun-
light and shade and pasted on the right of the second little
donkey the eternal bald and crowned profile [of Edward VII]
olive-green this time and framed with the caption POSTAGE
repeated on the two vertical strips on each side of the medal-
lion the imperial crown overlapping the word SEYCHELLES
the caption of the card in tiny red letters running among the
shadows the sand the sparkling vegetation what happiness
what a dream: FELICITE ISLAND—COCONUT OIL-MILL
and on the back the jagged arrogant handwriting as rigid in
pleasure in voluptuousness as in the years of virginity overlapping the printed letters (CARTE POSTALE—POST
KARTE—POST CARD—TARJETA POSTALE, Published by
Mr. S. S. Ohashi, Seychelles—Printed in Germany):

Dear Maman

We're at Mahu now and it's raining torrents. I'm writing you
from the shop of some sort of merchant. It's too bad about the
weather, for the stop here would have been so pretty. This
magnificent tropical vegetation enchants me. I won't mail a
letter here because they say it would only leave later from
Diego. Henri is fine and sends his love and kisses with mine

the rain falling overwhelming echoing and gray on the palm
trees the opal gulf the little donkeys the men with their ebony
faces their soaking shirts and trousers gray now sticking to their
skinny limbs with those paler folds winding interlacing like a

network of roots the warm rain it's too bad the torrential sound
the huge drops on the leaves taking refuge in the shop of some
kind of merchant probably the one who had sold her the postcard a Mr. S. S. Ohashi with yellow skin watching her writing
on a corner of a table or the counter the lady bending over,
her mysterious bust of white flesh swathed in lace that bosom
which already perhaps was bearing me in its shadowy taber-
nacle a kind of gelatinous tadpole coiled around itself with its
two enormous eyes its silkworm head its toothless mouth its
cartilaginous insect's forehead, me? . . . (pp. 339–41)

Claude Simon, in spite of his tendency to become more and
more autobiographical, has by no means exhausted his subject
matter. Like Faulkner and Proust, whom he so much resembles, he has behind him not only his own experience but
that of a whole region and a whole social class. It is to be
hoped that he will not attempt to exploit further his reminiscences of Spain and of World War II but continue to
anatomize the sufferings of a so-called peaceful world in
which the pangs of love, the anguish of loss, the tortures of
disease—not to mention all the burdens of social and economic
injustice—offer all too many subjects to the novelist. It speaks
well for Simon's future as an artist that in his latest novel he
presents these sufferings—and a few concomitant joys—
directly, with very little of the rather hackneyed "philosophiz-
ing" that marred some of his earlier books. *Histoire* is its own
commentary, and if we need any further commentary on its
order and disorder, we can turn to the epigraph that Simon
has borrowed for this book from Rilke:

*It submerges us. We organize it. It falls to pieces. We organize
it again and fall to pieces ourselves.*

7

Claude Mauriac

THE IMMOBILIZATION OF TIME

CLAUDE MAURIAC (b. 1914), eldest son of the novelist and man of letters François Mauriac (winner of the Nobel Prize for Literature in 1952), came late to the writing of novels: *Toutes les femmes sont fatales* (*All Women Are Fatal*), his first, did not appear until 1957. One can understand why the son of a novelist who had attained classic stature in his own lifetime would hesitate to compete with his father: all the more so because Claude admired François with a generosity rare in father-son relationships. It is pleasant to record that Mauriac *père*, with equal generosity, actively encouraged Mauric *fils* to embark on creative work after an already long and impressive career as a journalist-critic of literature and the films.

In view of Claude Mauriac's astonishing growth as a virtuoso of novelistic technique, it is curious to note how little concern for technique is displayed in his literary criticism. Although M. Mauriac told me in conversation (July 19, 1965) that he did not really think of himself as a New Novelist and that nothing new had been discovered since Joyce and Proust, it is especially his resolute exploration of technical possibilities that has compelled me to include him in this study. Indeed, his career to date seems to provide all the justification that technical experiment in the novel will ever need. Michel Butor

has pointed out that the experimental novel can be a research
—into new ways of knowing, feeling, and thinking. Claude
Mauriac appears to have learned a great deal from his experiments, not only about how to write novels but also about life
and about himself. According to my notes of our 1965 conversation, he "agrees that his concern with technical problems
has liberated him as regards *le fond* [content]."

Because Mauriac has learned so much about his purpose as
a novelist in the process of writing his novels, the device
employed in other chapters of this study—analyzing an
author's masterpiece first in considerable detail and then considering his other novels more briefly—cannot be made use
of here. Without doubt, Claude Mauriac's masterpiece is *La
Marquise sortit à cinq heures* (*The Marquise Went Out at
Five*), but we must begin at the beginning, with *All Women
Are Fatal*. This book, the least experimental of his novels,
introduces us to many of the characters in the three succeeding
novels, although Mauriac had no intention of writing a
tetralogy when it appeared. He told me that, in spite of his
dissatisfaction with *All Women*, he wrote the other novels, in
a sense, in order to make people read that first one.

It was not until the publication of the fourth novel,
L'Agrandissement ("The Enlargement," not yet translated into
English), in 1963 that Mauriac revealed, or perhaps discovered, that he had written a four-part sequence linked by
something more than a common protagonist, the novelist
Bertrand Carnéjoux. The alert reader, looking at the list of the
author's previous works given opposite the title page, was
now informed that Mauriac's four novels composed a tetralogy
entitled *Le Dialogue intérieur* ("The Interior Dialogue"). It
is a clever title, reminding the critic and perhaps the more
sophisticated general reader of the well-known term *monologue intérieur* ("interior monologue"), commonly used in
France to describe what is more frequently known in English
as "stream of consciousness." What Mauriac means by "interior dialogue" will be more fully discussed when we examine
L'Agrandissement, but essentially it refers, as one would
expect, to those rare moments when one character's unspoken

thoughts answer those of another with a coherence seldom found even in spoken dialogue. Actually, Mauriac intended to give his tetralogy the more accurate title *Le Temps immobile* ("Immobile Time"), but decided to reserve it for a selection of passages from the diary he has kept since 1930. In this projected work, which may have seen the light before my study does, the various epochs of Claude Mauriac's life will be presented as though they had all occurred simultaneously.

All Women Are Fatal did not appear in English until 1964, after translations of the second and third parts of the tetralogy, *Le Dîner en ville* (*The Dinner Party*) and *La Marquise*, had already been published. This first novel is divided into four parts:

I. The Beach at Rio, or the Uncertainties of Desire
   [afternoon, Rio de Janeiro, Bertrand 33]
II. An Evening in Society, or The Seriousness of Seduction
   [evening, Paris, Bertrand 38]
III. A Stroll in New York, or the Truths of Love
   [evening, New York, Bertrand 41]
IV. A Night of Love, or the Solitude of Pleasure
   [night, Paris, Bertrand 25]

The opening paragraph of Part I locates us firmly within the Joycean stream of consciousness of a single character— Bertrand Carnéjoux, as we eventually discover—which we will not leave for the remainder of the book:

> Two black holes instead of eyes, Mathilde is lying near me. With her heavy breasts, her slender waist, her long legs and above all her golden, downy, flawless skin, she'd be one of the loveliest girls I know if she weren't so expressionless. She keeps quiet. I've always liked quiet women. The sand is soft under my almost naked body. It yields under my belly and at the same time resists, embracing me in a supple matrix. Electric elasticity. Warmth. A thought, a hint of movement would be enough to make this pleasure explicit. (p. 11)

A man, then, is lying on Copacabana Beach, near the woman of the moment. He has known many other women, though the translator has inexplicably turned "girls I have known" into "girls I know." But of course he has known other beaches as well as other women, other women on other beaches. In the second paragraph, memory is at work, and we are reminded, as so often in this novel, of Proust:

> Le Piquey, so long ago. Behind the palings of the oyster beds, that sprinkling of white sails toward Arcachon. A speedboat buzzing across the Basin. Eyes half-closed, I spy on my red-headed friend Pascale Bressac, who is chastely getting dressed after swimming with me. (p. 11)

Thus the beach at Rio becomes peopled with many of the women he has desired—he will not admit to being capable of love—most of whom have been his mistresses. We learn of Francine, who has become a famous film actress in her thirties under the name France Éline; of the beautiful Christiane, taken from him by an older man, Jean-Jacques Limher; of a mysterious Edwige, now "out of reach, for good, apparently"; and of many others. Above all, we hear constantly of Marie-Prune, whom he has never possessed, whom he might have married, who has married his Cousin Thomas instead.

A few incidents punctuate his reverie. He calls Mathilde "my little insignificance," a phrase he used to employ lovingly with a girl named Sylvienne, but Mathilde, misunderstanding, goes off to their hotel in a huff. He meets a former mistress, English-speaking Cecily Peagson, who has grown old and ugly, along with her husband and some friends. As he lies alone or walks alone on the beach, his desire is aroused momentarily by woman after woman; he feels that two people can know each other more intimately in a single glance exchanged than through sexual intercourse. Finally, he literally bumps into a Brazilian girl, Amelhina, in the surf and recognizes her as the girl he noticed earlier for her resemblance to Marie-Prune; Part I ends with the prospect that Bertrand and Amelhina will become lovers.

Two themes important for the tetralogy are established in this opening section. One is the idea of Bertrand as a potential novelist who plans some day to write an *essai romanesque*, an essay in the form of a novel, tentatively and pretentiously

entitled *Phenomenology of Physical Love*. No doubt this corresponds to *All Women*. Bertrand is at present a journalist, in
Rio to report on the Carnival for his magazine, *Ring*.

The desire to become a creative writer might seem to imply
a conviction of one's own uniqueness, but Carnéjoux thinks of
"a work in which I would write not what I am the only person
capable of expressing, but what I need to say" (p. 13). This
concept prepares the way for the second theme: "Early one
morning of my nineteenth year, it was August, I had a revelation of the nothingness of my life" (p. 25). This seems to have
occurred soon after his first experience of sexual intercourse.
All men and all women are reduced to the status of interchangeable parts by sexual desire; yet, paradoxically, when
one woman singles him out as her partner, he quickly escapes,
for the moment, "the obsession of insignificance."

The final paragraph of Part I leaves us in a confusion
characteristic of the New Novel and perhaps imitated by
Mauriac from the work of Samuel Beckett, whom he greatly
admires. (See his essay on Beckett in *The New Literature*,
1959.)

> Where's she taking me? And where am I? On the Copaca-
> bana beach, living through all this? On the Saint-Tropez
> beach, remembering it? Unless I'm at my desk, dreaming
> about the *Essay in the Form of a Novel* I must bring myself
> to write one of these days. I've always been old and I'm still
> young. My lost fiancée [Marie-Prune] with the double coun-
> tenance of melancholy and fire slowly destroys herself. No
> doubt about it: I have a toothache. (p. 67)

In the third and fourth volumes of the tetralogy Mauriac will
employ a more daring method of reminding us that we are
reading a book, not experiencing life.

Part II takes place chiefly in a Paris *salon*, during an evening
party for a hundred people, given by Irène, Bertrand's mis-
tress-in-chief of the moment. Their affair has been going on for
three years, and Bertrand complains that he suffers agonies
of jealousy because of this twice-married woman, aging and
never beautiful, who nevertheless has fascinated a great
number of lovers. One would not expect Bertrand, on the

basis of the character established in Part I, to be capable of jealousy or of being, as he suspects, in love with Irène; few readers will be convinced that he suffers, and some may even think that Mauriac has attributed this feeling to Bertrand in order to vary the emotional tone of the book.

Basically, however, this rather tedious *soirée* is another Proustian device, like the beach in Part I, by which to surround Bertrand with his past. Many of the women present are former mistresses of his—his *troupeau*, his "flock," as he calls them—or women he has desired; many of the men have been or are lovers of his former mistresses, while some are rivals for Irène's favors. We learn from his reverie that Amelhina became his mistress and that he regrets he could not bring himself to marry her. For a fleeting moment, at the beginning of the episode, he considers the possibility of marrying Martine, Irène's pubescent daughter, whom, as we shall see, he does marry eventually. During the evening he learns that Marie-Prune, now a widow as the result of an automobile accident, has returned to Paris. He meets Pascale, the girl he used to swim with but was too young and shy to seduce twenty-two years ago. She has been married a long time and seems middle-aged. She says to him, "How charming he was, the young man you were . . ." (p. 102).

If Bertrand is jealous, he certainly achieves a multiple revenge, for during the afternoon he has made love to Chantal, a woman lawyer, at a *maison de passe* where he has taken three or four other women in the past—who the fourth was, if there was a fourth, he has completely forgotten. During the evening he dances with a young girl named Béatrice and discovers that she is the daughter of Ghislaine, long dead, the woman who distracted him at the moment, just before World War II, when he was on the point of proposing marriage to Marie-Prune. Bertrand makes an appointment with Béatrice for the next day, tells Irène that he is too tired to meet her later that night, and goes out, elated by whiskey and champagne, to look for a prostitute. Naturally, he has no difficulty in finding one; in the café where he sees her, she knows he has chosen her, without a word being spoken, almost before he does. He gives

his name as René and does not even catch hers. In *The Dinner
Party* we shall meet her again as his mistress Marie-Ange;
neither she nor Bertrand realizes that they have had intercourse together previously.

As Bertrand strolls home satiated, he still feels desire for
women he passes, although he is now physically incapable
of satisfying it:

> Desire beyond desire. Last solitude of the insatiable heart in
> a sated body. I see in this another proof that physical love
> has never been anything but a pretext or a chance solution,
> the answer to a metaphysical nostalgia. (p. 153)

Claude Mauriac comes closer to his father here than anywhere else in his work. A fundamental theme with François
Mauriac is the notion that all sexual desire prefigures the
ultimate desire—for the infinite, for God.

This brief *rapprochement* with his father, however, leaves
the essential Claude Mauriac untouched. Far more characteristic is Bertrand's conviction that his triumphs with women
are his not as an individual but as an undifferentiated male—
"what I call my successes, which are those of my sex" (p. 127).
As he overhears a woman say at the party, "There are no ugly
men" (p. 103). Bertrand, in conversation with an "old" novelist,
Jean-Jacques Limher, insists on one of the fundamental doc-
trines of the New Novel—fundamental, at any rate, with
Nathalie Sarraute and Alain Robbe-Grillet:

> "All of Western literature, which you continue to represent so
> brilliantly, is based not on what unites men but on what
> distinguishes them. The unique character of each human
> being is the postulate. The literature of the future will no
> longer be that of the individual but of the collective. Do you
> want me to tell you what your famous human person is? No
> one." (pp. 109–10)[1]

Equally fundamental to Mauriac's thought is a much more
existentialist statement of the "metaphysical nostalgia" theme:

[1] In French this ends with an epigrammatic play on words: *Voulez-
vous que je vous dise ce qu'est votre fameuse personne humaine?
Personne.*

Physical love, especially at the first shock, is the sole experience of *the other* that's afforded to man with this intensity. One of the only chances of escape. The only one, in any case, which carries him beyond the limits not only of his personality, but also of his genus and of the animal kingdom. The only possible transmutation, but a dizzying one. Hence a man and a woman who have slept together only once are linked forever, beyond all social conventions, beyond even the deepest inner revolutions. (pp. 128–9, with my corrections of an inadequate translation)

Since Bertrand's last thought in Part II is of Marie-Prune, we are hardly surprised to learn, at the beginning of Part III, that he and she have become lovers at last and indeed have been living together in Paris prior to Bertrand's assignment to New York. Marie-Prune is subject to extreme changes of mood, during which she becomes completely alienated from her lover. It was during one of these periods of alienation that Bertrand had to leave her, to begin a six-month tour of duty in New York for his magazine. For the first few weeks he has been consoling himself with Leslie, a New York girl of about twenty. But she has abruptly broken off with him, and on the evening when we are with him—first in Central Park, then in Greenwich Village and nearby neighborhoods—he is in, for him, the terrifying situation of having been without a mistress for some ten days. He is very conscious of his age, forty-one, and seems to lack both the will and the power to attract another woman—at least one who attracts him. Once again, like any man in the buses and streets of New York, he finds himself surrounded by attractive women, but none of them has shared a past with him. It is a moment, if ever there was one, for searching his innermost heart. He comes gradually to an astonishing conclusion. Far from never having been in love, he has unconsciously fallen in love over and over again: with Marie-Prune, of course; with Amelhina; with Pascale; with Christiane, Edwige, Leslie, perhaps even Irène, though he now denies he was ever jealous of her; and perhaps, above all, with Francine.

Sometimes, looking at Marie-Prune asleep, he has felt a

pang that death might separate them. This is one of the
reasons why he fears love:

> . . . Marie-Prune, if I love you, I no longer avoid despair. We'll
> die, Marie-Prune, we're going to die. Not love, Marie-Prune,
> not love. Death makes love impossible. (p. 167)

This leads to the related thought, "If not knowing how to
suffer is not knowing how to love, then I don't know a thing
about love . . ." (p. 184). Eventually he arrives, however reluctantly, at the contradictory thought that "Love saves us
from death" (p. 215). He sees that for the past fifteen years
he has been undergoing a slow sentimental education. Instead
of going forward to a new love, he should go back to one of
the old ones and make it the unique love. At last he accepts
the psychology of love that has become classic in French
literature—in Madame de La Fayette, Racine, Benjamin
Constant, Proust. "The novelty, still little recognized," the *only*
novelty in Bertrand's "modern" psychology of love, "lies in
this coexistence of several loves in us" (p. 223), and he cites
a passage from the letters of Julie de Lespinasse to support
the relative antiquity of this "novelty." He goes on to speak once
more of his projected book, now to be called *Truths of Love*:

> . . . where I'll say that I love Marie-Prune, that I've loved her
> nearly twenty years and learned it only tonight. That I'll
> always love Amelhina, perhaps Pascale and probably several
> others. (p. 225)

In spite of hankerings after Edwige and Francine, with both
of whom his love affairs have often recommenced, he seems
ready to

> . . . decide that Marie-Prune's the most attractive, not only of
> all the women I've met, but even of all those I might discover
> in the future. . . .
> Why should a girl be more desirable because I don't know
> her yet or know her only a little? . . . Have I ever exhausted
> Francine's nakedness, indefinitely demagnetized and re-en-
> chanted? Marie-Prune's keeps its mystery for me. A mystery
> which is less her own than that of the eternal woman whom

I must henceforth adore and celebrate under only these forms. . . .

All women in one, for better and worse. All of love's fatality in a single fatal woman. (p. 230)

The logical structure of Bertrand's thought in this passage has carried us a long way from stream-of-consciousness technique toward the analytic moralizing, almost in essay form, of the classical French novel. Part III, however, ends by returning to a more disjointed style and more cynical reflections. The third-last paragraph reads:

Thirty-five, all the same, thirty-five . . . [Marie-Prune's age, whereas Bertrand's mistresses have rarely been over twenty-five.] I know Francine's older. But it's not a question of marrying her. Don't commit this folly with Marie-Prune. (p. 233)

We shall hardly be surprised to find in *The Dinner Party* that, although Bertrand is now, startlingly enough, married, it is to someone much younger than Marie-Prune. About literature Bertrand is more consistently serious, and Part III ends with a reference to "The book in which I'll speak with precision about the multiplications of a unique love" (p. 233).

Part IV is the only portion of the novel placed out of chronological order. In it we are on the eve of World War II; Bertrand, born in 1914 like his creator, is twenty-five years old. He and Francine are spending the night in a *maison de passe*; they achieve mutual satisfaction two or three times. Sometimes Bertrand's consciousness clings very close to the matter in hand; at other times it is engaged in abstract meditations on physical love. We are given snatches of Francine's conversation from time to time; at other times we are made aware of the storm of pleasure that rages to a climax within her. But in general Part IV lives up to its subtitle "The Solitude of Pleasure." Not only is Bertrand isolated from Francine by his own pleasure, but the pleasure that he is careful to ensure for her isolates her from him and leaves him envious: "Man is always haunted by the unknown perfection of feminine pleasure" (p. 254).

Most of Part IV repeats themes that we are already too familiar with: in particular the anonymity of sexual desire. We hear from time to time of Bertrand's vacillating intention to propose marriage to Marie-Prune, then only nineteen, and of those who stand in his way: Francine, Ghislaine, and Aunt Edwige, the young wife of Bertrand's elderly Uncle Charles.

The one really new theme in Part IV is an unexpected sexual pantheism, so to speak:

> . . . it's something of the secrets of the twilight, of living water, of country fires, of the sky that I grasp by means of love. . . . For an instant, I've been snatched up by cosmic forces. . . . We don't know what to do with a landscape. But a woman, however prodigious . . . offers herself for the taking. . . . The possession of the world is in any man's reach: all he needs is to possess a woman. (pp. 292–3)

Already, we hear much of the book that Bertrand would have liked to write if the war were not about to intervene. In a long passage on pp. 304–6 he worries about the effect of this hypothetical book on its readers. Will it "seem to be the work of a naïve fool? A collection of banalities?" He fears "it would be a book without a soul." It may give the reader "an impression of asphyxiation." Paradoxically, it may be "pedantic . . . in its inevitable didacticism," and at the same time "scandalous." If it is not "excessively abstract," it may "slip from writing to mere pornography."

Vulnerable to all these criticisms *All Women* may be, yet it represents a brave attempt to treat sex with simultaneous clinical precision and philosophic abstractness—an aim different from but no less serious than that of D. H. Lawrence in *Lady Chatterley's Lover* (mentioned on pp. 278–9 of the Mauriac novel). The critic may legitimately wonder whether, instead of postponing the most nearly pornographic section to the last, as Joyce did in *Ulysses*, Mauriac should not have begun with it, putting the present Part IV in place of Part I. If this were done, the whole emphasis of the book would of course be changed: not, one must insist, because of the obscenity of Part IV, which contains not a single obscene word or image, but because in it the book reverts to a more mechanistic phase of Bertrand's thinking: at age twenty-five he is far indeed from the humanism of the Bertrand of forty-one.

I raised this objection in a letter to M. Mauriac, and he replied (letter dated June 26, 1967):

> The place of the fourth chapter of *Femmes Fatales*, chronologically the first, was purposely assigned to it, not in a cheap attempt to be "modern," which would only result in one's being *démodé*, but because many of the riddles posed in the preceding parts find their solutions in Part IV without Bertrand Carnéjoux's knowing what they are. It is a matter, above all, of studying—or making the reader conscious of—the phenomenon of forgetfulness. For instance: later he [Bertrand] no longer knows what importance Francine has had in his life, he has forgotten even the color of her hair, thinks he has never loved a blonde (or a brunette, I've forgotten), whereas she was a brunette (or a blonde), etc. The forgetfulness is henceforward mine. It has been added to that of my hero. So much so that I would be incapable, without a fresh reading and long researches, of explaining to you all the riddles of *Femmes Fatales*, but they *all* have their solutions, especially in the last chapter, and any attentive reader can find them. [my translation]

As a matter of fact, Bertrand first knew Francine as a blonde, until she gave up bleaching her hair and became a brunette (p. 237, badly translated or proofread). The *maison de passe* of Part IV is the same one in which Bertrand made love to Chantal, yet he could not remember having been there with Francine (pp. 93-4, 142). He forgets (p. 73) whom he first called "Hummingbird" (*Colibri* in French, which lends itself to tender variations such as *Cobrili* and *Librico*), but it seems likely (p. 275) that it was Francine. Again, in Part III of *All Women*, he remembers a soiled brassière but associates it with happiness (p. 170); we discover (p. 297) that it was Francine's. Such are some of the riddles solved in Part IV.

At this point, if a critic may be permitted to drop his mask of objectivity, I should like to insist upon my private belief in the uniqueness of human personality and upon romantic

love as the response to each other of two unique personalities.
From my own limited experience, I would also suggest that a
night of satisfying love-making, such as Francine and Bertrand's, consisting as it does of a series of shared orgasms, is
the least memorable of sexual experiences. "Happy is the
nation that has no history" says the proverbial phrase; conversely, those nights that were less than perfect, that aroused
our imaginations without satiating our senses, are the ones we
most vividly remember. From this fact as much as from the
abstract language in which they are presented comes the
dullness of the erotic moments in Part IV of *All Women Are
Fatal.* A little uniqueness would have been refreshing in the
midst of this attempt to render universal experience. Let us
not make the mistake, however, of confusing Bertrand with
his creator: in practice, Claude Mauriac creates more than
one strongly individual character and presents more than one
instance of true and lasting love.

Unless the notion of individuality is in part accepted, *The
Dinner Party* becomes impossible to read. It presents the
conversation and unspoken thoughts of eight characters seated
around a dinner table. Since no "stage directions" indicate
who is speaking or thinking at any given moment, we must
identify the speaker or thinker by virtue of his or her uniqueness, at any rate within the limited frame of reference of the
eight diners.

It is the fall of 1959. Reading clockwise around the round
dining table in Bertrand's apartment on the Île St-Louis, with
its view of the Seine and Notre Dame, we have the eight
diners, beginning with the hostess:

MARTINE CARNÉJOUX, twenty-four, Irène's daughter and Bertrand's wife, also known by her pet-name of PILOU. Her
dominant trait is devotion to her children, Jean-Paul and
Rachel, aged five and three respectively. She is fond of Bertrand also, but perfectly aware of his promiscuity. She is
taciturn, reserved, unwilling to say what she means.

ROLAND SOULAIRES, forty-three, a wealthy bachelor who
makes his money from the stock market. He has suffered all his

life from psychic impotence, having been able to conquer it with only one mistress, Marie-Louise. He has read widely in French and English literature, so that English phrases often appear in his interior monologue.

MARIE-ANGE VASGNE, twenty-three, unmarried, French-Canadian, a model with ambitions to become a film star. A farm girl, she was raped at the age of fourteen in a field of red clover, and apparently had to leave home to get rid of the resulting pregnancy. She has risen in the world by exploiting her beauty and the men attracted by it—first as a prostitute, then as a beauty-contest winner, and so on to modeling and acting.

JÉRÔME AYGULF, twenty, unmarried, a law student with ambitions to become a writer. He lives with his grandparents and plans to enter the family firm. He is very conscious of being the youngest and least distinguished person present, but he also feels that the others are out of date: they know nothing of science and represent a decaying class, the bourgeoisie, to which, in spite of his Communist sympathies, Jérôme has to admit he also belongs. He has been invited as a stopgap, being a childhood friend of Martine's, or rather of her younger sister; he is in love with Martine. He has red hair and an unconscious habit of picking his nose.

EUGÉNIE (GIGI) PRIEUR, nee VALERBES, sixty-six, widowed, the mother of one married daughter, lives alone on a small inheritance. She has been a shining light of the fashionable world all her life, noted for her beauty, her culture, her wit, her love affairs, and she is still a frequent dinner guest on the strength of her past reputation rather than her present failing powers. Her two greatest love affairs have been with Jean-Jacques Limher (she became pregnant by him and had an abortion) and with Gilles Bellecroix. She is both superstitious and genuinely religious.

BERTRAND CARNÉJOUX, forty-five, who has arranged this party so that Marie-Ange can meet influential people in the film world. (Martine thinks he has arranged it in honor of the successful cosmetic operation just performed on her nose.) Bertrand, characteristically, is being triply unfaithful to Martine—with Marie-Ange, with Colette (his secretary), and with Armande, the housemaid who is helping the butler (especially hired for the occasion) to serve the dinner.

LUCIENNE OSBORN, forty-one, second wife of the successful American film producer John Osborn; he had to refuse the dinner invitation but may arrive afterwards. During her first marriage, she was Bertrand's mistress on her rare visits to Paris from Chatellerault. She is the "little provincial" of *All Women Are Fatal*, but Bertrand, after twenty years, does not recognize her until dinner is almost over. A hypochondriac, a firm believer in sun-bathing, dieting, and horoscopes, she is devoted to her basset hound, Zig, and only a little less so to her skillful young lover, Léon-Pierre. Her husband is seventy-nine, but unweariedly unfaithful to her, as she to him.

GILLES BELLECROIX, forty-nine, successful screen writer and onetime unsuccessful novelist. A reformed rake, who at twenty-two became Gigi's last great love, he married ten years ago and has been unswervingly faithful to his young, jealous wife, Bénédicte, who is absent tonight because of illness. He is the adoring father of a son, Nicolas, not quite four years old. Gilles, who is still handsome, feels strongly attracted to Martine, and she to him, ever since they danced together at Bertrand's last party.

After reading this outline of the cast—a seating plan is included in both the French and the American editions—one can easily see how the various streams of consciousness may be differentiated. (Speeches, incidentally, are introduced by quotation marks and unspoken thoughts by ellipses.) Martine rarely has a thought unconnected with her children. Roland seems unnecessarily preoccupied with his impotence, even though the disturbing Marie-Ange is sitting immediately to his left. All references to red clover—and there are far too many—identify Marie-Ange's thoughts; also, she likes to call herself "Mariette" in her reverie. Jérôme constantly thinks of his youth and inferiority or of his great friend Raymond Frôlet, an impudent, brash young man for whom he has a callow admiration. Gigi thinks just as constantly of her age; in French one can often recognize either her speech or her thoughts by the phrase *"ah! mais alors"* (translated "believe me"). Bertrand's stream of consciousness is by far the richest and most varied, since he is the spokesman for Mauriac; he is meditating on his next novel, having published his first, *Sober Pleasures,* five years earlier. (The reader will have no difficulty in recognizing, from the frequent allusions to it, that *Sober Pleasures* closely resembles *All Women Are Fatal.*) Lucienne seems more of a caricature than any of the other characters: her stream of consciousness is always immediately recognizable through some reference to horoscopes or sun-bathing or Zig or Léon-Pierre. Gilles, like Martine, can never keep his mind off his family for long: Bénédicte and Nicolas recur endlessly; sometimes, however, his keen visual aware-ness or his rapid sketch of a "treatment" reminds us that he is a screen writer.

Other characters too have favorite words or phrases, Gilles's being *quoi?* and Roland's *d'accord* (translated as "well?" and "quite, quite" in the New York edition, p. 279). We can also recognize at least two individuals by the ways in which their streams of consciousness are presented typographically: Lucienne's without any punctuation at all, and Roland's with an over-abundance of parentheses.

In other words, *The Dinner Party* is far easier to read than it appears at first sight: in fact, Mauriac has made it easy at the risk of presenting characters who border on caricatures, stereotypes, or victims of obsession. Obviously, if Mauriac had meticulously identified each speaker or thinker, the reader would have been deprived of the satisfaction of puzzling everything out for himself. The respectable sale of this book in French and English shows that readers were willing to take the trouble. In the two books which followed, where the number of characters was not restricted to eight relatively immobile dinner guests, the reading public seems to have been less willing to accept the puzzle element.

The imaginary American professor in *L'Agrandissement* offers another justification for the non-identification of characters:

"When we walk in the street, we know nothing of the passers-by but their outward appearance and whatever the sight of them, when they don't remain invisible to us, makes us feel (desire, envy, irony, discomfort, repulsion, etc.) We know nothing of their identity, any more than our own identity is present to our minds. Their age, their social class are approximately known to us. But between them (of whom we know so little) and me (of whom they know no more), subtle links are forged in the time it takes to see and pass each other. More complete anonymity than that owed to the euphoria of a meal eaten in company and which legitimizes the practice followed by Bertrand Carnéjoux in *The Barricades of Paris*, and previously in *Lunch at the Bistro*, of not naming his protagonists. No one is still present to himself, lost as each one is in his 'thoughts,' obscure mental and bodily stirrings that are mingled indissolubly." (pp. 118–19, my translation)

Comparing *The Dinner Party* with its predecessor rather than its successors, we see that Mauriac's novelistic method has not really changed, but he has discovered how to combine greater unity with greater variety. Once again Proustian memory, which makes past and present appear simultaneous, has been combined with Joycean stream of consciousness. This time, however, instead of choosing four localities (or three at any rate) in which Bertrand can be surrounded by his past, Mauriac has settled on a single one. On the other hand, we are no longer confined to Bertrand's stream of consciousness alone but can range through that of seven other people as well. We have already noted some reasons why Bertrand's stream of consciousness is the richest of those presented in *The Dinner Party*: it should be added that Mauriac assumes his reader's familiarity with *All Women*, and therefore allows himself a richer range of allusion to Bertrand's past than would otherwise be possible. A careful reader of the earlier novel might well recognize Lucienne before Bertrand does. A *very* alert reader might even grasp the fact that "René" in the following passage and Marie-Ange's current lover, Bertrand, are one and the same:

. . . my real chance, the beginning of my rise to success, was not far off. I owe it to a young man in dinner clothes who had

gone in search of flesh late in the evening and chose me, on a
night when I was feeling blue. He did not give me any advice,
unlike most of those well-meaning, salacious gentlemen. But
his elegance, his manners, suddenly made me wish I were
worthy of a lover like him. If only I could have seen Paulo's
face, the morning I disappeared! The name of that customer
who was so quiet and well-bred was René. I never saw him
again, but I remember his name . . . (p. 141, with slight
corrections)

On page 148 we find that Bertrand remembers that night
too, but not the girl. If the reader is not in fact more alert
than Bertrand and Marie-Ange, he will have to read all the
way to pp. 27-8 of *L'Agrandissement* before becoming aware
of Mauriac's subtlety. As Proust has shown once for all,
novels about remembering are also novels about forgetting.
However, if something has been completely forgotten by his
characters, and if his readers do not catch his hints, an author
may feel compelled to step forward in his own person to
point out what has been forgotten; in effect, this is what
Mauriac does in the passage of *L'Agrandissement* just referred
to. Mauriac's latest novel, *L'Oubli* ("Forgetfulness"), is about
forgetting, but we shall see that, conversely, it is also about
remembering.

It may have occurred to some who have read thus far that
Gilles Bellecroix bears a close resemblance to what Bertrand
almost becomes in Part III of *All Women*. For instance, Gilles
says to himself, "Love is a refuge from other loves. A woman
is a refuge from women" (p. 301). Similarly, in the earlier
book, Bertrand had said, "To love a single creature will release me from loving them all by revealing true love to me"
(*All Women*, p. 231). No character named Gilles Bellecroix
appears in the earlier book, although there is a film director,
René Duclost, of about the same age and equally successful
with women. One wonders, too, whether Martine's personality
is not rather closely modeled on Marie-Prune's. Marie-Prune
is mentioned occasionally in *The Dinner Party*, but we learn
nothing more of her than that she has remained beautiful and
young-looking, none the worse for her break-up with Ber-

trand.[2] Perhaps Mauriac once intended to portray Bertrand's conversion to monogamy as the husband of Marie-Prune, but eventually changed his mind.

Be that as it may, what actually does take place in this novel during the three hours between the seating of the guests at table and their rising from it? In terms of overt action, very little. Much food is consumed and much champagne drunk; Bertrand impulsively gives his cuff-links to Jérôme and sends for another pair; some family photographs are looked at; a quotation from Proust is verified by a look at the text; Gigi cursorily reads a few palms. There is much showy talk of history, genealogy, and literature.

What, then, of "inner" action? What psychological changes occur in the eight diners? Again, very few. Most of the characters, after experiencing a flash of sexual desire, return to their *status quo*. When the guests stand up, Martine slips away to kiss her children and Gilles to telephone his wife and tell her he loves her: so much for their moment of mutual attraction. Bertrand, having realized who Lucienne is, feels drawn to her for a moment but then loses interest. Lucienne, panicked by talk of cancer during dinner, rushes off to look at herself in the bathroom mirror. Roland, attracted by Marie-Ange, realizes that he is happier alone with a provocative photograph of her as a cover girl than in company with the woman of flesh and blood. Marie-Ange, for her part, longs to make love with Jérôme, whose red hair reminds her of the man who raped her. Gigi, who has inwardly yearned toward each of the men at table in turn—even impotent Roland, for whose problem she feels she has a cure—wearily heads homeward, wishing she were sixty again. As for Jérôme, the youngest, he seems to have changed more than anybody except Marie-Ange, who for once has forgotten to be mercenary. He has gathered sufficient courage, largely due to the champagne, to speak at length about Tibet and the method of choosing a new Dalai Lama, and in general to take part in the dinner-table conversation. He feels greatly drawn to Bertrand after the cuff-

---

[2] Merloyd Lawrence, translator of *The Dinner Party*, renders her name as "Marie-Plum." Why not "Marie-Angel" for Marie-Ange, then?

links episode, and his feeling has momentary homosexual overtones. He becomes conscious of a possible homosexual feeling for Raymond Frôlet also. There is a comic moment when Marie-Ange deliberately rubs her knee against his and he thinks the contact was due to his clumsiness:

> . . . Good God! My knee just bumped into Marie-Ange's. I hope she didn't think I did it on purpose. Try to keep still. The plain, wholesome taste of bread. And what if she thinks that I think she nudged me? That would be even more embarrassing . . . (p. 278)

Jérôme yearns for his lost religious belief, and has been deeply impressed by Gigi's unshakable faith, especially as he has despised her until this revelation. His last recorded thoughts in the novel (p. 320) are ". . . In the name of the Father, the Son, and the Holy Ghost. As simple as cool water and wine . . ." (It is interesting to find that in *L'Agrandissement* Jérôme has become a talented film director.)

But throwing the emphasis so much on the presence or absence of narrative elements is foolish. Mauriac's musical culture seems to exist only on a popular level—a jam session at the Central Plaza in New York, Brazilian sambas, the popular hit *Toutes les femmes sont fatales*, which appears in *The Dinner Party* and *La Marquise* as well as in the book named for it. Nevertheless, it is not hard to find musical analogies for the structure of his books, especially since he travels in the footsteps of two writers so conscious of music as were Joyce and Proust. The four parts of *All Women* may be seen as "movements" that differ sharply in their tempos. *The Dinner Party* as a whole may be described as an octet; by far the most interesting passages are those in which a common theme is orchestrated for all eight different instruments at once. Among these themes are cancer, God, and palmistry, but mention of the date 1925 leads to the richest orchestration of all. The date, with its evocation of the "twenties," inspires every character, whether born before or after it, to meditate on time, age, and death (pp. 90–9). As Bertrand says to himself (p. 98), ". . . Everyone is playing his solo in a score that has no

unity other than its theme. . . ." He is referring only to the
words spoken aloud by the diners, but the full orchestration
includes their unspoken words also. At other moments, *all*
the diners fall silent, but their thoughts center on, for example,
Naples, which has just been mentioned.

Bertrand meditates a good deal on the next book he plans to
write, which, as usual, is the one we're reading: ". . . The
thoughts which go on behind conversations, yes, it would be
interesting to try to do something with them in my next
book . . ." (p. 205). In another passage, he suggests that such
a book would be self-defeating:

> . . . Our thoughts, or at least what we like to call by that
> name, are essentially alike. So similar that it would probably
> be hard to identify them if they were quoted anonymously.
> How can we be distinguished one from another if we are all
> the same? Interchangeable organisms whose presence is
> attested to only by brief signals, fleeting epiphenomena,
> flickering sparks of memory, emotion and fear. Why should
> our identities be differentiated, if we are all alike? . . . (p. 208)

The Dinner Party itself, as already suggested, serves to refute
this view, for the thoughts of the various characters are *not*
so very similar.

In conclusion, let us note the relevance of the concepts
"interior dialogue" and "immobilization of time" to *The
Dinner Party*. A passage on page 84 of *L'Agrandissement* explicitly draws attention to pp. 99–100 of *The Dinner Party*, on
which Gilles and Gigi exchange reminiscences of their long-
dead love affair without a word spoken aloud. This is the
classic example of interior dialogue in the tetralogy. There
are other, briefer exchanges between Gilles and Marie-Ange
(pp. 66–7) and between him and Martine (p. 282). Again,
Gilles and Bertrand think almost simultaneously of the night
Gilles danced with Martine (pp. 258–9). One wonders whether
Mauriac was aware of having included Gilles in *all* these tele-
pathic exchanges.

As for the immobilization of time, the first passage in the
tetralogy to refer to it (precisely the one reproduced in capitals
on pp. 100–1 of *L'Agrandissement*), will be found on page 67

of the French text: *"L'immobilisation du temps, mon cher, ni plus ni moins: l'immobilisation du temps."* Bertrand and Gilles are discussing what Bertrand calls "the magic in still photography," which he finds "superior to that of moving pictures," when Gilles makes this crucial remark. Unfortunately, the New York edition renders it as "The crystallization of time, old man, the crystallization of time. Nothing more, nothing less" (p. 74).

The whole of *The Dinner Party* in a sense immobilizes time. One character (Bertrand?), thinks, ". . . While dinner lasts, we are outside of time, saved from this plunge towards death or at least under the illusion that we are saved, which comes to the same thing" (p. 190). Bertrand and Gigi think more than once of all the other dinners eaten in this room through the centuries, including several parties that Gigi attended before the Carnéjouxs lived there. Furthermore, we are conscious, in observing the streams of consciousness of most of the characters, that time has stood still within them. Critical moments of their childhood or youth remain intact there, and they feel far younger than they look. Gigi is still twenty at heart. The reduction of the time represented in the novel to about three hours, or less than the time required to read it, may be described as at least a *near*-immobilization of time.

The time span of Mauriac's next novel, *The Marquise Went Out at Five*, is still further reduced—to a single hour, between five and six o'clock on a warm, thundery summer evening. Space is also restricted, but not to the narrow limits of a dining table. Unity of place is provided, instead, by the Carrefour de Buci, between the Seine and the Boulevard Saint-Germain, where five streets of old Paris intersect.

Throughout the hour, Bertrand is at his window overlooking the intersection. He has separated from Martine and left his fine apartment on the Quai d'Orléans to live in two miserable rooms on a second floor of the Rue de l'Ancienne-Comédie. He has also given up his post as editor-in-chief of *Ring* and is taking notes for his next novel, of which he knows only that it will be called *The Marquise Went Out at Five*. The epigraph to Mauriac's book, a quotation from André Breton's *First Surrealist Manifesto*, explains the title:

> *Monsieur Paul Valéry recently suggested anthologizing as many first sentences of novels as possible, from whose imbecility he expected a great deal. The most famous authors would be laid under contribution. Such a notion still honors Paul Valéry who not long since, apropos of novels, assured me that as far as he was concerned, he would never permit himself to write:* The Marquise went out at five.

As the hour begins, Bertrand still plans to have a genuine marquise in his book, but about halfway through he changes his mind:

> . . . Rose, the little salesgirl in the vegetable stall next door. Rose. Have I already had a girl with that name? Not exactly an imbecile, but a little peculiar. I'd like to put her in my book, but then I'll have to change the subject, the Marquise can't know her. This Carrefour, my Carrefour, now there's a beautiful subject, and what do I care about the Marquise anyway, I'll give up the Marquise, but I'll put Rose, along with my other neighbors, into my novel . . . (p. 156)

From this point on, his mental picture of his novel resembles quite closely the book we are reading, though it begins ". . . The Marquise went out at five." The "Marquise," however, turns out to be the elderly homosexual Zerbanian, of whom we have caught fleeting glimpses in the two previous novels, out "cruising" the neighborhood in search of a likely young man. Zerbanian speaks of himself in the third person as "the Marquise."

The technique of Mauriac's third novel seems at first glance identical with that of his second. Once again we have the mixture of dialogue and stream of consciousness, the two being distinguished by the same punctuation devices as before. This time, however, the method is applied to over seventy speaking and/or thinking characters, major and minor, in contemporary Paris; and we catch glimpses of many more "silent" ones. The problem of identifying a particular interior monologue is too often solved by having the character address himself or herself by name.

Contemporary Paris only receives about half our attention as readers; the Carrefour has been inhabited since at least the twelfth century, and nearly half the "novel" is devoted to a montage of documents dealing with the past history of the intersection.[3] Bertrand reflects: ". . . It would be good if in my next book I included a character fanatically interested in old Paris, about which he would know everything" (p. 49). But in fact we have already met this character, Claude Desprez, an autograph collector and dealer, on the first page of Mauriac's novel. At five o'clock he is standing on his balcony, from which he can see Bertrand at his window; they share the same cleaning woman, although they have not met. All the documents that Bertrand could possibly wish for are cited more or less verbatim as part of Desprez's stream of consciousness. Sometimes he may be thought to be reading the document cited, but when he goes down into the streets for a stroll and to buy some more tobacco (he is a chain-smoker who rolls his own cigarettes), he must be quoting from memory. At this point, the device seems a transparent and desperate one, but before the book ends we shall meet with a convincing explanation of the accuracy of the quotations.

La Marquise, Bertrand insists, will not resemble "in any way that abomination of abominations: the historical novel" (pp. 201–2). None of the history is novelized, except insofar as Desprez comments on it during his ruminations. What we have instead are "raw" documents, scattered through a novel of contemporary Paris. Sometimes the documents will have an immediate relevance, as when Desprez sees people going into and out of a shoe store and remembers the names of five shoemakers listed as living in the neighborhood in 1292 (pp. 214–15). The bulk of the documents, however, are "fed" into the book in chronological order, from 1180 to 1960. The fact that Mauriac gives them in their original syntax and orthography—usually either archaic or illiterate—presents problems

---

[3] The source of this novel is an unpublished MS, entitled *Les Barricades de Paris*, in which M. Mauriac combined his journal of the liberation of Paris (partly experienced at the Carrefour de Buci) with a similar montage of documents.

that Richard Howard, the translator, has coped with gallantly.
"Diplomatic" texts of this kind certainly offer a flavor of
authenticity, but one wonders whether such scholarly meticu-
lousness is really appropriate in a novel. On the other hand,
much of the documentation comes from police records; its
brutality or obscenity is made more palatable by preserving
the illiteracies of the spies and police officers who compiled it.

The preoccupation of Mauriac's characters with sexuality
has diminished but by no means disappeared in this novel.
Besides the promiscuous Zerbanian, we encounter a nameless
voyeur, almost a dwarf, who is obsessed by the breasts of the
women who pass by, as well as by the brassières in lingerie
shops; similar obsessions haunt the thoughts of a devout young
soap salesman who has received communion that morning and
is trying to keep his thoughts pure; Raoul Lieuvain, a sixteen-
year-old secondary-school student, is disturbed by the pornographic films he has just watched in an amusement arcade.
Patrice Reslaut, on the other hand, feels a pure love for his
classmate Valérie; unfortunately for him, she prefers the impure Raoul. Two pairs of lovers slip into hotels during the
hour; we follow fairly closely the perverse pleasure of one
pair: after they have made love together, the woman almost
forces the man to make love to a hotel employee in the next
room while she lies in bed pleasurably imagining and partly
overhearing what goes on next door.

The girl-watchers of the neighborhood have some interesting material on which to feast their eyes: notably, a
young girl in slacks who is running gracefully through the
crowds toward the subway; another girl, in a dress of imita-
tion leopard skin, walks, reading a magazine, in a stately way
through the passers-by, preceded by a bust of monumental
proportions. A husband with a shrewish wife watches from
his window and idealizes a harried secretary who would like
to attract her boss but fails, although she finds some other men
appreciative as she goes on an errand through the streets.

In general, the sexual relationships of the young and middle-
aged are treated with cynicism. A barman named Fred tries
to console a colleague named Riri who is brokenhearted be-

cause his girl left him; Fred thinks it is ridiculous to get upset over such an ordinary girl. A middle-aged woman named Jeanne bores two women friends with her unrequited passion for Desprez, who thinks of her as a nuisance when he thinks of her at all. The girl in the leopard-skin dress is too interested in a threatened divorce between two movie stars to keep an appointment with her lover. Rose, the somewhat deranged girl who sells vegetables, appears to be the mistress of both Bertrand and a gangster named Filledieux, who is in hiding nearby. A fellow crook waits throughout the hour for Filledieux, who has mistaken the day of their appointment. Three detectives, who have been informed of the planned meeting, wait for their quarry in vain.

One of these unhappy little affairs involves a violation of the unity of place. Gilbert and Simone, an unmarried couple who live together, have not been able to arrange simultaneous vacations. At Gilbert's insistence, Simone has gone on vacation alone. As he thinks of her between five and six, she is thinking of him on a beach far away—but this does not keep her from being unfaithful to him with a handsome young swimmer whom she has just met. There is one other violation of the unity of place: in some tropical country, a Frenchman is reminiscing about the Paris of his youth, but he can't for the life of him remember the name of the Carrefour de Buci.

Bertrand's wife, Martine, and his daughter, Rachel, now four, have just left him at five o'clock. Martine is still in love with her husband and glad of opportunities to bring the children to visit him. At least Bertrand no longer commits infidelities with women of her own circle, and he enjoys discussing his book, especially the matter of "interior dialogue," with her.

It is among the old people, however, that we find the most sympathetic portraits in this novel. A poetess—left over from the generation of Paul Éluard, Robert Desnos, and Jules Supervielle—who suddenly realizes that she has grown old, is presented rather cruelly, but three humbler old ladies win our sympathy. One, unnamed, who has just bought some nasturtiums at the flower market and insists on carrying them herself, is the recipient of boundless devotion from her grand-

son Max. Another, Mme Ginette, whose daughter has run
away from her husband, finds compensation in the tender
mutual care she and her deserted son-in-law, Cricri, lavish on
each other. She feels that her death is near and that no one
will remember her first love or her husband, both killed in
World War I, when she is dead. Mme Claire, proprietress of
the Hôtel du Valois, which is temporarily sheltering the perverse lovers, actually dies during the hour. She has almost forgotten Raymond, her much younger, unfaithful husband, and
thinks only of her dear cousin Laurent, more than sixty years
dead.

Most touching of all these old people is Roland Loubert,
who relates to a visitor the gentle death experienced two
months earlier by his wife Mathilde, his companion for fifty-
five years. He misses her terribly, yet it comforts him to think
that he was with her to the end and that she experienced no
death agony. Largely, no doubt, as a result of meditating on
this narrative, which he has based on an actual experience,
Bertrand undergoes a revelation. He regards it as "a revelation
of the same order" as the one that made him see his own
insignificance in *All Women*: "The acceptance of death, that's
it, its tranquil welcoming, where and when it will be time" (p.
304). Loubert has already told of his wife's acceptance:

> "She said: 'Well, now, Lord, am I going to meet you at last?
> The moment has already come to leave my dear husband . . .
> I accept it, Lord, I accept it, if I must. So now I shall be
> with you, My Lord.' " (p. 246)

Loubert's narrative seems to dominate the closing pages of the
book until, on pp. 286–302 of the New York edition, we find a
long passage of stream of consciousness clearly located in
Bertrand's mind. In it we find snatches from the speech and
thoughts of a great many of the characters in the novel; some
of these are reprises, some new material. We become aware
that Bertrand has been inventing rather than experiencing
much of what we have read so far. On page 301 he leaves a
blank space in which to record some fact which he has to
look up ". . . and which, in fact, by negligence or ignorance

I've omitted." For a few pages (302–7), the book returns to
its previous pretense of objectivity, but then Bertrand breaks
in again to explain that Roland and Mathilde Loubert are
"really" based on his cousins Gilbert and Agnès Louvet.

Whereupon (p. 309) Mauriac breaks in, in his own person:

> . . . Thus Bertrand Carnéjoux records in his novel, and I
> record in the novel in which I have given life and speech to
> Bertrand Carnéjoux, that impossibility of conceiving what
> seems so natural in others, what one has spent one's life
> fearing, knowing oneself ineluctably threatened by it in the
> beings one loves and in oneself: death. Out of his cousin
> Agnès, he has made the Mathilde of his book, and I myself
> know that this dying woman's real name was no more Agnès
> than it was Mathilde. A triple character, this Bertrand Car-
> néjoux, since he's supposed to write the books in which he
> himself plays a hero's part. A novelist animated by a novelist
> whom I (myself a novelist) have put into a novel in which,
> however, nothing was invented, a labyrinth of mirrors cap-
> turing some of life's sensations, feelings and thoughts . . .
> (pp. 309–10)

Mauriac continues this unexpected intervention by assuring
us that all the "documents" have been searched out and recorded "mechanically" by himself. He apologizes for the
"tinge of lechery and blood" that clings to "all or almost all"
the facts that have come to him, he insists, by chance and
without selection, conscious or unconscious. His autograph
dealer, Desprez, frequently comments on the sordidness of the
records available to him and regrets that, in a period when
French soldiers and police were torturing Algerian nationalists,
civilization seems to have made little if any progress. An unnamed psychotic, whose stream of consciousness we readers
enter a few times, believes that he is threatened by mysterious
invisible waves which are in some way the result of the
sufferings of children in the Warsaw Ghetto, in the extermination camps, and in France itself under the Pétain regime of
collaboration and the Nazi occupation.

The Carrefour itself, Mauriac tells us, was "chosen at
random, merely because my memories of the Liberation of

Paris had made it dear to me after having revealed it to me in the first place. . . ." He goes on to assure us that "Man has his states of grace which escape any chronicle. There have been perhaps saints, there have surely been saintly women and noble men in my neighborhood."

In effect, Mauriac is concluding his novel with the sort of apologia 'that in the nineteenth century would have appeared in a preface. The final paragraph begins with a summary of the three novels so far published and ends with what seems at first to be an unfortunate confusion between fact and fiction but is in actuality a humorous reference to the last sentence, for we already know that the Marquise did *not* go out at five:

> . . . Thus the story of Bertrand Carnéjoux, which in its first version concerned a single character and his selfish preoccupations, has rejoined, thanks to the eight guests of its sequel, more general truths, widening and deepening in this third part where a whole nation was raised up and perhaps resuscitated. The sound stilled, the fury faded, there remains—freedom. Thus the novel has in its penultimate pages gradually faded away, and disappeared, without masks or make-believe, giving way to the novelist who, if he has put himself directly into his book, has at the end purified it of its last traces of fiction by granting it a truth in which literal exactitude was preferred to literature. The Marquise did not go out at five . . .

Fortunately, the commentary on the three preceding novels which occupies the greater part of *L'Agrandissement* is pitched in a less rhetorical key than this rather magniloquent conclusion to what is undoubtedly its author's masterpiece.

Before passing on to the final volume of the tetralogy, let us assess the relative proportions of interior dialogue and immobilization of time in *The Marquise*. In regard to interior dialogue we find an interesting theoretical statement, not in Bertrand's stream of consciousness, but in Martine's:

> . . . Those child's stares that you catch fixed on you, how marvelous. A wordless but intense conversation, thanks to which an immediate and total communication is effected. Perfect interchange. Bertrand told me once that he'd like to write a whole book about a dialogue like that, between a little

girl and her daddy. He said: her daddy. But with me, her mommy, it would be even better. He said only his friend Nathalie Sarraute could express such tacit exchanges, so mysterious, although everyone has experienced them. He said almost no one understood Nathalie Sarraute because the inexpressible secrets she was trying to grasp at their living source in the depths of being were too new. He said I was one of the few people he knew who already had some understanding of these things. What a recompense it is when he talks to me like that . . . (pp. 61–2)

Mauriac has shown great cunning in making his statement of theory do double duty as an emotional link between Bertrand and Martine, but, in fact, interior dialogue is no more frequent in *The Marquise Went Out at Five* than in *The Dinner Party*. It is interesting to find Mauriac himself hinting at the similarity between interior dialogue and Mme Sarraute's sub-conversation.

Besides Rachel's unspoken communication with Martine, there are really only three instances of interior dialogue: Bertrand and an out-of-work Negro in the street below exchange sympathy in a glance, but Bertrand does not grasp the man's predicament and offer him help in getting a job (p. 15); Max answers mentally an unspoken question, "What will he do when he gets older?" put by his grandmother (p. 67); the two women friends, Jeanne and Henriette, are able to communicate silently, even though Jeanne now rather bores Henriette: ". . . Loving the same man [Bernard Freissane, not Claude Desprez] brought us closer together, until we don't even need to talk in order to communicate with each other . . ." (p. 135). We might add a generalized reference to Roland and Mathilde Loubert as "understanding each other without having to speak a word . . ." (p. 308).

On the other hand, even if *The Marquise* contained no explicit references to the immobilization of time—in fact, there are several—the entire book must be recognized as an attempt to achieve precisely this. Almost eight centuries of local history are focused upon this single hour through the device of interpolating documents. As Mauriac says himself in his concluding intervention:

> . . . I have imagined, written, completed my book without any preconceived idea save that of this theme: *the reality of time* both aggravated and *denied* by this crowd which from day to day, year to year, century to century, has unceasingly crossed the same Carrefour of my city. (p. 310, italics mine)

Much earlier in the novel, Desprez, watching from his balcony, expresses the same idea even more forcibly:

> . . . All it takes is for me to be watching . . . from this balcony for *them* to rise up out of the vacuum, *all duration canceled, time no longer passing, no longer existing, only this prodigious simultaneity*, offering to God's gaze the entire universe, and to mine this little part of the world. (pp. 70–1, my italics except for *them*)

Proust brought into a simultaneous relationship the past and the present of his narrator, Marcel; but Claude Mauriac has attempted, within the compass of a far shorter work than *À la recherche du temps perdu*, to impose simultaneity on eight centuries of Parisian history. The wonder is not that he has failed but that he has so nearly succeeded. As Desprez says to himself: ". . . O madness, my Carrefour is too big for me. I hoped that in a space so defined and restricted, I could exhaust reality, but I'm not able to." He feels that his mind is giving way under its self-imposed task, as the narrator of Michel Butor's *Degrés* (*Degrees*), published in French just a year before *La Marquise*, died under the strain of his. Butor's Pierre Vernier tried to trace all the antecedents of a single classroom hour in a *lycée*, including a goodly portion of the history of European culture. Probably Mauriac's book owes something to Butor's, but it seems to me more successful, perhaps because it is less of a novel than Butor's. In fact, in Bertrand's words, it is ". . . not so much a novel as a symphony, a poem, a film . . ." (p. 268).

L'Agrandissement (1963) is, to my mind, Claude Mauriac's most original work by far, and at least the equal in originality of any other work by the New Novelists. In this book, which he describes on the title page as a *roman*, a novel, he has at last arrived at the new form that he had sought in his earlier books: *l'essai romanesque*. What we encounter in *L'Agrandissement* is not merely an essay *in* the form of *a* novel but an essay *on* the form of *the* novel. In the three earlier novels of the tetralogy we observe Bertrand engaged in planning the novel that we happen to be reading, but in the fourth volume those of us who have followed him step by step thus far can observe him planning a novel *that we have already read*. Mauriac, who intervenes once again in his own person at the end of *L'Agrandissement*, tells us: "This book is the story of a gentleman who is asking himself how he's going to write a novel that I have already written" (p. 197). We are back near the beginning of the hour that unrolls before our eyes in *La Marquise*, but this time we stay with Bertrand—and indeed within *his* mind only—for the space of barely two minutes. To insist on its unity, the meditation of a single mind, Mauriac has had the entire book printed as a single paragraph filling 192 pages of large print.

Bertrand is thinking not only of the novel we have already read but of the one after that, the one we are now reading. We are, of course, reading Mauriac's novels, not Bertrand's; let us look at the corresponding titles in French:

Mauriac	Carnéjoux
LE DIALOGUE INTÉRIEUR	LA COMMUNICATION
I. *Toutes les femmes*	I. *Le Plaisir grave*
II. *Le Dîner en ville*	II. *Le Déjeuner au bistrot*
III. *La Marquise*	III. *Les Barricades de Paris*
IV. *L'Agrandissement*	IV. *Le Balcon (détail)*

The point of the title of the fourth volume is probably clear by now: "The Enlargement," a term borrowed from photography, refers to time rather than to space. The two minutes from the original hour are treated at almost as great length as the hour itself was in *La Marquise*. Bertrand's title, "The Balcony (detail)," reminds us of those illustrations in books on art which enlarge greatly a significant detail from a painting.

Mauriac's ultimate aim is to halt time altogether, but Bertrand indicates the futility of this aspiration:

> To enlarge a corner of the picture, which itself, in another, future book, could become the object of the same operation, and so, from enlargement to enlargement, I would obtain the essential detail, magnified to the point where I would no longer lose any of it. But this fragment would consist of innumerable particles. The most infinitesimal fraction of time conceivable still lasts too long for me to hope to exhaust it. (p. 73)

Bertrand is also aware (p. 177) that in the French movie industry the technical term for an enlargement is *gonflement* ("blow-up"), with its overtones of blowing up a balloon, or "inflation." "With the hope of exhausting the virtualities of every second, I spread out what was concentrated" (p. 177). The resultant diffusion may be fatal to art. Note that the "story" of *L'Agrandissement*, principally consisting of the mute interchange between Bertrand at his window and the Negro in the street below, occupies only four pages (23–6) of *La Marquise*, corresponding to pp. 13–16 of the New York translation. Brief passages from those pages are scattered throughout Bertrand's meditation.

L'Agrandissement is thus a kind of reprise of Mauriac's previous novel, but it is also a sort of afterword to the entire series, *Le Dialogue intérieur*. To the best of my recollection, Mauriac had never used the precise expression *dialogue intérieur* in any of his three previous novels. Therefore, he has seen fit not only to introduce us to the concept of interior dialogue but also to point out examples of its use in the three earlier books. Furthermore, as *L'Agrandissement* progresses, we learn from Bertrand's thoughts of a variety of possible applications of this term besides the "classic" one that we noted in *The Dinner Party* between Gigi and Gilles.

Let us look at the way in which Mauriac has chosen to introduce and define this new critical term. On page 14 a mysterious voice breaks into Bertrand's reverie with a single puzzling sentence. A moment later, on page 15, the voice breaks in again with a coherent statement: "Let us take note right away that there exists a form of interior dialogue akin to the interior monologue, if indeed it does not amount to the same thing. *In her seat between two male students Miss Fowling, the redhead, looks at herself in her mirror as if she were at home.*" We eventually discover that the mystery voice belongs to an unnamed American professor who is lecturing to a class on the works of Bertrand Carnéjoux, an author whom he believes to be overrated. Miss Fowling, a student with whom he is in love, draws some of her traits from a young, pretty redhead who is making up her face at her window just across the street from Bertrand.

The professor, a product of Bertrand's imagination, is allowed to continue his lecture from time to time; he has read the two novels which Bertrand has not yet written, and is familiar with the overall plan of the tetralogy, which he knows as *La Communication*. In order to belittle Bertrand's originality, he points out (pp. 40–7) Balzac's use of a similar device in part of his novella *Le Curé de Tours* (1832). Madame de Listomère's and the Abbé Troubert's unspoken thoughts are given in parentheses right after their spoken dialogue, and we can see that some of these thoughts answer each other as precisely as spoken dialogue could. The professor's voice is eventually silenced permanently, but not before he has given us a thorough and even pedantic introduction to his subject, as well as entertaining us by his infatuation for the aloof Miss Fowling, into whose contemptuous thoughts we are also permitted a glimpse. A male student amusingly wonders why the professor doesn't shut up and make use solely of interior dialogue to communicate with his class (p. 20).

The type of interior dialogue akin to interior monologue which the professor first mentioned consists of the intimate conversations we hold with ourselves in examining the different aspects of a problem (p. 16). These occur most frequently in Bertrand's first book. Bertrand himself meditates on the silent communication between animals and men, as well as on the fact that a child loses the power to communicate silently and deeply with adults as he learns to express himself more clearly in words (p. 29). Another type of interior dialogue is that of the heroes of a novel with the novelist, "who, if he has given them life, has nevertheless much to learn from them" (p. 53). And if one can hold a dialogue with fictional characters, why not with the dead? "Thanks to old papers, we talk to the dead and they answer us. Hence the emotion that autographs have always inspired in me" (p. 69).

We have already noted in *The Dinner Party* how a common experience can provoke interlocking responses: "a sight seen in common, a noise heard in common arousing the same associations of ideas, the same convergent interior monologues become or do not become interior dialogue, according to whether the interested parties feel that they are accomplices or not . . ." (*L'Agrandissement*, p. 93).

On page 104 we have a reprise of the passage in *All Women* (p. 169) where Bertrand bumps into a young woman in a New York bus: "A long enough interval occurs, before she's regained her balance, for our bodies to get acquainted. *They speak to each other* in an ardent and decisive dialogue." As Bertrand comments in the later book, "Dialogue: the word is there. . . . The continuity of our preoccupations is consoling. . . . We know, from the first book on, where we are going and what we are looking for" (p. 104).

Some of the variations in interior dialogue which figure at a late stage in Bernard's reverie seem paradoxical: "there exists too an interior dialogue which, instead of using the minimum of words to make itself understood, manifests itself on the contrary by the maximum of sentences . . ." (p. 113). Another paradox: ". . . in extreme youth, interior dialogue is not only possible without language but is anterior to it" (p. 121); on the other hand, once one has learned to talk, it is "As if interior dialogue demanded, in default of words, the possibility of speech" (p. 120). "In order that communication between two people may be possible, contact must be made, the current must not be cut off" (p. 121). ". . . I knew with the unique Marie-Prune that permanent form of exchange which continued, it seemed, even in our sleep, during which we remained tuned to the same wave length" (p. 173).

It is hardly possible to list in full all the subtle shades that

Bertrand's meditation imparts to the concept of interior dialogue. He even comes to doubt its validity: "to ask myself if
I haven't overdone things, if I haven't even purely and simply
invented the object of my search" (p. 153). Furthermore,
"since interior dialogue unfolds itself in instantaneity, to stretch
it out enough to express it is to betray it—so much so that
what I had thought to seize in its living truth has become
congealed" (p. 153).

Insistently he recurs to the first form of interior dialogue
mentioned by the professor he has imagined: "Why not choose
this technique for my novel: dialogue, but with oneself" (p.
172). L'Agrandissement may be viewed as mainly a combination of this type of interior dialogue with the type consisting
of an author's dialogue with his characters. "Dialogue with"
is a misleading phrase, no doubt; what Bertrand actually does
is to let each of his characters speak for a while in turn. We are
sure that they are characters of his creation even though they
may be based on people he has seen in the street a moment
before. Take the Negro, for instance: after giving a few lines
of his stream of consciousness, Bertrand breaks off, saying,
"Here begins the difficulty for the novelist who tries to reproduce as exactly, as faithfully as possible, to write being to
describe or nothing. . . . But what do I know of the life of a
Parisian working man or a young man of the black race? Inevitably weak parts of my novel, if I decide to compose it" (p.
13). Documentation and invention might help, but not very
much. "I could for the most part legitimately invent an old
lady who thinks herself a poet, because I sometimes think of
myself as a poet, because I too am growing old, and because
I've heard many old ladies speak and seen the way they live.
But a working man? But a black?" (p. 14). We see here the
germ of the poetess in The Marquise—or rather, since The
Marquise already exists, we see what may or may not have
been the origin of the poetess. There are insights into the possible genesis of several other characters from the earlier novel.
Regardless of whether Mauriac made the specific changes here
suggested in the course of composing The Marquise, we are
given an interesting picture of a novelist's mind at work and

sense the malleability of his raw material at this early stage.
Patrice Reslaut and Raoul Lieuvain, the two *lycée* students
who were in love with Valérie in *The Marquise*, appear in
L'Agrandissement as secondary-school teachers in their sixties,
both on the brink of retirement yet in love with another
Valérie, a colleague aged forty. Their stream of consciousness
and "mental age" differ little from those of their youthful
counterparts. Bertrand sums up his method thus: "As I talk
to myself, it is my characters who carry on a dialogue within
me. Eventual, possible characters, to whom I am giving a trial
run, ready to discard them if it seems to me more true to life
or convenient to replace them" (pp. 183–4). As the professor
says, "fragments which the author . . . had sacrificed in his
first work could rise again from the dead . . ." (p. 180).

We learn a little more about Carnéjoux the man, as well as
a great deal about Carnéjoux the author, in this last volume.
He is much more unhappy about his separation from Martine
and the children than he had seemed in *The Marquise*, and
much more contrite about his philandering in general. He even
castigates his first book: "There's nothing that seems less
comprehensible to me today than that hymn to physical love
that was my first *essai romanesque*" (p. 108). Not only the
book but the life reflected in it, "my impoverished life as a
young male," now seem to him utterly without interest. The
whole book purported to be about love, of which the young
man he then was understood nothing, not even its most physical aspect.

> Love as Marie-Prune, and then Martine, tardily revealed it to
> me—for before them, after Valérie whom I had never
> approached except with my eyes (and how respectfully!),
> after Valérie, or rather, no, her name was Pascale, after Pascale
> and until Marie-Prune there was nothing, nobody, no woman
> really loved, truly desired, or even possessed in other than
> illusory fashion. Nothing and nobody loved, except I myself
> who am nothing and nobody. . . . (pp. 108–9)

Love such as he had known as a young man takes one's mind
off death, in contrast to "true love, such as we feel for a wife

and children who are well-beloved and mortal, a love such that it makes death more intolerable than before" (p. 109).

As already indicated, Mauriac intervenes on page 197, and the final cadenza of the book presents us with Mauriac-Carnéjoux staring, as so often throughout *L'Agrandissement*, at his own hand—which could almost have become the subject of still another novel. We also note the telephone that has been ringing throughout the two minutes, the fly that has been buzzing about in a distracting way, the traffic light that has been marking time by its changes:

> Who thinks of what and looks at what? Sees only this monu-
> mental little finger big enough to fit in the ear of a giant?
> Man or animal? Nail or claw? Nail *and* claw. Man *and* animal.
> I come back from far away. It was only the smallest of my
> fingernails. It's only me, on my balcony, on a summer evening.
> Nail, balcony, evening, summer: nothing but what is certain
> and reassuring. Words in which I can have confidence. Yellow
> light. Red light soon. The telephone stops ringing. The fly
> comes to rest on an ivy leaf. Simple, incontestable words for
> things that are true and undeniable . . . (p. 200; ellipsis
> Mauriac's)

L'Oubli ("Forgetfulness," 1966, not yet translated), Mauriac's fifth and last novel to date, stands apart from the tetralogy. Like each of the other four novels, it is a tour de force, but it leaves me with the uneasy feeling that it is not much more than that. Perhaps the strong element of parody in the book prevents me from giving full recognition to the profound insights into the workings of memory and forgetfulness that the work also contains.[4]

L'Oubli parodies for us two very different forms of literature: on the one hand, the *ciné-roman* or film novel of Alain Robbe-Grillet, and especially the world-famous *Last Year at Marienbad*; on the other hand, to some extent, the classic crime stories of Maurice Leblanc (1864–1941) about Arsène

---

[4] In a letter to me dated January 6, 1969, M. Mauriac wrote: "*L'Oubli* is for me a serious book, the most serious [*grave*] of all; I should like to give it a sequel. . . . The final pirouette was a way of escaping. . . ."

Lupin, the gentleman burglar who eventually turns detective.

Nicolas, the hero of *L'Oubli*, is, once again, a novelist, but he also writes stage plays. His *Les Oiseaux* ("The Birds") may resemble Claude Mauriac's first play *La Conversation* ("The Conversation," 1964; not yet translated), and he and Mauriac have both written a play entitled *Ici, maintenant* ("Here, Now"; not yet translated). During the action of *L'Oubli*, which takes place during the night of August 4 to 5, 1966, his latest novel, unnamed, is spoken of as unfinished. As usual, it very much resembles the book we are reading:

"And your novel? The novel you've begun, what's it about?"

"It doesn't much matter what it's about. One always tells the same story. The interesting part is the way in which it's told. What I'm trying to do is, how shall I put it . . . A sort of intellectual crime novel, without cops or robbers—or just enough of them to keep the reader's interest. The reader is so to speak the detective, if you see what I mean."

"Not very well . . ."

"How can I explain it to you . . . I don't like, in some present-day novels, the indeterminacy deliberately contrived by the author, who accepts in advance all possible interpretations. Who profits undeservedly from all possible analyses. From all possible investigations. I shan't provide, any more than they do, the answers to the riddles, to the series of riddles which will make up my novel, but I'll proceed in such a way that there will be a single explanation for each mysterious point, one that any halfway intelligent and attentive reader can arrive at for himself if he reads me carefully and pays attention to the hints I give. Every allusion, every image, every question the reader will meet with should be or at any rate can be elucidated, understood, answered. Nothing that can't be justified, explained. Not a line. The variety of levels, of close-ups and long shots—for it's as much a film as a novel— their variety, the element of mystery, sometimes even the element of crime thriller, in the plot ought, if I don't slip up, to balance the more subtle parts. In any case, I'd like people not to take me too seriously . . ." (pp. 38–9, my translation)

Nicolas is conscious of being shadowed as he goes to a cocktail party at the home in Passy of Simone Brouges, whom we have heard of but not seen in the tetralogy. Everybody of importance is supposed to leave Paris in August, but the party is very well attended. During it, Nicolas has two experiences, perhaps even three, that set his memory working. The most startling of these involves his being approached by a beautiful woman, apparently much younger than he, who insists that they have known each other intimately in the past (as the second man insists to the woman in *Last Year at Marienbad*); she and he leave the party to have dinner together at a restaurant which he has often visited in the past. The second experience is seeing a yellow rose pinned to the corsage of a woman who is "almost old"; he does not recognize her, but suddenly he sees the rose stuck into the neck of a sweater instead of pinned to a pink blouse (pp. 16, 19). The third and most trivial "experience"—the first in point of time—is his noticing and regretting that the pretty housemaid isn't wearing a lace cap (p. 12).

Nicolas—who is separated from his wife, Marthe, and their son, David, now on the brink of puberty—has been very conscious of his age lately and is deeply flattered by the advances made to him by this beautiful unknown woman. At dinner and as they dance in the restaurant, he tries to identify her with each of the women whom he remembers as his mistresses. None of the faces or bodies fits, but suddenly the pet name "Manou" comes to him and he calls her that mentally, though not aloud, for the rest of the book. Almost simultaneously she mentions "our little hotel at Senlis" (p. 45).

After dinner, they make an appointment to meet at Nicolas's apartment about one in the morning. Nicolas insists on walking home alone through the rainy streets, though Manou offers to drive him. The neighborhood is the one Nicolas grew up in after his father bought a pharmacy in Paris, but his earliest memories are of the small town of Senlis and the big château and park of the Duval family nearby.

The walk home naturally arouses many memories. Once home, Nicolas reads the newspapers, with their stories of the Vietnam war and other current events. He telephones Simone Brouges to ask who the young woman is, but Simone cannot identify her and promises to call back after asking her husband. While Nicolas awaits Simone's call and the arrival of Manou, he sleeps fitfully and dreams about his past. Part of his dream is a session of psychoanalysis during which a doctor, resembling the photograph of Jung that hangs on his wall, questions him. When Simone returns his telephone call, it is to say that the mysterious young woman was a gate-crasher.

Whether Nicolas dreams or wakes, the free association of ideas brings back to him everything that he wants to know. Unfortunately, he does not succeed in retaining all of the dream after he wakes up or in making all the connections between what he remembers and what has happened to him earlier in the night. We readers, however, have been privileged to inhabit his mind, both waking and sleeping, and can remember and make connections if we wish. Furthermore, we can penetrate Manou's mind—something impossible for Nicolas. On pp. 214-20 her thoughts are given on the right half of the page, parallel with Nicolas's on the left. We thus discover that, so far as she knows, she has never met Nicolas before; she is a sort of female Arsène Lupin:

> . . . I'm a thief and a liar, never, never had I seen him before this evening, I invented everything to gain his confidence, everything . . . (p. 220)

When she sees that he is sound asleep after their love-making —which has given her unexpected pleasure, although he is neither young nor handsome—she steals what she has come for.

We follow her from the apartment to where she meets two male accomplices, and then we discover something we may have suspected for a long time. Her name really *is* Manou, for she is none other than Emmanuèle Duval, only five years younger than Nicolas; he used to sneak into her parents' park in Senlis and tell her the plots of the Arsène Lupin stories, which she was then too young to read but whose titles she learned by heart (pp. 222-3). In his dream of reverie, Nicolas remembered the only day on which she ever spoke to him, reciting to him all the titles while an oriole sang. (The song of the oriole is one of the most frequently recurring leitmotivs in the novel.) In return he whispered into her ear a magic phrase that he has never been able to remember (pp. 141–3). Manou remembers the phrase, although she does not connect it with Nicolas. What was it? The reader is confronted with an ambiguity, but it would seem that the phrase is "Nijni-Novgorod," the name of the Russian city, which has been recurring throughout the book (p. 223). In sum, then, she has told the truth while believing she was lying: she and Nicolas had met before, at Senlis, and "Nijni-Novgorod" was a sacred phrase for them, though not, as she pretends, a pet name for her breasts (p. 208).

As for the yellow rose, that association clarifies itself eventually. The woman who has always been fond of yellow roses and whom Nicolas failed to recognize at Simone's party is named Marie-Stéphane. She was a friend of another of Nicolas's loves, Marie-Hortense, blond and alcoholic. For a long time it is Marie-Hortense who preoccupies Nicolas's memory and leads him on a false trail, for he loved her and not her friend, though both of them loved him. Nicolas associates fear with Marie-Stéphane, yet the fear did not begin with her.

As for the housemaid and the cap, they form part of an elaborate complex of associations, including an agate marble and a female breast with a beauty spot on it. In picking up a dropped marble, twelve-year-old Nicolas was struck by an opening door; the housemaid who opened it bent over to comfort him, giving him a glimpse of her untrammeled breasts and her beauty spot (pp. 191–2). Was it this same housemaid or another whose face he caught sight of amid the tall grass of the Duvals' park? The relevant quotation gives us a good idea of the cinematic technique so frequently used in *L'Oubli*, especially in the dream sequences:

> Cooing of a turtle-dove. Face lying in the crushed tall grass, seen upside down, very blond hair, lace cap.
> It's not Marie-Stéphane. It can't be Marie-Stéphane. The moaning of the turtle-dove becomes more and more insistent. Face of the young woman suddenly screwed up and as though tortured. (pp. 133–4)

Obviously this housemaid, whose name was possibly Véro-nique, was having an orgasm when Nicolas came upon her, though he could not see the cause of it because of the tall grass. The sight of her face frightened him, as well it might frighten an inexperienced boy, but why that face became associated with Marie-Stéphane, who was a brunette, is more than at least one "halfway intelligent and attentive" reader can say after two readings of L'Oubli. Guillemette was the Duvals' housemaid's name, apparently (p. 195). She re-sembled the famous French revolutionary and victim of the guillotine, Mme Roland, whose portrait hangs on Nicolas's wall.

Many things that Nicolas is not looking for surge up from his dreams, including the face of his beloved cousin Bertrand, born the same year as himself. As Nicolas tells Manou, since the death of this cousin at the age of fourteen, he, Nicolas, has not been able to believe in his own existence or in any-thing. "In anything but women, that is to say in nothing and nobody. Pleasure took the place of happiness" (p. 201).

Another scene that rises up during the dream-psychoanalysis recalls a vision that haunts the wave-obsessed psychotic in The Marquise:

"I've never recovered from it, never."
"From that train?"
"A long, long freight train, in the Gare d'Austerlitz, with children, little boys, behind the bars, at every opening those children's faces. French policemen here and there along the platform. French, yes. That must have been in 1942." (p. 179)

Mauriac very likely drew this memory from his own experi-ence, but in certain passages he employs a unique device for intruding in his own person: the left half of the page is used, the right half being entirely blank. For instance, after Nicolas has seen Bertrand in his dream:

. . . No more novel here, it's too serious, the real name, the real dates, as for my grandmother.
BERTRAND GAY-LUSSAC, Bor-

deaux, 5 December 1914.—
Paris, 23 July 1928 . . . (p.
199)

When both halves of the page are filled, the left "voice" is not Mauriac's; but when *only* the left column is used, Mauriac apparently is speaking directly to us.

Whole pages or parts of pages are left blank. At the same time, when Nicolas's memory altogether refuses to function, the right column seems to be reserved mainly for memories surging up from deeper levels of Nicolas's unconscious than the memories that run right across the page in normal typography. The protests of outraged readers quarreling with the author—be he Nicolas or Mauriac—occupy the right column also. It is interesting to note the division of the page into two columns for similar purposes in Raymond Queneau's *Les Enfants du limon.*

In addition to the element of parody, there are two kinds of highly contemporary reference that help give *L'Oubli* the air of a self-conscious, almost "gimmicky" tour de force One is the use of precise quotations from French newspapers of August 4 and 5, 1966—August 6 being the twenty-first anniversary of the dropping of the first atomic bomb on Hiroshima. The suffering of Vietnamese children in American bombing raids is associated with that of French Jewish children under the Nazis in 1942 and with that of children everywhere throughout history. (In passing, let us note the beautiful passages in which the babyhood of Pablo, fourteen-month-old child of Nicolas's Spanish maid-of-all-work, Dolorès, is recorded.) Since the *achevé d'imprimer* of *L'Oubli* is given as October 13, 1966, the novel must have been written at astonishing speed: there are several references to its having "written itself," in fact; see especially page 237.

We have already noted that Manou stole something; she also left a note saying, "Forget me." Later, her two accomplices and another man, in order to divert suspicion from her, broke into Nicolas's apartment, handcuffed Nicolas, threw things about, and pretended to steal what she had already stolen, a dossier containing the "plans for the New Novel"! But when

Nicolas's friend Henri comes to keep an early-morning appointment and frees Nicolas, the *real* plans are found safe behind the portrait of Mme Roland. Nicolas expects a telephone call from Manou, whose note has disappeared in the scuffle, so he begs Henri to notify the other members of Les Treize (The Thirteen) that the plans are safe. The members include "Nathalie" [Sarraute]; "the two Jeans" [??]; "Alain" [Robbe-Grillet]; "the three Claudes" [Simon, Mauriac, and perhaps Ollier]; "Samuel" [Beckett], who is "the first among us since James [Joyce] died . . ."; "Robert" [Pinget]; "Michel" [Butor] (pp. 228–9). Nicolas himself must be one of the Thirteen, but a couple of others are left unnamed. *L'Histoire des Treize* is a trilogy of novels by Balzac concerning members of a secret society called *Les Treize*; he names only five of the Thirteen.

Obviously this highly topical ending, which the outraged reader in the right column protests vigorously, is extremely humorous and reinforces the impression of Sternean humor and eccentricity that one occasionally suspected were lurking beneath the surface in earlier Mauriac novels. This ending also, like so many others in the New Novel, reminds us that what we are reading is "only" a novel. But somehow the whole tone of *L'Oubli* led us to expect a less slapstick ending. The irony of Nicolas's last *spoken* words provides what to me is a more suitable tone on which to end:

> "I need to be alone. I've spent a night . . . You can't imagine . . . A marvelous night. A night I'll never forget. With an unforgettable woman." (p. 233)

Claude Mauriac, then, is an inheritor of Proust and Joyce. From the former he takes his preoccupation with time and its indispensable human accompaniment, memory; by a skillful manipulation of memory he endeavors to immobilize all time and make it simultaneous. From Joyce Mauriac takes the interior monologue and endeavors to refine it into an interior dialogue, somewhat in the manner of Nathalie Sarraute.

Like almost all the New Novelists, Mauriac is contemptuous

of plot, which he calls "anecdote," and of character discrimination. Although not completely interchangeable, his characters —especially when their sexual lives undergo scrutiny—are not sharply differentiated. For instance, there is not too great a difference between the *voyeur* and the soap salesman in *The Marquise*, or between them and Raoul Lieuvain or even Zerbanian. In fact, there are two almost identical passages on pp. 80-1 and 85-6 of *L'Agrandissement*, one of which describes "the permanent ballet of young women" seen by Lieuvain at the Carrefour de Buci and the other "the permanent ballet of young men" seen at the same place by Zerbanian. Similarly, the four old ladies who are dying or near death in *The Marquise*—Mme Claire, the unnamed grandmother, Mme Ginette, and Mathilde—are not very easily separated from one another by the reader.

Mauriac's real subject matter, as he very well knows, is that of the lyric poet: universal human experience. Love, death, and the experiences of being young and growing old, along with those of forgetting and remembering, are the stuff of all his novels. Like all the novelists treated in this book— whether they have published poems or not—he seeks to apply the methods of poetry and music to the novel. Hence his disregard of narrative and character presentation. In their place we find an emphasis on verbal refrains and repetitions, on themes and leitmotivs, on metaphors and recurrent imagery, on the orchestration through diverse instruments of a single melody or harmony. Like many of the other New Novelists, he has been tempted by the tremendous poetic possibilities of the modern cinema.

Such are the qualities that Mauriac possesses in common with his fellow New Novelists. Does his work contain anything that is unique? As we know, Mauriac himself does not believe in the uniqueness of the individual; it is therefore, from his point of view, useless for us to stress his insistence that his basic material is drawn from personal experience, however much rearranged. All we can do here is to note once again that as author he intervenes personally in three of his novels to insist upon the authenticity of their raw material.

In any case, it is the artist's vision, not his raw material, that makes a work of art unique.

And it is precisely in his artistic vision that we can isolate Mauriac's uniqueness. To say that Mauriac, or at any rate his novelist-hero, constantly reassesses his own past, giving it new meanings and judging it by new standards, is in fact to say that Mauriac is an heir of Proust and his Bertrand Carnéjoux an inheritor of Proust's Marcel. But when Mauriac and/or Carnéjoux constantly reassesses his already completed novels, giving them new meanings and reaching fresh value judgments about them, we have moved into an entirely new novelistic dimension. Nicolas of *L'Oubli* puts it very tritely when he says, "One always tells the same story" (p. 38). Far more significant is a passage from page 21 of *L'Agrandissement* in which Bertrand is thinking of his own work:

> One ought to feel delivered, liberated, by what one has already written. But I never feel myself scot-free. I must say and resay, write and rewrite, repeat myself indefinitely in order to find myself in the end (there is no end) with the same impression of uneasiness and guilt. Literary avowals: confessions without absolution.

It is particularly significant that the next sentence evokes for us the opening page of the entire tetralogy: "And so Pascale Bressac is wading forever, her long red hair hanging down her back." We begin to grasp the full meaning of Claude Mauriac's admission, cited at the beginning of this chapter, that, in spite of his dissatisfaction with *All Women*, he wrote the other novels, in a sense, in order to make people read that first one.

Perhaps we can go on to claim much more than Mauriac does: each succeeding novel in the tetralogy sets its predecessors in a new light and makes it possible not only for us but for their author to understand them in a new way. If this claim can be at all substantiated, and I think this study has gone a long way toward doing so, we have discovered something that seems without parallel in the history of the novel. Novelists, playwrights, and narrative poets have all written works in which a central incident or group of incidents has been viewed from many different angles, but I am not aware that any sequence of works has yet been written, except by Mauriac, in which each succeeding work, and especially the last, has constituted a literary critique of all its predecessors.

8

Robert Pinget

THE BUILDING MATERIAL

ROBERT PINGET is the author of a number of interesting novels and one great one, *L'Inquisitoire* (*The Inquisitory*), 1962. His first novel, published ten years earlier, bore the title *Mahu ou le matériau* ("*Mahu or The* [Building] *Material*"). The subtitle of this earlier book suggests an aim that has been realized in *L'Inquisitoire*, that of presenting to the reader the materials from which a novel—or many novels—may be constructed without the author's having imposed an arbitrary form upon them. This sounds like an abdication of what the traditional novelist has considered to be his true function, namely to make an artistic order out of the chaos of life. And in fact *Mahu* hardly deserves to be called a novel, nor is it so described on the title page. As the author confesses in the second-last paragraph, "The first part [of this book], between you and me, is an aborted novel. . . ." The second part is no more than a series of sketches from life, possessing no unity except that of the sensibility which has recorded them.

L'Inquisitoire succeeds where *Mahu* failed because of one paradoxical fact: though no form is imposed upon the building materials themselves, their presentation to the reader does adhere to an arbitrary and rather limited form, that of question and answer. A retired manservant, unnamed, is being questioned by at least two officials: the only first-person

pronoun employed in the questions occurs on page 273, where
the old man is asked, "Do you think we're interrogating you
for fun, tell all that you saw. . . ." As the old man is very
deaf, the questions are in the form of written notes, which he
calls *billets*. His replies are given orally and recorded by a
woman on a stenographic machine (p. 449). A slight familiarity with French legal practice suggests that the interrogation
is being carried out by a *juge d'instruction* (examining magistrate) and one or more of his assistants. The ostensible cause
for the interrogation is the disappearance of a male secretary
who worked for the old man's joint former employers, whom
he usually calls *ces messieurs* ("those gentlemen"). We have
not been reading very long, however, before we conclude that
the interrogators are engaged in what is popularly called "a
fishing expedition," and that they are primarily interested in
the habits and associates of "those gentlemen," who are plainly
a homosexual couple, though the old man refuses to say so.[1]
Homosexual relations in private on the part of consenting
adults are not punishable under the Code Napoléon, but the
two employers have a number of dubious associates. The old
man suggests that complicated schemes for tax evasion may be
involved, while the interrogators at one point seem to suspect
drug addiction in the couple and some of their friends. The
possibility of male prostitution is also explored.

But the questions range far more widely than this: some
of them are so irrelevant that it seems impossible to fit them
into a realistic context, even if French law permits a latitude
of interrogation unheard of in Anglo-Saxon procedure. (It
should be noted that Pinget has a law degree.) For instance,
the old man is asked to give a detailed inventory of the
furniture in virtually every room of the château where he was
employed. He is also instructed to describe in some detail the
layout of the streets in the nearby village of Sirancy and the

[1] M. Pinget comments on this sentence: "The homosexuality of those
gentlemen is altogether a side issue. The word 'homosexuality,' furthermore, is never used by the servant. Consequently, your drawing attention to it at the start seems to me to mislead your readers." Letter of
July 14, 1965; my translation.

neighboring town of Agapa. For a number of pages (306–26), he is compelled to describe in detail each building in the *place* or main square of Sirancy and to list the tenants in each. Then he is interrogated in more detail about each tenant or family.

At one point the old man offers a hardly satisfactory explanation of the peculiar technique employed by his interrogators. He is being questioned in detail about the contents of the attic rooms and finally balks at describing the last of them:

> I've had enough of your system you're trying to make me make mistakes over details you'd do better to ask me about important things (p. 390)[2]

(Note that both questions and answers, while sometimes containing interior punctuation—commas only—lack all end punctuation, whether periods or question marks.)

Obviously, many of the questions could have been answered by the interrogators themselves through the use of a map or a directory or by investigation on the spot. We should regard questions of this type as narrative devices employed by Pinget rather than as part of his attempt to present the interrogation as realistically as possible. In regard to realism, however, one has to concede that the method offers gain as well as loss. Even if many of the questions seem eccentric, the answers build up a most convincing picture of a whole area as seen through the eyes of one man who has lived all his life there and has become a more acute observer as his deafness increased. From one aspect, *L'Inquisitoire* offers us Balzac's method modernized and reduced to a kind of shorthand. The publishers of *L'Inquisitoire*, Les Éditions de Minuit, prepared a little brochure of eight pages for free distribution to their friends and the author's: *Nomenclature des personnes de Sirancy-la-Louve d'Agapa et des environs mentionnés dans le procès-verbal.* They were kind enough to send me a copy of this "list of names of persons . . . mentioned in the record,"

---

[2] These page numbers refer to the original French edition. I had made my own translations of the passages quoted before Donald Watson's translation, *The Inquisitory*, appeared in 1966. Because of the "British" flavor of his version, I have retained my own.

which contains names, nicknames, or other identification for over six hundred characters in the novel, more than a quarter the number in the *Comédie humaine*. It would be even more useful to Pinget's readers and critics if it also included the hundred or more street names and names of places referred to in the book. *L'Inquisitoire*, it should be noted, is shorter than many a novel by Balzac, for, although it contains 483 pages of text, the print is large and the questions and answers are spaced out like the dialogue of a play.

Pinget's Balzacian preoccupation has been evident in his work from the beginning. His first publication, a volume of brief, rather Surrealist sketches, *Entre Fantoine et Agapa* ("Between Fantoine and Agapa"), 1951, is already localized in his imaginary territory, a sort of Barsetshire or Yokna-patawpha County, and characters and place names recur from book to book. As in Balzac or Faulkner or Zola, some of the details given about a character in one book are contradicted by those in another; also, some persons and places of business have been transferred from Fantoine to Sirancy as the cycle has developed, though Fantoine continues to be referred to. Sometimes, *L'Inquisitoire* clarifies problems posed by earlier books: in particular, *Baga* (1958) will remain a puzzle to someone who has not also read both the play *Architruc* and page 282 of *L'Inquisitoire*.

This Balzacian multiplicity of characters underlines another paradox, of content rather than form, which will be found in *L'Inquisitoire* and in some of the earlier novels. In spite of his obvious concern to present a picture of contemporary society by studying the microcosm of Agapa and its hinterland, Pinget is also fascinated by the solitary individual, isolated from society by eccentricity, by a physical handicap, or by some psychic trauma. Clope of *Clope au dossier* and Monsieur Levert of *Le Fiston* are cases in point. So is the deaf old re-spondent of *L'Inquisitoire*. Yet it is only in this last novel that the technical problem of presenting both the isolated indi-vidual and the multitudinous group is successfully overcome. Once again, the question-and-answer technique seems to re-solve the dilemma. Whatever he reveals or conceals about others, the old man almost necessarily reveals a great deal about himself by the way he answers the questions and by the extent to which he passes or refuses to pass judgment upon his employers, fellow servants, neighbors, acquaintances, and friends—these last being few indeed.

Not only do we obtain indirect information of this kind about him: because of the freedom which Pinget grants to the interrogators, we obtain a great deal of direct information. At times a question—usually irrelevant—will evoke a sort of free-association, stream-of-consciousness response: for instance, the reply on pp. 219–22 to the question, "How do you pass your days," meaning how he passes them now that he has retired. After the answer to this question has rambled on for some time, the interrogator breaks in, "Very sorry to interrupt your meditation you must answer"; we realize that indeed it is a private meditation rather than an answer that we have been reading.

The most startling insight into the old manservant is not provided until halfway through the novel. The interrogator has just led him through a long, circumstantial, and irrelevant account of a wedding celebration—the bride being a niece of Marthe, who is still cook to "those gentlemen" and one of the old man's few real friends. The old man has spoken of the memories that this festivity evoked in him; finally he is asked, "Have you ever been married" (p. 246). He tries to avoid the question but is forced to answer. The reader has assumed up to this moment that the old servant is a confirmed bachelor; now it turns out that he had been married for ten years, his wife having died ten years ago. Furthermore, he had a son, Claude, who died of meningitis at the age of eight, two years before his mother.

As the interrogation about his married life proceeds, a macabre tangle of superstitions is unraveled. The old man and his wife, Marie, were employed throughout their married life by a wealthy couple named Emmerand. The Emmerands were convinced spiritualists, the wife being a medium. The old man does not doubt for a moment that Mme Emmerand spoke with the dead, but he always thought this was a dangerous thing to do; in fact, he cannot understand why he did not leave the Emmerands when he realized what they devoted their lives to. Marie was unwilling to quit because their employers were so kind and also because she herself became interested in spiritualism. The old man is convinced that Mme Emmerand was responsible for his son's death because she "wanted another dead person to talk to especially a child she knew"; he also blames her for Marie's death. Furthermore, both the Emmerands are now dead; the old man stuck pins in their photographs to bring this about, believing that he was inspired by God. He is also haunted by visions of the devil, in whom he implicitly believes; in fact, he sees the devil stand beside one of his interrogators and touch him (pp. 254-5). The old man is convinced that the Emmerands deliberately chose to live near the haunted Forest of Grance and another place with an evil reputation in local folklore, the quarry of Vaguemort and the empty farmhouse of the same name. He becomes very excited and insists that the farm must be burned, that he himself will burn it. The interrogator then asks if the old man drinks a lot; he admits he does but insists that he is not an alcoholic and that his mind is in no way affected.

Eventually the interrogation resumes its routine progress. But Pinget has one more surprise for us. After the detailed description of the Château de Broy (the home of "those gentlemen") that the old man has given us, it turns out that there is an older part of the château, *le donjon*, which he has not described at all (p. 429). At first he insists that nobody lives there any more except the caretaker and his family, but eventually he admits that a certain Monsieur Pierre, a friend of "those gentlemen," lives there also. M. Pierre is "a saint." He has very little share in the lives and associations of "those gentlemen," living by himself and devoting himself entirely to the study of the heavens. Since the old man, in his malapropistic way, calls him an *"astronogue,"* it is hard to be sure whether M. Pierre is an astrologer (*astrologue*) or an astronomer (*astronome*). The account of the saintliness of M. Pierre appears with peculiar effect hard on the heels of a long, detailed description of one of "those gentlemen's" wild evening parties, full of hard drinking and ending in homosexual and heterosexual promiscuity.

The old man's indirect self-revelations permeate all his answers: it is this fact which makes the numerous inventories far from tedious, for he cannot help offering his personal associations with this or that piece of furniture, work of art, or building. "Those gentlemen" are passionate collectors of art and antiques, to such an extent that they don't have enough space to display their collection and must store many valuable paintings and pieces of furniture in the attic rooms. The old man's comments on a piece in the main *salon* are typical:

> . . . the glass-fronted cabinet is a converted wardrobe one of those mastodons from Normandy that take a whole day to clean and besides the cornice on top is loose, nearly every time you got up on the stepladder to dust it one false move and bingo it would start to come down . . . (p. 191)

His comments on the paintings are often delightfully shrewd:

> . . . above the sofa there's a picture that covers the whole wall it's religious the Circumcision of the first of January a crowd of people from the Bible standing in a church with big columns they surround Jesus who is held by his mother she presents him to the priest who bends over to cut him, the people around don't know what to do with themselves they see that they're being looked at that's what I don't like in those paintings . . . (p. 192)

Of a worm-eaten wooden sculpture of the Virgin, probably medieval, he remarks:

> . . . it was a bargain, that sort of thing is greatly admired today you might say that the crummier it is the better they call that rustic . . . (p. 194)

Sometimes his comments on the art works are amusingly prudish, such as those on a painting which appears to be by Rubens or one of his imitators:

> . . . a dame seated on a chariot she has nothing on but a crown of leaves she's laughing as she squeezes the tip of one breast with one hand, in the other she's raising a wine cup that's

turning upside down you see the wine spilling around her
stool which is ornamented with grapes and vine leaves, there
are men and women in poses they are sucking grapes or
giving them to each other and around the chariot children are
dancing and looking at the dames one of them puts his hand
on the behind of one of the dames, you wonder really what
the people who made those paintings were thinking of today
at least for instance in the cinemas it's forbidden for those
under sixteen to see risqué films we have more decency all
the same . . . (p. 118)

While Pinget's catalogues of "things" give his backgrounds
the solidity that Robbe-Grillet so much desires, Pinget does
not share Robbe-Grillet's existentialist view of man's alienation
from things; on the contrary, he saturates them in human
associations—the old man's or their owners':

> . . . an armchair with an oval back and straight legs that
> doesn't go with the others, covered in white silk with green
> floral designs those gentlemen kept it in memory of a dead
> woman friend who had left a legacy to them . . . (p. 198)

The old man's attitude on sexual matters in general presents
an odd contrast with his prudery about the subjects of paintings and his delicacy in the choice of words to describe sexual
acts. He refuses to judge the sexual habits of others on the
untranslatable ground that *les questions sentiment c'est person-
nel* (p. 274). Although he is rather frank about the sex life of
an earlier employer, d'Eterville, who is heterosexual, he refuses
to be specific about the homosexuality of "those gentlemen."
The interrogator of the moment asks him why:

> Because
> Answer
> Because it isn't the same people don't understand a thing
> about it and you ought to tell the truth and it isn't easy so it's
> better to say nothing
> Why not
> Because those things I realize that they're thus and so even
> if you have difficulty talking about them they're real and don't
> concern anybody except those who do them, and to go and
> mix morals up with the business that's the dirty part and I

don't want to talk about it with you because I don't know
you (p. 275)

At times, the old man answers or meditates to himself in
a vein which can only be described as philosophical. These
answers and reflections deal, in his own uneducated and
highly colloquial language, with some of the key problems
of the New Novelists: reality, memory, consciousness, knowledge. On page 299 the interrogator accuses him of making
no effort to tell the truth; he replies:

> On the contrary, I do make an effort I even try too hard
> and the truth remains to one side, what I no longer know or
> what I don't yet know or what you forget to ask me . . . (pp.
> 299–300)

A little later he is asked to try to remember:

> Remember remember does one remember you've done two
> or three things you've not seen many more hardly half of it
> stays in your head, those things in the past do you remember
> them you tell about them someone in your head has changed
> them during the years it isn't them any more since they're
> still there, when they happened you weren't trying to re-
> member them you had other worries and when they come back
> to us ten twenty years later they've been remade no one would
> recognize them any more you don't know who it is that gives
> them this appearance, no they're no longer memories they're
> something you must have wished for even unhappiness is
> wished for without knowing . . . , if I think of Marie and our
> child in my head it's unhappiness but when I was with them
> I wasn't unhappy . . . that's what unhappiness is do you see
> it's not in life it's afterwards in your head . . . (pp. 300–1)

A little farther on he says:

> . . . the truth [reality?] is to have under your eyes something
> that you don't see because you've something else to do, and
> to love your family that's it it's not to think about it and to
> go and empty the chamber pots and wax the salon and work
> in the garden and go back to your room at night dead beat
> without even thinking of having your wife because when you
> think of it it's already too late . . . (p. 303)

Much later there is a final outburst that sums up the profound ambiguity of this book which tells us so much and yet so little. The interrogator, in a moment of exasperation, writes, "It is difficult to believe you after your evasions and your continual omissions," to which the old man replies:

> I don't care I don't care a bit in fact I'm pleased, all this rubbish that Mademoiselle taps out on her machine it's as though it wasn't me who said it you're dragging things out of me I know what's coming these are things that should be done in private and that don't interest anyone except depraved people like you, yes depraved I say if I hadn't had to tell about them or if I'd told about them calmly taking my time they wouldn't have been the same instead like that you're going to make use of them against those gentlemen or other people or me, things get digested slowly and before they're digested they can do harm they aren't understood you're tempted to spit them out before that when a person has no experience he's like that always in a hurry to jump to conclusions from bits and pieces and all our judgments are false as a matter of fact, but with time everything gets digested nothing is poisonous there's only this idiotic hurry that stupefies us bit by bit no let me alone for a moment till I get it all off my chest, stupefies us that's the right word don't you think I don't realize it, I think about it all the time in the café you see someone do something right away you draw conclusions from it a crazy idea there are no conclusions except those that you imagine on the spur of the moment or that you force to call themselves conclusions, the real ones don't resemble them at all they combine with all the rest and that's life but it happens slowly and you see with your questions sometimes I fall into the trap knowingly, it happens that I fall into the trap and give my opinion and draw conclusions even though I know it's all bunkum to do that until a hundred years have gone by or maybe ever that's what I think, as if you were in a hurry to get life over with well I'm not you understand, in spite of everything I'm not soon I'll go back to my room and tomorrow back to the bistro which isn't always much fun but I want it to last forever so there (pp. 449–50)

Thus this book, which consists almost entirely of answers, reminds us that, in the current cliché, "there are no answers."

Like so many contemporary novels, especially those of the French New Novelists, *L'Inquisitoire* is self-destructive. One thing it cannot destroy, however, is the experience the reader undergoes in reading it, an experience that can be repeated with profit and enjoyment, probably many times. It is high time to take this book a little less seriously and to emphasize some of the pleasure that can be derived from it. Two of the great pleasures one draws from more traditional novels can be found in abundance here: the naïve enjoyment of being told stories, and the more sophisticated one of discovering between the lines the author's sly humor.

Although the book lacks a sustained narrative, it is crammed with short and long narrative passages. Almost every character whose name comes up during the interrogation has his or her story; it may be the merest gossip or hearsay, but the old man relates it anyway, often with gusto. One example will have to stand for literally hundreds:

> Beside the church is the newspaper kiosk as I said the sales-woman is old lady Attention she's been there for years she doesn't change, her husband has been paralyzed for ten years he used to be a shoemaker I don't know what she can earn with her papers they have two rooms on the Camp Road in an annex, at the time when he was working I used to give him my shoes to mend he had a shop in Bapluie Street almost at the corner of Grands-Traversots, he had traveled a lot as a young man having been to Istambull [*sic*] as a steward on a ship then he was porter in a hotel out there, he was more or less married and he came home when the war started the first one I mean leaving his wife and child that he never saw again you remember the foul-up over papers and passports at that time, he continued to travel after the war as far as Denmark where he learned shoemaking with a guy who nearly strangled him over a woman, he came back home and married Denise Vantard his present wife that is she was a modiste then she wouldn't hear of his going in for shoemaking and he went to work at Romain Prout's the shoe store on Chavirat Street where he stayed maybe four or five years before going back to shoemaking, his wife had given up the fashion shop to be manager of the little perfume shop on Garances Place and

when her husband got ill she quit to take over the kiosk a
year or two after (p. 321)

Many of the little life stories appended to the names of
characters are much briefer and less eventful than this one;
others are longer. Occasionally the interrogation elicits a long
and circumstantial story, such as that of the German servant
Johann who murdered three young women, two with the help
of accomplices, in order to practice necrophilia with them (pp.
283–94). As already mentioned, the account of the last nighttime garden party which the old man witnessed at the Château
de Broy is long and full. At first the old man is reluctant to go
into details, but eventually he warms to his work and laughs
over one or two bawdy incidents; the account, including the
preparations for the *fête de nuit*, takes up thirty pages (pp.
398–428). The account of the wedding of Marthe's niece,
equally circumstantial, offers a bourgeois counterpoise, full of
wholesome sentiment, to the bohemian revels of the aristocracy (pp. 228–44).

As for the humor, it is to be found at a number of levels.
First, the basic structure of the novel contains an implicitly
humorous element that the reader becomes keenly aware of
from time to time: the contrast between the coldly impersonal
written questions and the warmly personal spoken answers.
Then, much of the old man's colloquial speech is either consciously or unconsciously humorous. As we have seen in his
comments on works of art, he has an acute sense of the ridiculous; his prudery, though, falls into the category of unconscious humor, as do his numerous malapropisms and the other
manifestations of his inadequate education.

Pinget, like Fielding and Dickens, shows endless ingenuity
in the coinage of proper names. Sometimes these are appropriate for their bearers, like the last name of Sophie Narre
(*narre*, "narrates"), one of the chief gossips of the neighborhood, or that of Douglas Hotcock, a somewhat promiscuous
American actor. Others amuse by their sheer incongruity, like
the name of the local bishop, Monseigneur Bougecroupe
("Budgebottom"). Some of the geographical names sound

highly indecorous, such as that of the River Chie, too closely related to the French verb *chier* ("to shit"). The efforts of the parish priest of Sirancy, l'abbé Quinche, to provide less offensive etymologies from the Latin for Chie and some other place names only heighten the humor. The patron saint of the Cathedral of Agapa, Sainte Fiduce, suggests financial stability rather than devotion. It should be noted also that the former Place de la Cathédrale is now called Place Karl-Marx and that Marx's statue has replaced that of Sainte Fiduce. The name Agapa itself suggests Greek *agapē* ("love"), a deliberately ironic derivation. Many of the street names in Agapa and Sirancy show a similar ingenuity.

Like many New Novels—and also *Tristram Shandy* and *Finnegans Wake*—*L'Inquisitoire* displays a roughly circular form. The first "question" (p. 7) is *Oui ou non répondez* ("Answer yes or no"); it is also the last one (p. 489), to which the old man's reply is *Je suis fatigué* ("I'm tired"). The opening implies that the questioning has already gone on for some time and the close does not necessarily imply that the questioning is over. In spite of the hint of cyclic form, life does not fit into a neat pattern even here.

When he reaches the end which is no end, the reader may be tempted to ask himself a naïve question: "Is this book optimistic or pessimistic?" Naïve questions are not always easy to answer, if only because they oversimplify. The answer this time is easy, however: "Neither." The old man sees the world as made up of good, bad, and indifferent people. Against a sadist like Johann must be balanced a saint like Monsieur Pierre. Most people, like "those gentlemen," cannot be painted black or white. Also, in spite of his unlucky life, the old man has no wish to die. Life may be meaningless, or its meaning may escape us, but it is livable. And the book ends with a vision of happiness, a dream that the old man has had one day of meeting his wife and child and going to visit M. Pierre and talking endlessly with him about the stars. It is the nearest thing to a vision of heaven that the old man is capable of. The interrogator asks him several times, "Had you fallen asleep in the café?" but the old man insists "I don't know any more," as if he were unwilling to admit that it was a dream and not a prophetic vision. On this characteristically ambiguous note of "I don't know any more," *L'Inquisitoire* draws to a close.

The earlier works can be dealt with more briefly; inevitably the critic looks for anticipations of *L'Inquisitoire* as well as for false trails that Pinget had to abandon later. Yet, we must recognize the autonomy of each book: the Balzacian analogy has very limited application, for Pinget has never announced or in fact embarked upon a cycle resembling *La Comédie humaine* or Zola's *Les Rougon-Macquart*. Some of his books about the Fantoine-Agapa-Sirancy area are realistic, but others —especially *Mahu*, *Graal Flibuste*, and *Baga*—while making reference to some of the same people and places, diverge into a world of fantasy. One might say that they are anchored to earth at one corner only, while the rest floats freely in an atmosphere of imagination.

Mahu (1952) falls into two distinct parts. Part I, *"Le Romancier"* ("The Novelist"), is an aborted novel; Part II, *"Mahu bafouille"* ("Mahu Stammers," or "Mahu Talks Nonsense"), is perhaps sufficiently described for the moment by its title. Part I begins with Mahu saying, "Here is this story, I don't understand any of it. . . ." In the next paragraph he adds:

> So I'm telling this story, but there's also Latirail, he writes novels. He tells me sometimes how he goes about it; that causes me a lot of complications; it's all very well for him to explain his characters to me, but I am perhaps one of them myself when I think about it? (pp. 9–10)[3]

And so we plunge into a wildly irrational world in which Mahu has fourteen brothers, all called Frédy, and the postmaster of Sirancy, Sinture, makes everyone write to everyone else in care of General Delivery (*poste restante*) and read their letters in the post office. The mailman is forbidden to deliver any letters, so that businessmen try to avoid the post office by sending letters hidden in packages via rail freight.

[3] Here and elsewhere in this chapter, unless the reader is informed otherwise, the page numbers refer to the original French edition and the translations are mine.

The basic idea, however, is that Latirail, a Mlle Lorpailleur, and Mahu himself, in a sense, are all novelists whose characters come to life as soon as they "create" them; also, when they write about "real" people, they seem to be able to control their actions. An added complication is supplied by Sinture, who insists that he is dictating Latirail's novel; when Mahu mentions this to Latirail, however, he is met with an incredulous denial.

This power of creation leads to several comic entanglements: for instance, Latirail decides to change a character's name from Fion to Bouchèze; to his dismay, he soon reads in a local paper that Bouchèze has been arrested on the charge of strangling Fion. Flann O'Brien, the Irish humorist, gave some of his characters similar creative powers in *At Swim-Two-Birds* (London, 1939; New York, 1951) and worked out the consequences with a sort of insane logicality. Pinget, however, soon gives up and has Mahu say goodbye to all his characters, telling them to shift for themselves (p. 102).

Behind all this fooling, one can detect a serious critique of realism in the novel. Latirail is desperately anxious to write truthfully, realistically. Unfortunately, having written that fifteen-year-old girls wash their hair in vinegar, he learns from his wife that nowadays they use Dop shampoo instead. Besides, she says, ten years from now they may be using something else. She has put her finger on one of the disadvantages of the realistic method. Furthermore, if one's aim is realism, why not write about "real" people such as Sinture and Mahu? And, if the pretensions of the realist have any meaning, why shouldn't his "created" characters have a real existence also? Conversely, Mahu meets someone who thinks that it is impossible to write novels at all: one cannot put oneself in the place of other people.

Accordingly, in Part II Mahu makes no attempt to tell a story. Instead, he gives a series of autobiographical sketches. The setting is now Paris instead of Sirancy, but the point of view is that of the eccentric Mahu, so that the real world seems almost as odd as the imagined one. Latirail and his wife, Ninette, appear in the sketches from time to time, but no attempt is made to give a sustained narrative; one might almost call the second part a collection of essays, in a rather Surrealist vein. Mahu can hardly stick to one subject for two paragraphs together. As examples of the fantastic range of topics in these little chapters or essays, take numbers 21 and 22 of Part II. The first deals humorously with the problems of eating at an Arab restaurant and watching a belly dancer at the same time; it apparently records an "actual" experience when Mahu was a guest of the Latirails. Mahu dislikes doing two things at once and gets hopelessly confused between them:

> The mutton of the couscous is as hard as wood, it's interesting how she makes her rolls of fat move although it's soft. (pp. 160–1)

In Chapter 22 Mahu imagines what it would be like to go about on stilts: he would wear an overcoat long enough to hide his feet; he could cross the street without waiting for the red light because all the drivers would stop to look at him. He could buy the wood already sawed and make the stilts himself; he likes the smell of wood; he'll give his godchildren presents made of wood, wooden books.

> When one likes something, one hesitates to make a present of it; one doesn't know whether one likes this wood or the person; one would prefer that the person should be in the wood so that one could like both at once. (p. 165)

As usual, Mahu's mind (if one can call it that) has veered from one subject to another with unpredictable eccentricity.

In the final chapter, of Part II and of the book, Mahu confides to us that he lied a lot at the beginning but that the truth is now "ripe." A few characters like Latirail and Ninette are really friends of his, and in Part II he has distorted very little of what passes between them. Part I, it is true, is an abortive novel:

> . . . but no matter, it served as preliminary scales for me, what matters to me is not singing well but hearing my voice without bronchitis, you know what bronchitis is like, there are a lot of little whistling sounds.

There, I've nothing more to say, yet everything remains
with me, I've won. (p. 212)

The reader, however, may have lost. Mahu's (or Pinget's)
struggle toward self-expression retains the reader's interest
with difficulty, if at all. One admires the French publisher for
his readiness to encourage the slightest glimmer of talent and
envies the French novelist who can learn his trade at the
publisher's expense. Even a French publisher's patience is
limited, however; one notes without surprise that Pinget had
a different publisher for each of his first four books: either
Jarnac or La Tour de Feu for *Entre Fantoine et Agapa*; Robert
Laffont for *Mahu*; Gallimard for *Le Renard et la boussole*; and
finally Les Éditions de Minuit for *Graal Flibuste*. One wonders
how much longer French publishers can afford to take such
risks; meanwhile, the experimental novelist has an easier time
getting published in France than he would have in the
English-speaking world. In America or England a Pinget
might have lost heart before producing *Graal Flibuste*, let
alone *L'Inquisitoire*.

Le Renard et la boussole ("The Fox and the Compass"),
1953, described as a novel on the title page, is a far richer
and more interesting book than *Mahu* but no less disorderly.
The general impression received by the reader is of an attempt
to force a sharply observed impressionistic record of a visit
to modern Israel into a fictional frame which is replete with
Pinget's fantasy. The medley of styles and subject matters
shows brilliant virtuosity, but the mixture becomes too rich
and heterogeneous to be readily digestible.

The narrator of *Le Renard* is a Mahu-like eccentric who
bears the improbable name of John Tintouin Porridge. He used
to work in a hat factory until he became allergic to felt; now
he works for private customers when there is work for him;
the rest of the time he cultivates his "talents"—for writing and
painting among other things. When he returns from Israel (pp.
186–7), we discover that he lives in Fantoine, yet he is surrounded by all the characters of Part I of *Mahu*, including

Mahu himself, who told us in the earlier book that he spent only his summer vacations in Fantoine. In *L'Inquisitoire*, Sinture and others of the *Mahu* characters are unequivocally located in Sirancy; while Agapa appears as a large town throughout the novels, Pinget seems to have vacillated between Sirancy and Fantoine as the location for his typical village.

Having introduced himself at the beginning of the book, John does not quite know what to do next. "What is a true story?" he asks. As for simple stories, he detests them. When one begins a story, the best thing is to say, "I was born."

> My heart is full of beginnings that always prove abortive. And I have no end in view, either. (p. 10)

He rambles on until one morning a phrase from the Bible sticks in his head:

> . . . something like *Beware of the little foxes* and also something about vines, yes, the foxes in the vines. (p. 21)

In the King James (Authorised) Version, the passage from the *Song of Solomon*, 2:15, runs, "Take us the foxes, the little foxes, that spoil the vines"; it gave Lillian Hellman the title for her play *The Little Foxes*. This phrase stirs John's imagination: suddenly he sees the fox meeting an old Jew who is going to Jerusalem; the fox asks to be allowed to follow the Jew like a dog; the Jew agrees; they sleep on the docks while waiting for the departure of their ship. Reynard attracts John, who feels that they are kindred spirits, both prowlers.

Then John's attention is distracted to other things: he receives a commission to paint the Creation for a suburban elementary school; the first images that he splashes on his canvas are kangaroos and motorcycles—dozens of both— followed by a wild medley of animals, skyscrapers, factories, and the signs of the zodiac. One day, while still working on this painting, he sees a poster in the street offering reduced rates for a vacation in Palestine; on the spur of the moment he decides to go, although he is not a Jew. His vision of Reynard and the Wandering Jew comes back to him and during his voyage he decides to include them in his story.

The Jew is given the name David; he is old, wise, calm, scholarly, devout, and impoverished; he has never seen "his" country before. Thanks to his presence, we are given a dual view of Israel: as it appears to the Gentile tourist, John, and as it appears to the "returning" exile, the pilgrim David. In presenting David's view of Israel, which appears authentic to a non-Jewish reader, Pinget relies heavily upon the Old Testament, whose words haunt David as he sees the places with which they are associated. Reynard's viewpoint does not add much to the other two because it tends to merge with John's; Reynard too is a "Christian," who thinks of Christ as "The Great Fox." John also encounters another alter ego, the Jewish painter Benjamin, who compiles an album of sketches dealing with the adventures of David and Reynard. One cannot help suspecting that Pinget, once a painter himself, has a sheaf of similar sketches tucked away among his belongings. Many of John's experiences read like passages from Pinget's autobiography; one would be very surprised to learn that Pinget had never been to Israel or had never had the experience of being a solitary Gentile among a large group of Jews. The reader gains a warm and living awareness of the virtues and faults of the Jewish people as seen through Christian eyes.

When the liner reaches Israel and the travelogue proper begins, the reader is subjected to at least three styles of discourse: the realistic narrative of David's and John's experiences as they visit the holy places of their respective religions and such institutions of modern Israel as the kibbutzim or farm colonies; a rather pompous lecture in textbook style delivered by *un homme positif*, a sort of Babbitt, on his return from Israel; and a series of adventures in the realm of imagination which take us into the past history of Palestine. Among the characters whom we encounter in these last excursions (besides Jesus) are Suleiman the Magnificent, the Saracen ruler; a Roman Emperor, appropriately at´ Caesarea; the Pharaoh of the Book of Exodus; the Sire de Joinville, historian of the Crusades; Mary Magdalene. Also, regardless of geography, we find ourselves for a while in the company of Don Quixote and Sancho Panza, to whom David and Reynard roughly correspond. (This Quixote-Panza analogy is implicit rather than explicit in Pinget's next two books, *Graal Flibuste* and *Baga*.)

These three main styles are interrupted from time to time by other "voices," notably that of John back at home after his travels and wondering how to write about them, but also those of others who seem to have little to do with the main narrative. An encounter of David's with a flock of she-goats while he is swimming prompts the insertion of a court report, dated 1611, dealing with the prosecution of various French peasants for acts of bestiality with she-goats and other animals; this interruption has more relevance than others, such as a radio interview with a certain Chevalier du Toc, "author of a remarkable work on the soul," made largely inaudible by the drilling and hammering which go on in the studio simultaneously. At times one is reminded of *Finnegans Wake* by these abrupt shifts of speaker and subject.

When John definitively returns to Fantoine, his narrative is under no better control. There is a ten-page circumstantial account of his first day in Fantoine, full of eating and drinking and pointless errands, which is reminiscent of many passages in the old man's evidence throughout *L'Inquisitoire*. Suddenly we find ourselves in the midst of an imaginary autopsy on Joan of Arc, who turns out to have been a man. Then John describes the clutter in his room, but the description does not fill as much space in his book as he had hoped. Next comes a discussion of his book with Mlle Lorpailleur, the novelist. She is profoundly disappointed with John's account of the book and gives him a little lesson in how to begin a novel. Each of her examples begins, "I was born," and the stations in life into which she is born become more and more absurd, culminating in a page of compound adjectives and compound nouns such as *prie-Dieu, garde-crotte, chauffe-bain, prête-nom, lance-torpille* ("prayer stool, mudguard, water heater, figurehead, torpedo tube"), none of which satisfies even so eccentric an author as John Tintouin Porridge. John gives her a cup of tea to revive her, and she then recites some of her poems, each one more Surrealist than the last. John, exhausted, says

goodbye to her. He had hoped to finish his book in a blaze of
glory, with a synthesis or even a moral, but his ideas have
given out and the book ends in a babble of phrases linked
only by free association. The last sentence of all is the same
as the first, "My name is John Tintouin Porridge."

A book like *Le Renard* or *Mahu* is in one sense beyond
criticism: if a half-demented character like Mahu or John
were to write a book, this is doubtless the sort of book he
would write. On the other hand, Mahu's and John's constant
self-questioning about the nature of reality and the validity
of the accepted modes of representing it in literature parallels
that of many twentieth-century novelists, including of course
Pinget himself. The most serious criticism to be leveled
against *Le Renard* is not the lack of unity of style and subject
so much as the lack of consistency in the presentation of John:
we expect him to be consistently irrational, but during the
voyage to Israel and his travels about that country he appears
altogether too rational; we do not see his shipmates and the
contrasts presented by the Holy Land through his eyes but
through Pinget's. A piece of non-fiction seems to have been
forced into a fictional framework, to the detriment of both.

Ulysses stands as a permanent witness to the fact that unity
of style and viewpoint is not a *sine qua non* of the novel;
nevertheless, an unpracticed novelist violates this unity, these
unities, at his peril. *Graal Flibuste* and *Baga* suggest that
Pinget had at least temporarily learned this lesson: each of
these works is a fantasy, but the freedom granted to their
matter is counterbalanced by the strict classicism of their
manner and their almost undeviating adherence to first-person
narration.

Graal Flibuste, 1956,[4] is a work so nearly unique as to be
almost indescribable. It relates the travels in an imaginary
world of an unnamed narrator and his coachman, Brindon; yet
the realm they explore can in part be located geographically

[4] An *édition intégrale* (complete edition), containing sixteen new
chapters (inserted at three different points in the work), was published
in 1966.

in relation to the "real" town of Agapa. For instance, the temple of the god Graal Flibuste (whose name might be roughly translated as "Grail Filibuster" or "Grail Freebooter") is located in a gloomy, rat-infested valley, Le Chanchèze, that is referred to in a number of Pinget's books. Brindon reappears fleetingly in *L'Inquisitoire* (pp. 262–3), along with his horse Clotho, as the coachman of Mme de Nutre, an eccentric old aristocrat who refused to buy herself an automobile. He is described as *un brave type* ("a swell guy") who used to eat in the kitchen with the servants at the Château de Broy and tell stories about the countries he had seen, having traveled a great deal with his former master. One wonders whether this master is the unnamed narrator of *Graal Flibuste* or whether the earlier book is an alcoholic dream which incorporates such memories of the everyday world as Mme de Nutre's coachman, horse, and carriage. The latter hypothesis is supported by the opening of *Graal Flibuste* (pp. 7–9), which consists of an untitled passage in italics describing the falling asleep of a lonely alcoholic who has no companion except a very old cat.[5] If the remainder of the book consists of this drunkard's dream or dreams, he must have been a man of considerable culture and education, for some of the narrator's reflections and conversation display a high level of both. The alcoholic might even be the M. Levert of *Le Fiston*, for he thinks, just before he falls asleep: "*So many years, so many years with this bottle because of a letter that did not arrive. . . .*"

At any rate, once this brief prologue is over, we are in the land of the god Graal Flibuste and his numerous fellow gods and goddesses. We can reject this world with impatience if we wish, but those who continue with the book will find it permeated by a strange charm. No consistent allegorical interpretation of the two travelers' adventures seems possible; although there are passages of parody and perhaps even satire, the work seems chiefly an exercise in pure narration and description. To draw parallels with the fantasy worlds of J. R. R. Tolkien or Lord Dunsany would be misleading, however:

[5] Page references are to the 1966 complete edition.

Pinget does not burden himself with a plot or a consistent morality. His chief delight seems to lie in the creation of new words and new images, which in turn beget new gods and a new flora and fauna. One recalls John Tintouin Porridge's painting of the Creation and reflects that *Graal Flibuste* contains a vastly exaggerated extension of the literal view of artistic "creation" played with in Part I of *Mahu*. Why should the novelist be limited to creating characters who must function according to the rules of a real world where it matters whether one uses vinegar or Dop shampoo? Why should he not create a whole new world for his characters to live in? It may surprise us that the author of *Graal Flibuste* should so wholeheartedly adopt the literary convention of realism in *L'Inquisitoire*, but we must remember that even in the latter book he does not confuse realism with reality. Since both books are works of fiction, the adventures in *Graal Flibuste* are just as real or unreal as those in *L'Inquisitoire*; what is important for Pinget is that, having written the former book wholeheartedly in an anti-realist convention, he has gained a deeper, clearer understanding of the realist convention, as he shows in the latter book.

Pinget's delight in words for their own sake, which we have noted in the place and personal names of *L'Inquisitoire*, finds its fullest outlet in the two chapters devoted to the genealogy of Graal Flibuste, where we find the following:

> Prak begat Flop.
> Flop begat Duic.
> Duic begat Poutousse [Louse coughs].
> Poutousse begat Nouille [Noodle].
> Nouille begat Vertige [Vertigo] ... (p. 72)

and so on. In the next chapter Brindon complains:

> "It's very vulgar, what you are saying."
> "My dear man, I'm not saying, I'm relating. Vulgar? You astonish me. Vulgarity is never laughable; it saddens me, personally. You are passing judgment on what only requires your attention, you know. Don't disappoint me."
> "I'm against bric-à-brac."

"That's why you don't perceive the great beauty of the world."

"If this genealogy is one of its splendors, I certainly admit that I don't understand."

"That's not the point, Brindon. There isn't a beauty here and an ugliness there; there's the total effect, the mechanism of the total effect. Think big, my dear man, think big." (pp. 73–4)

But Brindon insists that he likes *le vécu* ("what has been lived").

This passage seems Pinget's defense of the book as a whole. Brindon's role as the down-to-earth Sancho Panza, a foil to the narrator's Don Quixote, also stands out clearly. At a later stage Brindon questions the narrator very sharply. "What do you expect from your experiences?" he asks (p. 147). To which the answer eventually emerges, "To find out what I am. . . ." "But, sir," answers Brindon, "who will tell you that if not I? . . . Or anybody else, no matter who?" "Brindon, you are a great philosopher" (pp. 148–9). In effect, Brindon is propounding here an existentialist view of personality.

These "philosophic" discussions play only a small part in the book, however. More characteristic are the descriptions of strange flora and fauna: little flowers with human faces that sing in chorus, tiger-birds and horse-swans, monkey-butterflies. The pair encounter strange shapeless animals called *"bloues,"* which exist only to be eaten, like the "shmoo" invented by the American cartoonist Al Capp; rather similar are the "mud-hares" which have only one ear and owe their delicious taste when eaten to the amount of mud that they eat. A whole chapter (pp. 219–23) is devoted to some remarkable flora.

Then there are the adventures with people, almost all unexpected and instructive: for instance, the apparently simple peasant named Jasmin, who cultivates his kitchen-garden during the day but organizes *partouses* (an argot word for sex orgies) every evening. (The *fête de nuit* in *L'Inquisitoire* is a sort of *partouse* also.) Brindon and the narrator are persuaded to participate in these orgies, and the narrator at least learns a great deal about human nature from his experiences—

which are, however, not described. "'Bed,' as Jasmin used to say, 'teaches us more about anyone than the longest speeches.' That is true" (p. 134). Among Jasmin's collaborators is an elderly nymphomaniac, the Duchesse de Bois-Suspect, familiar to readers of *L'Inquisitoire*. She gives a highly improbable account of her life, beginning with her birth in the little town of Nutre, where the wives kill their husbands after the third or fourth child. Eventually the orgies begin to pall on both travelers and they move on, but not toward any particular goal.

Graal Flibuste does not end; it merely stops, for there is no allegory to be completed and no plot to be resolved. Well before the finish, the reader has grown accustomed to discontinuity, for the climax of more than one of the "adventures" about which our interest has been aroused is never related, though it may be alluded to later.[6] This characteristic of the narrative is particularly reminiscent of dreams, in which tension may be endlessly built up without achieving a resolution. The dream world of *Graal Flibuste*, however, is essentially benign, containing very little of the guilt that haunts our own dreams or the dreamlike fictional world of Kafka. One might also describe the book as a prose poem; one chapter, "The Love-Quest of the Witch Vaoua" (pp. 75–9), is in fact written in free verse, reminding us of Queneau's use of the same technique in Part III of *Saint Glinglin*.

Baga too is the history of a dream world, a somewhat grimmer one than that of *Graal Flibuste*, but this time there is no prologue to hint to us that it *is* a dream world. The book begins with the flat statement, "I am a king." Admittedly, the narrator goes on to modify this assertion:

> Yes, a king. I am king of myself. Of my filth. I and my filth we have a king. I mean the filth of my mind. For I have a mind. (p. 7)

As the book continues, however, he insists more and more that he is a king in literal truth, not in metaphor. He has a minister, Baga, and a court routine; he receives ambassadors from the

[6] This is true of the complete edition as well as of the original one.

neighboring kingdom of Novocordie; he goes to war in person against Novocordie, leading his forces in his father's old taxi. Only at page 66 does he suggest that much of the account of the war is false, going on to insist, however, that a war did take place, although he was defeated rather than victorious. He is writing all this, he says, for the benefit of his nephews, one of whom will succeed him; writing is a difficult business:

> Decidedly, I lack method. Should one narrate as if things were over and done with or as if they were still going on? Sometimes I imagine that I am in process of doing what I am writing about. (p. 42)

He may, in effect, be inventing his life as he writes about it.

After the war, the king becomes a hermit in the forest for a time but decides that he is unfitted for such a life and returns to Baga. He confesses that he loves Baga and cannot live without him, although he does not desire him physically.

At this point there is a curious break in the narrative. The next chapter begins:

> This from another point of view. There is no palace or garden. There is a cave. In it, King Gnar. He has a counselor who is a serpent. As has been said somewhere.
>
> King Gnar is in possession of the hermit's letters. He reads them. (p. 92)

King Gnar belongs to the mythological part of *Graal Flibuste*, which is thus linked explicitly with *Baga*. There are five letters in all, love letters of a sort: the first begins very tenderly with "Dear soul," but the tone grows rapidly colder, so that the third begins "Dear Madam" and the fifth "Dear pus," the hermit-king having now discovered that he has contracted gonorrhea from his relations with the woman to whom he is writing. The series of letters stands revealed as an exercise in "black" humor.

In the next chapter the king adopts an orphan, Rara, and tries to remake him in his own image; but soon the king finds himself in prison, for no stated reason. He keeps a diary describing, among other things, his efforts to build a raft in order to escape. The dating of the diary becomes more and more eccentric: after reaching November 30, it goes on to the thirty-first and eventually to the sixty-first.

In the following chapter the king is on trial, apparently before God. The charge seems to be his love for Baga. Eventually, rather than confess in detail, the king asks to be condemned at once. He is led away by the guards.

Next follows "the intermezzo of the picnic," describing an official visit from Conegrund, the queen of Dualie. She is treated to a picnic which she turns into an orgy, eating and drinking with gross appetite and finally solacing herself with the king's Negro dishwasher.

In the second-last chapter, the king goes to a convent, turns into a woman, and becomes a nun. As Sister Angèle he/she keeps a pious diary. Sister Angèle becomes interested in a beautiful young girl named Marie, but the latter, instead of being won to the religious life, goes away with her lover. However, four months later Marie returns to live in the convent and expiate her sins. Sister Angèle realizes too late that she is in love with Marie. The diary which records this experience manages to be outrageously comic in its portrayal of the naïve piety and concupiscence of "Sister Angèle," with its constant refrain of "Drove away the evil thought." But the evil thoughts return and eventually refuse to be driven away.

In the final chapter the narrator becomes a man again and returns to Baga, who, faithful as ever, has been building him a new château in his absence. Their life together resumes its course after Baga has given him a scolding, and the book ends with Baga bringing him his tea next morning.

With *Baga*, as with *Graal Flibuste*, no allegorical interpretation seems possible. One must accept the book "as is," content to shake with helpless laughter at the black and blasphemous humor of the hermit's letters and Sister Angèle's diary, and to pick up little nuggets of philosophy from the Quixote-Panza dialogue of the narrator and Baga.

Yet it is possible to see *Baga* as in part a realistic study of hallucination. On page 282 of *L'Inquisitoire* the deaf servant describes an eccentric old man among his employers' acquaintances:

Those gentlemen called him Architruc a sort of screwball there's no other word for it he said he was king of somewhere or that he had been a king, Marthe thought that he was mad his servant too who accompanied him in his travels as he said but without a penny where could he travel to, he called him his minister in my opinion he must have been a sort of former Russian you remember they were all princes of somewhere those gentlemen let him think that they believed it yes I remember him and the minister they must have died soon after, those gentlemen never heard tell of them any more

On page 136 of *Baga* Queen Conegrund calls the narrator "*Architruc*" ("Archthingamajig," a sort of pun on *Archiduc*, the French for "Archduke"), the only time he is ever named. Hence the unnamed "minister" in *L'Inquisitoire* is undoubtedly Baga; if Marthe was right in thinking Architruc mad, then *Baga* may be his attempt at a literal record of his imagined adventures.

Pinget has also written a one-act play entitled *Architruc* (1961), containing four characters: the King; Baga, a minister; the Cook; Death. In this, we see Baga trying to entertain his master for an hour before dinner. Neither of them ever suggests that Architruc's kingship is imaginary, yet Baga's entertainment consists of a series of disguises, the first being that of an ambassador from the king of Novocordie; both Architruc and Baga share in the play-acting for a while, but the former keeps forgetting his kingly protocol and has to be coached by Baga, who must therefore lay aside his ambassadorial role for the moment. Baga's next appearance is as Architruc's Aunt Estelle; carried away by his feminine role, he tries to seduce the King, who remains virtuous. Next, Baga says he will disguise himself as God; he soon returns in the costume of a judge, ready to enact the Last Judgment. This project explains the trial chapter in *Baga*, but Architruc balks at enacting a similar scene in the play. The King feels ill and lies down; Baga suggests it is time for his master to adopt an heir, and they run through an amusing scene with Baga as the little boy and the King as the adoptive father. But the King is bored and dissatisfied, he wants a change, he still hopes for freedom and a new life. Baga packs a bag for their projected trip and then goes offstage to prepare his last disguise before dinner. Before he has time to return, Death enters in full medieval array of skeleton and shroud; the King mistakes him for Baga at first, but Death lays him low with his scythe. In answer to the King's dying cries, Baga, thinking he has grown impatient, calls out: "There we are. I'm coming." The curtain falls.

For all its originality, this play reminds one strongly of Beckett's *Waiting for Godot*: Baga and the King seem to be killing time by their play-acting, as Vladimir and Estragon do with their elaborate attempts at conversation. Each pair has been together so long that they find it hard to devise some new way of passing the time—until nightfall in Beckett's play, until dinner in Pinget's. One might say that in Pinget's play, although the two main characters are not waiting for him, "Godot" does come in the shape of Death. *Architruc* is a valid and interesting play in its own right, although the ending seems a little crude; but an audience familiar with *Baga* might find it more compelling than an unprepared one would. As we shall see, almost all of Pinget's plays to date are either byproducts or anticipations of his novels.

Pinget's last two novels before *L'Inquisitoire—Le Fiston*, 1959, and *Clope au dossier*, 1961—resemble each other very closely but represent a sharp break with their predecessors. In these new works, Pinget has gone far toward accepting the convention of realism, but at the core of each stands a solitary character—M. Levert, Clope—who sheds uncertainty upon everything around him. Each of these recluses is engaged, like so many of the protagonists of *le nouveau roman*, in writing something: Levert, an interminable letter, constantly recommenced and never posted, to his only son, who has disappeared; Clope, an equally interminable *dossier* to exculpate himself from a charge of murdering an old woman, who, he claims, committed suicide in his garden while he was firing at a bird, or at any rate in the air.

In each of these short but densely populated novels we find

a high proportion of impersonal, omniscient narrative and description presenting, in pedestrian detail, fragments from the life and surroundings not only of the central character but of other people, whose connections with him range from relative intimacy to total indifference—in some cases to ignorance of his very existence. One assumes that the observer of these impersonally recorded facts is the traditionally omniscient author until one finds quotations from the impersonal passages recurring in Levert's letter and Clope's porings over his dossier. There are also unsettling moments when the impersonal, omniscient observer—whoever he may be—suddenly abandons either his impersonality or his omniscience by confessing an interest in a character or partial ignorance of a character's actions or motives. In other words, the consistency of viewpoint that has become a fetish with critics of the novel—and to a large extent with novelists too—since the time of Henry James is constantly and doubtless systematically violated by Pinget in these two novels. In *L'Inquisitoire*, on the other hand, as we have seen, a totally consistent viewpoint is adopted.

The purpose behind this confusion of viewpoints, one presumes, is once more to criticize and call in question the convention of realism. The impersonally omniscient viewpoint is particularly open to criticism because it lulls the reader, and even the author, into the complacent notion that everything about a given person or situation can be known in real life, which is patently untrue. Pinget, having discovered in himself a remarkable gift for precisely this type of impersonal circumstantial narration, doubtless feels honor-bound to put the reader on his guard at intervals; it cannot be denied, however, that as a result the reader's task is made considerably more difficult.

Le Fiston, the longer and more complex of these two similar novels, introduces a technical device for which it is difficult to recall a precedent in the history of the novel; at about the halfway point, the book breaks off and begins again in the first person:

I'm starting over. I must have made a mistake at the beginning. I questioned Sophie Narre yesterday or the day before and other people other days and besides that I've thought it over, son, I decided it would be better to start everything over than to compromise your return by a mistake, you never know, maybe a half hour's mistake. Or that lousy bottle. Or maybe if I hadn't actually seen or known, the Moules for instance if there were only two of them and if Aunt Pacot or Alice or someone else wasn't maybe actually there. I'm starting over. This letter will never be mailed. I think in the part about Roger and his wife they might have gone back to Le Rouget with those friends on another day. (pp. 69–70; 80)[7]

Clearly, this forms a part of one of M. Levert's letters to his son; but in the first half of the book the Moule brothers, Aunt Pacot, and Alice were present only in the impersonal omniscient narration; furthermore, M. Levert himself was dealt with in the third person except when the reader was being presented with the first-person stream of consciousness which seemed to constitute M. Levert's letter, properly speaking. Must we then conclude that the entire book, third person "omniscient" as well as first person, is written by M. Levert? Apparently we must. At any rate, there seems no doubt that the entire second half must be read as the work of M. Levert.

But, as hinted in the quotation above, the second half of *Le Fiston* reveals an even more shocking abyss to the trusting reader: a great deal of the information he has been given in the first half is contradicted or altered in the second. The events that followed the funeral of Marie Chinze, which opens the book, were almost all erroneously related. The wife of Roger Chinze, Marie's elder brother, did not become ill on the way home; it was a friend of hers to whom this happened. Alice and her mother, Aunt Pacot, did not have a revealing encounter with Alice's lover, Georges. The curé did not have lunch at home and then go to visit a sick old woman. And so

[7] All quotations from *Monsieur Levert*, tr. Richard Howard (New York: Grove Press, 1961). The first page number refers to this edition; the number after the semicolon refers to *No Answer*, tr. Richard N. Coe (London: John Calder, 1961), a much less faithful translation than Howard's.

on and so on. Not merely the events but various identifications
of persons and even smaller details are contradicted: the curé's
maid's name is Martha, not Odette; Odette is someone else
entirely, the wife of Louis, who owns a *bistro*; not only were
there just two Moule brothers at the funeral, but the third
brother is one-legged, not one-armed. Most confusing of all,
perhaps, is the visit paid to Levert by his niece Francine. In
the first half she is a little girl who comes with her mother to
visit him at his country house, the Villa des Roches, at four
o'clock. In the second half, she is a girl of seventeen who
visits him at five o'clock, in his town house in Sirancy, after
her mother's death. An error, not of an hour but of a whole
decade, seems to have crept in here. A possible explanation,
not necessarily to be given any weight, is offered by Levert's
brother-in-law:

> And what about his work, is he going on with it? that's more
> upsetting than all the rest if you ask me, I'll bet he's been
> copying the same page for the last ten years. (pp. 25–6; 27)

It is indeed possible that Levert has been rewriting his account
of the day of Marie Chinze's funeral throughout a decade.
Faced with such contradictions within *Le Fiston* itself, we
can make light of the fact that in *L'Inquisitoire* (p. 158)
Levert's son is called Philippe, whereas in *Le Fiston* he is
called Gilbert; perhaps the deaf servant's memory (or Pinget's) had failed him.

Confronted with the realization that "omniscient" narrative
can prove to be nescient, the reader wonders what rock he can
still cling to in the whirlpool that is *Le Fiston*. Ignoring for
the moment the obvious consideration that in a work of fiction
nothing has to be true, we may say that at least Levert had a
son who left him and disappeared without trace. Probably not
even the son could give the "real" reasons for their falling-out.
Levert offers many, ranging from the son's attachment to his
dead mother, who had become a drug addict, to the trivial
notion that the son did not like the new curtains in his room.
It seems "certain" that the son became a drunkard after the
mother's death and that the father drank with him to try to

retain some hold on him; also, after the son's departure to
seek "a new life," the father drank in the son's favorite bar,
hoping that Gilbert would return there. The letter at times
grows so incoherent that it seems as though Levert is drinking
while he writes. At one point, for a few lines, the syllables
become scrambled in a kind of spoonerism; it is hard to sort
them out until one realizes that this passage is a reprise of the
opening lines of the book: "The shoemaker's daughter is dead"
(p. 7 of New York edition) becomes "The doeshaughter's
baker is mead" (p. 64). (The corresponding pages in the
London edition are 5 and 76.)

The obsession with the funeral of Marie Chinze, the shoemaker's daughter, is partially explained by the suggestion
that she was M. Levert's illegitimate daughter, but Levert
himself never offers any positive assurance that he even had
sexual relations with her mother. Nevertheless, the story of
Marie's unhappy love affair with a certain Léon, as remembered by Minet, her younger brother, is the most moving
narrative passage in the book. This occurs in the first half and
is balanced in the second half by the story of a happy love
affair between Georges's sister, Margot, and her brother's
friend, Rodolphe. These two short interludes appeal to the
reader's emotions far more effectively than the maunderings of
M. Levert, who has only one thing to say, however many different ways he may find to say it. What should be the highly
personal heart of the book remains bloodless beside these little
impersonal narratives on the periphery.

The deaf servant in L'Inquisitoire succeeds where M. Levert
fails, in taking us into the very core of his being. There are
other failures in Le Fiston too which are redressed in L'Inquisitoire. The earlier book contains a number of inventories of
furniture and descriptions of houses, all of which are boring
because of their impersonality. On the other hand, similar descriptions in L'Inquisitoire pulse with life because of their
deeply felt human associations. Among all this deadwood,
however, Le Fiston contains one huge slab of "building
material" that achieves an existential solidity: the description
of the local cemetery in which M. Levert takes a walk at night.

It is seen impersonally rather than through his eyes, but a cemetery is such an evocative place that it can stand on its own, especially as so many of the family names have taken on authenticity through their recurrence in Pinget's work. (The passage occurs at pp. 55–60 of the New York edition and at pp. 66–72 of the London one.) At the heart of this description lies the unadorned notation: "Next Germaine Levert *née* Pisson 1900–1940. Next an empty plot. Next . . ." (p. 59; 71). One assumes that the empty plot awaits "Edouard Levert called home to God the twelfth twelfth twelfth nineteen hundred and so on" (p. 121; 146). As the last sentence of the book says, "Except for what is written there is death."

And what *is* written?

> . . . for instance, at various dates which I do not give in order, the unexpected arrival of my niece, meeting woman in the woods, the news of the funeral, the tedious pursuit of unknown persons of both sexes [Alice, Aunt Pacot, Roger, the two Moules, and others?], the memory of the houses my wife and I lived in, the visit to a cemetery, the confusion at different dates and for different reasons of characters relating facts and gestures of other characters at such and such a date, the substitution of names, the writing of a letter, and the urgent duty of creating for myself other habits putting me outside the range of any emotion henceforth. The success has surpassed my hopes, it seems that the cycle is complete, the revolution has not been bloody. (pp. 121–2; 146–7)

In such an ambiguous book, one is not prepared to accept the last sentence of this quotation at face value; nevertheless, it is possible to believe that Levert has written himself out of his anguish into a sort of tranquillity; it is also possible, since he continues to write to his son for a few pages more, to believe the contrary.

In 1959, the same year as *Le Fiston*, Pinget published a play on the same subject as the novel, *Lettre morte*.[8] One cannot exactly describe it as a dramatization of the novel, although many passages are identical or similar in both works.

---

[8] "Dead Letter," tr. Barbara Bray, in Robert Pinget, *Plays*, Vol. 1 (London: John Calder, 1963).

Rather, the whole subject has been reworked, more simply, for dramatic presentation. The play is in two acts, one taking place in a bar, the other in a post office. The barman and the post-office clerk are to be played by the same actor. Most of both acts consists of a dialogue between Levert and the good-natured young employee, who tries to comfort him but admits that he himself has left his parents. In the first act, the two other characters in the cast make their only appearance; they are a touring actor and actress, Fred and Lili, who act out various portions of the vulgar, sentimental comedy, *The Prodigal Son*, that they are performing at the local theatre. In such a play, naturally, the son *does* return in response to his father's letters. As Martin Esslin writes in *The Theatre of the Absurd* (New York: Anchor Books, 1961), p. 197:

> Here the worn-out convention of boulevard theatre, where everything happens as it should, is cruelly confronted with that of the Theatre of the Absurd where nothing happens at all and where the lines of dialogue do not flit wittily to and fro like ping-pong balls but are as repetitious and inconclusive as in real life. . . .

Clope au dossier ("Clope on File," or "Clope at His File"), a work that can exert a compulsive attraction upon a receptive reader, remains in the end a mystery. Why is Clope keeping a dossier on himself and how much of the novel's contents are we to consider as forming part of this file? The only punishable act that Clope seems to have committed is to fire a shot from his garden in a fairly thickly inhabited area and to bring down a wild goose from a flight passing overhead. Although there are vague hints at the end of the novel that something more sinister may have occurred, we must turn to a play of which Clope is the protagonist, *Ici ou ailleurs*,[9] also published in 1961, to find something more specific. In Act II of the play, Clope tells Pierrot that an old woman committed suicide in or near his garden, the shot going off virtually simultaneously with the one that he fired in the air. Pierrot, however, is not

[9] "Clope," tr. Barbara Bray, in Robert Pinget, *Plays*, Vol. 1.

convinced that Clope is telling the truth, and we have seen in
Clope au dossier that some of his neighbors think the old man
is out of his mind. Clope seems to be haunted by a dead
woman at the end of the novel, but the ghost is identified at
one point (p. 132) with his mother, who had been dead for
years before the mysterious shot. One really does not know
what to believe, but at any rate the novel concerns itself
almost entirely with the day on which the shot was fired at
the wild goose, just as *Le Fiston* focuses on the day of Marie
Chinze's funeral. Clope, like M. Levert, is regarded by his
neighbors as a man who has begun to brood because he has no
regular work to do, though he is by no means as wealthy as
Levert. (Incidentally, on p. 84 of *Clope au dossier* we learn
that Levert was found dead in a ditch the year before.)

The approximately 130 pages of the novel are divided into
six enormous paragraphs. The first of these "paragraphs" or
chapters (pp. 7–39) deals with the actual shooting of the wild
goose by Clope and with what a number of other characters
were doing at the time they heard (or did not hear but could
have heard, or did not hear and could not possibly have heard)
the shot. The first group of three men—Mortin, Philippard,
and Dansot, nicknamed "Verveine"—happen to be discussing
Clope's eccentricity and saying that "They'll finish by taking
him away" when the shot goes off. Simone Brize, the wife of
a certain Pierrot who is doubtless Pierre Moule of *Le Fiston*,
does not hear the shot as she prepares lunch for herself and
her little son, Guillaume. Judge Pommard's maid hears the
shot, but the judge himself does not, being immersed in a legal
document. Among others who hear it is an old, one-eyed
beggar named Toupin who plays a barrel-organ on the bridge.
We then see what most of these characters were doing earlier
in the morning. Finally we are shown the galley of a big cargo
boat where Pierrot and his fellow cooks are working, quarreling, and discussing the girls they will go with in the next port.

Almost all this chapter is presented in impersonal omniscient
narrative, but an occasional phrase is interjected that suggests a personal point of view: *"Tympan détraqué"* ("Ear-
drum out of order"), for instance, which pops up from

nowhere on page 19 and recurs throughout the book, especially in Clope's final soliloquy. Notice also the chain of free associations with the word *"temps"* (pp. 27–8), which appears to be Clope's. Elsewhere the phrase *"Du nerf"* ("Courage!" or "Try hard") seems to be a leitmotiv for Clope.

The second paragraph or chapter (pp. 39–64) deals entirely with Simone *née* Brize, telling us how her day began on this Monday, apparently so fateful for Clope. We get an extraordinarily faithful picture of the exasperating, not-quite-comic routine gone through by the mother of a small boy who is not yet housebroken, in a miserable little apartment. He urinates on her bed, has to be coaxed into eating and allowing himself to be washed and dressed, and spills ink all over his clean clothes as soon as he is left alone for a moment. In this chapter, again, everything seems to be told impersonally—except while Simone is washing herself. Then, suddenly, we become conscious of a narrator:

> She takes the wash-glove hanging on a string above the sink with other things a pair of pants a rag a towel she soaks it in warm water, she rubs it with Marseille soap from the soap-dish on the wall, she begins with her face. Then under the arms then that's it here we are her pink breasts turning brown at the tips let's savor it, she rinses, then more soap from the soap-dish let's savor it she passes the wash-glove between her legs that's it her thighs ah she's separating them, she bends over. Simone's ass. Pink plump melting. . . . (pp. 51–2)

The book contains no other quite so drastic violation of impersonality, but the use of the first person on page 88 and in one or two other places should also be noted. These sometimes humorous failures in impersonality are accompanied by occasional failures in omniscience, both in this chapter and elsewhere. Rather whimsically, the narrator cannot keep track of all the pots of water that Simone must heat on the gas stove in order to wash Guillaume and herself:

> . . . a rag soaked in the hot water what hot water the remainder or if not she must have put on some more to heat before after the second washing of the little fellow. . . . (p. 59)

This becomes a sort of running gag, as there are other references to the problematical hot water on pp. 51 and 63. There is not a single reference to Clope in this chapter, but Simone is a lonely figure in the absence of her husband and thus resembles Clope somewhat.

No reference is made to Clope in the next chapter (pp. 64–87) either; it consists entirely of a conversation between Toupin, the organ-grinder, and old Pommard, the father of the judge, both of whom are in their seventies. They have not met for a long time; during the interval, Toupin has slipped down in the social scale while Pommard has risen by virtue of his children's success; yet they were more or less equals in their youth. They talk about the good old days, when the seasons were much warmer than they are now; about their military service; about the younger generation and how much more selfish and lazy it is than theirs; about their wives, Toupin's living and Pommard's dead; about the first automobiles they remember and the current folly of trying to explore the moon; and finally about the girls they used to know, including Germaine Pisson, the late Mme Levert. Both speak indistinctly, having trouble with their teeth, and find that their memories are no longer reliable; still, they are glad to be alive.

This whole chapter was turned into a radio play with very little alteration except for the addition of street noises and barrel-organ music; it was published as *La Manivelle* in 1960, accompanied by an adaptation into English on facing pages, written by Samuel Beckett. Beckett's version, which reads very much like an excerpt from a play by Sean O'Casey, was first broadcast by the British Broadcasting Corporation's Third Programme on August 23, 1960, and bears the title *The Old Tune*. It has been reprinted in the London edition of Pinget's *Plays*, Vol. 1, 1963.

The fourth chapter (pp. 88–107) describes the bridge on which Toupin has set up his barrel-organ and a painter named Maurice Legendre his easel. In the middle of this Monday morning various people, mostly women going to the market, pass over the bridge and speak to Toupin or Legendre. We see

Mme Philippard, Mme Dansot, and others; also Simone Brize again. The chapter finishes by turning to Mme Mortin, not in mid-morning, but at dawn, when she was awakened by noises from the maid's room; she knows very well that the maid's lover is there, and she roams the house and garden, obviously dissatisfied with her husband.

The fifth chapter (pp. 107–24) begins, "Simone when she goes to bed what does she think about." Obviously this implies a narrator, but the rest of the chapter is strictly impersonal in viewpoint, though it evokes a most intimate picture of Simone's reveries and dreams, in which she longs for Pierrot, imagines their love-making, fears a rival, finds herself married in a dream to Jean, a former suitor. She feels she would rather be beaten every day or be dead than endure these constant separations, but she realizes that Pierrot likes his life and the prostitutes of the ports he visits. She feels that she is not perverse enough for him and begins to imagine some of the things she might do; then, full of revulsion, she thinks of herself as an unworthy mother who will bring bad luck to Guillaume. In another dream she imagines herself married to her son. Eventually Guillaume's crying awakens her in terror.

It is impossible to summarize all the thoughts and emotions that pass through Simone's consciousness within this quite short chapter. One can only describe it as a masterpiece of psychological realism, without pausing to inquire too closely just what the word "realism" means here. Clope is mentioned once as she remembers her wedding:

> Even Monsieur Clope had given her that table mat which had come to him from his mother he said with a trembling in his voice. Monsieur Clope. (p. 120)

Finally, in the sixth chapter, there is Clope's soliloquy as he puts the finishing touches to the dossier that he faintly hopes will prove his innocence, so that "they" will be unable to do anything to him. He broods over some of the seemingly pointless details already recorded in the book, but mainly he is reliving his search all over his garden and in the river behind it for proofs; he does not seem to have found much except the tortoise-shell frame of an old pair of spectacles; he sees the ghost of a woman doing her washing and the ghost of his mother—unless they are both the same. At one point he thinks of hanging himself, at another of hiding in a loft, but the only hint of what causes his fear and his obsessions is a phrase on page 126: *morte par ce coup venait de se flan-quer une balle* ("dead by that shot had just put a bullet into herself"). The book dies away in a murmur of "no time left no time left no time left."

The reader of *Clope au dossier* closes the book with the feeling that he has a lot of building material here, of impressive solidity, if he could only erect it into a coherent structure. The comings and goings of the little village (neither Agapa nor Sirancy, perhaps Fantoine?) within hearing of Clope's shot and Toupin's barrel-organ are vividly suggested, though not exhaustively set forth. A whole phase of Simone Brize's life has been defined with an accuracy that her own memories will never supply when she looks back on it. Toupin and old Pommard are archetypes of the garrulous old man, yet each is sharply individualized. Are we to imagine that Clope has reconstructed these people's lives on a certain Monday out of his memory, his imagination, and the interminable small talk and gossip with which village folk relive in excruciating detail each moment of their own and others' lives? And if he is capable of such clear, firm reconstruction, why is his own reverie so incoherent and imprecise?

Pinget's major creative efforts since 1962 have been devoted to what one might call "the Mortin cycle." This series of works, which revolves around still another semi-recluse and failed writer similar to Clope and Monsieur Levert, consists of the following:

1. A dramatic monologue entitled *L'Hypothèse* (*The Hypothesis*), published in a volume of plays along with *Ici ou ailleurs* and *Architruc* in 1961

2. *Autour de Mortin* (*About Mortin*), a series of dialogues for radio, first printed in September 1965[10]
3. A novel, *Quelqu'un* (*Someone*), published December 1965, winner of the Prix Femina, and thus the first of Pinget's works to reach a really wide circle of readers
4. *Le Libera* ("The *Libera* [*nos, Domine*]"), a novel published in 1968

The last of these is only peripherally concerned with Mortin, but it reveals ("suggests" or "hints" might be a better word) that the anonymous narrator of *Quelqu'un* may be Mortin. At any rate, Alexandre Mortin appears in *Le Libera* as the sole proprietor of a *pension* (boarding house) that was the joint property of the narrator and his friend Gaston in *Quelqu'un*. Several of the boarders are named in both books. One, Vérassou, is spoken of as dead in *Le Libera*, whereas he was definitely alive throughout *Quelqu'un*; hence Gaston may be thought of as having died between the epoch of *Quelqu'un* and that of *Le Libera*.

But the careful reader of the Mortin books must become convinced of a fact that he was beginning to suspect in earlier Pinget novels: far from seeking a Balzacian consistency—which Balzac himself sometimes missed either through a failure of memory or through his pursuit of some overriding artistic goal—Pinget scarcely bothers his head about consistency in chronology, topography, characterization, or even nomenclature. To take the last point first, there is, for example, a pharmacist nicknamed Verveine in both *Clope au dossier* and *Le Libera*; in the former book, his real name is given as Dansot, in the latter as Cruze. Other instances of such minor inconsistencies have been noted earlier, along with some confusion between the inhabitants of Fantoine and Sirancy.

A preoccupation with exact chronology has been one of the hallmarks of realism in the novel: think of *Tom Jones*, or even

---

[10] Both *The Hypothesis* and *About Mortin*, as well as *Architruc*, appear in Robert Pinget, *Plays*, Vol. 2, tr. Barbara Bray (London: Calder and Boyars, 1967). The translation is basically effective but marred by errors in proper names ("Biaule" for "Bianle," *passim*; "Trutaz" for "Truitaz") and by a more serious muddle on p. 99.

of *Ulysses,* for all its large component of fantasy. To Pinget, however, chronology means nothing. Anything in the past is almost always identified by his characters as having happened "ten years ago," neither more nor less. It is quite impossible to fit the years at the *pension* into the outline of Mortin's life given in *Autour de Mortin.* Furthermore, although *Quelqu'un* seems to be earlier in time than *Le Libera,* there is mention in the former book of renting a television set, which would identify the period as post-World War II. Yet the only war referred to in *Le Libera* is the 1914–18 one. In fact, it is impossible to recall, throughout Pinget's *oeuvre,* a single unequivocal reference to World War II.

As for consistency in characterization, the whole burden of *Autour de Mortin* is that this shibboleth of novelists involves outrageous falsification. The core of this little masterpiece is a series of eight "recorded" interviews with people who claim to have known the late Monsieur Mortin. Not only can the interviewees not agree about matters of hearsay—such as whether Mortin was a bachelor or a widower, childless or the father of one or more legitimate or illegitimate children— but they contradict each other on matters of direct personal observation: some say he was cheerful and talkative, others that he was gloomy and taciturn. We cannot even discover from their evidence whether he was an original author or a mere plagiarist. For once, Pinget seems to have taken infinite pains to convey an illusion of realism: if these dialogues were broadcast by competent professional actors, it would be easy for the radio audience to believe in the authenticity of the interviews and of Mortin. Yet, the more one accepts the sincerity of the speakers, the more confused one becomes about the "real" character of Mortin. But then, the people we meet in life, as opposed to literature, are often at least as hard to characterize as Mortin, so that the illusion of realism is here linked with the elusiveness of reality.

In a letter of July 14, 1965, to me M. Pinget, referring to himself in the third person, spoke of *"sa hantise . . . des efforts à accomplir pour sonder la seule réalité qui soit, son âme . . ."* ("his being haunted . . . by the efforts required to fathom the only reality there is, his soul . . ."). Ultimately, Mortin and all the other solitary figures who sit writing, writing, in the novels of Pinget must be surrogates for the author. The narrator of *Quelqu'un*, whoever he may be, sounds very like the author of *L'Inquisitoire* when he writes:

> Who is questioning me? Nobody, good Lord. Don't let them come and tell me that I'm answering questions. Because they've said that. They had said that. About my other lives, when I tried to rid myself of them. He's answering questions, see. It must be the police. It sounds like the police, he's compelled to answer, he's being coerced, hunted down. Stupid blunders like that. I really must have gone the wrong way about wording it. To have deceived myself that much, to give such a wrong impression. What a nuisance! Talent is what I'm always short of. In short, I don't want to give the impression that I'm answering questions. (p. 17)

A few pages later, the narrator writes:

> In one of my other lives, watch it, I've never had more than one, I mean my other accounts [*exposés*], I said that I was king of my filth. (p. 30)

This is almost a direct quotation from the opening words of *Baga*—already quoted earlier in this chapter.

In restrospect, *Quelqu'un* may prove to be Pinget's most successful effort "to fathom the only reality," though its introversion makes it a less immediately attractive book than *L'Inquisitoire*. The latter probes deeply into the soul (*âme* = soul, psyche, mind, spirit, essence, heart—it is untranslatable by any single English word) of the old servant and therefore, by extension, into the soul of its author and of all of us. But *Quelqu'un* approaches closer to its author because it is the record of a writer writing. The narrator—Mortin or another— is not a professional author: as a hobby, since he has retired from the business world and Gaston takes care of the management of the *pension*, he is at work on

> . . . a treatise on plants. Not at all technical, not at all literary. Observations that I have made. I haven't yet mentioned a

quarter, a tenth of the plants in our part of the country. . . .
(p. 14)

But on the day described in *Quelqu'un* he cannot find the piece of paper which has written on it the piece of information that he needs to continue his book, and he hunts high and low for it through the house and garden. Why he should then sit down and write an account of his fruitless search for the piece of paper, struggling with his faulty memory to reconstruct the entire day, is never clearly explained. Nor need it be: the search for the piece of paper becomes a pretext for the reconstruction of a whole way of life, not merely that of the somewhat alienated narrator but of all the inhabitants of the boarding house. The nearest approach to an explanation offered is the following, which reminds one of M. Levert:

> I have an amateur's interest in botany. From time to time I write an account of my life in order to be rid of it, to set free my mind. What I'm doing at the moment is different, though not very. I say that I'm looking for a paper that I need for my botany manuscript and I'm afraid of having to talk about my life in this connection, but if the occasion presents itself, I will talk about it, especially about those around me. Simple, isn't it? Makes sense, doesn't it? Yes. The one and only thing that bothers me is preciseness. (pp. 38–9)

It is a cruelly hot day in July, and many of the boarders have already gone on vacation, as has the cook, leaving the maid, Marie, in charge. All through the year, those who have not yet gone on vacation tell themselves and each other that it is time they went: "*Ça vous changera les idées.*" The literal translation of the French cliché is "That will change your ideas for you" (meaning something like the English "That will make a nice change for you"), but of course nobody's ideas ever do change, and as the table conversation at lunch or dinner stumbles on, everybody knows what everybody else is going to say next. The only real change of ideas occurs one summer when everybody has gone away except the narrator and a retarded adolescent nicknamed Fonfon: the narrator rents a television set for a month and shares Fonfon's delight in the serial exploits of a Captain Corcoran.

It is with Fonfon that the narrator has his most satisfactory relationship; as he says on page 127, apart from sheer necessity, Fonfon is his chief reason for continuing with the *pension*; sensitive as he is to fancied slights from others, he knows that even when Fonfon disobeys him it is not out of malice. But in spite of his general disgust with his surroundings and himself, the narrator is revealed as something of a saint. Because of his own sensitivity, he is aware when the feelings of others are hurt by their fellow boarders, and he tries to soothe the ruffled ones.

Quelqu'un is almost as difficult to render a coherent account of as Beckett's *The Unnamable*, since the same events and the same themes for meditation are repeated over and over again. When the narrator loses the thread of his story, he tends to go back to eight o'clock in the morning, when he was awakened by Marie. He first writes *"Je me suis levé à huit heures. . . ."* ("I got up at eight") on page 11 of the original French edition; this is then repeated on pp. 26, 39, 52, 57, 181, and 190. After harking back for the last time, he decides on page 191 that he has recommenced too far back. Clearly, since the book ends on page 257, the longest, most circumstantial account of his day occurs between pp. 57 and 181. This trick of beginning again from the beginning has been encountered already in Butor's *Degrees*, but it has a totally different effect there. Pinget's narrator insists on the poorness of his memory, and goes back to the beginning in order to stimulate the recall of some detail that has eluded him. Part of his difficulty lies in the fact that one day so closely resembles another: on the day he is trying to remember, as we have noted, some of the boarders are on vacation, yet during one meal which he describes they are all at the table. When he discovers his error, he does not bother to cross out what he has written. Part of the book's curious effect comes from this refusal to erase anything. We have the sensation of being present during the creation of a work of art—as we do in Robbe-Grillet's *La Maison de rendez-vous*—instead of reading the finished product with all the false starts eliminated. This, in effect, is a new way of supplying us with the raw material.

As always in Pinget, there are a few longer "set-pieces" in the midst of the fragmentary confusion, the *caca* ("pooh-pooh" or some such baby language for excrement), as the narrator often calls it. One is the description of lunch, pp. 122–47: the narrator takes us around the table, describing each of the boarders (including those who are in fact away on vacation), their typical conversation, Fonfon's clumsiness and the reaction of the boarders to it, the hostility between the maid and some of the boarders, and so on. The whole episode is described in a dryly humorous way:

> Generally speaking when we talk of the butcher Madame Cointet says to her husband you remember the roast beef on the Borromean Islands. They went there thirty years ago, long before coming to stay with us. At Isola Bella, the menu of June 25th, I forget why, and that roast beef that melted in your mouth, and the dessert, and the flowers on the island, the boat-trip on the lake, and it goes on with Lugano and Montreux. And when they say the wrong thing, Reber corrects them though she's never been there—she knows the story by heart. (p. 136)

Occasionally the humor could be described as "black":

> Sometimes it's Vérassou who takes over. . . . He talks about what he's seen at the hospital or what he's been told, incurable cases, amputations, highway accidents with details that take away my appetite or what's left of it but not theirs, not at all, especially the women. Like mustard or pickles, it makes their mouths water, they ask for more, they want more details. They eat their tainted meat and lick their chops. Does the subconscious imagine that it's chomping on the sawn-off leg or the testicle that's being torn off? (p. 138)

The mood may even change to the pathetic, though not for long:

> Tut, tut, I said, there's no more vinegar, I'll get some in the kitchen. I went there. And there I saw this dreadful thing, Marie weeping as she chewed her beefsteak. She didn't even

pretend to wipe her eyes or to be gagging, she didn't look at
me, she didn't stop chewing. I pretended I hadn't seen anything and I took the vinegar from the cupboard. I leant over
the sink so as not to spill all over the place and I filled the
thingamajig. I said to myself, I've got to say something to her,
I've got to think of something, I can't let her go on crying
like that. And the thingamajig overflowed. Marie yelled that's
it, dump the works in the sink, then everyone'll say that it's
me wastes the groceries. I was saved. I brought the vinegar
back to the dining room. She's crying, I said to Gaston. He
said she'll piss less. It didn't bother him at all, or the others.
Did they mean it wasn't their affair, that it was because of
me? I kept my trap shut. (pp. 142–3)

Another of these set-pieces is devoted to the boarding-house
photograph album, full of bittersweet memories. It begins
with the photographs taken when Gaston and the narrator
first met again after many years and decided to go into business together. First there is the narrator, taken by Gaston;
then Gaston, taken by the narrator, then both of them together:

Third photo, below, Gaston and I at the same spot. We had
asked a passer-by, a cyclist who was wheeling his machine
along the sidewalk. He put down his bike and took us. In it
you can see better than ever that my smile is false and Gaston's
isn't. At least I see it. I almost remember too saying to myself
let's get closer to him, make it look nice, but not too close so
as not to be ridiculous. And you can see that the upper part of
me is closer to him, but my feet are farther to the left and
I'm almost losing my balance. It's lousy to know yourself the
way I do, you never get any pleasure, never a surprise. (p. 200)

Perhaps no passage better reveals the narrator's anguished,
self-hating self-consciousness; yet he goes on hoping against
hope for a miracle: for example, that the impact of television
will "save" Fonfon, bring him out of his retarded state; but
Gaston and he can't afford a television if they're going to get
the washing machine that Gaston has his heart set on. As the
album shows, they used to take the boarders for picnics on
weekends in earlier days, until it became a bore like everything else. The narrator wonders if they couldn't do something
similar now to brighten all their lives:

As I said to Gaston, since we haven't succeeded in putting new heart into ourselves all these years, let's think up something for our guests, to see them happy will smarten us up a bit perhaps. He answered say, you get bright ideas, do you think I came down in the last shower, my washing machine, don't you understand. I had pulled another boner. (p. 254)

And so the book stumbles to a close which is not in any sense a conclusion. The same old mistakes will be repeated tomorrow; the "little future" that the narrator tried to plan will never come. After dinner,

Reber serves the coffee. Two lumps of sugar for Apostolos, two for me, one for Gaston. I don't take any. She [Reber] went back to her knitting. Gaston was leafing through the prospectus of the washing machine which has a permanent place on the Moroccan pedestal table. Apostolos suggested a game of bezique to me. Courage. She married the king of hearts with the queen of diamonds. She told me I play better than Madame Cointet, it's odd because she's such a habitual card player. Marie came back to gather up the cups. She must be bored alone in the kitchen, she was looking for something to say. She couldn't find anything and I was too fed up to find it for her. She went out again. Bezique. No, you've made another mistake, it's queen of spades and knave of diamonds, not the opposite, you see you've done the opposite. She said it's funny, every time I make the same mistake. Then we spoke of going off on vacations. Reber was leaving the beginning of September, Apostolos wasn't leaving. She wouldn't put on her beautiful dress.

This time it's finished.

The little future is done for.

Say what I did after the women had gone up to their rooms again. Gaston was in his armchair, looking preoccupied. I said to him why don't you go visit your mother, that would change your ideas for you. He said to me she's not feeling well, my sister will go and look after her. He went to sort his bills. (pp. 256–7)

Le Libera, whose title refers to a litany, "O Lord, deliver us," from the Roman Catholic burial service, vies in difficulty

with some of Pinget's earliest works. Subject and object seem
to have become fused or confused, so that it is impossible to
be sure who is telling the story or precisely what the story is.
At first we think we are reading a sort of mystery story about
the strangling of a child in the woods near Fantoine, the
inevitable ten years ago. Later we begin to think that that
child or another was not strangled but run over by a truck at a
dangerous crossing in the village. Or that a third child or the
same one wandered off and was drowned in the river. There
are also a number of alternative stories about a number of
alternative adults. We begin to realize that we are hearing
the voices of the village gossips spinning their unreliable and
mutually contradictory yarns, day in, day out, without respite.
Those not addicted to Pinget would be prepared to bet that
he could not keep this sort of thing going for over two hundred pages; or that, if he could, no sane man could be found
to read it all. Sane or not, I read *Le Libera* at somewhere near
twice my normal speed for absorbing colloquial French. How
is such a book ever to be translated into colloquial British
or American idiom, though? Short of the collaboration of a
writer of Beckett's stature, as in the translation of *La Manivelle*, one feels that the task is flatly impossible. I here and
now offer my *mea culpa* for the mistranslations I am about
to commit.

One thing that we notice very soon about this book is the
extraordinary number of paragraphs beginning with "*Ou
que . . .*" ("Or that . . ."), introducing alternative versions of
every piece of gossip. Obviously each gossip would categori-
cally assert the truth of her version, so there must be *somebody*
desperately trying to set things down as he has heard them.
Occasionally toward the end there seems to be a voice saying
"Write . . ." and another saying "Don't interrupt me," but
whose they are never becomes clear. The narrative technique
of *Le Libera* can be seen as a logical development of that of
Le Fiston: the more recent book simply offers the reader a
much greater choice among conflicting versions of each
episode.

As the names slip and slide, Odette becoming Monette and

then Odette again, Mlle Ronzière becoming Mlle Lozière, Apostolos becoming Apollonios, and so on indefinitely, one begins to notice the insouciant formula of one or more of the gossips: *moi les noms vous savez* (approximately meaning "you know me when it comes to names").

One always assumes that the gossips are women, though Verveine the pharmacist, one of the most inveterate gossips of all, is in fact male. At any rate, their chatter is studded with euphemisms appropriate to pious old women of both sexes. One absolutely indispensable, all-purpose word is *parfaitement* (literally meaning "perfectly," but probably best rendered in English by "just so"). Doubtless the speaker makes a pregnant pause, which her audience fills with "just so." For instance, a Jesuit is alleged to have been seen committing pederasty with an altar boy; this is how the gossips phrase it:

> . . . in short one evening during the mission Madame Moineau returning home very late from the sewing circle had noticed a sound of panting in a hedge, she had been afraid but suddenly recognized in the moonlight the Rev. Father in the act of just so [*parfaitement*] the Tourniquet boy, that's where the love of children was leading him, he hadn't heard her in the heat of the action you may well say, she had gone away on tiptoe and as soon as she was home had alerted several of those ladies by telephone, what should she do, warn the parish priests, the police, the whole kit and caboodle [*tout le tremblement*]. . . . (p. 132)

Or again, *parfaitement* becomes the equivalent of the male genitals in the following passage:

> . . . in parenthesis Passavoine is still a handsome man and I've heard it said that as regards the just so [*le parfaitement*] he's all there . . . not like that poor Magnin to name only him who it seems is no bigger than that and stupid into the bargain. . . . (p. 109)

Another favorite expression is *qui vous savez* ("you know who"), which rounds off many a sentence with intimacy and conviction. Unfortunately, we readers usually haven't the

faintest notion who is meant, nor can we be sure that the
hearer, or even the speaker, knows either.

Suddenly, in the midst of this welter of innuendo, we come
on a paragraph (Who can have written or spoken it? Did it
write or speak itself in the confusion of subject and object?)
that cuts through it all incisively, judging it and finding it
wanting:

> Which would amount to saying that the whole psycho
> psychi life of our little society rested on one or two sentences
> in the air, some trumped-up assertions about no matter who
> and no matter what, emanating from two or three people at
> most who, generally without knowing it, would have set the
> tone for conversations for years past or, better still, for the
> behavior of our fellow citizens, yes it surely was funny, this
> network of gossip and absurd notions had conditioned our
> existence so thoroughly that a stranger settling among us
> would not have resisted it long and having come to practice the
> profession of baker let's say he would infallibly have branched
> off into that of child murderer for example, his responsibility
> having nothing to do with the matter, which would explain
> among other things why our scribblers who set out to be
> critics or novelists should have remained at the stage of
> writing newspaper serials or meteo [meteorological?] columns,
> poetry anthologists included, such was Mortin's opinion. . . .
> (p. 145)

We see that the judgment is ultimately attributed to Mortin,
but this does not, of course, make him the author of the
passage.

In comparison with the stylistic unity of *Quelqu'un*, we
should note the variety of styles in *Le Libera*: although the
gossipy style is preponderant, the passage just quoted is not
particularly colloquial except for the "*psycho psychi*" phrase,
which occurs frequently elsewhere in the book. The user
clearly cannot remember whether the word he wants is
"psychological" or "psychic" or possibly "psychiatric," and is
not in any case sure how to pronounce any of them. Besides
this fairly literate style and the usual folksy one, we find
pastiches of other styles, including the stilted passage on pp.
208–11 which begins:

Which was none other than the faithful relation by Sister Lorpailleur (it's Edmée, is it not?) of those [i.e., the relations] existing between Monnard and the schoolmistress. . . . (p. 208)

The great comic set-piece in *Le Libera*, the account of the annual concert given in the coach house of Alexandre Mortin's *pension* by Mlle Lozière and her pupils, is a treasury of contorted styles. The passage (pp. 158–75) manages to be pathetically dignified and wildly funny all at the same time. Pinget addicts will find other set-pieces involving lunch parties at the Château de Bonne-Mesure, with Mlle Ariane in fine fettle, and at the Château de Broy with its "campy" inhabitants.

Various hints toward the end of the novel lead one to believe that the whole book may have been put together by Mortin, the *raté*, the failed writer—this passage especially, recalling "Except for what is written there is death" in *Le Fiston*:

> And one could have wondered what Mortin was up to just then in his room, he was *au courant* with the relations . . . with the affair and having announced pompously to his guests that he had undertaken to reconstruct the drama, perhaps he was putting down something, who knows . . . he was so secretive, he hardly ever opened up, tinkering with rough drafts in his room then, disjointed elements of what might have been . . . who knows and his nose so buried in it that an impartial reader would have racked his brains over it, odds and ends mixed up with glimmerings. . . .
>
> And his nose so buried in it that death must have surprised him in that position. . . . (p. 212)

The book ends with a funeral, whether Mortin's or someone else's, possibly that of the dead child. The last page dies away in disjointed, cryptic sentences, the third-last of which, significantly, is *Plus question de finir* ("No question now of finishing").

And indeed there is no question now of finishing this account of Pinget's career as a novelist. Fifty years of age in 1970, he seems at the height of his powers, with twenty books at least still waiting to be written. Even if his life's work were completed, it would be difficult to give a final assessment here. So much time must be spent explaining—and, where it cannot be explained, describing—the work of a difficult, unfamiliar writer like Pinget that little margin is left for evaluation.

Fortunately, the usually reticent M. Pinget has put his aspirations as a writer on record in a letter to me of July 14, 1965. In it he speaks of

> . . . *la passion de l'auteur pour l'invention, son obsession des destins individuels, sa hantise de l'imagination et des efforts à accomplir pour sonder la seule réalité qui soit, son âme, et enfin son amour illimité de la langue française.*
>
> . . . the author's passion for fictional creation, his obsession with the destinies of individuals, his being haunted by imagination and by the efforts required to fathom the only reality there is, his soul, and finally his limitless love of the French language.

These are lofty aspirations, yet few living writers could claim to have translated them into achievement more faithfully than Robert Pinget has. What this emotional outburst inevitably overlooks is the whole other side of Pinget's artistic self—his irony, his humor, his malice, his sophistication, his at least partly deliberate obscurity. If I have succeeded in illuminating this other aspect, even to the detriment of the more idealistic side, I can rest partially content.

Plus question de finir must interrupt our consideration not only of *Le Libera* and Robert Pinget but of the New Novel as a whole. *Le nouveau roman* may have come to an end as a literary movement, but Pinget and our other six writers are still pursuing the inner logic of their development as artists. A critic simply dare not make predictions about the future of writers who are still alive and growing, regardless of their age. Nor can this book end with a chapter smugly labeled "Conclusion." Let it stop rather than finish, in true New Novel fashion, with the words

PLUS QUESTION DE FINIR

Selective Bibliography

Each author's work is listed in chronological order of first publication in France. All his or her major prose fiction and a few significant volumes of poetry, drama, autobiography, and criticism have been included. Wherever possible, titles of English translations are given, indented, immediately after the French works to which they correspond. Where both American and British translations (or editions of the same translation) exist, they are listed in order of publication date. Monographs on a particular author are recorded immediately below the list of his works. At the end of the author bibliography, a list of more general works is given, including all the books known to me in French and English that are exclusively concerned with the New Novel. The inclusion of a book in this general listing does not necessarily mean that I am in any way indebted to it. (P = Paris; L = London; NY = New York.)

BUTOR, MICHEL, 1926–

Passage de Milan. P: Les Éditions de Minuit, 1954.
L'Emploi du temps. P: Minuit, 1957.
    Passing Time, tr. Jean Stewart. NY: Simon and Schuster, 1960.
    Passing Time, tr. Jean Stewart. L: Faber and Faber, 1961.
La Modification. P: Minuit, 1957.
    Second Thoughts, tr. Jean Stewart. L: Faber and Faber, 1958.
    A Change of Heart, tr. Jean Stewart. NY: Simon and Schuster, 1959.

Degrés. P: Gallimard, 1960.
> *Degrees*, tr. Richard Howard. NY: Simon and Schuster, 1961.
> *Degrees*, tr. Richard Howard. L: Methuen, 1962.
Répertoire. P: Minuit, 1960. (Essays)
Mobile: Étude pour une représentation des États-Unis. P: Gallimard, 1962.
> *Mobile: Study for a Representation of the United States*, tr. Richard Howard. NY: Simon and Schuster, 1963.
Répertoire II. P: Minuit, 1964. (Essays)
> *Inventory: Essays*, ed. and with a foreword by Richard Howard. NY: Simon and Schuster, 1968. (Translated by various hands, mainly from *Répertoire* and *Répertoire II*.)
Portrait de l'artiste en jeune singe, capriccio. P: Gallimard, 1967. (A partly autobiographical fantasy)
Répertoire III. P: Minuit, 1968. (Essays)

ABOUT BUTOR
Albérès, R.-M. (René Marill). *Michel Butor.* P: Éditions universitaires, 1964.
Charbonnier, Georges. *Entretiens avec Michel Butor.* P: Gallimard, 1967.
Raillard, Georges. *Butor.* P: Gallimard, 1968.
Roudaut, Jean. *Michel Butor, ou le Livre futur, proposition.* P: Gallimard, 1964.
Roudiez, Léon S. *Michel Butor.* NY: Columbia University Press, 1965.

MAURIAC, CLAUDE, 1914–

Conversations avec André Gide (extraits d'un journal). P: Éditions Albin Michel, 1951.
> *Conversations with André Gide*, tr. Michael Lebeck. NY: George Braziller, 1965.
Toutes les femmes sont fatales. P: Albin Michel, 1957.
> *All Women Are Fatal*, tr. Richard Howard. NY: Braziller, 1964.
> *Femmes Fatales*, tr. Henry Wolff. L: Calder and Boyars, 1966.
L'Alittérature contemporaine. P: Albin Michel, 1958.
> *The New Literature*, tr. Samuel I. Stone. NY: Braziller, 1959. (Includes essays on Robbe-Grillet and Mme Sarraute)
Le Dîner en ville. P: Albin Michel, 1959.

The Dinner Party, tr. Merloyd Lawrence. NY: Braziller, 1960.

Dinner in Town, tr. Merloyd Lawrence. L: John Calder, 1963.

La Marquise sortit à cinq heures. P: Albin Michel, 1961.

   The Marquise Went Out at Five, tr. Richard Howard. NY: Braziller, 1962.

   The Marquise Went Out at Five, tr. Richard Howard. L: Calder and Boyars, 1966 [1967].

L'Agrandissement. P: Albin Michel, 1963.

L'Oubli. P: Éditions Bernard Grasset, 1966.

Théâtre. P: Grasset, 1968. (Five plays)

PINGET, ROBERT, 1920–

Entre Fantoine et Agapa. Nouvelle édition, P: Les Éditions de Minuit, 1966. (This volume of short fiction was completed in 1951 and published in that or the following year, but details about place, publisher and date conflict in my sources.)

Mahu ou le matériau. P: Robert Laffont, 1952. Now published by Minuit.

   Mahu or The Material, tr. Alan Sheridan-Smith. L: Calder and Boyars, 1966 [1967].

Le Renard et la boussole. P: Gallimard, 1953.

Graal Flibuste. P: Minuit, 1956. Édition intégrale, P: Minuit, 1966.

Baga. P: Minuit, 1958.

   Baga, tr. John Stevenson. L: Calder and Boyars, 1967.

Le Fiston. P: Minuit, 1959.

   Monsieur Levert, tr. Richard Howard. NY: Grove Press, 1961.

   No Answer, tr. Richard N. Coe. L: John Calder, 1961.

Lettre morte. P: Minuit, 1959. (Play based on *Le Fiston*)

   "Dead Letter," tr. Barbara Bray, in *Plays*, Vol. 1.

La Manivelle, pièce radiophonique; texte anglais de Samuel Beckett. P: Minuit, 1960.

   "The Old Tune," adapted by Samuel Beckett, in *Plays*, Vol. 1.

Clope au dossier. P: Minuit, 1961.

Ici ou ailleurs, suivi de Architruc et de L'Hypothèse. P: Minuit, 1961. (Three plays)

   For *Ici et ailleurs*, see "Clope," tr. Barbara Bray, in *Plays*, Vol. 1. For the others, see "Architruc" and "The Hypothesis," both tr. Barbara Bray, in *Plays*, Vol. 2.

L'Inquisitoire. P: Minuit, 1962.

The Inquisitory, tr. Donald Watson. L: Calder and Boyars, 1966.
The Inquisitory, tr. Donald Watson. NY: Grove Press, 1967.
Autour de Mortin, suite radiophonique. P: Minuit, 1965.
"About Mortin," tr. Barbara Bray, in *Plays*, Vol. 2.
Plays, Vol. 1. L: John Calder, 1963.
Three Plays. NY: Hill and Wang, 1966. (Same as *Plays*, Vol. 1)
Plays, Vol. 2. L: Calder and Boyars, 1967.
Quelqu'un. P: Minuit, 1965.
Someone, a translation of *Quelqu'un*, "in preparation" by Calder and Boyars.
Le Libera. P: Minuit, 1968.
Passacaille. P: Minuit, 1969. (Not discussed in Pinget chapter.)

QUENEAU, RAYMOND, 1903–

Le Chiendent. P: Gallimard, 1933.
   The Bark-Tree, tr. Barbara Wright. L: Calder and Boyars, 1968.
Gueule de pierre. P: Gallimard, 1934.
Les derniers jours. P: Gallimard, 1936.
Chêne et chien. P: Denoël, 1937. (Novel in verse)
Odile. P: Gallimard, 1937.
Les Enfants du limon. P: Gallimard, 1938.
Un rude hiver. P: Gallimard, 1939.
   A Hard Winter, tr. Betty Askwith. L: John Lehmann, 1948.
Les Temps mêlés (Gueule de pierre II). P: Gallimard, 1941.
Pierrot mon ami. P: Gallimard, 1942.
   Pierrot, tr. J. Maclaren-Ross. L: John Lehmann, 1950.
Loin de Rueil. P: Gallimard, 1944.
   The Skin of Dreams, tr. H. J. Kaplan. Norfolk, Conn.: New Directions, 1948.
Exercices de style. P: Gallimard, 1947. Nouvelle édition, revue et corrigée, P: Gallimard, 1964.
   Exercises in Style, tr. Barbara Wright. L: Gaberbocchus, 1958. (Distributed in the U.S. by New Directions.)
Saint Glinglin, précédé d'une nouvelle version de Gueule de pierre et des Temps mêlés. P: Gallimard, 1948.
Bâtons, chiffres et lettres. P: Gallimard, 1950. P: Gallimard, Collection "idées," 1965. (Essays; the 1965 edition differs considerably from the original)
Petite cosmogonie portative. P: Gallimard, 1950. (A didactic poem)

Le Dimanche de la vie. P: Gallimard, 1951.
Si tu t'imagines 1920–1951. P: Gallimard, 1952. (Collected poems, including *Chêne et chien*)
Zazie dans le métro. P: Gallimard, 1959.
    Zazie, tr. Barbara Wright. L: Bodley Head, 1960.
    Zazie, tr. Barbara Wright. NY: Harper, 1960.
Cent mille milliards de poèmes. P: Gallimard, 1961. (Ten sonnets, each line of which is printed on a separate strip of paper, so that any version of line 1 can be combined with any version of line 2, any version of line 3, etc. This makes possible the manufacture of one hundred trillion different sonnets by U.S. reckoning, or a hundred billion, British style.)
Les Œuvres complètes de Sally Mara. P: Gallimard, 1962.
Les Fleurs bleues. P: Gallimard, 1965.
    Between Blue and Blue, tr. Barbara Wright. L: Bodley Head, 1967.
    Blue Flowers, tr. Barbara Wright. NY: Atheneum, 1967.
Le Vol d'Icare. P: Gallimard, 1968.

ABOUT QUENEAU
Bens, Jacques. *Queneau.* P. Gallimard, 1962.
Bergens, Andrée. *Raymond Queneau.* Genève: Librairie Droz, 1963.
Cahiers du Collège de 'Pataphysique, dossier 20.
Gayot, Paul. *Raymond Queneau.* P: Éditions universitaires, 1967.
Guicharnaud, Jacques. *Raymond Queneau.* NY: Columbia University Press, 1965.
Queneau, Raymond. *Entretiens avec Georges Charbonnier.* P: Gallimard, 1962.
Queval, Jean. *Essai sur Raymond Queneau.* P: Pierre Seghers, 1960.
Simonnet, Claude. *Queneau déchiffré (Notes sur "le Chiendent").* P: Julliard, 1962.

ROBBE-GRILLET, ALAIN, 1922–

Les Gommes. P: Les Éditions de Minuit, 1953.
    The Erasers, tr. Richard Howard. NY: Grove Press, 1964.
    The Erasers, tr. Richard Howard. L: Calder and Boyars, 1966.
Le Voyeur. P: Minuit, 1955.

The Voyeur, tr. Richard Howard. NY: Grove Press, 1958.

The Voyeur, tr. Richard Howard. L: John Calder, 1959.

La Jalousie. P: Minuit, 1957.

Jealousy, tr. Richard Howard. NY: Grove Press, 1959.

Jealousy, tr. Richard Howard. L: John Calder, 1959.

Dans le labyrinthe. P: Minuit, 1959.

In the Labyrinth, tr. Richard Howard. NY: Grove Press, 1960.

In the Labyrinth, tr. Christine Brooke-Rose. L: Calder and Boyars, 1967 [1968].

L'Année dernière à Marienbad, ciné-roman. P: Minuit, 1961.

Last Year at Marienbad, tr. Richard Howard. NY: Grove Press, 1962.

Last Year at Marienbad, tr. Richard Howard. L: John Calder, 1962.

Instantanés. P: Minuit, 1962. (Short fiction)

Snapshots and Towards a New Novel, tr. Barbara Wright. L: Calder and Boyars, 1965.

Snapshots, tr. Bruce Morrissette. NY: Grove Press, 1968.

L'Immortelle, ciné-roman. P: Minuit, 1963.

Pour un nouveau roman. P: Minuit, 1963. (Essays)

For a New Novel, tr. Richard Howard. NY: Grove Press, 1965.

Snapshots and Towards a New Novel (see above).

La Maison de rendez-vous. P: Minuit, 1965.

La Maison de Rendez-vous, tr. Richard Howard. NY: Grove Press, 1966.

The House of Assignation, tr. A. M. Sheridan-Smith. L: Calder and Boyars, 1970.

ABOUT ROBBE-GRILLET

Alter, J. V. *La Vision du monde d'Alain Robbe-Grillet*. Geneva: Librairie Droz, 1966.

Bernal, Olga. *Alain Robbe-Grillet: le roman de l'absence*. P: Gallimard, 1964.

Miesch, J. *Robbe-Grillet*. Éditions universitaires, 1965.

Morrissette, Bruce. *Alain Robbe-Grillet*. NY: Columbia University Press, 1965.

Morrissette, Bruce, *et al.* "Introductory Essays" in *Two Novels by Robbe-Grillet: Jealousy and In the Labyrinth*. NY: Grove Press, 1965.

Morrissette, Bruce. *Les Romans de Robbe-Grillet*. P: Minuit, 1963.

Stoltzfus, Ben F. *Alain Robbe-Grillet and the New French Novel.* Carbondale, Ill.: Southern Illinois University Press, 1964.

SARRAUTE, NATHALIE, 1901–

Tropismes. P: Robert Denoël, 1939. P: Les Éditions de Minuit, 1957. (Short fiction; the 1957 edition contains some new "tropisms")
    Tropisms and The Age of Suspicion, tr. Maria Jolas. L: John Calder, 1963.
    Tropisms, tr. Maria Jolas. NY: George Braziller, 1967.
Portrait d'un inconnu. P: Robert Marin, 1948. P: Gallimard, 1956.
    Portrait of a Man Unknown, tr. Maria Jolas. NY: Braziller, 1958.
    Portrait of a Man Unknown, tr. Maria Jolas. L: John Calder, 1959.
Martereau. P: Gallimard, 1953.
    Martereau, tr. Maria Jolas. NY: Braziller, 1959.
    Martereau, tr. Maria Jolas. L: John Calder, 1964.
L'Ère du soupçon. P: Gallimard, 1956. (Essays)
    The Age of Suspicion, tr. Maria Jolas. NY: Braziller, 1963.
    Tropisms and The Age of Suspicion (see above).
Le Planétarium. P: Gallimard, 1959.
    The Planetarium, tr. Maria Jolas. NY: Braziller, 1960.
    The Planetarium, tr. Maria Jolas. L: John Calder, 1961.
Les Fruits d'or. P: Gallimard, 1963.
    The Golden Fruits, tr. Maria Jolas. NY: Braziller, 1964.
    The Golden Fruits, tr. Maria Jolas. L: John Calder, 1965.
Le Silence, suivi de Le Mensonge. P: Gallimard, 1967. (Plays)
Entre la vie et la mort. P: Gallimard, 1968.
    Between Life and Death, tr. Maria Jolas. NY: Braziller, 1969.
    Between Life and Death, tr. Maria Jolas. L: Calder and Boyars, 1970.

ABOUT SARRAUTE
Cranaki, Mimica, and Yvon Belaval. *Nathalie Sarraute.* P: Gallimard, 1965.
Micha, René. *Nathalie Sarraute.* P: Éditions universitaires, 1966.
Temple, Ruth Zabriskie. *Nathalie Sarraute.* NY: Columbia University Press, 1968.

Simon, Claude, 1913–

Le Tricheur. P: Éditions du Sagittaire, 1946. (Not discussed in Simon chapter.)

La Corde raide. P: Sagittaire, 1947. (Autobiography)

Gulliver. P: Calmann-Lévy, 1952.

Le Sacre du printemps. P: Calmann-Lévy, 1954.

Le Vent: Tentative de restitution d'un retable baroque. P: Les Éditions de Minuit, 1957.

    The Wind, tr. Richard Howard. NY: George Braziller, 1959.

L'Herbe. P: Minuit, 1958.

    The Grass, tr. Richard Howard. NY: Braziller, 1960.

    The Grass, tr. Richard Howard. L: Jonathan Cape, 1961.

La Route des Flandres. P: Minuit, 1960.

    The Flanders Road, tr. Richard Howard. NY: Braziller, 1961.

    The Flanders Road, tr. Richard Howard. L: Cape, 1962.

Le Palace. P: Minuit, 1962.

    The Palace, tr. Richard Howard. NY: Braziller, 1963.

    The Palace, tr. Richard Howard. L: Cape, 1964.

Histoire. P: Minuit, 1967.

    Histoire, tr. Richard Howard. NY: Braziller, 1968.

    Histoire, tr. Richard Howard. L: Cape, 1969.

La Bataille de Pharsale. P: Minuit, 1969. (Not discussed in Simon chapter.)

ABOUT SIMON

See the books by Janvier and Sturrock listed below.

GENERAL

Barrère, Jean-Bertrand. *La Cure d'amaigrissement du roman.* P: Albin Michel, 1964.

Bloch-Michel, Jean. *Le Présent de l'indicatif.* P: Gallimard, 1963.

Boisdeffre, Pierre de. *Où va le roman?* P: Del Duca, 1962.

Champigny, Robert. *Pour une esthétique de l'essai, analyses critiques (Breton, Sartre, Robbe-Grillet).* P: Minard, 1967.

Cruickshank, John, ed. *The Novelist As Philosopher: Studies in French Fiction 1935–1960.* L, NY: Oxford University Press, 1962. (Essays on Robbe-Grillet and Queneau, the latter a particularly fine one by Martin Esslin.)

Frohock, W. M. *Style and Temper: Studies in French Fiction 1925–1960*. Cambridge, Mass.: Harvard University Press, 1967. (Chapter 7, "Continuities in the 'New Novel.'")

Janvier, Ludovic. *Une Parole exigeante: le nouveau roman*. P: Minuit, 1964. (Chapters on Butor, Robbe-Grillet, Sarraute, Simon.)

Le Sage, Laurent. *The French New Novel: An Introduction and a Sampler*. University Park, Pa.: Pennsylvania State University Press, 1962. (Selections from Butor, Pinget, Robbe-Grillet, Sarraute, Simon, and others.)

Nadeau, Maurice. *Le Roman français depuis la guerre*. P: Gallimard, 1963.

Nadeau, Maurice. *The French Novel Since the War*, tr. A. M. Sheridan-Smith. L: Methuen, 1967. (Chapter 14, "The 'Nouveau Roman'"; an appendix of "Critical Texts" by Butor, Queneau, Robbe-Grillet, Sarraute, and others.)

Peyre, Henri. *French Novelists of Today*. NY: Oxford University Press, 1967. (Chapter XII, "Main Trends Since World War II. The 'New Novel.'")

Ricardou, Jean. *Problèmes du nouveau roman*. P: Éditions du Seuil, 1967.

Sturrock, John. *The French New Novel: Claude Simon, Michel Butor, Alain Robbe-Grillet*. L, NY: Oxford University Press, 1969.

Zants, Emily. *The Aesthetics of the New Novel in France*. Boulder, Colo.: University of Colorado Press, 1968. (Butor, Robbe-Grillet, Sarraute.)

Zeltner-Neukomm, Gerda. *Die eigenmächtige Sprache: Zur Poetik des Nouveau Roman*. Olten und Freiburg: Walter-Verlag, 1965. (Butor, Pinget, Robbe-Grillet, Sarraute, Simon, and Beckett.)

SPECIAL ISSUES OF PERIODICALS DEALING
WITH THE NEW NOVEL

Esprit, nouvelle série, nos. 7–8 (July–August 1958).

L'Esprit Créateur, Vol. VII, no. 2 (Summer 1967). Pub. at Lawrence, Kansas.

Revue des lettres modernes, nos. 94–99 (1964).

Yale French Studies, no. 24 (Summer 1959).

Index

3 1382 00016 3399

Y COLLEGE LIBRARY

AS   PQ 671 .M39 c.1

Mercier, Vivian, 1919-
  The new novel from Queneau
to Pinget.

BT.
ASHC

10/73

LANSING COMMUNITY COLLEGE LIBRARY
419 N. CAPITOL AVENUE
LANSING, MICHIGAN 48914